제4판

교원임용고시
영미문학 필독서

literature

유희태 영미문학 ④

# 영미문학 문제은행

임용영어수험생 대다수가 선택하는 전공영어의 보통명사

LSI 영어연구소 유희태 박사 저

박문각 임용 동영상강의 www.pmg.co.kr

박문각

# 머리말

# Preface

≪유희태 영미문학 4-영미문학 문제은행≫(4판)은 ≪유희태 영미문학 1-영미문학개론≫, ≪유희태 영미문학 2-영미소설의 이해≫, ≪유희태 영미문학 3-영미문학 기출≫의 자매집이다. 『유희태 영미문학』 시리즈의 가장 핵심 교재인 ≪영미문학개론≫에서 문학 공부의 기초가 되는 공시적 방법론과 통시적 방법론을 시, 소설, 드라마, 그리고 비평에 구체적으로 적용하여 이론을 확립한다. 하지만 교원임용시험은 일반론적인 이론을 중심으로 테스트하는 대학원 시험과는 다르게, 매우 구체적인 형태의 문항이 출제되기 때문에 단순히 이론을 많이 안다고 해서 시험문제가 잘 풀리는 것은 아니다.

따라서 ≪영미문학개론≫에서 배운 이론을 임용시험에 최적화된 실전 문제를 통해 점검해 보는 것은 필수적이다. 이 ≪문제은행≫은 그런 부분을 충족시켜주는 교재라 할 수 있다. 따라서 ≪영미문학개론≫과 함께 ≪문제은행≫을 같이 공부하는 것이 교원임용시험을 준비하는 데 매우 유용할 것이다.

전공 공부를 등한시하면 임용시험에서 합격할 가능성은 거의 없다. 전공(전문적 지식)과 외국어(실용적 수업능력) 실력을 동시에 평가하여 어느 하나에 치우치지 않는 전문적 지식인으로서 교사를 양성하려는 현재의 임용시험은 하루아침에 준비될 수 없기 때문이다.

이 4판 작업을 하면서 많은 분들의 도움을 받았다. 원고를 보기 좋은 최종 결과물로 만들어 준 박문각의 변수경 님과 교재에 실린 시, 소설, 드라마, 비평, 수필 지문이 가지고 있는 함축 의미와 문화적 맥락, 그리고 문학적 감성 등을 두고 토론하고 때로는 논쟁을 했던 LSI 영어연구소의 Sean Maylone 수석연구원에게 고마움을 전한다. 아무쪼록 이 ≪문제은행≫ 4판 교재가 수험생 여러분의 합격에 도움이 되기를 깊은 마음으로 바란다.

2023년 11월 LSI 영어연구소에서

유희태

차례

# Contents

## Part 01 기본이론문제 1



## Part 02 기본이론문제 2



## Part 03 실전모의고사

## 모범답안

유희태 영미문학 ❹

# 영미문학 문제은행

Part

# 01

## 기본이론문제 1

# 01 회 기본이론문제 1

모범답안 p.4

[1-5] First, identify each of the following as literal or figurative. Second, if figurative, identify what sort of figure(s) of speech is(are) employed. Also, explain what is being compared to what.

**01**

> The strongest oaths are straw
> To the fire i' the blood.

**02**

> The tawny-hided desert crouches watching her.

03

Let us eat, drink, and be merry, for tomorrow we may die.

04

Let us eat, drink, and be merry, for tomorrow we shall die.

05

Dorothy's eyes, with their long brown lashes, looked very much like her mother's.

**[6-7] Identify each of the following quotations as literal or figurative. If figurative, identify literal and figurative terms respectively. In addition, explain the meaning of it.**

Example

> I wouldn't squeal to the policemen.

- Literal or figurative: figurative
- Literal term: I
- Figurative term: a pig or any animal that squeals
- Meaning: Apparently to this speaker, telling the policemen his information is a subhuman, low-life, perhaps cowardly act. Also suggests negative attitude toward policemen.

## 06

> The Orange County ladies live in furnished souls.

- Literal or figurative: ______________________
- Literal term: ______________________
- Figurative term: ______________________
- Meaning: ______________________

## 07

> Tom is a real snake when it comes to the have-not.

- Literal or figurative: ______________________
- Literal term: ______________________
- Figurative term: ______________________
- Meaning: ______________________

**08** Identify the figure of speech employed in the underlined part and explain its meaning.

> LET us go then, you and I,
> When the evening is spread out against the sky
> Like a patient etherized upon a table;
> Let us go, through certain half-deserted streets,
> The muttering retreats
> Of restless nights in one-night cheap hotels

**[9-10] Identify the figure of speech employed in the underlined parts ⓐ and ⓑ and explain their meaning respectively.**

ⓐ He clasps the crag with crooked hands;
Close to the sun in lonely lands,
Ringed with the azure world, he stands.

The wrinkled sea beneath him crawls;
He watches from his mountain walls,
ⓑ And like a thunderbolt he falls.

**09** ______________________

**10** ______________________

# 02회 기본이론문제 1

모범답안 p.5

[1-2] First, identify each of the following as literal or figurative. Second, if figurative, identify what sort of figure(s) of speech is(are) employed. Also, explain what is being compared to what.

**01**

> O tenderly the haughty day
> Fills his blue urn with fire;

**02**

> It is with words as with sunbeams—the more
> they are condensed the deeper they burn.

**[3-8] Identify the figure of speech at work in the following excerpts and identify the literal referents. Also, explain the meaning of the given excerpt. Use complete sentences.**

**03**

The apple of his eye was Beatrice, for whom he wrote the sonnets.

**04**

This letter of recommendation is the keystone of her application packet to university.

**05**

The car lurched itself into the driveway belching smoke.

**06**

You must watch for that salesman, he is like a shark.

**07**

Cigar smoke flew around the room and lay down to curl around the guests' feet loyally.

**08**

Under the eaves, pigeons could be heard gossiping loudly.

**09** Identify the figure(s) of speech employed in the underlined part and explain their meaning.

> Bent double, like old beggars under sacks,
> Knock-kneed, coughing like hags, we cursed through sludge
> Till on the haunting flares we turned our backs

# 03회 기본이론문제 1

모범답안 p.6

**01** Identify the figure of speech at work in the following excerpts and identify the literal referents. Also, explain the meaning of the given excerpt. Use complete sentences.

> The students suddenly became sharp as knives when passing meant going home early.

---

---

---

**02** Identify the figure(s) of speech employed in the underlined parts ⓐ and ⓑ and explain its meaning respectively.

> But ⓐ someone still was yelling out and stumbling
> And floundering like a man in fire or lime.—
> Dim through the misty panes and thick green light,
> ⓑ As under a green sea, I saw him drowning.

---

---

---

---

---

**03** What figures of speech do you find in the underlined part? How do they contribute to its meaning?

> O Rose, thou art sick!
> <u>The invisible worm</u>
> <u>That flies in the night,</u>
> <u>In the howling storm,</u>
>
> <u>Has found out thy bed</u>
> <u>Of Crimson joy,</u>
> And his dark secret love
> Does thy life destroy.

# 04회 기본이론문제 1

모범답안 p.7

**01** Identify figure(s) of speech used in the underlined parts and explain their meaning respectively.

A poem should be palpable and mute
Like a globed fruit,

ⓐ Dumb
As old medallions to the thumb,

ⓑ Silent as the sleeve-worn stone
Of casement ledges where the moss has grown—

A poem should be wordless
Like a flight of birds.

**02** **In the underlined parts the speaker uses a paradox as a figure of speech. Explain the meaning of the paradox.**

> <u>A poem should be motionless in time</u>
> <u>As the moon climbs,</u>
>
> Leaving, as the moon releases
> Twig by twig the night-entangled trees,
>
> Leaving, as the moon behind the winter leaves,
> Memory by memory the mind—

**03** Identify figure of speech used in the underlined part and explain its meaning.

> Shall I compare thee to a summer's day?
> Thou art more lovely and more temperate.
> Rough winds do shake the darling buds of May,
> <u>And summer's lease hath all too short a date.</u>

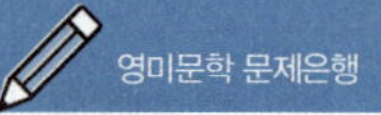


# 05회 기본이론문제 1

모범답안 p.7

**[1-2] Read the poem and follow the directions.**

True ease in writing comes from art, not chance,
As those move easiest who have learned to dance.
'Tis not enough no harshness gives offense,
The sound must seem an echo to the sense;
Soft is the strain when Zephyr gently blows,
And the smooth stream in smoother numbers flows;
But when loud surges lash the sounding shore,
The hoarse rough verse should like the torrent roar.
When Ajax strives some rock's vast weight to throw,
The line too labors, and the words move slow;
Not so, when swift Camilla scours the plain,
Flies o'er the' unbending corn, and skims along the main.
Hear how Timotheus' varied lays surprise,
And bid alternate passions fall and rise!

**01** There are four classical allusions in the poem. What do these allusions enable the poet to achieve?

**02** Write down the theme of the poem in your own language. In addition, where does the poet illustrate this theme concretely? Give at least two examples.

## 03 Read the poem and follow the directions.

When my mother died I was very young,
And my father sold me while yet my tongue
Could scarcely cry "'weep! 'weep! 'weep! 'weep!"
So your chimneys I sweep, and in soot I sleep.

There's little Tom Dacre, who cried when his head
That curled like a lamb's back, was shaved, so I said,
"Hush, Tom! never mind it, for when your head's bare,
You know that the soot cannot spoil your white hair."

And so he was quiet, and that very night,
As Tom was a-sleeping he had such a sight!
That thousands of sweepers, Dick, Joe, Ned, and Jack,
Were all of them locked up in coffins of black;

And by came an Angel who had a bright key,
And he opened the coffins and set them all free;
Then down a green plain, leaping, laughing they run,
And wash in a river and shine in the Sun.

Then naked and white, all their bags left behind,
They rise upon clouds, and sport in the wind.
And the Angel told Tom, if he'd be a good boy,
He'd have God for his father and never want joy.

And so Tom awoke; and we rose in the dark
And got with our bags and our brushes to work.
Though the morning was cold, Tom was happy and warm;
So if all do their duty, they need not fear harm.

How do the speaker's and the poet's attitudes toward the speaker's lot in life differ? Specifically, how are the meanings of the poet and the speaker different in lines 7-8, and 24? Write your answer by relating those answer to the dramatic irony.

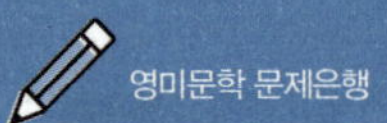


# 06회 기본이론문제 1

모범답안 p.8

[1-3] Identify the figure(s) of speech employed in the underlined part and explain its meaning respectively.

**01**

An aged man is but a paltry thing,
A tattered coat upon a stick

**02**

The rose-lipped girls are sleeping
In fields where roses fade.

**03**

Only the monstrous anger of the guns.

**04** Identify what sort of figure(s) of speech is(are) employed. Also, explain what is being compared to what.

A yellow leaf, from the darkness
Hops like a frog before me.
Why should I start and stand still?

[5-8] Read the poem and follow the directions.

I met a traveller from an antique land
Who said: Two vast and trunkless legs of stone
Stand in the desert. Near them, on the sand,
Half sunk, a shattered visage lies, whose frown
And wrinkled lip, and sneer of cold command
Tell that its sculptor well those passions read
Which yet survive, stamped on these lifeless things,
The hand that mocked them and the heart that fed.
And on the pedestal these words appear:
"My name is Ozymandias, king of kings:
Look on my works, ye Mighty, and despair!"
Nothing beside remains. Round the decay
Of that colossal wreck, boundless and bare
The lone and level sands stretch far away.

**05** In line 8, whose hand? and whose heart? What figure of speech is used in "hand" and "heart"?

______________________________

______________________________

______________________________

**06** Ozymandias was an ancient Egyptian tyrant. This poem was first published in 1817. Explain the symbolic meaning of "Ozymandias" in the poem.

______________________________

______________________________

______________________________

**07** Write down the main theme of the poem.

**08** Paraphrase the poem.

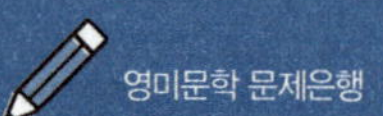


# 07회 기본이론문제 1

모범답안 p.9

**[1-2] Identify the figure(s) of speech employed in the poem and explain its meaning respectively.**

**01**

The sea awake at midnight from its sleep
And round the pebbly beaches far and wide
I heard the first wave of the rising tide

**02**

Folding clothes
I think of folding you
Into my life.

[3-5] Identify the figure(s) of speech employed in the underlined part and explain its meaning respectively.

## 03

Call it a day, I wish they might have said
To please the boy by giving him the half hour
That a boy counts so much when saved from work.
His sister stood beside them in her apron
To tell them "Supper." <u>The saw,</u>
<u>As if to prove saws knew what supper meant,</u>
<u>Leaped out at the boy's hand</u>

## 04

<u>We paused before a house that seemed</u>
<u>A swelling of the ground:</u>
<u>The roof was scarcely visible.</u>
<u>The cornice but a mound</u>

Since then—'tis Centuries—and yet
Feels shorter than the Day
I first surmised the Horses' Heads
Were toward Eternity

## 05

When you are old and grey and full of sleep
And nodding by the fire, take down this book,
And slowly read, and dream of the soft look
Your eyes had once, and of their shadows deep;

[6-7] Read the poem and follow the directions.

Who hath not seen thee oft amid thy store?
Sometimes whoever seeks abroad may find
Thee sitting careless on a granary floor,
Thy hair soft-lifted by the winnowing wind;
Or on a half-reap'd furrow sound asleep,
Drows'd with the fume of poppies, while thy hook
Spares the next swath and all its twined flowers:
And sometimes like a gleaner thou dost keep
Steady thy laden head across a brook;
Or by a cyder-press, with patient look,
Thou watchest the last oozings hours by hours.

**06** How many sorts of imagery are used in the poem above? Give examples of each.

______________________________

______________________________

______________________________

**07** Identify the main figure of speech used in the poem above. Also, explain what is being compared to what.

______________________________

______________________________

______________________________

# 08회 기본이론문제 1

모범답안 p.10

**[1-4] Read the poem and follow the directions.**

When getting my nose in a book
Cured most things short of school,
It was worth ruining my eyes
To know I could still keep cool,
And deal out the old right hook
To dirty dogs twice my size.

Later, with inch-thick specs,
Evil was just my lark:
Me and my coat and fangs
Had ripping times in the dark.
The women I clubbed with sex!
I broke them up like meringues.

Don't read much now: the dude
Who lets the girl down before
The hero arrives, the chap
Who's yellow and keeps the store
Seem far too familiar. Get stewed:
Books are a load of crap.

**01** Explain the three stages in the speaker's life.

______________________________________________

______________________________________________

______________________________________________

______________________________________________

______________________________________________

**02** Paraphrase the first stanza in your words.

There was a time when reading ______________________________

______________________________________________

______________________________________________

______________________________________________

______________________________________________

**03** Paraphrase the second stanza in your words.

Later, already having to wear ______________________________

______________________________________________

______________________________________________

______________________________________________

______________________________________________

**04** Paraphrase the final stanza in your words.

I don't read much any more because now I ______________________________

______________________________________________________________

______________________________________________________________

______________________________________________________________

______________________________________________________________

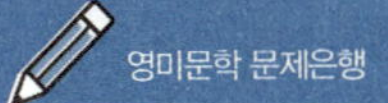


# 09회 기본이론문제 1

모범답안 p.11

[1-3] Identify the figure(s) of speech employed in the poem and explain its meaning respectively.

**01**

> I am—yet what I am, none cares or knows;
> My friends forsake me like a memory lost;

**02**

> The fog comes
> On little cat feet.

**03**

> When it comes the landscape listens,
> Shadows hold their breath.

[4-5] Read the poem and follow the directions.

**Cross**

My old man's a white old man
And my old mother's black.
If ever I cursed my white old man
I take my curses back.

If ever I cursed my black old mother
And wished she were in hell,
I'm sorry for that evil wish
And now I wish her well

My old man died in a fine big house.
My ma died in a shack.
I wonder were I'm gonna die,
Being neither white nor black?

**04** Explain what different denotations the title has and what connotations are linked to each of them.

**05** The language in the poem, such as "old man," "ma," and "gonna," is plain and even colloquial. Is it appropriate to the subject?

# 10회 기본이론문제 1

모범답안 p.12

[1-2] Identify the figure of speech employed in the poem and explain its meaning.

**01**

> My heart is like an apple tree
> Whose boughs are bent with thickest fruit

______

______

______

**02**

> The Soul selects her own Society—
> Then shuts the door—

______

______

______

## 03 Read the poem and follow the directions.

There is no frigate like a book
To take us lands away,
Nor any coursers like a page
Of prancing poetry.
This traverse may the poorest take
Without oppress of toll;
How frugal is the chariot
That bears a human soul!

The above poem uses an extended metaphor throughout its length. Identify the corresponding metaphoric and literal figures compared. What significance is this comparison meant to communicate to the readers? Use direct reference from the poem, but no more than SIX consecutive words.

# 11 회 기본이론문제 1

모범답안 p.12

**01** Read the passage and follow the directions.

Whoever has made a voyage up the Hudson must remember the Catskill Mountains. They are a dismembered branch of the great Appalachian family, and are seen away to the west of the river, swelling up to a noble height, and lording it over the surrounding country. Every change of season, every change of weather, indeed, every hour of the day, produces some change in the magical hues and shapes of these mountains, and they are regarded by all the good wives, far and near, as perfect barometers. When the weather is fair and settled, they are clothed in blue and purple, and print their bold outlines on the clear evening sky; but sometimes, when the rest of the landscape is cloudless, they will gather a hood of gray vapors about their summits, which, in the last rays of the setting sun, will glow and light up like a crown of glory.

At the foot of these fairy mountains the voyager may have descried the light smoke curling up from a village whose shingle roofs gleam among the trees, just where the blue tints of the upland melt away into the fresh green of the nearer landscape. It is a little village of great antiquity, having been founded by some of the Dutch colonists, in the early times of the province, just about the beginning of the government of the good Peter Stuyvesant (may he rest in peace!), and there were some of the houses of the original settlers standing within a few years, with lattice windows, gable fronts surmounted with weathercocks, and built of small yellow bricks brought from Holland.

In that same village, and in one of these very houses (which, to tell the precise truth, was sadly time-worn and weather-beaten), there lived many years since, while the country was yet a province of Great Britain, a simple, good-natured fellow, of the name of Rip Van Winkle. He was a descendant of the Van Winkles who figured so gallantly in the chivalrous days of Peter Stuyvesant, and accompanied him to the siege of Fort Christina. He inherited, however, but little of the martial character of his ancestors.

Summarize the passage above with 3-4 sentences.

**02** Read the poem and follow the directions.

**The Death of the Ball Turret Gunner**

From my mother's sleep I fell into the State,
And I hunched in its belly till my wet fur froze.
Six miles from earth, loosed from its dream of life,
I woke to black flak and the nightmare fighters.
When I died they washed me out of the turret with a hose.

Who is the speaker? What has happened to him? Use examples to support your writing.

# 12 회 기본이론문제 1

모범답안 p.13

[1-3] Read the passage and answer the questions.

The opinions of this junto were completely controlled by Nicholas Vedder, a patriarch of the village, and landlord of the inn, at the door of which he took his seat from morning till night, just moving sufficiently to avoid the sun and keep in the shade of a large tree; <u>so that the neighbors could tell the hour by his movements as accurately as by a sundial</u>. It is true he was rarely heard to speak, but smoked his pipe incessantly. His adherents, however (for every great man has his adherents), perfectly understood him, and knew how to gather his opinions. When anything that was read or related displeased him, he was observed to smoke his pipe vehemently, and to send forth short, frequent and angry puffs; but when pleased, he would inhale the smoke slowly and tranquilly, and emit it in light and placid clouds; and sometimes, taking the pipe from his mouth, and letting the fragrant vapor curl about his nose, would gravely nod his head in token of perfect approbation.

**01** What is the general tone of the passage above?

______________________________

______________________________

______________________________

**02** Identify the figure of speech at work in the underlined part. In addition, explain what is being compared to what and the meaning of it. Use complete sentences.

**03** Explain the characteristics of the character, Nicolas Vedder in approximately 2 or 3 sentences.

## [4-7] Read the passage and follow the directions.

Turkey was a short, pursy Englishman of about my own age, that is, somewhere not far from sixty. ⓐ In the morning, one might say, his face was of a fine florid hue, but after twelve o'clock, meridian—his dinner hour—it blazed like a grate* full of Christmas coals; and continued blazing—but, as it were, with a gradual wane—till 6 o'clock, P. M. or thereabouts, after which I saw no more of ⓑ the proprietor of the face, which gaining its meridian with the sun, seemed to set with it, to rise, culminate, and decline the following day, with the like regularity and undiminished glory. There are many singular coincidences I have known in the course of my life, not the least among which was the fact, that exactly when Turkey displayed his fullest beams from his red and radiant countenance, just then, too, at that critical moment, began the daily period when I considered his business capacities as seriously disturbed for the remainder of the twenty-four hours. Not that he was absolutely idle, or averse to business then; far from it. The difficulty was, he was apt to be altogether too energetic. There was a strange, inflamed, flurried, flighty recklessness of activity about him. He would be incautious in dipping his pen into his inkstand. All his blots upon my documents, were dropped there after twelve o'clock, meridian. Indeed, not only would he be reckless and sadly given to making blots in the afternoon, but some days he went further, and was rather noisy. At such times, too, his face flamed with augmented blazonry, as if cannel coal had been heaped on anthracite*. He made an unpleasant racket with his chair; spilled his sand-box; in mending his pens, impatiently split them all to pieces, and threw them on the floor in a sudden passion; stood up and leaned over his table, boxing his papers about in a most indecorous manner, very sad to behold in an elderly man like him.

** grate: a frame of iron bars to hold a fire*
** anthracite: hard[stone] coal*

**04** What is the general tone of the passage above?

______________________________________________

**05** Explain the main problem of the character Turkey mentioned by the speaker in the passage.

______________________________________________

______________________________________________

______________________________________________

**06** Identify the figure of speech at work in the underlined part ⓐ. In addition, explain what is being compared to what and the meaning of it. Use complete sentence.

______________________________________________

______________________________________________

______________________________________________

**07** What does the underlined ⓑ refer to?

______________________________________________

## [8-9] Read the passage and follow the directions.

Nippers was a whiskered, sallow, and, upon the whole, rather piratical-looking young man of about five and twenty. I always deemed him the victim of two evil powers—ambition and indigestion. The ambition was evinced by a certain impatience of the duties of a mere copyist, an unwarrantable usurpation of strictly professional affairs, such as the original drawing up of legal documents. The indigestion seemed betokened in an occasional nervous testiness and grinning irritability, causing the teeth to audibly grind together over mistakes committed in copying; unnecessary maledictions, hissed, rather than spoken, in the heat of business; and especially by a continual discontent with the height of the table where he worked. Though of a very ingenious mechanical turn, Nippers could never get this table to suit him. He put chips under it, blocks of various sorts, bits of pasteboard, and at last went so far as to attempt an exquisite adjustment by final pieces of folded blotting-paper. But no invention would answer. If, for the sake of easing his back, he brought the table lid at a sharp angle well up towards his chin, and wrote there like a man using the steep roof of a Dutch house for his desk:—then he declared that it stopped the circulation in his arms. If now he lowered the table to his waistbands, and stooped over it in writing, then there was a sore aching in his back. In short, the truth of the matter was, Nippers knew not what he wanted. Or, if he wanted any thing, it was to be rid of a scrivener's table altogether. Among the manifestations of his diseased ambition was a fondness he had for receiving visits from certain ambiguous-looking fellows in seedy coats, whom he called his clients. Indeed I was aware that not only was he, at times, considerable of a ward-politician, but he occasionally did a little business at the Justices' courts, and was not unknown on the steps of the Tombs*. I have good reason to believe, however, that one individual who called upon him at my chambers, and who, with a grand air, he insisted was his client, was no other than a dun, and the alleged title-deed, a bill. ⋯

It was fortunate for me that, owing to its peculiar cause—indigestion—the irritability and consequent nervousness of Nippers, were mainly observable in the morning, while in the afternoon he was comparatively mild. So that Turkey's paroxysms* only coming on about twelve o'clock, I never had to do with their eccentricities at one time. Their fits relieved each other like guards. When Nippers' was on, Turkey's was off; and vice versa. This was a good natural arrangement under the circumstances.

** the Tombs: name of a prison*

** paroxysm: any sudden, violent outburst; a fit of violent action or emotion*

**08** Translate the underlined part into Korean.

**09** What is the general tone of the passage above?

# 13 회 기본이론문제 1

모범답안 p.14

[1-5] Read the <A> and <B> and follow the directions.

A

**"Out, Out — "**

The buzz-saw snarled and rattled in the yard
And made dust and dropped stove-length sticks of wood,
Sweet-scented stuff when the breeze drew across it.
And from there those that lifted eyes could count
Five mountain ranges one behind the other
Under the sunset far into Vermont.
And the saw snarled and rattled, snarled and rattled,
As it ran light, or had to bear a load.
And nothing happened: day was all but done.
Call it a day, I wish they might have said
To please the boy by giving him the half hour
That a boy counts so much when saved from work.
His sister stood beside them in her apron
To tell them 'Supper'. At the word, the saw,
As if to prove saws knew what supper meant,
Leaped out at the boy's hand, or seemed to leap—
He must have given the hand. However it was,
Neither refused the meeting. But the hand!
The boy's first outcry was a rueful laugh.
<u>As he swung toward them holding up the hand</u>
<u>Half in appeal, but half as if to keep</u>
<u>The life from spilling. Then the boy saw all—</u>
Since he was old enough to know, big boy
Doing a man's work, though a child at heart—

He saw all spoiled. 'Don't let him cut my hand off—
The doctor, when he comes. Don't let him, sister!'
So. But the hand was gone already.
The doctor put him in the dark of ether.
He lay and puffed his lips out with his breath.
And then—the watcher at his pulse took fright.
No one believed. They listened at his heart.
Little—less—nothing!—and that ended it.
No more to build on there. And they, since they
Were not the one dead, turned to their affairs.

B

She should have died hereafter.
There would have been a time for such a word.
Tomorrow, and tomorrow, and tomorrow
Creeps in this petty pace from day to day
To the last syllable of recorded time.
And all our yesterdays have lighted fools
The way to dusty death. Out, out, brief candle.
Life's but a walking shadow, a poor player
That struts and frets his hour upon the stage,
And then is heard no more. <u>It is a tale</u>
<u>Told by an idiot, full of sound and fury,</u>
<u>Signifying nothing.</u>

**01** What is the main theme of the poem <A>?

___

___

___

**02** What is the tone of the passage <B>?

______________________________________________

**03** What is the figure of speech used in the underlined part of the poem <A>?

______________________________________________

**04** What is the figure of speech used in the underlined part of the <B>? What is compared to what? Explain the meaning of it.

______________________________________________

______________________________________________

______________________________________________

**05** The title of the poem <A> is an allusion to the passage <B>. Explain the function of the allusion.

______________________________________________

______________________________________________

______________________________________________

______________________________________________

______________________________________________

**06** Read the poem and follow the directions.

**Loveliest of Trees**

Loveliest of trees, the cherry now
Is hung with bloom along the bough,
And stands about the woodland ride
Wearing white for Eastertide.

Now, of my threescore years and ten,
Twenty will not come again,
And take from seventy springs a score,
It only leaves me fifty more.

And since to look at things in bloom
Fifty springs are little room,
About the woodlands I will go
To see the cherry hung with snow.

How old is the speaker? Identify the theme of the poem, providing supporting clues that reveal this. Use specific references to the poem.

유희태 영미문학 ④

# 영미문학 문제은행

Part

# 02

# 기본이론문제 2

# 01 회 기본이론문제 2

모범답안 p.15

**[1-3] Read the poem and follow the directions.** [25 points]

My galley, chargèd with forgetfulness,
Thorough* sharp seas in winter nights doth pass
'Tween rock and rock; and eke* mine enemy, alas,
That is my lord, steereth with cruelness;
And every oar a thought in readiness,
As though that death were light in such a case.
An endless wind doth tear the sail apace
Of forced sighs and trusty fearfulness.
A rain of tears, a cloud of dark disdain,
Hath done the weared cords great hinderance;
Wreathèd with error and eke with ignorance.
The stars be hid that led me to this pain;
Drownèd is Reason that should me comfort,
And I remain despairing of the port.

** Thorough: Through*
** eke: also*

**01** **What type of poem is the poem above?** [5 points]

**02** **What is the rhyme scheme of the poem?** [10 points]

**03** **Fill in the blank with TWO words.** [10 points]

> The poem is constructed around an ____________ of a ship in a perilous storm which is compared to a spurned love.

**[4-6] Read the poem and follow the directions.** [25 points]

One day I wrote her name upon the strand,
But came the waves and washèd it away:
Again I wrote it with a second hand,
But came the tide and made my pains his prey.
Vain man (said she) that dost in vain assay
A mortal thing so to immortalise;
For I myself shall like to this decay,
And eke my name be wipèd out likewise.
Not so (quod I); let <u>baser things</u> devise
To die in dust, but you shall live by fame;
My verse your virtues rare shall eternise,
And in the heavens write your glorious name:
Where, when as Death shall all the world subdue,
Our love shall live, and later life renew.

**04** **What is the rhythm of the poem?** [5 points]

**05** **What is the rhyme scheme of the poem?** [10 points]

**06** What does the underlined "baser things" represent? Write your answer in 10 words or less. [10 points]

**[7-10] Read the poem and follow the directions.** [50 points]

**Sonnet 19**

ⓐ Devouring Time, blunt thou the lion's paws,
And make the earth devour her own sweet brood;
Pluck the keen teeth from the fierce tiger's jaws,
And burn the long-liv'd Phoenix in her blood;
Make glad and sorry seasons as thou fleets,
And do whate'er thou wilt, swift-footed Time,
To the wide world and all her fading sweets;
But I forbid thee one more heinous crime:
ⓑ O, carve not with the hours my love's fair brow,
Nor draw no lines there with thine antique pen!
Him in thy course untainted do allow
For beauty's pattern to succeeding men.
Yet do thy worst, old Time! Despite thy wrong
My love shall in my verse ever live young.

**07** What is the rhyme scheme of the poem? [10 points]

**08** Identify the figures of speech used in the underlined ⓐ and ⓑ respectively. [10 points]

**09** What is the main theme of the poem? [10 points]

**10** Paraphrase the lines 9-12. [20 points]

# 02회 기본이론문제 2

모범답안 p.16

**[1-4] Read the poem and follow the directions.** [45 points]

As virtuous men pass mildly away,
  And whisper to their souls to go,
Whilst some of their sad friends do say,
  "Now his breath goes," and some say, "No."

So let us melt, and make no noise,
  No tear-floods, nor sigh-tempests move;
'Twere profanation of our joys
  To tell the laity our love.

ⓐ <u>Moving of th' earth</u> brings harms and fears;
  Men reckon what it did, and meant;
But trepidation of the spheres,
  Though greater far, is innocent.

Dull sublunary lovers' love
  —Whose soul is sense—cannot admit
Of absence, 'cause it doth remove
  The thing which elemented ⓑ <u>it</u>.

But we by a love so much refined,
  That our selves know not what it is,
Inter-assurèd of the mind,
  Care less, eyes, lips and hands to miss.

<u>Our two souls therefore, which are one,</u>
  <u>Though I must go, endure not yet</u>
<u>A breach, but an expansion,</u>
  <u>Like gold to aery thinness beat</u>.

If they be two, they are two so
  As stiff twin compasses are two;
Thy soul, the fix'd foot, makes no show
  To move, but doth, if th' other do.



**01** **In the first stanza, what is compared to what?** [10 points]

**02** **What does the underlined ⓐ Moving of th' earth refer to?** [10 points]

**03** **What does the underlined ⓑ it refer to?** [5 points]

**04** **Explain the meaning of the paradox and simile used in the sixth stanza.** [20 points]

[5-7] **Read the poem and follow the directions.** [30 points]

Drink to me only with thine eyes
  And I will pledge with mine.
Or leave a kiss but in the cup
  And I'll not look for wine.
The thirst that from the soul doth rise
  Doth ask a drink divine;
But might I of Jove's nectar sup,
  I would not change for thine.

I sent thee late a rosy wreath,
  Not so much hon'ring thee
As giving it a hope that there
  It could not withered be;
But thou thereon did'st only breathe,
  And sent'st it back to me,
Since when <u>it</u> grows and smells, I swear
  Not of itself, but thee.

**05** **Who is the speaker of the poem?** [10 points]

**06** **What does the underlined "it" refer to?** [5 points]

**07** **Fill in the blanks with appropriate words.** [15 points]

The speaker creates a romantic tone by catering to one's senses as if he will win Celia over by appealing to her senses. Beginning with ___ⓐ___, the speaker asks Celia to look into his eyes, suggesting intimate eye contact. The speaker then calls on the sense of ___ⓑ___ for a kiss, physical affection between two people. Next comes the speaker's appeal to ___ⓒ___ with wine and nectar, one a delicacy of man, the other a delicacy of the gods. Finally, the scent of the roses pleases the sense of ___ⓓ___. Each of these is associated with romance: gazing into the other's eyes, giving a kiss, the flavorful wine, and the fragrant roses; thus, the speaker's appeal to the senses is an elegant call to romance.

**08** **Read the poem and follow the direction.** [10 points]

Go, lovely Rose—
Tell her that wastes her time and me,
That now she knows,
When I resemble her to thee,
How sweet and fair she seems to be.

Tell her that's young,
And shuns to have her graces spied,
That hadst thou sprung
In deserts where no men abide,
Thou must have uncommended died.

Small is the worth
Of beauty from the light retired:
Bid her come forth,
Suffer herself to be desired,
And not blush so to be admired.

Then die—that she
The common fate of all things rare
May read in thee;
How small a part of time they share
That are so wondrous sweet and fair!

**What is the main theme of the poem?**

**[9-10] Read the poem and follow the directions.** [15 points]

> Death, be not proud, though some have called thee
> Mighty and dreadful, for, thou art not so,
> For, those, whom thou think'st, thou dost overthrow,
> Die not, poor death, nor yet canst thou kill me.
> From rest and sleep, which but thy pictures be,
> Much pleasure, then from thee, much more must flow,
> And soonest our best men with thee doe go,
> Rest of their bones, and soul's delivery.
> Thou art slave to Fate, Chance, kings, and desperate men,
> And dost with poison, warre, and sickness dwell,
> And poppy, or charms can make us sleep as well,
> And better then thy stroke; why swell'st thou then?
> One short sleep past, we wake eternally,
> And death shall be no more; death, thou shalt die.

**09** **Identify the figurative language used in line 5 and explain the meaning of it.** [10 points]

______________________________

______________________________

______________________________

**10** **Identify the figure of speech commonly used in lines 1 and 4.** [5 points]

______________________________

______________________________

______________________________

# 03회 기본이론문제 2

모범답안 p.18

**[1-3] Read the poem and follow the directions.** [20 points]

Get up, get up for shame, the blooming morn
Upon her wings presents the god unshorn.
  See how Aurora throws her fair
  Fresh-quilted colours through the air:
  Get up, sweet slug-a-bed, and see
  The dew bespangling herb and tree.
Each flower has wept and bow'd toward the east
Above an hour since: yet you not dress'd;
  Nay! not so much as out of bed?
  When all the birds have matins said
  And sung their thankful hymns, 'tis sin,
  Nay, profanation to keep in,
Whereas a thousand virgins on this day
Spring, sooner than the lark, to fetch in May.

Come, let us go while we are in our prime;
And take the harmless folly of the time.
  We shall grow old apace, and die
  Before we know our liberty.
  ⓐ <u>Our life is short, and our days run</u>
  <u>As fast away as does the sun;</u>
And, ⓑ <u>as a vapour or a drop of rain</u>
<u>Once lost, can ne'er be found again,</u>

So when or you or I are made
A fable, song, or fleeting shade,
All love, all liking, all delight
Lies drowned with us in endless night.
Then while time serves, and we are but decaying,
Come, my Corinna, come, let's go a-Maying.

**01** **What is the main theme of the poem?** [10 points]

**02** **Identify the figurative language used in the underlined ⓐ.** [5 points]

**03** **Identify the figurative language used in the underlined ⓑ.** [5 points]

**[4-5] Read the poem and follow the directions.** [20 points]

My mother bore me in the southern wild,
And I am black, but O! my soul is white;
White as an angel is the English child:
But I am black as if bereav'd of light.

My mother taught me underneath a tree
And sitting down before the heat of day,
She took me on her lap and kissed me,
And pointing to the east began to say.

Look on the rising sun: there God does live
And gives his light, and gives his heat away.
And flowers and trees and beasts and men receive
Comfort in morning joy in the noonday.

And we are put on earth a little space,
That we may learn to bear the beams of love,
And these black bodies and this sun-burnt face
Is but a cloud, and like a shady grove.

For when our souls have learn'd the heat to bear
The cloud will vanish we shall hear his voice.
Saying: come out from the grove my love & care,
And round my golden tent like lambs rejoice.

Thus did my mother say and kissed me,
And thus I say to little English boy.
When I from black and he from white cloud free,
And round the tent of God like lambs we joy:

I'll shade him from the heat till he can bear,
To lean in joy upon our fathers knee.
And then I'll stand and stroke his silver hair,
And be like him and he will then love me.



## 04 Fill in the blanks. [15 points]

The poem centers on a spiritual awakening to a divine love that transcends ___ⓐ___. The speaker internalizes ___ⓑ___ and applies it in his relations with the outer world; specifically, Blake shows us what happens when the boy applies it to his relationship with a white child. The results are ambivalent. The boy explains to his white friend that they are equals, but that neither will be truly free until they are released from the constraints of the physical world. He imagines himself shading his friend from the brightness of God's love until he can become accustomed to it. This statement implies that the black boy is better prepared for heaven than the white boy, perhaps because of the greater burden of his dark skin has posed during earthly life. This is part of the consoling vision with which his mother has prepared him, which allows his suffering to become a source of ___ⓒ___ rather than shame.

## 05 What is the rhyme scheme of the poem? [5 points]

**[6-7] Read the poem and follow the directions.** [25 points]

O my Luve's* like a red, red rose,
That's newly sprung in June:
O my Luve's like the melodie,
That's sweetly play'd in tune.

As fair art thou, my bonie lass*,
So deep in luve am I;
And I will luve thee still, my dear,
Till a' the seas gang dry.

Till a' the seas gang* dry, my dear,
And the rocks melt wi' the sun;
And I will luve thee still, my dear,
While the sands o' life shall run.

And fare-thee-weel, my only Luve!
And fare-thee-weel, a while!
And I will come again, my Luve,
Tho' 'twere ten thousand mile!

** luve: love*
** bonny lass: pretty girl*
** gang: go*

## 06 **Paraphrase the lines 5-6.** [15 points]

______________________________

______________________________

______________________________

**07** What is the main figure of speech used in the third stanza? [10 points]

**[8-10] Read the poem and follow the directions.** [35 points]

Is this a holy thing to see,
In a rich and fruitful land,
Babes reduced to misery,
Fed with cold and usurous hand?

Is that trembling cry a song?
Can it be a song of joy?
And so many children poor?
It is a land of poverty!

And their sun does never shine.
And their fields are bleak and bare.
And their ways are fill'd with thorns.
It is eternal winter there.

For wheree'er the sun does shine,
And wheree'er the rain does fall:
Babe can never hunger there,
Nor poverty the mind appall.

**08** **What is the primary objective of the poem? Write your answer in less than 10 words.** [10 points]

**09** In the first stanza, the speaker contrasts the "rich and fruitful land" with the actions of a "cold and usurous hand." Why does the speaker use the contrast? Write your answer in 20-30 words. [15 points]

**10** What does the failing crops and sunless fields symbolize? Write your answer using the given words below. [10 points]

| wasting, nation's resources, public's, future |
|---|

# 04회 기본이론문제 2

모범답안 p.20

**[1-4] Read the poem and follow the directions.** [40 points]

When I have fears that I may cease to be
Before my pen has glean'd my teeming brain,
<u>Before high-piled books, in charactery,</u>
<u>Hold like rich garners the full ripen'd grain;</u>
When I behold, upon the night's starr'd face,
Huge cloudy symbols of a high romance,
And think that I may never live to trace
Their shadows, <u>with the magic hand of chance</u>;
And when I feel, fair creature of an hour,
That I shall never look upon thee more,
Never have relish in the faery power
Of unreflecting love;—then on the shore
Of the wide world I stand alone, and think
Till Love and Fame to nothingness do sink.

## 01 Fill in the blanks with a proper word each. [10 points]

In the poem, the speaker contemplates all of the things that he wants in life: ______ⓐ______, and ______ⓑ______.

______________________________

______________________________

______________________________

**02** **Identify the figure of speech used in the eighth line.** [5 points]

**03** **Paraphrase the third and fourth lines of the poem.** [15 points]

**04** **Fill in the blanks with appropriate words.** [10 points]

> In lines 1, 2, 3, 5, 11, 14, the speaker uses temporal indicators as the first word of each of these lines, creating a feeling of expectation through the use of ___ⓐ___. In line 5, ___ⓑ___ the night by turning its stars into a "face" allows the speaker to interact with it as he would a real person.

**[5-6] Read the poem and follow the directions.** [25 points]

When we two parted
In silence and tears,
Half broken-hearted
To sever for years,
Pale grew thy cheek and cold,
Colder thy kiss;
Truly that hour foretold
Sorrow to this.

The dew of the morning
Sank chill on my brow—
It felt like the warning
Of what I feel now.
Thy vows are all broken,
And light is thy fame:
I hear thy name spoken,
And share in its shame.

<u>They name thee before me,</u>
<u>A knell in mine ear</u>;
A shudder come o'er me—
Why wert thou so dear?
They know not I knew thee,
Who knew thee too well:—
Long, long shall I rue thee,
Too deeply to tell.

In secret we met—
In silence I grieve,
That thy heart could forget,
Thy spirit deceive.
If I should meet thee
After long years,
How should I greet thee?—
With silence and tears.

**05** **What does the repetition of "silence and tears" at the beginning and end of the poem denote? Write your answer in about 10 words.** [10 points]

______________________________

______________________________

______________________________

**06** **Identify the figure of speech used in the underlined part and explain the meaning of it.** [15 points]

______________________________

______________________________

______________________________

**[7-10] Read the poem and follow the directions.** [35 points]

I am: yet what I am none cares or knows,
ⓐ <u>My friends forsake me like a memory lost</u>;
I am the self-consumer of my woes,
ⓑ <u>They</u> rise and vanish in oblivious host,
Like shades in love and death's oblivion lost;
And yet I am! and live with shadows tossed

Into the nothingness of scorn and noise,
Into the living sea of waking dreams,
Where there is neither sense of life nor joys,
But the vast shipwreck of my life's esteems;
And e'en the dearest—that I loved the best—
Are strange—nay, rather stranger than the rest.

**07** **Fill in the blanks with appropriate terms.** [5 points]

> The poem above consists of two stanzas of ____ⓒ____ each. The second stanza follow the ababcc rhyme scheme, while the first stanza's rhyme scheme is ____ⓓ____.

**08** **What does the underlined ⓑ They refer to?** [5 points]

**09** Identify the figure of speech used in the underlined ⓐ and explain the meaning of it. [15 points]

**10** What is the poem about? Write your answer using the given words below. [10 points]

| exploration, meaning, value, an isolated |
| --- |

# 05회 기본이론문제 2

모범답안 p.21

**[1-4] Read the poem and follow the directions.** [40 points]

The sea is calm tonight.
The tide is full, the moon lies fair
Upon the straits—on the French coast the light
Gleams and is gone; the cliffs of England stand,
Glimmering and vast, out in the tranquil bay.
Come to the window, sweet is the night air!
Only, from the long line of spray
Where the sea meets the moon-blanched land,
Listen! you hear the grating roar
Of pebbles which the waves draw back, and fling,
At their return, up the high strand,
Begin, and cease, and then again begin,
With tremulous cadence slow, and bring
The eternal note of sadness in.

<u>The Sea of Faith</u>
<u>Was once, too, at the full, and round earth's shore</u>
<u>Lay like the folds of a bright girdle furled.</u>
But now I only hear
Its melancholy, long, withdrawing roar,
Retreating, to the breath
Of the night-wind, down the vast edges drear
And naked shingles of the world.

Ah, love, let us be true
To one another! for the world, which seems
To lie before us like a land of dreams,
So various, so beautiful, so new,
Hath really neither joy, nor love, nor light,
Nor certitude, nor peace, nor help for pain;
And we here as on a darkling plain
Swept with confused alarms of struggle and flight,
Where ignorant armies clash by night.

**01** As precisely as possible, define the implied scene: What is the speaker's physical location? Whom is he addressing? What is the time of day? [10 points]

**02** Identify figures of speech used in the underlined part and explain the meaning of the part. [12 points]

**03** Discuss the imagery in the last three lines. Are the "armies" figurative or literal? [13 points]

**04** What is the overall tone of the poem? [5 points]

**[5-8] Read the poem and follow the directions.** [35 points]

My aspens dear, whose airy cages quelled,
Quelled or quenched in leaves the leaping sun,
All felled, felled, are all felled;
ⓐ <u>Of a fresh and following folded rank</u>
<u>Not spared, not one</u>
<u>That dandled a sandalled</u>
<u>Shadow that swam or sank</u>
<u>On meadow and river and wind-wandering weed-winding bank</u>.

O if we but knew what we do
When we delve or hew—
Hack and rack the growing green!
Since country is so tender
To touch, her being so slender,
ⓑ <u>That, like this sleek and seeing ball</u>
<u>But a prick will make no eye at all,</u>
Where we, even where we mean
To mend her we end her,
When we hew or delve:
After-comers cannot guess the beauty been.

**05** **In the underlined part ⓐ, metaphor is used. Explain it.** [12 points]

**06** **What is the overall tone of the poem?** [5 points]

**07** **Fill in the blanks with appropriate words** [5 points]

___ⓒ___ is a poetic rhythm designed to imitate the rhythm of natural speech. The above poem is written in ___ⓒ___, in which the number of accents in a line are counted, but the number of syllables are not. The result is that the poet is able to group accented syllables together, creating striking ___ⓓ___ effects. In the third line, for example, the heavy recurrence of the accented words "all" and "felled" strike the ear like the blows of an ax on the tree trunks.

**08** **In the underlined part ⓑ, a startling and painful image is used. What is this? Why does the poet use the image?** [13 points]

[9-10] **Read the poem and follow the directions.** [25 points]

That is no country for old men. The young
In ⓐ <u>one another's arms</u>, birds in the trees
—ⓑ <u>Those dying generations</u>—at their song,
ⓒ <u>The salmon-falls</u>, the mackerel-crowded seas,
Fish, flesh, or fowl commend all summer long
Whatever is begotten, born, and dies.
Caught in that ⓓ <u>sensual music</u> all neglect
ⓔ <u>Monuments of unaging intellect</u>.

An aged man is but a paltry thing,
A tattered coat upon a stick, unless
Soul clap its hands and sing, and louder sing
For every tatter in its mortal dress,
Nor is there singing school but studying
Monuments of its own magnificence;
And therefore I have sailed the seas and come
To the holy city of Byzantium.

**09** **Which one is different from the rest in terms of meaning?** [10 points]

**10** **Paraphrase the second stanza of the poem. Write your answer in about 50 words.** [15 points]

# 06회 기본이론문제 2

모범답안 p.23

**[1-3] Read the poem and follow the directions.** [30 points]

Little thinks, in the field, yon red-cloaked clown,
Of thee from the hill-top looking down;
The heifer that lows in the upland farm,
Far-heard, lows not thine ear to charm;
The sexton, tolling his bell at noon,
Deems not that great Napoleon
Stops his horse, and lists with delight,
Whilst his files sweep round yon Alpine height;
Nor knowest thou what argument
Thy life to thy neighbor's creed has lent.
All are needed by each one;
Nothing is fair or good alone.
I thought the sparrow's note from heaven,
Singing at dawn on the alder bough;
I brought him home, in his nest, at even;
He sings the song, but it pleases not now,
For I did not bring home the river and sky;—
He sang to my ear,—they sang to my eye.
The delicate shells lay on the shore;
The bubbles of the latest wave
Fresh pearls to their enamel gave;
And the bellowing of thc savagc sea
Greeted their safe escape to me.
I wiped away the weeds and foam,
I fetched my sea-born treasures home;
But <u>the poor, unsightly, noisome things</u>
Had left their beauty on the shore,
With the sun, and the sand, and the wild uproar.

**01** **Fill in the blanks below using the given words below.** [10 points]

The thematic idea of the poem is "nothing is fair or good alone." Transcendentalists believed the nature and the universe was like a circle, perfect and whole. They believed that a life force connected everything. The speaker of the poem describes examples of artifacts (or creatures) that ______________________________.

removed, natural place, have lost, natural beauty

______________________________

______________________________

______________________________

**02** **In the poem above, the poet indicates the true way to appreciate the wonders of the natural world. Explain it by mentioning at least one example.** [15 points]

______________________________

______________________________

______________________________

**03** **What does the underlined "the poor, unsightly, noisome things" refer to?** [5 points]

______________________________

______________________________

______________________________

**[4-7] Read the poem and follow the directions.** [30 points]

Lay your sleeping head, my love,
Human on my faithless arm;
Time and fevers burn away
Individual beauty from
Thoughtful children, and ⓐ the grave
Proves the child ephemeral:
But in my arms till break of day
Let the living creature lie,
Mortal, guilty, but to me
The entirely beautiful.

ⓑ Soul and body have no bounds:
To lovers as they lie upon
ⓒ Her tolerant enchanted slope
In their ordinary swoon,
Grave the vision Venus sends
Of supernatural sympathy,
Universal love and hope;
While an abstract insight wakes
Among the glaciers and the rocks
The hermit's carnal ecstasy.

Certainty, fidelity
On the stroke of midnight pass
Like vibrations of a bell
And fashionable madmen raise
Their pedantic boring cry:
Every farthing* of the cost,
All the dreaded cards foretell,
Shall be paid, but from this night
Not a whisper, not a thought,
Not a kiss nor look be lost.

**farthing: a British coin which is no longer in use. 1/4 penny.*

**04** What does the underlined ⓐ the grave / Proves the child ephemeral mean? [10 points]

**05** What does the underlined ⓑ Soul and body have no bounds: / To lovers as they lie upon mean? [10 points]

**06** What does the underlined ⓒ Her refer to? [5 points]

**07** What is the tone of the third stanza? [5 points]

**[8-10] Read the poem and follow the directions.** [40 points]

Tell me not, in mournful numbers,
  Life is but an empty dream!—
For the soul is dead that slumbers,
  And things are not what they seem.

Life is real! Life is earnest!
  And the grave is not its goal;
Dust thou art, to dust returnest,
  Was not spoken of the soul.

Not enjoyment, and not sorrow,
  Is our destined end or way;
But to act, that each to-morrow
  Find us farther than to-day.

Art is long, and Time is fleeting,
  And our hearts, though stout and brave,
Still, like muffled drums, are beating
  Funeral marches to the grave.

<u>In the world's broad field of battle,</u>
  <u>In the bivouac* of Life,</u>
<u>Be not like dumb, driven cattle!</u>
  <u>Be a hero in the strife</u>!

<u>Lives of great men all remind us</u>
  <u>We can make our lives sublime,</u>
<u>And, departing, leave behind us</u>
  <u>Footprints on the sands of time;</u>

** bivouac: a military encampment made with tents or improvised shelters, usually without shelter or protection from enemy fire.*

**08** **What is the rhythm of the poem?** [10 points]

______________________________

______________________________

______________________________

**09** **What is the figure of speech used in the first two lines of the fifth stanza? Also, explain the speaker's main idea expressed in the stanza.** [15 points]

______________________________

______________________________

______________________________

**10** **Explain the speaker's main idea expressed in the sixth stanza.** [15 points]

In the stanza, the speaker tells the reader that ______________________________

______________________________

______________________________

______________________________

# 07회 기본이론문제 2

모범답안 p.26

**[1-2] Read the poem and follow the directions.** [20 points]

I like to see it lap the miles,
And lick the valleys up,
And stop to feed itself at tanks;
And then, prodigious, step

Around a pile of mountains,
And, supercilious, peer
In shanties by the sides of roads;
And then a quarry pare

To fit its sides, and crawl between,
Complaining all the while
In horrid, hooting stanza;
Then chase itself down hill

And neigh like Boanerges;
Then, punctual as a star,
Stop—docile and omnipotent—
At its own stable door.

**01** **What does the underlined "it" refer to?** [5 points]

**02** **Paraphrase the poem in about 50 words.** [15 points]

**03** **Read the poem and follow the directions.** [15 points]

I'm nobody! Who are you?
Are you nobody, too?
Then there's a pair of us—don't tell!
They'd banish—you know!

How dreary to be somebody!
How public like a frog
To tell one's name the livelong day
To an admiring bog!

**Who does the speaker satirize in the poem? Why?**

**[4-7] Read the poem and follow the directions.** [38 points]

Call the roller of big cigars,
The muscular one, and bid him whip
In kitchen cups ⓐ concupiscent curds.
Let the wenches dawdle in such dress
As they are used to wear, and let the boys
Bring flowers in last month's newspapers.
ⓑ Let be be finale of seem.
The only emperor is the emperor of ice-cream.

Take from the dresser of deal,
Lacking the three glass knobs, that sheet
On which she embroidered fantails once
And spread it so as to cover her face.
If her horny feet protrude, they come
To show how cold she is, and dumb.
Let ⓒ the lamp affix its beam.
The only emperor is the emperor of ice-cream.

**04** **What does the underlined ⓐ represent?** [10 points]

**05** Paraphrase the underlined ⓑ Let be be finale of seem. [15 points]

**06** Fill in the blank with an appropriate word [5 points]

In the poem above, the speaker tells the reader about the thematic contrast between life and ____________. The poem is broken up into two stanzas that can be labeled as the "life" and ____________ stanzas of the poem. The form and content of the poem support this idea, and both compliment each other to form a poem divided not just physically by its break in stanzas, but also by the content of each stanza and its respective meaning.

**07** What does the underlined ⓒ the lamp symbolize? [8 points]

**[8-10] Read the poem and follow the directions.** [27 points]

What thoughts I have of you tonight, Walt Whitman, for I walked down the sidestreets under the trees with a headache self-conscious looking at the full moon.
ⓐ <u>In my hungry fatigue, and shopping for images, I went into the neon fruit supermarket, dreaming of your enumerations!</u>
<u>What peaches and what penumbras! Whole families shopping at night!</u> Aisles full of husbands! Wives in the avocados, babies in the tomatoes!—and you, Garcia Lorca, what were you doing down by the watermelons?

I saw you, Walt Whitman, childless, lonely old grubber, poking among the meats in the refrigerator and eyeing the grocery boys.
I heard you asking questions of each: Who killed the pork chops? What price bananas? Are you my Angel?
I wandered in and out of the brilliant stacks of cans following you, and followed in my imagination by the store detective.
We strode down the open corridors together in our solitary fancy tasting artichokes, possessing every frozen delicacy, and never passing the cashier.

Where are we going, Walt Whitman? The doors close in an hour. Which way does your beard point tonight?
(I touch your book and dream of our odyssey in the supermarket and feel absurd.)
Will we walk all night through solitary streets? The trees add shade to shade, lights out in the houses, we'll both be lonely.
Will we stroll dreaming of the lost America of love past blue automobiles in driveways, home to our silent cottage?
Ah, ⓑ <u>dear father</u>, graybeard, lonely old courage-teacher, what America did you have when Charon quit poling his ferry and you got out on a smoking bank and stood watching the boat disappear on the black waters of Lethe?

02

**08** **Fill in the blanks with appropriate words.** [12 points]

The speaker thinks of Walt Whitman as he ______ⓒ______. Speaking to an imagined Whitman, the speaker enters a ______ⓓ______, and notices all of the families shopping. He imagines he sees ______ⓔ______, a Spanish poet and playwright, shopping for watermelons. The speaker addresses Whitman again, and imagines that he sees him shopping for meat and asking questions of ______ⓕ______. He wanders around the stacks of cans, and imagines that he's being followed by ______ⓖ______. He then imagines that he and Whitman sample the food in the supermarket without paying for it. The speaker feels lost, and asks Whitman ______ⓗ______. He thinks of Whitman's book and feels silly. He then asks Whitman a number of big life questions.

**09** What does the speaker make a comment on in the underlined ⓐ? [10 points]

**10** What or who does the underlined ⓑ dear father refer to? [5 points]

MEMO

literature

유희태 영미문학 ❹

# 영미문학 문제은행

Part

# 03

# 실전모의고사

# 01 회 실전모의고사

모범답안 p.28

**01** **Read the excerpt from a fiction and follow the directions.** [4 points]

For all her sleek beauty, Edith Bradin was a grave, slow-thinking girl. There was a streak in her of that same desire to ponder, of that adolescent idealism that had turned her brother socialist and pacifist. Henry Bradin had left Cornell University, where he had been an instructor in economies, and had come to New York to pour the latest cures for incurable evils into the columns of a radical weekly newspaper.

"Why, Edith!" He rose quickly and approached her in surprise, removing his eye-shade. He was tall, lean, and dark, with black, piercing eyes under very thick glasses. They were far-away eyes that seemed always fixed just over the head of the person to whom he was talking.

He put his hands on her arms and kissed her cheek.

"What is it?" he repeated in some alarm.

"I had a dance party across at Delmonico's, Henry," she said excitedly, "and I couldn't resist tearing over to see you."

"I'm glad you did."

"You should have come earlier," interrupted Bartholomew, Henry's co-worker. ⓐ "<u>We had a regular vaudeville</u>."

"Did you really?"

"A serenade," said Henry. "A lot of soldiers gathered down there in the street and began to yell at the sign."

"Why?" she demanded.

"Just a crowd," said Henry, abstractedly. "All crowds have to howl. They didn't have anybody with much initiative in the lead, or they'd probably have forced their way in here and smashed things up."

"Yes," said Bartholomew, turning again to Edith, "you should have been here."

"Are the soldiers all set against the socialists?" demanded Edith of her brother. "I mean do they attack you violently and all that?"

Henry replaced his eye-shade and yawned. "The human race has come a long way, but most of us are throw-backs; the soldiers don't know what they want, or what they hate, or what they like. They're used to acting in large bodies, and they seem to have to make demonstrations. So it happens to be against us. There've been riots all over the city to-night. It's May Day, you see."

"You're glad to see me, Henry?"

"Why, sure."

"You don't seem to be."

"I am."

"I suppose you think I'm a—a waster. Sort of ⓑ the World's Worst Butterfly."

Henry laughed. "Not at all. Have a good time while you're young. Why? Do I seem like the priggish and earnest youth?"

"No—" she paused, "—but somehow I began thinking how absolutely different the party I'm on is from—from all your purposes. It seems sort of—of incongruous, doesn't it?—me being at a party like that, and you over here working for a thing that'll make that sort of party impossible ever any more, if your ideas work."

"I don't think of it that way. You're young, and you're acting just as you were brought up to act. Go ahead—have a good time?"

**Explain what Bartholomew means when he says "We had a regular vaudeville". Do NOT copy more than FOUR consecutive words from the passage. Second, describe what Edith has done to make herself feel like "the World's Worst butterfly".**

## 02 Read the poem and follow the directions. [4 points]

Give up sitting dutifully at your desk. Leave
your ⓐ house or apartment. Go out into the world.

It's all right to carry a notebook but a cheap
one is best, with pages the color of weak tea
and on the front a kitten or a space ship.

Avoid any enclosed space where more than
three people are wearing ⓑ turtlenecks. Beware
any ⓒ snow-covered chalet* with deer tracks
across the muffled tennis courts.

Not surprisingly, ⓓ libraries are a good place to write.
And the perfect place in a library is near an aisle
where a child a year or two old is playing as his
mother browses ⓔ the ranks of the dead.

Often he will pull books from the bottom shelf.
The title, the author's name, the brooding photo
on the flap mean nothing. Red book on black, gray
book on brown, he builds a tower. And the higher
it gets, the wider he grins.

You who asked for advice, listen: When the tower
falls, be like that child. Laugh so loud everybody
in the world frowns and says, "Shhhh."

Then start again.

** chalet: a traditional shepherd's hut*

Identify the ONE thing among ⓐ–ⓑ that is different from the rest in terms of the context of the poem. Second, explain what the speaker's "advice" in stanza six is. Do NOT copy more than FOUR consecutive words from the poem.

## 03 Read the excerpt from a play and follow the directions. [4 points]

NORA (*a little nervous*) Take no notice of it, Jack; they'll go away in a minute.

*Another knock, followed by the voice of Captain Brennan*

Capt. Brennan Commandant Clitheroe, Commandant Clitheroe, are you there? A message from General Jim Connolly.

Clitheroe Damn it, it's Captain. Brennan.

Nora (*anxiously*) Don't mind him, don't mind, Jack. Don't break our happiness··· Pretend we're not in··· Let us forget everything to-night but our two selves!

Clitheroe (*reassuringly*) Don't be alarmed, darling; I'll just see what he wants, an' send him about his business.

Nora (*tremulously—putting her arms around him*) No, no. Please, Jack; don't open it. Please, for your own little Nora's sake!

Clitheroe (*Rising to open the door*) Now don't be silly, Nora.

*Clitheroe opens the door, and admits Capt. Brennan in the full uniform of the Irish Citizen Army. He carries a letter in his hand. When he comes in, he smartly salutes Clitheroe.*

Capt. Brennan (*giving the letter to Clitheroe*) A dispatch from General Connolly.

Clitheroe (*reading*) "Commandant Clitheroe is to take command of the eighth battalion of the ICA*, which will assemble to proceed to the meeting at nine o'clock. He is to see that all units are provided with full equipment: two days' rations and fifty rounds of ammunition. At two o'clock a.m. the army will leave Liberty Hall for a reconnaissance attack on Dublin Castle.—Command Gen. Connolly."

Clitheroe (*in surprise, to Capt. Brennan*) I don't understand this. Why does General Connolly call me Commandant?

Capt. Brennan The Staff appointed you Commandant, and the General agreed with their selection.

Clitheroe When, did this happen?

Capt. Brennan A fortnight ago.

Clitheroe How is it word was never sent to me?

Capt. Brennan Word was sent to you··· I myself brought it.

Clitheroe Who did you give it to, then?

Capt. Brennan (*after a pause*) I think I gave it to Mrs. Clitheroe, there.

Clitheroe Nora, d'ye hear that? (*Nora makes no answer. There is a note of hardness in his voice.*) Nora··· Captain Brennan says he brought a letter to me from General Connolly, and that he gave it to you···. Where is it? What did you do with it?

Nora (*running over to him, and pleadingly putting her arms around him*) Jack, please Jack, don't go out to-night and Ill tell you; I'll explain everything···. Send him away, an' stay with your own little red-lipp'd Nora.

Clitheroe (*removing her arms from around him*) None o' this nonsense, now; I want to know what you did with the letter? Why didn't you give me the letter? What did you do with it?··· What did you do with the letter?

Nora (*flaming up and standing on her feet*) I burned it, I burned it. That's what I did with it! Is General Connolly and the Citizen Army goin' to be your only care?

** ICA : Irish Citizen Army*

**Describe what important news Clitheroe missed? Do NOT copy more than FOUR consecutive words from the passage. Second, explain Nora's emotional change shown in the stage directions.**

# 02회 실전모의고사

모범답안 p.29

**01** **Read the excerpt from a short story and follow the directions.** [4 points]

[A] Myers was travelling through France in a first-class rail car on his way to visit his son in Strasbourg, who was a student at the university there. He hadn't seen the boy in eight years. There had been no phone calls between them during this time, not even a postcard since Myers and the boy's mother had gone their separate ways—the boy staying with her. The final breakup was hastened along, Myers always believed, by the boy's malign interference in their personal affairs.

The last time Myers had seen his son, the boy had lunged for him during a violent quarrel. Myers' wife had been standing by the sideboard, dropping one china plate after the other on to the dining-room floor. Then she'd gone on to the cups. "That's enough," Myers had said, and at that instant the boy charged him. Myers sidestepped and got him in a headlock while the boy wept and pummelled Myers on the back and kidneys. Myers had him, and while he had him he made the most of it. He slammed him into the wall and threatened to kill him. He meant it. "I gave you life," Myers remembered himself shouting, "and I can take it back!"

[B] Thinking about that horrible scene now, Myers shook his head as if it had happened to someone else. And it had. He was simply not that same person. These days he lived alone and had little to do with anybody outside his work. At night he listened to classical music and read books on waterfowl decoys.

He lit a cigarette and continued to gaze out the train window, ignoring the man who sat in the seat next to the door and who slept with a hat pulled over his eyes. It was early in the morning and mist hung over the green fields that passed by outside. Now and then Myers saw a farmhouse and its outbuildings, everything surrounded by a wall. He thought this might be a good way to live—in a remote old house surrounded by a wall.

He stayed awake and began to think of the meeting with his son, which was now only a few hours away. How would he act when he saw the boy at the station? Should he embrace him? He felt uncomfortable with that prospect. Or should he merely offer his hand, smile as if these eight years had never occurred, and then pat the boy on the shoulder? Maybe the boy would say a few words—"I'm glad to see you. How was your trip?" And Myers would say—something. He really didn't know what he was going to say.

**Explain what can be inferred about Myers' character from his interest in the "remote old house surrounded by a wall" in the underlined selection. Second, what was the last direct interaction in <A> that was shaping Myers' contemplation of the reunion?**

## 02 Read the poem and follow the directions. [4 points]

April. And the air dry
As the shoulders of a water buffalo.

Grasshoppers scratch at the dirt,
rub their wings with thin legs
flaring out in front of the soldiers
in low arcing flights, wings a blur.

The soldiers don't notice anymore,
seeing only the wreckage of the streets,
bodies draped with sheets, and the sun,
how bright it is, how hard and flat and white.

It will take many nails from the coffinmakers
to shut out this light, which reflects off everything:
the calloused feet of the dead, their bony hands,
their pale foreheads so cold, bright in the sun.

**Explain the need for nails in the last stanza. Then, complete the commentary below by filling in the blank with the ONE most appropriate word from the poem.**

Commentary

The poet repeatedly states the sun's __________ light that emphasizes and reveals the tragedy of the war.

**03** **Read the excerpt from a play and follow the directions.** [4 points]

*Gallimard, a civil servant of the French embassy in China discusses Vietnam with his colleague Toulon in Gallimard's home. A Chinese spy and opera singer named Song Liling eavesdrops.*

TOULON They're killing ⓐ <u>him</u>.

GALLIMARD Who? I'm sorry? What?

TOULON Bother you to come over at this late hour?

GALLIMARD No··· of course not.

TOULON Not after you hear my secret. Champagne?

GALLIMARD Um.. thank you.

TOULON You're surprised. There's something that you've wanted, Gallimard. No, not a promotion. Next time. Something in the world. You're not aware of this, but there's an informal gossip circle among intelligence agents. And some of ours from some of the Americans—

GALLIMARD Yes?

TOULON That the U.S. will allow the Vietnamese generals to stage a coup··· and assassinate President Diem.

*The chime rings again. Toulon freezes. Gallimard turns upstage and looks at Butterfly, who slowly and deliberately clips a flower off its stem. Gallimard turns back towards Toulon.*

GALLIMARD I think··· that's a very wise move!

*Toulon unfreezes.*

TOULON It's what you've been advocating. A toast?

GALLIMARD Sure. I consider this a vindication.

TOULON Not exactly. "To the test. Let's hope you pass."

*They drink. The chime rings again. Toulon freezes. Gallimard turns upstage, and Song clips another flower.*

GALLIMARD (*To Toulon*) The test?

TOULON (*Unfreezing*) It's a test of everything you've been saying. I personally think the generals probably will stop the Communists. And you'll be a hero. But if anything goes wrong, then your opinions won't be worth a pig's ear. I'm sure that won't happen. But sometimes it's easier when they don't listen to you.

GALLIMARD They're your opinions too, aren't they?

TOULON ⓑ Personally, yes.

GALLIMARD So we agree.

TOULON But my opinions aren't on that report. Yours are. Cheers.

*Toulon turns away from Gallimard and raises his glass. At that instant Song picks up the vase and hurls it to the ground. It shatters. Song sinks down amidst the shards of the vase, in a calm, childlike trance. She sings softly, as if reciting a child's nursery rhyme.*

SONG "The whole world over, the white man travels, setting anchor, wherever he likes. Life's not worth living, unless he finds, the finest maidens, of every land…"

**Identify the person referenced in the underlined ⓐ. Second, explain what can be inferred from the repeated stage direction *"Toulon freezes"*. Third, explain the meaning of the underlined words in ⓑ.**

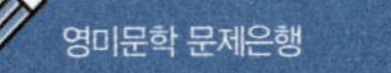



# 03회 실전모의고사

모범답안 p.30

**01** **Read the poem and follow the directions.** [4 points]

I like the generosity of numbers.
The way, for example,
they are willing to count
anything or anyone:
two pickles, one door to the room,
eight dancers dressed as swans.

I like the domesticity of addition—
add two cups of milk and stir—
the sense of plenty: six plums
on the ground, three more
falling from the tree.

And multiplication's school
of fish times fish,
whose silver bodies breed
beneath the shadow
of a boat.

Even subtraction is never loss,
just addition somewhere else:
five sparrows take away two,
the two in someone else's
garden now.

There's an amplitude to long division,
as it opens Chinese take-out
box by paper box,
inside every folded cookie
a new fortune.

And I never fail to be surprised
by the gift of <u>an odd remainder</u>,
footloose at the end:
forty-seven divided by eleven equals four,
with three remaining.

Three boys beyond their mothers' call,
two Italians off to the sea,
one sock that isn't anywhere you look.

**In the fourth stanza, the poet employs a paradox. Explain it. Second, identify the TWO consecutive words from the poem that best correspond to the underlined words.**

## 02 Read the excerpt from a fiction and follow the directions. [4 points]

He stopped opposite the child, and the two regarded each other. The dog hesitated for a moment, but presently he made some little advances with his tail. The child put out his hand and called him. In an apologetic manner the dog came close, and the two had an interchange of friendly pattings and waggles. The dog became more enthusiastic with each moment of the interview, until with his gleeful caperings he threatened to overturn the child. Whereupon the child lifted his hand and struck the dog a blow upon the head.

This thing seemed to overpower and astonish the little dark-brown dog, and wounded him to the heart. He sank down in despair at the child's feet. When the blow was repeated, together with an admonition in childish sentences, he turned over upon his back, and held his paws in a peculiar manner. At the same time with his ears and his eyes he offered a small prayer to the child.

Presently he struggled to his feet and started after the child.

He looked so comical on his back, and holding his paws peculiarly, that the child was greatly amused and gave him little taps repeatedly, to keep him so. But the little dark-brown dog took this chastisement in the most serious way, and no doubt considered that he had committed some grave crime, for he wriggled contritely and showed his repentance in every way that was in his power. He pleaded with the child and petitioned him, and offered more prayers.

At last the child grew weary of this amusement and turned toward home. The dog was praying at the time. He lay on his back and turned his eyes upon the retreating form.

Presently he struggled to his feet and started after the child. The latter wandered in a perfunctory way toward his home, stopping at times to investigate various matters. During one of these pauses he discovered the little dark-brown dog who was following him with the air of a footpad.

The child beat his pursuer with a small stick he had found. The dog lay down and prayed until the child had finished, and resumed his journey. Then he scrambled erect and took up the pursuit again.

On the way to his home the child turned many times and beat the dog, proclaiming with childish gestures that he held him in contempt as an unimportant dog, with no value save for a moment. For being this quality of animal the dog apologized and eloquently expressed regret, but he continued stealthily to follow the child. His manner grew so very guilty that he slunk like an assassin.

**Describe the meaning of the underlined "interview". Second, explain the meaning of the figure of speech employed in the last sentence of the excerpt as it is intended by the narrator.**

## 03 Read the excerpt from a play and follow the directions. [4 points]

*Three Spanish women talk about men.*

Hellena Ah!—would I had never seen my mad gentleman—and yet for all your laughing I am not in love—and yet this small acquaintance, o'my conscience, will never out of my head.

Valerie Ha, ha, ha—I laugh to think how thou art fitted with a lover, a fellow that, I warrant, loves every new face he sees.

Hellena *Hum*—he has not kept his word with me—and may be taken up—that thought is not very pleasant to me—what the Duce should this be now that I feel?

Valerie What is't like?

Hellena Nay, the Lord knows—but if I should be hanged, I cannot choose but be angry and afraid, when I think that mad fellow should be in love with any body but me—What to think of myself I know not—Would I could meet with some true damn'd Gipsy, that I might know my fortune.

Valerie Know it! there's nothing so easy; thou wilt love this wandering inconstant till thou find'st thy self hanged about his Neck, and then be as mad to get free again.

Florence Yes, Valeria; we shall see her bestride* his baggage-horse, and follow him to the Campaign.

Hellena So, so; now you are provided for, there's no care taken of poor me—But since you have set my heart a wishing, I am resolv'd to know for what.

Florence Art thou mad to talk so? Who will like thee well enough to have thee, that hears what a mad wench* thou art?

| | |
|---|---|
| Hellena | Like me! I don't intend, every he that likes me shall have me, but he that I like: I shou'd have staid* in the Nunnery still, if I had lik'd my Lady Abbess as well as she lik'd me. No, I came thence, not *(as my wise Brother imagines)* to take an eternal farewell of the world, but to love and to be belov'd; and I will be belov'd, or I'll get one of your men, so I will. |
| Valerie | Am I put into the number of lovers? |

** bestride: sit on or ride on*
** wench: young girl*
** staid: stayed*

**Explain Valerie's criticism of Hellena's new lover. Do NOT copy more than FOUR consecutive words from the passage. Second, identify where Hellena was previously.**

# 04회 실전모의고사

모범답안 p.31

**01** **Read the excerpt from a novel and follow the directions.** [4 points]

The grass-plot before the jail, in Prison Lane, on a certain summer morning, not less than two centuries ago, was occupied by a pretty large number of the inhabitants of Boston; all with their eyes intently fastened on the iron-clamped oaken door. Amongst any other population, or at a later period in the history of New England, the grim rigidity that petrified the bearded physiognomies of these good people would have augured some awful business in hand. It could have betokened nothing short of the anticipated execution of some noted culprit, on whom the sentence of a legal tribunal had but confirmed the verdict of public sentiment. But, in that early severity of the Puritan character, an inference of this kind could not so indubitably be drawn. It might be that a sluggish bond-servant, or an undutiful child, whom his parents had given over to the civil authority, was to be corrected at the whipping-post. It might be that a Quaker, or other heterodox religionist was to be scourged out of the town, or an idle and vagrant Indian, whom the white man's fire-water* had made riotous about the streets, was to be driven with stripes* into the shadow of the forest. It might be, too, that a witch, like old mistress Hibbins, was to die upon the gallows. In either case, there was very much the same solemnity of demeanor on the part of the spectators; as befitted a people amongst whom religion and law were almost identical, and in whose character both were so thoroughly interfused, that the mildest and the severest acts of public discipline were alike made venerable and awful. Meagre and cold was the sympathy that a transgressor might look for, from such bystanders, at the scaffold*. On the other hand, a penalty, which, in our days, would infer a degree of mocking infamy and ridicule, might then be invested with almost as stern a dignity as the punishment of death itself.

** fire-water: high-proof whiskey*

** stripes: rod or whip*

** scaffold(=gallows): platform on which a criminal is executed by hanging*

**What is the most distinct difference the excerpt draws between a child being scolded publicly during that time in Boston in comparison with today? Second, explain the meaning of the underlined words. Do NOT copy more than FOUR consecutive words from the excerpt.**

03

## 02 Read the poem and follow the directions. [4 points]

I used to lie on the floor for hours after
school with the phone cradled between
my shoulder and my ear, a plate of cold
rice to my left, my school books to my right.
Twirling the cord between my fingers
I spoke to friends who recognized the
language of our realm. Throats and lungs
swollen, we talked into the heart of the night,
toying with the idea of hair dye and suicide,
about the boys who didn't love us,
who we loved too much, the pang
of the nights. <u>Each sentence was
new territory, like a door someone was
rushing into</u>, the glass shattering
with delirium, with knowledge and fear.
My Mother never complained about the phone bill,
what it cost for her daughter to disappear
behind a door, watching the cord
stretching its muscle away from her.
Perhaps she thought it was the only way
she could reach me, sending me away
to speak in the underworld.
As long as I was speaking
she could put my ear to the tenuous earth
and allow me to listen, to decipher.
And these were the elements of my Mother,
the earthed wire, the burning cable,

as if she flowed into the room with
me to somehow say, Stay where I can reach you,
the dim room, the dark earth. Speak of this
and when you feel removed from it
I will pull the cord and take you
back towards me.

**Explain what the speaker tells the reader by employing the figure of speech simile in the underlined selection. Second, complete the commentary by filling each blank with the ONE most appropriate word from the poem respectively.**

Commentary

The speaker reaches a certain age and her sense of family is replaced by the importance of ___ⓐ___. Her mother is willing to give her space as long as she is willing to communicate somehow. The ___ⓑ___ is a main symbol for her relationship with her mother.

## 03 Read the excerpt from a play and follow the directions. [4 points]

| | |
|---|---|
| Cardinal | Sit: thou art my best of wishes. Please tell me, what trick did thou invent to come to Rome without thy husband? |
| Julia | Why, my lord, I told him I came to visit an old anchorite* here, for devotion. |
| Cardinal | Thou art a witty false one; I mean, to him. |
| Julia | You have prevail'd with me beyond my strongest thoughts: I would not now find you inconstant. |
| Cardinal | Do not put thyself to such a voluntary torture, which proceeds out of your own guilt. |
| Julia | How, my lord? |
| Cardinal | Sooth, generally; for women, a man might strive to make glass malleable, ere he should make them fixed. |
| Julia | So, my lord. |
| Cardinal | We had <u>need go borrow that fantastic glass, invented by Galileo the Florentine, to view another spacious world in the moon, and look to find a constant woman there.</u> |
| Julia | This is very well, my lord. |
| Cardinal | Why do you weep? Are tears your justification? The self-same tears will fall into your husband's bosom, lady. With a loud protestation that you love him above the world. Come, I'll love you wisely: That's jealousy; since I am very certain you cannot make me cuckold. |
| Julia | I'll go home to my husband. |

| | |
|---|---|
| Cardinal | You may thank me, lady: I have taken you off your melancholy perch, bore you upon my fist, and shew'd you game, and let you fly at it. I pray thee kiss me.—When thou weren't with thy husband, thou weren't watch'd like a tame elephant:—(still you are to thank me)—thou hadst only kisses from him, and high feeding; But what delight was that? 'twas just like one that hath a little fingering on the lute, yet cannot tune it:—still you are to thank me. |
| Julia | You told me of a piteous wound in the heart, and a sick liver, when you wooed me first. |

** anchorite: hermit*

**Identify the figure of speech employed in the underlined selection and what point the Cardinal is making with it. Second, what is the relationship between Julia and the Cardinal?**

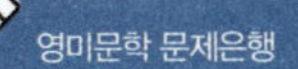


# 05회 실전모의고사

모범답안 p.32

**01** **Read the poem and follow the directions.** [4 points]

Is the scent of apple boughs smoking
in the woodstove what I will remember
of the Red Delicious I brought down, ashamed

that I could not convince its limbs to render fruit?
Too much neglect will do that, skew the sap's
passage, blacken leaves, dry the bark and heart.

I should have lopped* the dead limbs early
and watched each branch with a goshawk's eye,
patching with medicinal pitch, offering water,

compost* and mulch*, but I was too enchanted
by pear saplings, flowers and the pasture,
too callow to believe that death's inevitable

for any living being unloved, untended.
What remains is this armload of applewood
now feeding the stove's smolder. Splendor

ripens a final time in the firebox, a scarlet
harvest headed, by dawn, to embers.
Two decades of shade and blossoms—tarts

and cider, bees dazzled by the pollen,
spare elegance in ice—but what goes is gone.
Smoke is all, through this lesson in winter

regret, I've been given to remember.
Smoke, and Red Delicious apples redder
than a passing cardinal's* crest or cinders.

** lop: cut off*
** compost: fertilizer*
** mulch: covering of decaying leaves*
** cardinal: bird with bright red feathers*

**Explain what "this lesson" is. Second, for how long has the speaker appreciated the apple tree?**

03

**02** **Read the excerpt from a play and follow the directions.** [4 points]

| | |
|---|---|
| Thomasina Coverly | Septimus, they are not speaking of carnal embrace, are you, Mama? |
| Lady Croom | Certainly not. What do you know of carnal embrace? |
| Thomasina | Everything, thanks to Septimus. In my opinion, Mr Noakes's scheme for the garden is perfect. It is a Salvator! |
| Lady Croom | What does she mean? |
| Richard Noakes | *(Answering the wrong question)* Salvator Rosa, your ladyship, the painter. He is indeed the very exemplar of the picturesque style. |
| Captain Edward Brice | Hodge, what is this? |
| Septimus Hodge | <u>She</u> speaks from innocence not from experience. |
| Brice | You call it innocence? Has he ruined you, child? *(Pause)* |
| Septimus | Answer your uncle! |
| Thomasina | *(To Septimus)* How is a ruined child different from a ruined castle? |
| Septimus | On such questions I defer to Mr Noakes. |
| Noakes | *(Out of his depth)* A ruined castle is picturesque, certainly. |
| Septimus | That is the main difference. *(To Brice)* I teach the classical authors. If I do not elucidate their meaning, who will? |
| Brice | As her tutor you have a duty to keep her in ignorance. |
| Lady Croom | Do not dabble in paradox, Edward, it puts you in danger of fortuitous wit. Thomasina, wait in your bedroom. |

| | |
|---|---|
| Thomasina | *(Retiring)* Yes, mama. I did not intend to get you into trouble, Septimus. I am very sorry for it. It is plain that there are some things a girl is allowed to understand, and these include the whole of algebra, but there are others, such as embracing a side of beef* that must be kept from her until she is old enough to have a carcass of her own. |
| Lady Croom | One moment. |
| Brice | What is she talking about? |
| Lady Croom | Meat. |
| Brice | Meat? |
| Lady Croom | Thomasina, you had better remain. Your knowledge of the picturesque obviously exceeds anything the rest of us can offer. Mr Hodge, ignorance should be like an empty vessel waiting to be filled at the well of truth—not a cabinet of vulgar curios*. |

** a side of beef: lover*
** curios: curious objects*

**Identify who the underlined "she" is. Second, explain the meaning of figurative language used in the underlined words in Lady Croom's line. Do NOT copy more than THREE consecutive words from the passage.**

## 03 Read the excerpt from a fiction and follow the directions. [4 points]

On the short walk from the churchyard to her car, Mrs. Crasthorpe was aware of a profound humiliation. A lone mourner at her husband's funeral, she had sensed it first in the modest country church he had insisted upon for what he had called his obsequies. A woman cleric unknown to Mrs. Crasthorpe had conducted a bleak service, had said the necessary words in an accent that appalled Mrs. Crasthorpe, and then had scuttled off without so much as a glance in Mrs. Crasthorpe's direction. Two men were waiting, leaning on their shovels in the nearby graveyard, and within minutes had returned the clay to where they had dug it from, making a little mound, the coffin gone forever and with it Arthur, all of it a mockery. She was wrong, Mrs. Crasthorpe knew, to blame Arthur for the arrangements he'd put in hand before he went, but she'd become used to blaming him in his lifetime and couldn't help doing so still.

She was a woman of fifty-nine who declared herself to be forty-five because forty-five was what she felt. She had married a considerably older man, who had died in his seventy-second year. She had married him for his money, but, in spite of the comfort and convenience this had brought, Mrs. Crasthorpe believed that in marriage she had failed to blossom. Always a rosebud was how, privately, she thought of herself; and there was, in Mrs. Crasthorpe, a lot of privacy, there always had been. She knew she would tell no one, not ever, that Arthur had been buried without a decent sendoff, just as she'd told no one that she was the mother of a son or that there had been, in the late years of her marriage, Tommy Kildare and Donald.

"I shall relish my widowhood," she asserted, aloud and firmly, in her car. "I shall make something of it."

A light rain became heavier as she drove, the ________________ slushing it away, a sound she particularly disliked. In the driving mirror, which she glanced at now and then, her blonded hair, her gray-blue eyes, the curve of her generously full lips pleased Mrs. Crasthorpe. She liked the look of herself, and always had.

She turned on the radio to suppress the noise of the windscreen wipers, wondering as she did so why Arthur had chosen to be buried in such an obscure place, wondering what it was she hadn't listened to when she'd been told. Faintly, on some foreign station, popular music passed from tune to tune, each one known to Mrs. Crasthorpe, since they were of her time.

**Explain Mrs. Crasthorpe's primary opinion of Arthur's funeral. Second, what is implied concerning Tommy Kildare and Donald in the context of the story? Third, fill in the blank of the second-to-last paragraph with the TWO most appropriate consecutive words from the excerpt.**

________________________________________________

________________________________________________

________________________________________________

________________________________________________

________________________________________________

# 06회 실전모의고사

모범답안 p.33

**01** **Read the poem and follow the directions.** [4 points]

My brother kept
in a frame on the wall
pictures of every motorcycle, car, truck:
in his rusted out Impala convertible
wearing his cap and gown
waving
in his yellow Barracuda
with a girl leaning into him
waving
on his Honda 350
waving
on his Honda 750 with the boys
holding a beer
waving
in his first rig*
wearing a baseball hat backwards
waving
in his Mercury Montego
getting married
waving
in his black LTD
trying to sell real estate
waving
back to driving trucks
a shiny new rig
waving

on his Harley Sportster
with his wife on the back
waving
his son in a car seat
with his own steering wheel
my brother leaning over him
in an old Ford pickup
and they are
waving
holding a wrench a rag
a hose a shammy
waving.

My brother helmetless
rides off on his Harley
waving
my brother's feet
rarely touch the ground—
waving waving
face pressed to the wind
no camera to save him.

** rig: big truck*

**Through listing vehicles, what important biographical details are revealed? Second, describe the major event alluded to in the last stanza.**

**02** **Read the excerpt from a novel and follow the directions.** [4 points]

[A] Columbia City was not so very far away, even once she was in Chicago. What, pray, is a few hours—a few hundred miles? She looked at the little slip bearing her sister's address and wondered. She gazed at the green landscape, now passing in swift review, until her swifter thoughts replaced its impression with vague conjectures of what Chicago might be.

When a girl leaves her home at eighteen, she chooses one of two ways. Either she falls into saving hands and becomes better, or she rapidly assumes the cosmopolitan standard of virtue and becomes worse. Of an intermediate balance, under the circumstances, there is no possibility. The city has its cunning wiles, no less than the infinitely smaller and more human tempter. There are large forces which allure with all the soulfulness of expression possible in the most cultured human. The gleam of a thousand lights is often as effective as the persuasive light in a wooing and fascinating eye. Half the undoing of the unsophisticated and natural mind is accomplished by forces wholly superhuman. A blare of sound, a roar of life, a vast array of human hives, appeal to the astonished senses in equivocal terms. Without a counsellor at hand to whisper cautious interpretations, what falsehoods may not these things breathe into the unguarded ear! Unrecognised for what they are, their beauty, like music, too often relaxes, then weakens, then perverts the simpler human perceptions.

[B] Caroline was possessed of a mind rudimentary in its power of observation and analysis. ⓐ Self-interest with her was high, but not strong. It was, nevertheless, her guiding characteristic. Warm with the fancies of youth, pretty with the insipid prettiness of the formative period, possessed of a figure promising eventual shapeliness and an eye alight with certain native intelligence, she was a fair example of the middle American class—two generations removed from the emigrant. Books were beyond her interest—knowledge a sealed book. In the intuitive graces she was still crude. She could scarcely toss her head gracefully. Her hands were almost ineffectual. The feet, though small, were set flatly. And yet she was interested in her charms, quick to understand the keener pleasures of life, ambitious to gain in material things. ⓑ A half-equipped little knight, venturing to reconnoitre the mysterious city and dreaming wild dreams of some vague, far-off supremacy, which should make it prey and subject—the proper penitent, grovelling at a woman's slipper.

** reconnoitre: survey of enemy's area*

**Identify which way shown in <A> is likely to be chosen by the main character judging from the underlined ⓐ. Second, who is compared to the underlined "A half-equipped little knight" in ⓑ and why?**

**03** **Read the excerpt from a play and follow the directions.** [4 points]

*John is visiting to Ian's therapy clinic.*

Ian And how does it feel in the house? When you're there.

John I'm a little uneasy.

Ian *(Nods)* Okay.

John But. that's… that's also to do with… Like, when Mari was alive, you know, we had… stopped communicating. But now… she's gone, I really feel like there was a lot of communication. Even though, it wasn't… verbal… I suppose. You know, when you're young. And you're told about… what to expect I suppose. It is kind of happy ever after. But it's… you know, it's weird to accept what happiness really is, you know, or what it is… nothing is ever like anyone expects, is it, you know? Like, it's not a fairy tale… I mean, it has to be just kind of ordinary, you know? A bit boring even, otherwise it's probably not real, you know?

Ian Yeah…?

John No, it's, it's just that… we probably had it, you know? I mean when I think of it, really, we… we had it all, you know? But it's, it's hard to… accept… that this is it. You… you go… searching, not *searching*, I wasn't going anywhere searching for anything, but, I think I was always slightly… waiting… you know? This is something I probably wouldn't even have admitted before, you know? But maybe I felt that when we were married, and all settled in and eh… maybe even before we found out that we couldn't, that Mari couldn't, have children, I think that maybe even before that… I felt that I had kind of settled for second best, you know? I mean I mean I look at it now, and man, these are old feelings. Just fucking there all the time, for… all the way along. *(Silence)* That's terrible, isn't it? I mean, she was there. And I was there. And in that, there's obviously, the presence of… you know, a living person, Ian.

| | |
|---|---|
| Ian | John, you felt what you felt··· |
| John | (*Slight self-disgust*) Yeah but, what··· who the fuck did I think I was? I believe that··· we had a huge importance in each other's lives. You see, we'd, I think, we'd been slightly left behind, a little bit, you know? All our··· all our friends, they, you know, they had families. And, that··· that··· bound them together, you know? And, you see, I think that that··· that we were··· we were slightly left behind a little bit maybe. And that we felt that there was something kind of wrong with us, not anything serious or really wrong, but that there was a whole··· you know, a whole experience, a whole way, maybe, of··· of relating to everything, that wasn't··· it wasn't available to us. (*Suddenly*) It was a pain in the fucking hole to tell you the truth! |

**Explain what can be inferred about where John's wife is. Then, what was it about their friends that made John and Mari feel "left behind"?**

# 07회 실전모의고사

모범답안 p.35

**01** **Read the poem and follow the directions.** [4 points]

The turquoise* pool rose up to meet us,
its slide a silver afterthought down which
we plunged, screaming, into a mirage of bubbles.
We did not exist beyond the gaze of a boy.

Shaking water off our limbs, we lifted
up from ladder rungs across the fern-cool
lip of rim. Afternoon. Oiled and sated,
we sunbathed, rose and paraded the concrete,

danced to the low beat of "Duke of Earl"*.
Past cherry colas, hot-dogs, Dreamsicles,
we came to the counter where bees staggered
into root beer cups and drowned. We gobbled

cotton candy torches, sweet as furtive kisses,
shared on benches beneath summer shadows.
Cherry. Elm. Sycamore. We spread our chenille
blankets across grass, pressed radios to our ears,

mouthing the old words, then loosened
thin bikini straps and rubbed baby oil with iodine
across sunburned shoulders, tossing a glance
through the chain link at an improbable world.

* *turquoise: blue*

* *Duke of Earl: a 1962 US number-one hit song*

Identify the figure of speech used in the first line and explain the meaning as intended by the speaker of the poem. Second, describe ONE detail from the last two stanzas that indicates the limits of the paradise described in the poem.

**02** **Read the excerpt from a play and follow the directions.** [4 points]

JO I'd better go in now. Thanks for carrying my books.

BOY Were you surprised to see me waiting outside school?

JO Not really.

BOY Glad I came?

JO You know I am.

BOY So am I.

JO Well, I'd better go in.

BOY Not yet! Stay a bit longer.

JO All right! Doesn't it go dark early? I like winter. I like it better than all the other seasons.

BOY I like it too. When it goes dark early it gives me more time for— (*He kisses her.*)

JO Don't do that. You're always doing it.

BOY You like it.

JO I know, but I don't want to do it all the time.

BOY Afraid someone'll see us?

JO I don't care.

BOY Say that again.

JO I don't care.

BOY You mean it too. You're the first girl I've met who really didn't care. Listen, I'm going to ask you something. I'm a man of few words. Will you marry me?

JO Well, I'm a girl of few words. I won't marry you but you've talked me into it.

BOY How old are you?

JO Nearly eighteen.

BOY And you really will marry me?

JO I said so, didn't I? You shouldn't have asked me if you were only kidding me up. (*She starts to go.*)

BOY Hey! I wasn't kidding. I thought you were. Do you really mean it? You will __________ me?

JO I love you.

BOY How do you know?

JO I don't know why I love you but I do.

BOY I adore you. (*Swinging her through the air.*)

JO So do I. I can't resist myself. [Deleted..]

BOY I've got something for you.

JO What is it? A ring!

BOY This morning in the shop I couldn't remember what sort of hands you had, long hands, small hands or what. I stood there like a damn fool trying to remember what they felt like. (*He puts the ring on and kisses her hand.*) What will your mother say?

JO She'll probably laugh.

BOY Doesn't she care who her daughter marries?

JO She's not marrying you, I am. It's got nothing to do with her.

BOY She hasn't seen me.

JO And when she does?

BOY She'll see a coloured boy.

JO No, whatever else she might be, she isn't prejudiced against colour. You're not worried about it, are you?

BOY So long as you like it.

JO You know I do.

BOY Well, that's all that matters.

**Fill in the blank with the ONE word from the excerpt. Second, what is the Boy's anxiety regarding meeting Jo's mother? Do NOT copy more than THREE consecutive words from the excerpt.**

03

## 03 Read the excerpt from a novel and follow the directions. [4 points]

When I saw Finn waiting for me at the corner of the street I knew at once that ⓐ <u>something had gone wrong</u>. Finn usually waits for me in bed, or leaning up against the side of the door with his eyes closed. Moreover, I had been delayed by the strike. I hate the journey back to England anyway; and until I have been able to bury my head so deep in dear London that I can forget that I have ever been away I am inconsolable. So you may imagine how unhappy it makes me to have to cool my heels at Newhaven, waiting for the trains to run again, and with the smell of France still fresh in my nostrils. On this occasion too the bottles of cognac which I always smuggle had been taken from me by the Customs, so that when closing time came I was utterly abandoned to the torments of morbid self-scrutiny. The invigorating objectivity of true contemplation is something which a man of my temperament cannot achieve in unfamiliar towns in England, even when he was not also to be worrying about trains. Trains are bad for the nerves at the best of times. What did people have nightmares about before there were trains? So all this being considered, it was an odd thing that Finn should be waiting for me in the road.

As soon as I saw Finn I stopped and put the cases down. They were full of French books and very heavy. I shouted "Hey!" and Finn came slowly on. He never makes haste. I find it hard to explain to people about Finn. [deleted..]

When Finn came up to me at last I indicated one of the cases for him to carry, but he did not pick it up. Instead he sat down it and looked at me in a melancholy way. I sat down on the other case, and for a little while we were silent. I was tired, and reluctant to ask Finn any questions; he would tell all soon enough. He loves trouble, his own or other people's without discrimination, and what he particularly likes is to break bad news. [deleted..]

As he looked at me so sadly my heart sank.

"What is it?" I said at last.

"She's thrown us out," said Finn.

I could not take this seriously; it was impossible. "Come now," I said kindly to Finn. "What does this really mean?"

"She's throwing us out," said Finn. "Both of us, now, today."

"But why?" I asked. "What have we done?"

"It's not what we have done, it's what she's after doing," said Finn. "She's going to get married to a fellow, who is very rich."

This is a blow. I was wondering, where can we go? [deleted..]

I ought to have taken care of her. ⓑ This metamorphosis must have been a long time preparing, only I had been dull to see it. A girl like Magdalen can't be transformed overnight. I all of sudden felt an impulse to propose marriage. However, it was not in my nature to make myself responsible for other people. I found it hard enough to pick my own way along.

**Describe what the content of the underlined "something had gone wrong" in ⓐ is. Second, explain what the underlined "This metamorphosis" in ⓑ is. Do NOT copy more than THREE consecutive words from the excerpt.**

# 08회 실전모의고사

모범답안 p.36

**01** **Read the excerpt from a novel and follow the directions.** [4 points]

When the shadow of the sash appeared on the curtains it was between seven and eight o' clock and then I was in time again, hearing the watch. It was Grandfather's and when Father gave it to me he said *I give you the mausoleum of all hope and desire; it's rather excruciatingly apt that you will use it to gain the reducto absurdum of all human experience which can fit your individual needs no better than it fitted his or his father's. I give it to you not that you may remember time, but that you might forget it now and then for a moment and not spend all your breath trying to conquer it. Because no battle is ever won he said. They are not even fought. The field only reveals to man his own folly and despair, and victory is an illusion of philosophers and fools.*

Through the wall I heard Shreve's bedsprings and then his slippers on the floor hishing. I got up and went to the dresser and slid my hand along it and touched the watch and turned it face-down and went back to bed. But the shadow of the sash was still there and I had learned to tell almost to the minute, so I'd have to turn my back on it, feeling the eyes animals used to have in the back of their heads when it was on top, itching. *It's always the idle habits you acquire which you will regret.* Father said that. *Christ was not crucified; he was worn away by a minute clicking of little wheels.* Father said that *Cunning and serene. If you attend Harvard one year, but dont see the boat-race, there should be a refund.* Let Jason* have it. Give Jason a year at Harvard.

Shreve stood in the door, putting his collar on, his glasses glinting rosily, as though he had washed them with his face. "You taking a cut this morning?"

"Is it that late?"

He looked at his watch. "Bell in two minutes."

"I didn't know it was that late." He was still looking at the watch, his mouth shaping. "I'll have to hustle. I can't stand another cut. The dean told me last week—" He put the watch back into his pocket. Then I quit talking.

"You'd better slip on your pants and run," he said. He went out.

I got up and moved about, listening to him through the wall. He entered the sitting-room, toward the door.

"Aren't you ready yet?"

"Not yet. Run along. I'll make it."

He went out. The door closed. His feet went down the corridor.

* *Jason: The narrator's younger brother*

**Explain the relation between the narrator and Shreve. Second, complete the commentary below by filling in the blank with the ONE word from the excerpt.**

Commentary

The __________ is for the narrator a symbol of repetition as much as of the continual movement.

**02** **Read the poem and follow the directions.** [4 points]

My son's very graceful; he has perfect balance.
He's not competitive, like my sister's daughter.

Day and night, she's always practicing.
Today, it's hitting softballs into the copper beech*,
retrieving them, hitting them again.
After a while, no one even watches her.
If she were any stronger, the tree would be <u>bald.</u>

My son won't play with her; he won't even ride bicycles with her.
She accepts that; she's used to playing by herself.
The way she sees it, it isn't personal:
whoever won't play doesn't like losing.

It's not that my son's inept, that he doesn't do things well.
I've watched him race: he's natural, effortless—
right from the first, he takes the lead.
And then he stops. It's as though he was born rejecting
the solitude of the victor.

My sister's daughter doesn't have that problem.
She may as well be first; she's already alone.

** copper beech: a tree that has dark purple leaves*

**Explain what the underlined "bald" means. Second, why is the niece "alone", according to the speaker's implied judgement?**

______________________________________________

______________________________________________

______________________________________________

## 03 Read the excerpt from a play and follow the directions. [4 points]

*Africa, 19th Century. Clive, a British colonial administrator is talking with Harry.*

HARRY It is safe, I suppose?

CLIVE They won't go far. This is very much my territory and its broad daylight. Joshua will keep an open eye.

HARRY Well I must give them a hundred. You don't know what this means to me, Clive. A chap can only go on so long alone. I can climb mountains and go down rivers, but what's it for? For Christmas and England and games and women singing. This is the empire, Clive. It's not me putting a flag in new lands. It's you. The empire is one big family. I'm one of its black sheep, Clive. And I know you think my life is rather dashing. But I want you to know I admire you. This is the empire, Clive and I serve it. With all my heart.

CLIVE I think that's about a hundred.

HARRY Ready or not, here I come!

*He goes.*

CLIVE Harry Bagley is a fine man, Joshua. He travels to places about which very little is known. You should be proud to know him. He will be in history books.

JOSHUA Sir, while we are alone.

CLIVE Joshua of course, what is it? You always have my ear. Any time.

JOSHUA Sir, I have some information. The stable boys are not to be trusted. They whisper. They go out at night. They visit their people. Their people are not my people. I do not visit my people.

CLIVE Thank you, Joshua. They certainly look after Beauty. I will be sorry to have to supplant them.

JOSHUA They carry knives.
CLIVE I appreciate this, Joshua, very much.
JOSHUA Your wife.
CLIVE Thank you, Joshua.
JOSHUA Are you going to hide?
CLIVE Yes, yes I am. Thank you. Keep your eyes open Joshua.
JOSHUA I do, sir.

**Identify Harry's job as can be inferred from the excerpt. Second, what problem does Joshua describe and what is Clive's suggested solution? Do NOT copy more than FOUR consecutive words from the passage.**

# 09회 실전모의고사

모범답안 p.37

**01** **Read the poem and follow the directions.** [4 points]

*I don't know if we're in the beginning*
*or in the final stage.*
*—Tomas Tranströmer*

Rain is falling through the roof.
And all that prospered under the sun,
the books that opened in the morning
and closed at night, and all day
turned their pages to the light;

the sketches of boats and strong forearms
and clever faces, and of fields
and barns, and of a bowl of eggs,
and lying across the piano
the silver stick of a flute; everything

invented and imagined,
everything whispered and sung,
all silenced by cold rain.

The sky is the color of gravestones.
The rain tastes like salt, and rises
in the streets like a ruinous tide.
We spoke of millions, of billions of years.
We talked and talked.

> Then a drop of rain fell
> into the sound hole of the guitar, another
> onto the unmade bed. And after us,
> the rain will cease or it will go on falling,
> even upon itself.

**There is a main tone shift in the poem. Identify the line the tone shift comes to pass. Second, complete the commentary below by filling in the blanks with the same ONE most appropriate word from the poem.**

Commentary

> The speaker tells the reader that the world ultimately does not care if you __________, and everything will just go on the way it always has after you __________.

## 02 Read the excerpt from a novel and follow the directions. [4 points]

[A] I first met him in Piraeus. I wanted to take the boat for Crete and had gone down to the port. It was almost daybreak and raining. A strong sirocco* was blowing the spray from the waves as far as the little cafe, whose glass doors were shut. The cafe reeked of brewing sage and human beings whose breath steamed the windows because of the cold outside. Five or six seamen, who had spent the night there, muffled in their brown goat-skin reefer-jackets, were drinking coffee or sage and gazing out of the misty windows at the sea. The fish, dazed by the blows of the raging sea, had taken refuge in the depths, where they were waiting till calm was restored above. The fishermen crowding in the cafes were also waiting for the end of the storm, when the fish, reassured, would rise to the surface after the bait. Soles, hog-fish and skate* were returning from their nocturnal expeditions. Day was now breaking.

[B] The glass door opened and there entered a thick-set, mud-bespattered, weather-beaten dock labourer with bare head and bare feet.

"Hi! Kostandi!" called out an old sailor in a sky-blue cloak. "How are things with you?"

Kostandi spat. "What d'you think?' he replied testily. "Good morning—the bar! Good night—my lodgings! That's the sort of life I'm leading. No work at all!"

Some started laughing, others shook their heads and swore.

"ⓐ This world's a life-sentence," said a man with a moustache who had picked up his philosophy from the Karagiozis* theatre. "Yes, a life-sentence. Be damned to it."

A pale bluish-green light penetrated the dirty window-panes of the cafe and caught hands, noses and foreheads. It leapt on to the counter and lit the bottles. The electric light faded, and the proprietor, half-asleep after his night up, stretched out his hand and switched off.

03

There was a moment's silence. All eyes were turned on the dirty-looking sky outside. The roar of the waves could be heard and, in the cafe, the gurgling of a few hookahs. The old sailor sighed; "I wonder what has happened to Captain Lemoni? May God help him!" He looked angrily at the sea, and growled: "God damn you for a ⓑ destroyer of homes!" He bit his grey moustache.

** sirocco: a hot, fast Mediterranean wind*
** skate: a kind of fish*
** Karagiozis: A puppet shadow-play given in cafes*

**Explain the meaning of the metaphor used in the underlined ⓐ. Second, identify the TWO most appropriate consecutive words from [A] that BEST match the underlined words in ⓑ.**

## 03 Read the excerpt from a play and follow the directions. [4 points]

AMANDA Why do you go to the movies so much, Tom?

TOM I like a lot of adventure.

*AMANDA looks baffled, then hurt.*

AMANDA Most young men find adventure in their careers.

TOM Then most young men are not employed in a warehouse.

AMANDA The world is full of young men employed in warehouses and offices and factories.

TOM Do all of them find adventure in their careers?

AMANDA They do or they do without it! Not everybody has a craze for adventure.

TOM Man is by instinct a lover, a hunter, a fighter, and none of these instincts are given much play at the warehouse!

AMANDA Man is by instinct! Don't quote instinct to me! Instinct is something that people have got away from! It belongs to animals! Christian adults don't want it!

TOM What do Christian adults want, then, Mother?

AMANDA Superior things! Things of the mind and spirit! Only animals have to satisfy instincts! Surely your aims are somewhat higher than theirs! Than monkeys—pigs—

TOM I reckon they're not.

AMANDA You're joking. However, that isn't what I wanted to discuss.

TOM (*Rising*) I haven't much time.

AMANDA You have five minutes. I want to talk about Laura.

TOM All right! What about Laura?

AMANDA We have to be making some plans and provisions for her. She's older than you, two years, and nothing has happened. She just drifts along doing nothing. It frightens me terribly how she just drifts along.

TOM I guess she's the type that people call "a home girl".

| | |
|---|---|
| AMANDA | There's no such type, and if there is, it's a pity! That is unless the home is hers, with a husband! |
| TOM | What? |
| AMANDA | Oh, I can see the handwriting on the wall as plain as I see the nose in front of my face! It's terrifying! More and more you remind me of your father's behavior! He was out all hours without explanation!—Then left! Good bye! And me with the bag to hold. I saw that letter you got from the Merchant Marine. I know what you're dreaming of. I'm not standing here blindfolded. Very well, then. Then do it! But not till there's somebody to take your place. |

**Describe the concern Amanda has for Laura. Second, complete the commentary by filling in the blank with the ONE most appropriate word from the excerpt.**

Commentary

Amanda endeavors to make Tom feel guilty for his __________ abandonment, because she fears history repeating itself.

# 10회 실전모의고사

모범답안 p.39

**01** **Read the poem and follow the directions.** [4 points]

All week she's cleaned
someone else's house,
stared down her own face
in the shine of copper—
bottomed pots, polished
wood, toilets she'd pull
the lid to—that look saying

*Let's make a change, girl.*

But Sunday mornings are hers—
church clothes starched
and hanging, a record spinning
on the console, the whole house
dancing. She raises the shades,
washes the rooms in light,
buckets of water, Octagon soap.

<u>*Cleanliness is next to godliness*</u>…

Windows and doors flung wide,
curtains two-stepping
forward and back, neck bones
bumping in the pot, a choir
of clothes clapping on the line.

*Nearer my God to Thee…*

She beats time on the rugs,
blows dust from the broom
like dandelion spores, each one
a wish for something better.



**Explain the meaning of the underlined *"Cleanliness is next to godliness"*. Second, identify ONE instance of personification from the first three stanzas that illustrates the main character's pleasant emotion.**

## 02 Read the excerpt from a story and follow the directions. [4 points]

"You can imagine how a blue cheek would go over with the funeral home." Ray quickly inserted his fingers in the half-opened mouth, pushed the tongue back, brought his hand out again almost immediately, and closed the jaw with his palm. Then he gripped the head above the hairline and turned it counterclockwise away from the window. The head stayed where he put it.

"He hasn't got any false teeth."

"Good."

"Notice how I was careful not to touch the skin except where I had to. Wherever you touch him, that part's going to turn color, so you've got to be careful."

"How will they get this yellow out of him? He seems pretty discolored already."

"They have ways. Yellow's easier than blue, and yellow's not our fault. They'll have him laid out looking like the picture of health. Don't worry. He'll be the healthiest-looking man at the funeral."

Just then Roth heard a sound of rubber-soled shoes shrieking on the vinyl of the outer hall. Then Miss Trigg, the head nurse, came shrieking through the door frame. He and Ray started like grave robbers.

"He's not quite ready yet," Ray said.

Roth's hand was gripping the iron barrel of the intravenous rack. He could see the woman pause in the doorway and speak to someone out of sight. Miss Trigg yanked the sheet, covering the toes, and quickly tucked it in across the bottom.

"She's coming in," Roth said.

"I'm sorry," Miss Trigg said, partially blocking the woman at the foot of Mr. Tilney's bed, "you'll have to wait until the doctor arrives." Two girls, one about twelve, one about sixteen, had come in behind the woman. They looked at Miss Trigg expectantly.

"Has there been any change?" the woman said. The sixteen-year-old girl was watching Roth as he wheeled the intravenous rack against the wall. She had brown fluffy hair down to her shoulders. Miss Trigg seemed to be at a loss for words. The older girl gave her a frightened look and suddenly stepped around her and planted herself beside the deadman's bed.

"The doctor should be here any minute, Mrs. Houk," Miss Trigg said. "I'm sorry." They were all looking at the body now.

The woman's expression was haggard, resigned, immediately resigned, faintly disgusted. "It'll be all right," she said. Then the older girl threw herself upon the swollen, yellow man and desperately kissed the rigid face. Her back heaved up and down.

"Oh, Daddy," she sobbed. "Oh, Daddy, Daddy."

**Explain what Roth is being trained to do. Next, describe the tone shift at the story's end.**

## 03 Read the excerpt from a play and follow the directions. [4 points]

Candy The bartender's quite nice.
David Candy, you're talking about a date, not a lifetime commitment.
Candy Don't you ever wish you had a lover?
David I have many lovers.
Candy Not lover lovers.
David Pul-lease!
Candy Everybody needs somebody.
David Need I remind you there was a time that you and I were lovers.
Candy That was different.
David We had nothing but sex in common.
Candy Don't you ever see someone and it's like this thing goes off in your head and you just want to be with them all the time?
David No.
Candy Deep down you want someone to be special for you.
David I'm quite capable of being special for myself. What you're talking about doesn't exist, Candy.
Candy What about my parents?
David Your parents are The Munsters* in normal clothes.
Candy You're wrong, David. It's love. Two people going completely gaga over each other.
David You watched too much 60s television.
Candy David, you need to be loved.
David I have my friends.
Candy It's not the same.
David Are you saying my relationships with you and Bernie are invalid?
Candy Bernie? Right. He's psycho.
David Candy..?
Candy I saw the blood on the face cloth.
David He was in a fight.
Candy That's healthy?

| | |
|---|---|
| David | Let's not discuss this. You've always hated him. |
| Candy | Because he's weird, David. Weird. |
| David | Drop it. |
| Candy | Do you love him? |
| | (*Brief pause*) |
| David | He's my friend. |
| Candy | Do you love me? |
| | (*Pause*) |
| David | That's not the right word. |
| Candy | You love me. |
| David | There's no such thing. |
| Candy | I know you love me. |
| David | Then why do you have to ask. |
| Candy | *(Pause)* I'm going to bed. *Candy exits.* |

* *The Munsters: an American television citcom from the 1960s*

**Describe Candy's reason for referencing her parents. Second, what specific example does Candy bring up to criticize Bernie?**

# 11 회 실전모의고사

모범답안 p.40

**01 Read the excerpt from a novel and follow the directions.** [4 points]

[A] Lord, how time flies. Nel hardly recognized anybody in the town any more. Now there was another old people's home. Look like this town Medallion just kept on building homes for old people. Every time they built a road they built a old folks' home. You'd think folks was living longer, but the fact of it was, they was just being put out faster.

Nel hadn't seen the insides of this most recent one yet, but it was her turn in Circle Number 5 to visit some of the old women there. The pastor visited them regularly, but the circle thought private visits were nice too. There were just nine colored women out there, the same nine that had been in the other one. But a lot of white ones. White people didn't fret about putting their old ones away. It took a lot for black people to let them go, and even if somebody was old and alone, others did the dropping by, the floor washing, the cooking. Only when they got crazy and unmanageable were they let go.

Nel had been really active in church only a year or less, and that was because the children were grown now and took up less time and less space in her mind. For over twenty-five years since Jude walked out she had pinned herself into a tiny life. She spent a little time trying to marry again, but nobody wanted to take her on with three children, and she simply couldn't manage the business of keeping boyfriends.

[B] In the meantime the Bottom had collapsed. Everybody who had made money during the war moved as close as they could to the valley, and the white people were buying down river, cross river, stretching Medallion like two strings on the banks. Nobody colored lived much up in the Bottom any more. White people were building towers for television stations up there and there was a rumor about a golf course or something. Anyway, hill land was more valuable now, and those black people who had moved down right after the war* and in the fifties couldn't afford to come back even if they wanted to.

Just like that, white people had changed their minds and instead of keeping the valley floor to themselves, now they wanted a hilltop house with a river view and a ring of elms. The black people, for all their new look, seemed awfully anxious to get to the valley, or leave town, and abandon the hills to whoever was interested. It was sad, because the Bottom had been a real place. These young ones kept talking about the community, but they left the hills to the rich white folks. Maybe it hadn't been a community, but it had been a place. Now there weren't any places left, just separate houses with separate televisions and separate telephones and less and less dropping by. These were the same thoughts she always had when she walked down into the town.

** the war: the World War I*

**Describe the difference between White and Black people in relation to old folks' home as shown in the underlined part in <A> and identify the ONE word from <B> that BEST explains the reason of the difference. Then, explain how the Bottom village has changed in terms of resident composition.**

## 02 Read the poem and follow the directions. [4 points]

When death comes
like the hungry bear in autumn;
when death comes and takes all the bright coins from his purse

to buy me, and snaps the purse shut;
when death comes
like the measle-pox

when death comes
like an iceberg between the shoulder blades,

I want to step through the door full of curiosity, wondering:
what is it going to be like, <u>that cottage of darkness</u>?

And therefore I look upon everything
as a brotherhood and a sisterhood,
and I look upon time as no more than an idea,
and I consider eternity as another possibility,

and I think of each life as a flower, as common
as a field daisy, and as singular,

and each name a comfortable music in the mouth,
tending, as all music does, toward silence,

and each body a lion of courage, and something
precious to the earth.

When it's over, I want to say all my life
I was a bride married to amazement.
I was the bridegroom, taking the world into my arms.

When it's over, I don't want to wonder
if I have made of my life something particular, and real.

I don't want to find myself sighing and frightened,
or full of argument.

I don't want to end up simply having visited this world.

**Identify to what the underlined "that cottage of darkness" refers. Second, complete the commentary by filling in the blank with the ONE most appropriate word from the poem. If necessary, change the word form.**

Commentary

In the poem the speaker does not live a passive live. Rather, she enjoys every moment as an active participant, not as a(n) ______________.

## 03 Read the excerpt from a play and follow the directions. [4 points]

*Three persons are talking about their company's current issues.*

Jeffrey Skilling God, if you could hear yourself, 'Build more fucking powerplants.' No imagination, go crazy—What about wind farms or hydroelectric plants…?!

Claudia Roe *Wind farms?!* I'm sorry, I thought I was the only woman in the room.

Skilling We don't need the hard stuff.

Roe India, Africa—huge power requirements in the future—

Skilling That will take *years*! You really want to pay for people to go build pipelines along disputed borders, tribes with AK47s? You want that fucking *mess*—?

Roe I think in the most volatile areas in the world it might be worth controlling their energy supply, yes.

Skilling Scratching around in the dirt. I'm not talking about pushing on an industry already in place. I'm trying to tell you… Ken, you've seen some changes in business since you started.

Ken Lay Sure. I'm as old as the plains.

Skilling Well, it's time to evolve again. We *have to. America doesn't have the natural resources any more.* Not really. And that's good, that's fine. We have intellectual capital, and the best of it in the world. Look at the societies that *do* have the raw materials, how modern do they feel, really? Then take a landlocked, barren country like Switzerland. What do they do? They invent banking. We should be coming up with new ideas. About everything. Employ the smartest people we can find. And have 'em free to look at whatever they want, free from the old assumptions about what this company is.

03

| | |
|---|---|
| Roe | Sounds like hippy talk to me. |
| Skilling | I'm not gonna patronise you by pretending you believe what you just said. |
| Lay | You got one idea about trading. |
| Skilling | I got plenty of ideas. Mark-to-market, energy trading, that's just the beginning. |
| Roe | I can push through natural gas deals we already have experience of. You want power? Enron*. India? Enron. South America? Enron. |
| Skilling | Countries are meaningless. It's all going to be virtual. Oil and land run out. |
| Roe | In which case, don't you think it's worth being the only people in the world with power plants?! |
| Skilling | There is a whole, glistening, green industry above what you're talking about that no one's even thought of yet. |
| Roe | Except you (!) |

*Silence. Lay leans back.*

| | |
|---|---|
| Lay | You see, I'm like Claudia. I like holding things. In our father's day, a man worked and he saw himself in his work. If he made a table, he saw himself in the table he made. It was part of him, and he of it. I *am* oil and pipelines. |

* *Enron: name of an energy company*

**Identify the TWO most appropriate consecutive words from the passage that BEST match the underlined "wind farms or hydroelectric plants". Second, explain the main disagreement between Skilling and Roe. Do Not copy more than FOUR consecutive words from the passage.**

# 12 회 실전모의고사

모범답안 p.42

**01** **Read the story and follow the directions.** [4 points]

It was a cloudy afternoon with an Italian butcher selling a pound of meat to a very old woman, but who knows what such an old woman could possibly use a pound of meat for?

She was too old for that much meat. Perhaps she used it for a bee hive and she had five hundred golden bees at home waiting for the meat, their bodies stuffed with honey.

"What kind of meat would you like today?" the butcher said. "We have some good hamburger. It's lean."

"I don't know," She said. "Hamburger is something else."

"Yeah, it's lean. I ground it myself. I put a lot of lean meat in it."

"Hamburger doesn't sound right," she said.

"Yeah," the butcher said. "It's a good day for hamburger. Look outside. It's cloudy. Some of those clouds have rain in them. I'd get the hamburger," he said.

"No," she said. "I don't want any hamburger, and I don't think it's going to rain. I think the sun is going to come out and it will be a beautiful day, and I want a pound of liver."

The butcher was stunned. He did not like to sell liver to old ladies. There was something about it that made him very nervous. He didn't want to talk to her any more.

He reluctantly sliced a pound of liver off a huge red chunk and wrapped it up in white paper and put it into a brown bag. It was a very unpleasant experience for him.

He took her money, gave her the change, and went back to the poultry section to try and get a hold of his nerves.

By using her bones like the sails of a ship, she passed outside into the street. She carried the liver as if it were victory to the bottom of a very steep hill.

She climbed the hill and being very old, it was hard on her. She grew tired and had to stop and rest many times before she reached the top.

At the top of the hill was the old woman's house: a tall San Francisco house with bay windows that reflected a cloudy day.

She opened her purse which was like a small autumn field and near the fallen branches of an old apple tree, she found her keys.

**Identify the ONE sentence from the excerpt that reveals the major character's bodily condition by employing a figure of speech. Second, describe the butcher's reaction to the old woman's order. Do NOT copy more than FOUR consecutive words from the excerpt.**

## 02 Read the poem and follow the directions. [4 points]

Someone had propped a skateboard
by the door of the classroom,
to make quick his escape, come the bell.

For it was February in Florida,
the air of instruction thick with tanning butter*.
Why, my students wondered,

did the great dead poets all live north* of us?
Was there nothing to do all winter there
but pine* for better weather?

Had we a window, the class could keep an eye
on the clock and yet watch the wild plum
nod with the absent grace of the young.

We could study the showy scatter of petals.
We could, for want of a better word, call it "snowy."
The room filled with stillness, flake by flake.

Only the dull roar of air forced to spend its life indoors
could be heard. <u>Not even the songbird
of a cell phone chirped</u>. Go home,

I wanted to tell the horse on the page.
You know the way, even in snow
gone blue with cold.

** tanning butter: suncream*
** north: US North*
** pine: wish*

**Explain the students' opinion of why there were few great Floridian poets. Second, write ONE word from the poem that corresponds to the underlined part. Third, complete the commentary by filling in the blank with the ONE most appropriate word from the poem.**

Commentary

The poem depicts a dark __________ setting that reflects on the attitudes of the speaker and her students.

## 03 Read the excerpt from a play and follow the directions. [4 points]

| | |
|---|---|
| MARLENE | I came up this morning and spent the day in Ipswich. I went to see Mother. |
| JOYCE | Did she recognize you? |
| MARLENE | Are you trying to be funny? |
| JOYCE | No, she does wander. |
| MARLENE | She wasn't wandering at all, she was very lucid, thank you. |
| JOYCE | You were very lucky then. |
| MARLENE | Fucking awful life she's had |
| JOYCE | Don't tell me. |
| MARLENE | Fucking waste. |
| JOYCE | Don't talk to me. |
| MARLENE | Why shouldn't I Talk? Why shouldn't I talk to you? Isn't she my mother too? |
| JOYCE | Look, you've left, you've gone away, we can do without you. |
| MARLENE | I left home, so what, I left home. People do leave home. It is normal. |
| JOYCE | We understand that, we can do without you. |
| MARLENE | We weren't happy. Were you happy? |
| JOYCE | Don't come back. |
| MARLENE | So it's just your mother is it, your child, you never wanted me around, you were jealous of me because I was the··· |
| JOYCE | Here we go. |
| MARLENE | ···little one and I was clever. |
| JOYCE | I'm not clever enough for all this psychology. If that's what it is. |
| MARLENE | Why can't I visit my own family without all this? |
| JOYCE | Aah. Just don't go on about Mum's life when you haven't been to see her for how many years. I go and see her every week. |

| | |
|---|---|
| MARLENE | It's up to me. Then I don't go and see her every week. |
| JOYCE | Somebody has to. |
| MARLENE | No they don't. Why do they? |
| JOYCE | How would I feel if I didn't go? |
| MARLENE | A lot better. |
| JOYCE | I hope you feel better. |
| MARLENE | It's up to me. Women have always been expected to fulfill certain roles, regardless of individual temperament, and women have been excluded from other experiences and possibilities in life. The roles have been determined for the convenience of men. This made me angry. And I was determined to succeed in the male-dominated world even if it meant me choosing between career and family. And I made my choice. As I instructed the newly engaged Jeanine whom I interviewed that she should not tell her potential employers that she is getting married, because they will assume that she will leave her job to have children. My sister Joyce was different and she made her choice too! |

**Explain why Joyce is mainly angry with Marlene. Do NOT use more than FOUR consecutive words from the excerpt. Second, what is implied to occur if Jeanine tells her company of her marriage plan? Do not use more than FOUR consecutive words from the excerpt.**

# 13회 실전모의고사

모범답안 p.43

**01** **Read the provided short story and follow the directions.** [4 points]

The closest thing to tumbleweed in New York City is the people.

I say this out loud to the woman next to me because I think she is from Arizona.

Whenever it starts to rain I think end of the world. Whenever the telephone rings or someone calls me by name I think Leonidas* at Thermopylae or Custer at Little Bighorn.

What this speaks to I try not to think about.

Don't try to trick me into being happy, is what the woman says back.

We are in a museum when we say this to each other. This particular room in the museum has windows for walls and you can see the weather from anywhere inside it.

This is not just me talking, I say. I pause a moment and then keep talking about the weather until I hear myself say, One bolt of lightning and it's everyone out of the pool time.

I think I've known this woman for years. I think we met in college and have tried since then to get away from each other. The problem is one or the other of us has nothing better to do at any given time. Then I think we came to New York two months ago to help the poor or feed the poor, something with the poor.

The trouble with me is I think too much and don't know anything.

I don't know why this is, though I suspect it's my own fault.

Outside the rain is coming down like it's angry with someone. Like someone had made fun of the rain's mother.

We are sitting on a bench surrounded by twenty giant speakers arranged in an oval. From the speakers a children's choir sings in a foreign language that might be Latin. When you walk from speaker to speaker you hear a different voice, which is why it's in the __________, I think. When you are outside the oval you can't distinguish one voice from the next. To me, the voices all sound the same, even the different ones.

The woman next to me is looking out the window, watching the passerby tramp through gaping puddles, watching the rain like she's never seen it fall down before.

This is when I say something about the homeless, something that sounds like at least they'll have a bath today. Why I say this is because I don't know how she'll react and I'm curious.

Between the choirboys and rainfall the woman can't hear me, though, and from the look on her face I can tell she's making her mind up about something, something that might include leaving me here on this bench to go play in the rain, eventually finding her way west to feed the poor of Tempe or Phoenix or wherever it is she's from and that maybe if I'm lucky she'll call when she gets there.

** Leonidas: King of Sparta who lost the battle of Thermopylae*

**Oftentimes the literary devices and imagery chosen by a narrator reflect her/his inner state, motivations, and concerns. In the story, identify the use of personification employed by the narrator. Additionally, explain the inner state reflected in the use of this personification. Then, fill in the blank with the ONE most appropriate word from the story above.**

## 02 Read the poem and follow the directions. [4 points]

Because all this food is grown in the store
do not take the leaflet.
Cabbages, broccoli and tomatoes
are raised at night in the aisles.
Milk is brewed in the rear storage areas.
Beef produced in vats in the basement.
Do not take the leaflet.
Peanut butter and soft drinks
are made fresh each morning by store employees.
Our oranges and grapes
are so fine and round
that when held up to the lights they cast no shadow.
Do not take the leaflet.

And should you take one
do not believe it.
This chain of stores has no connection
with anyone growing food someplace else.
How could we have an effect on local farmers?
Do not believe it.

The sound here is Muzak*, for your enjoyment.
It is not the sound of children crying.
There is a lady offering samples
to mark Canada Cheese Month.
There is no dark-skinned man with black hair beside her
wanting to show you the inside of a coffin.
You would not have to look if there was.
And there are no Nicaraguan heroes
in any way connected with the bananas.

Pay no attention to these people,
The manager is a citizen.
All this food is grown in the store.

** Muzak: recorded music that is played as background music in shops or restaurants*

**Describe the thematic idea of the poem. Second, identify who the underlined "these people" are.**

## 03 Read the excerpt from a play and follow the directions. [4 points]

B Oh, stop it! It's downhill from sixteen on! For all of us!

C Yes, but···

B What are you, twenty something? Haven't you figured it out yet? (*Demonstrates*) You take the breath in··· you let it out. The first one you take in you're upside down and they slap you into it. The last on e··· well, the last one you let it all out··· and that's it. You start··· and then you stop. Don't be so soft. I'd like to see children learn it—have a six-year-old say, I'm dying and know what it means.

C You're horrible!

B Start in young; make 'em aware they've got only a little time. Make 'em aware they're dying from the minute they're alive.

C Awful!

B Grow up! Do you know it? Do you know you're dying?

C Well, of course, but···

B (*Ending it*) Grow up.

A (*Wobbling, shuffling in*) A person could die in there and nobody'd care.

B (*Bright*) Done already!

A A person could die! A person could fall down and break something! A person could die! Nobody would care!

B (*Going to her*) Let me help you.

A Get your hands off me! A person could die for all anybody'd care.

C (*To herself, but to be overheard*) Who is this··· person? A person could do this, a person could do···

B It's a figure of speech.

C (*Mildly sarcastic*) No. Really?

B (*Not rising to it*) So they tell me.

A (*Flailing about*) Hold on to me! Do you want me to fall?! You want me to fall!

B Yes, I want you to fall; I want you to fall and shatter in··· ten pieces.

C Or five, or seven.

| | |
|---|---|
| A | Where's my chair? (*Sees it perfectly well.*) Where's my chair gone to? |
| B | (*Playing the game*) Goodness, where's her chair gone to?! Somebody's taken her chair! |
| C | (*Realizing*) What?! |
| A | (*Does she know? Probably*) Who's got my chair? |
| C | I'm sorry! |
| B | (*Placating*) There's your chair. Do you want your pillow? |
| A | I want to sit down. |
| B | Yes, yes. Here we go. (*Gently lowers A into the vacated armchair.*) |

**Based on the above discussion, which of the three women can be inferred to be the oldest and which the youngest? Second, the excerpt above reveals Character B's practical personality. Describe the part that demonstrates her to be as such.**

# 14 회 실전모의고사

모범답안 p.44

**01** **Read the excerpt from a story and follow the directions.** [4 points]

Assuredly a badger is the animal that one most resembles in this trench warfare, that drab-coated creature of the twilight and darkness, digging, burrowing, listening; keeping itself as clean as possible under unfavourable circumstances, fighting tooth and nail on occasion for possession of a few yards of honeycombed earth. What the badger thinks about life we shall never know, which is a pity, but cannot be helped; it is difficult enough to know what one thinks about, oneself, in the trenches. Parliament, taxes, social gatherings, economies, and expenditure, and all the thousand and one horrors of civilization seem immeasurably remote, and the war itself seems almost as distant and unreal. A couple of hundred yards away, separated from you by a stretch of dismal untidy-looking ground and some strips of rusty wire-entanglement, lies a vigilant, bullet-spitting enemy. It would not be advisable to forget for enemy soldiers, but one's mind does not dwell on their existence.

Much more to be thought about than the enemy over yonder or the war all over Europe is the mud of the moment, the mud that at times engulfs you <u>as cheese engulfs a cheesemite</u>. In Zoological Gardens one has gazed at an elk or bison loitering at its pleasure more than knee-deep in a quagmire of greasy mud, and one has wondered what it would feel like to be soused and plastered, hour-long, in such a muck-bath. One knows now. In narrow-dug support-trenches, when thaw and heavy rain have come suddenly atop of a frost, when everything is pitch-dark around you, and you can only stumble about and feel your way against streaming mud walls, then at least you are in a position to understand thoroughly what it feels like to wallow.

When one is not thinking about mud one is probably thinking about estaminet. An estaminet is a haven that one finds in agreeable plenty in most of the surrounding townships and villages, flourishing still amid roofless and deserted houses, patched up where necessary in rough-and-ready fashion, and finding a new and profitable tide of customers from among the soldiers who have replaced the bulk of the civil population. An estaminet is a sort of compound between a wine-shop and a coffee-house, having a tiny bar in one corner, a few long tables and benches, a prominent cooking stove, generally a small grocery store tucked away in the back premises, and always two or three children running and bumping about at inconvenient angles to one's feet.

**Explain the meaning the simile of the underlined part is intended to convey. Do NOT copy more than FOUR consecutive words from the passage. Second, identify the major setting other than the battlefield in the given excerpt.**

## 02 Read the poem and follow the directions. [4 points]

It mounts at sea, a concave wall
  Down-ribbed with shine,
And pushes forward, building tall
  Its steep incline.

Then from their hiding rise to sight
  <u>Black shapes</u> on boards
Bearing before the fringe of white
  It mottles towards.

Their pale feet curl, they poise their weight
  With a learn'd skill.
It is the wave they imitate
  Keeps them so still.

The marbling bodies have become
  Half wave, half men,
Grafted it seems by feet of foam
  Some seconds, then,

Late as they can, they slice the face
  In timed procession:
Balance is triumph in this place,
  Triumph possession.

The mindless heave of which they rode
  A fluid shelf
Breaks as they leave it, falls and, slowed,
  Loses itself.

Clear, the sheathed bodies slick as seals
  Loosen and tingle;
And by the board the bare foot feels
  The suck of shingle.

They paddle in the shallows still;
  Two splash each other;
Then all swim out to wait until
  The right waves gather.

Describe to what the underlined "Black shapes" refer. Second, the second-to-last stanza features a unique sound device several times. Identify this poetic device and provide TWO specific instances of its usage.

## 03 Read the excerpt from a play and follow the directions. [4 points]

Robert We've never talked seriously about our marriage before.

Hester What is there to say about it?

Robert A great deal.

Hester I don't agree. Marriages are things of feeling. They'd better not be talked about.

Robert Real marriages can stand discussion!

Hester Rob!

Robert What?

Hester That wasn't nice.

Robert Wasn't it?

Hester (*suddenly frightened*) What's the matter, Rob? I'll talk as seriously as you please. Do I love you? Yes. Am I going to make you a good wife? I hope so, though I am only twenty and may make mistakes. Are you going to be happy with me? I hope that, too, but you'll have to answer it for yourself.

Robert I can't answer it.

Hester What can't you?

Robert Because I'm not sure of it.

Hester Aren't you, Rob?

Robert These things are better faced before than after.

Hester What is it you're trying to say?

Robert If only we could be sure!

Hester (*stunned*) So that's it!

Robert Are you so sure you want to marry me?

Hester How can I be—now?

Robert Marriage is such a serious thing. You don't realize how serious.

Hester Don't I?

Robert No··· I hope you won't think harshly of me··· And, mind you, I haven't said I wanted to break things off··· I only want···

Hester Please, Rob!
Robert No. You've got to hear me out.
Hester I've heard enough, thank you!
Robert I'm only trying to look at this thing···
Hester Seriously··· I know···
Robert Because, after all, the happiness of three people is affected by it.
Hester Three?
Robert As Mother said, before dinner.
Hester So you talked this over with your mother?
Robert Isn't that natural?
Hester Is your mother the third?
Robert Wouldn't she be?
Hester Yes, I suppose she would··· I think you might tell me what else she had to say.
Robert It was all wise and kind. You may be as hard as you like on me, but you mustn't be hard on poor splendid lonely Mother.
Hester *(savage—under her breath)* So she's lonely, too!
Robert You will twist my meaning!
Hester You said "lonely".
Robert Perhaps I did. But Mother didn't. You know, she never talks about herself.
Hester I see. What else did she say about us?
Robert Well, you haven't been very interested in planning our future. She notices such things.

**Explain the conflicting perspectives Robert and Hester hold regarding a marriage discussion. Then, outline Hester's attitude toward her future mother-in-law as is implied in the underlined.**

# 15 회 실전모의고사

모범답안 p.45

**01 Read the excerpt from a short story and follow the directions.** [4 points]

"But this was the strange thing: as the days went by, we who were left worked harder and harder, and yet did we get less and less to eat in our Sea Valley tribe."

"But what of the goats and the corn and the fat roots and the fish-trap?" spoke up Afraid-of-the-Dark, "what of all this? Was there not more food to be gained by man's work?"

"It is so," grandfather Long-Beard agreed. "Three men on the fish-trap got more fish than the whole tribe before there was a fish-trap. The more food we were able to get, the less food did we have to eat."

"But was it not plain that the many men who did not work ate it all up?" Yellow-Head demanded.

Long-Beard nodded his head sadly and said. "Dog-Tooth's dogs were stuffed with meat, and the men who lay in the sun and did no work were rolling in fat, and, at the same time, there were little children crying themselves to sleep with hunger biting them with every wail. When we grumbled, Big-Fat arose and with the voice of God said that God had chosen the wise men to own the land and the goats and the fish-trap and that without these wise men we would all be animals, as in the days when we lived in trees.

“And there arose one who became a singer of songs for the king Dog-Tooth. Him they called the Bug, because he was small and ungainly of face and limb and excelled not in work or deed. He loved the fattest marrow bones, the choicest fish, the milk warm from the goats and the first corn that was ripe. And thus, becoming singer of songs to the king, he found a way to do nothing and be fat. And when the people grumbled more and more, and some threw stones at the king’s grass house, the Bug sang a song of how good it was to be a Fish-Eater. In his song he told that the Fish-Eaters were the chosen of God and the finest men God had made. He sang of the Meat-Eaters tribe as pigs and crows, and sang how fine and good it was for the Fish-Eaters to fight and die doing God’s work, which was the killing of Meat-Eaters. The words of his song were like fire in us. And we clamoured to be led against the Meat-Eaters. And we forgot that we were hungry, and why we had grumbled, and were glad to be led by Tiger-Face over the divide, where we killed many Meat-Eaters and were content.”

**In the allegorical story above, explain what actual position Big Fat represents in society. Second, explain the meaning of the underlined words. Do NOT copy more than THREE consecutive words from the passage.**

## 02 Read the poem and follow the directions. [4 points]

**Walking through a field with my little brother Seth**

I pointed to a place where kids had made angels in the snow.
For some reason, I told him that a troop of angels
had been shot and dissolved when they hit the ground.

He asked who had shot them and I said a farmer.

Then we were on the roof of the lake.
The ice looked like a photograph of water.

Why he asked. Why did he shoot them.

I didn't know where I was going with this.

They were on his property, I said.

When it's snowing, the outdoors seem like a room.

Today I traded hellos with my neighbor.
Our voices hung close in the new acoustics.
A room with the walls blasted to shreds and falling.

We returned to our shoveling, working side by side in silence.

But why were they on his property, he asked.

03

**Identify the two similes used to describe the setting of the given poem. Second, complete the commentary below by filling in the blank with SIX consecutive words from the poem.**

Commentary

In the given poem, the speaker is telling his little brother dark lies on a walk through the snow. These lies are believed by him and drawing in his imagination. This is implied when he brings up the subject again saying ________________________________.

## 03 Read the excerpt from a play and follow the directions. [4 points]

| | |
|---|---|
| FLOYD BARTON | What's wrong with that woman you got? |
| RED CARTER | Her mama ain't taught her how to cook. She know how to do everything else, but she can't cook. At first I thought she was lying. I come to find out it was the truth. I told her, "Come here, baby, I'm gonna show you this one time." Told her, "Pay attention." Then I showed her how to make biscuits. That's the only thing she can cook. That's why I'm getting fat. You hungry? We can go down there right now and get some biscuits. |
| FLOYD BARTON | You ought to teach her how to open up a can of beans. I don't want no woman who can't cook. She ain't too much good for me. She might be good for somebody, but much as I like to eat she ain't good for me. That's what got me so mad when they __________ me, cause I was gonna miss Vera's cooking. I asked the police say, "I done nothing. What you arresting me for?" He say, "I'm arresting you in advance. You gonna do something." I just look at him and told him, "Well, boss, you right, cause if I had my druthers I'd cut you every which way but loose." He just laughed, cause he know a black man ain't never had his druthers. They took me down there and beat me with them rubber hoses till I said uncle. I told him say, "If I ever meet you out in the back by the alley one day we gonna have some fun." Give me ninety days for vagrancy. |
| RED CARTER | One time they arrested me for having too much money. I had more money than the law allowed. Must have··· cause the police arrested me, put me in jail. Told me if I had that much money I must have stole it somewhere. |

| | |
|---|---|
| FLOYD BARTON | They got you coming and going. Put me in jail for not having enough money, and put you in jail for having too much money. Ain't no telling what they going to do next. *(FLOYD takes out his .38.)* That's why I got this here. |
| CANEWELL | That ain't gonna do nothing but get you arrested for carrying a loaded weapon. |
| BARTON | You allowed to carry a loaded weapon, you just can't hide it. You can carry it in your hand. That's your best bet. See, you can carry it like this here and walk right on by the police. They can't do nothing to you. But even if you be carrying a empty pistol they can take and put you in jail for carrying a concealed weapon. |

**Describe the experience of injustice Red Carter relates in the above excerpt. Do NOT copy more than THREE consecutive words from the passage. Second, fill in the blank with the ONE most appropriate word from the excerpt.**

# 16회 실전모의고사

모범답안 p.47

**01** **Read the excerpt from a play and follow the directions.** [2 points]

*The scene is Mrs. Mal's lodgings at Bath. Present, Lydia Languish. Enter Mrs. Mal and Sir Absolute.*

| | |
|---|---|
| MRS. MAL | There, Sir Absolute, there sits the deliberate simpleton who wants to disgrace her family, and lavish herself on a fellow not worth a shilling. |
| Lydia | Madam, I thought you once— |
| MRS. MAL | You thought, miss! I don't know any business you have to think at all: thought does not become a young woman. But the point we would request of you is, that you will promise to forget this fellow; to illiterate him quite from your memory. |
| Lydia | Ah, madam! our memories are independent of our wills. It is not so easy to forget. |
| MRS. MAL | But I say it is, miss; there is nothing on earth so easy as to forget, if a person chooses to set about it. I'm sure I have as much forgot your poor dear uncle as if he had never existed—and I thought it my duty so to do; and let me tell you, Lydia, these violent memories don't become a young woman. |
| Sir Absolute | Why, sure she won't pretend to remember what she's ordered not! Ay, this comes of her reading! |
| Lydia | What crime, madam, have I committed to be treated thus? |

| | |
|---|---|
| MRS. MAL | Now don't attempt to extirpate yourself from the matter; you know I have proof controvertible of it. But tell me, will you promise to do as you're bid? Will you take a husband of your friends' choosing? |
| Lydia | Madam, I must tell you plainly that had I no preference for any one else, the choice you have made would be my aversion. |
| MRS. MAL | Oh, there's nothing to be hoped for from you! You're as headstrong as an allegory on the banks of Nile. |

**Complete the commentary by filling in each blank with the ONE most appropriate word.**

Commentary

In the dialogue above, humorous effect is created by malapropism, which is the use of an incorrect word in place of a word with a similar sound. Two examples of malapropism in this passage are "____ⓐ____" which should be obliterate and "allegory" which should be ____ⓑ____.

## 02 Read the poem and follow the directions. [4 points]

Life is a nice place (They change
the decorations
every season; and the music,
my dear, is just too
marvellous, they play you
anything from birds to Bach. And
everyday the Host
arranges for some clever sort
of contest and they give
the most
fantastic prizes; I go absolutely
green. Of course, celebrities abound;
I've seen Love waltzing around
in amusing disguises.) to
visit. But
I wouldn't want to live there.

**Explain the irony employed in the first line by mentioning the general tone of the poem.**

## 03 Read the excerpt and follow the directions. [4 points]



Jim stepped to the washstand in the corner and washed his hands and combed water through his hair with his fingers. Looking into the mirror fastened across the corner of the room above the washstand, he peered into his own small grey eyes for a moment. With a towel he dried the soap and dropped the thin bar into a paper bag that stood open on the bed. A Gillette razor was in the bag, four pairs of new socks and another grey flannel shirt. He glanced about the room and then twisted the mouth of the bag closed. For a moment more he looked casually into the mirror, then turned off the light and went out the door.

He walked down narrow, uncarpeted stairs and knocked at a door beside the front entrance. It opened a little. A woman looked at him and then opened the door wider—a large blonde woman with a dark mole beside her mouth.

She smiled at him. "Mw-ter Nolan," she said.

"I'm going away," said Jim.

"But you'll be back, you'll want me to hold your room?"

"No. I've got to go away for good. I got a letter telling me."

"You didn't get no letters here," said the woman suspiciously.

"No, where I work. I won't be back. I'm paid a week in advance."

<u>Her smile faded slowly</u>. Her expression seemed to slip toward anger without any great change. "You should of give me a week's notice," she said sharply. "That's the rule. I got to keep that advance because you didn't give me no notice."

"I follow," Jim said. "That's all right. I didn't know how long I could stay."

The smile was back on the landlady's face. "You been a good quiet roomer," she said, "even if you ain't been here long. If you're ever around again, come right straight here. I'll find a place for you. I got sailors that come to me every time they're in port. And I find room for them. They wouldn't go no place else."

"I'll remember, Mrs. Meer. I left the key in the door."

**Explain why the landlady's smile faded slowly and give the reason for its return.**

_______________

_______________

_______________

_______________

_______________

03

## 04 Read the passage and follow the directions. [4 points]

[A] "For God's sake," he said, hearing her, but not turning round. "Don't make supper for me. I'm going out." At that point, Mary Maloney simply walked up behind her husband and without any pause she swung the big frozen leg of lamb high in the air and brought it down as hard as she could on the back of his head. She might just as well have hit him with a steel club.

A few minutes later she got up and went to the phone. She knew the number of the police station, and when the man at the other end answered, she cried to him, "Quick! Come quick! Patrick's dead!"

"You mean Patrick Maloney's dead?"

"I think so," she sobbed. "He's lying on the floor and I think he's dead."

"Be right over," the man said.

[B] The car came very quickly, and when she opened the front door, four policeman walked in. She knew them—because they worked with her husband—and she fell right into a chair, the one who was called O'Malley, kneeled by the body.

"Is he dead?" she cried.

"I'm afraid he is. What happened?"

Briefly, she told her story about going out to the grocer and coming back to find him on the floor. While she was talking, crying and talking, Noonan discovered a small patch of congealed blood on the dead man's head. He showed it to O'Malley who got up at once and hurried to the phone.

The four men searching the rooms seemed to be growing weary, a trifle exasperated.

[C] "Look, Mrs. Maloney. You know that oven of yours is still on, and the meat's still inside."

"Oh dear me!" she cried. "So it is!"

"I better turn it off for you, hadn't I?"

When the sergeant returned the second time, she looked at him with her large, dark tearful eyes. "Jack Noonan," she said. "Yes?"

[D] "Would you do me a small favor—you and these others? Here you all are, and good friends of dear Patrick's too, and helping to catch the man who killed him. You must be terribly hungry by now because it's long past your suppertime. Why don't you eat up that lamb that's in the oven. It'll be cooked just right by now." They were persuaded to go into the kitchen and help themselves.

"She wants us to finish it. She said so. Be doing her a favor."

"Okay then. Give me some more."

"That's the hell of a big club the guy must've used to hit poor Patrick," one of them was saying. "The doc says his skull was smashed all to pieces just like from a sledgehammer."

"That's why it ought to be easy to find."

**Identify the section (A, B, C, D) where the dramatic irony is revealed. Then, explain how this irony happens within the whole context.**

# 17회 실전모의고사

모범답안 p.48

**01** **Read the excerpt from a story and follow the directions.** [2 points]

Kino awakened in the near dark. The stars still shone and the day had drawn only a pale wash of light in the lower sky to the east. The roosters had been crowing for some time, and the early pigs were already beginning their ceaseless turning of twigs and bits of wood to see whether anything to eat had been overlooked. Outside the brush house in the tuna clump, a covey of little birds chittered and flurried with their wings.

Kino's eyes opened, and he looked first at the lightening square which was the door and then he looked at the hanging box where Coyotito slept. And last he turned his head to Juana, his wife, who lay beside him on the mat, her blue head-shawl over her nose and over her breasts and around the small of her back. Juana's eyes were open too. Kino could never remember seeing them closed when he awakened. Her dark eyes made little reflected stars. She was looking at him as she was always looking at him when he awakened.

Kino heard the little splash of morning waves on the beach. It was very good. Kino closed his eyes again to listen to his music. Perhaps he alone did this and perhaps all of his people did it. His people had once been great makers of songs so that everything they saw or thought or did or heard became a song. That was very long ago.

** tuna: thicket*

**Complete the commentary below by filling in the blank with the ONE most appropriate word from the excerpt above.**

Commentary

The protagonist reveals his love for his wife through the story. The writer employs the metaphor of __________ to illustrate how the protagonist views his beloved wife.

03

## 02 Read the poem and follow the directions. [4 points]

**A Little Boy Lost**

"Nought* loves another as itself*,
Nor venerates another so,
Nor is it possible to thought*
A greater than itself to know.

"And, Father*, how can I love you
Or any of my brothers more?
I love you like the little bird
That picks up crumbs around the door."

The priest sat by and heard the child;
In trembling zeal he seized his hair,
He led him by his little coat,
And all* admired the priestly care.

And standing on the altar high,
"Lo, what a fiend is here!" said he:
"One who sets reason up for judge
Of our most holy mystery."

The weeping child could not be heard,
The weeping parents wept in vain:
They stripped him to his little shirt,
And bound him in an iron chain,

And burned him in a holy place
Where many had been burned before;
The weeping parents wept in vain.
Are such things done on Albion's* shore?

** nought: nothing*
** another as itself: another thing like itself*
** to thought: to think*
** Father: God*
** all: all people*
** Albion: Great Britain*

**In the first two stanzas, the boy reasons that the limitations of both human understanding and human nature prevent one from ever truly loving another, including God, more than oneself. The last line of the third stanza is sarcastic. Explain the sarcasm. Second, in the poem what does the poet mainly condemn? Write your answer in ONE sentence.**

## 03 Read the passage and follow the directions. [4 points]

"Do you believe in magic?" he asks. "There was that Old Negro woman on Royal Street, oh way back, when we were just beginning. She wanted money. Remember? I had to sit down, I felt that sick and dizzy. You said it was nerves. You said it was not eating. You said I was making it up. Imagining things."

"I don't remember."

"After that we were never happy."

"I don't remember."

"All right," he says, "all right. Anyway, we have a healthy kid."

"That's a lot."

They turn up McAlister Drive, passing the brick dormitories, the broad-shadowed quadrangles. It is late summer. The students have all gone home. He bends his head passing under the mimosas. the low-hanging boughs.

"Was there really a black woman?" she asks.

"I had to sit down, I was that sick. And the next day we found out you were pregnant. Remember now? And then things just happened like they happened. She sang a song in Royal Street."

"I remember you were scared. Like a boy. I remember you wanted the baby dead."

"No."

"'There are ways,' you said. 'I know people,' you said."

"No. The Negro woman. She sang a song and I got sick."

"You wanted him dead. I don't remember a woman."

They have come to a corner, the streetlamps glimmering through the heavy leaves of trees. A bus flashes past and disappears into mist and dark.

"I think you made that up," she says, "About the black woman."

"After she sang, you never made it," he says. "Not one time."

"I was morning sick."

"Not one time."

"She didn't take my hand. She never sang to me."

"You remember then?"

He drives his fist against a stop sign and sinks to one knee in pain. He looks up at her. "There was a woman," he says slowly. "She took my hand. On Royal Street. She sang a song."

"She never took my hand."

"It was never any good again. Not once."

"Not never," she says. "Just never for you."

"Liar," he says. "Never again in your life."

She turns to him then and her eyes burn through the mist. "All right," she says, "all right. I remember the woman. She was horrible, all wrinkles and bad smell. When she took your hand her eyes shone red in the dark like a swamp animal."

"No," he says. "She was just an old beggar."

"When she crooned, there was death in her voice. She made you a dead man, and you didn't know."

"I don't remember."

"You remember, all right. After that, touching you was a night-mare. You stunk of the grave, a deader man than my father."

"There was never a woman. Or not like that. I made her up, an excuse."

**Identify the most important symbol revealing the couple's broken relationship. Second, of what part of their relationship is the couple most positive?**

**04** **Read the excerpt from a play and follow the directions.** [4 points]

*The staff of a small movie theater talking as they work.*

ROSE It was nice meeting you Toni.

TONI Yeah. You too.

ROSE (*to Sam*) Did you tell him about Dinner Money?

SAM Uh—what? No. Wait—

ROSE What did you do last night? Did you take it all?

SAM I thought that—he just started working here, so…

ROSE Well. Exactly, dumbass. You have to explain it to him.

SAM It's just—we have no idea if Toni's going to be cool with it and—

ROSE He *has* to be cool with it. *(Toni is trying to look like he's not listening.)*

SAM Hey. Toni.

TONI Yeah.

SAM At the end of every shift you're gonna get Dinner Money. It's just a little extra cash. We always split it three ways or two ways if there's just two of us. It can be anywhere from you know ten bucks on a weeknight to like thirty bucks on the weekend.

TONI Oh. Cool. So it's like a per diem*?

ROSE A what?

SAM No. Uh. Well. Kind of. It's kind of like a per diem. It's just…our boss Steve doesn't know about it.
*(A weird pause)*

TONI Steve doesn't give it to us?

*Rose looks at Sam. Sam struggles to find the right way to say it.*

SAM When we… when we take the tickets, we just kind of… you know when you tear them in half and put the other half in the bin, well—

TONI Yeah. Sure.

SAM Well, sometimes we take like, uh, like ten percent of those stubs, and we, uh, we, uh, resell them.

| | |
|---|---|
| | *(A pause)* |
| SAM | And then we take ten percent of the, uh, the, uh··· cash for the night. |
| ROSE | As Dinner Money. |
| SAM | We call it Dinner Money. |

**per diem: a specific amount of money given to an individual per day*

**Describe what "dinner money" is as it is discussed in the given excerpt. Next, identify who the newest staff member is.**

# 18회 실전모의고사

모범답안 p.50

**01** **Read the excerpt from a short story and follow the directions.** [2 points]

In the quiet and empty corridor, during the quiet hour of early afternoon, Joe was like a shadow, small even for five years, sober and quiet as a shadow. Another in the corridor could not have said just when and where he vanished, into what door, what room. But there was no one else in the corridor at this hour. He knew that. He had been doing this for almost a year, ever since the day when he discovered by accident the toothpaste which the dietitian used.

Once in the room, he went directly on his bare and silent feet to the washstand and found the tube. He was watching the pink worm coil smooth and cool and slow onto his parchmentcolored finger when hc heard footsteps in the corridor and then voices just beyond the door. With the tube in his hand and still silent as a shadow on his bare feet he crossed the room and slipped beneath a cloth curtain which screened off one corner of the room. Crouching, he heard the dietitian and her companion enter the room.

The dietitian was nothing to him yet, save a mechanical adjunct to eating, food, the diningroom, the ceremony of eating at the wooden forms, coming now and then into his vision without impacting at all except as something of pleasing association and pleasing in herself to look at. He knew the voice of her companion also: It was that of a young interne from the county hospital who was assistant to the parochial doctor who took the responsible of orphans.

Below is an analysis of the story above. Fill in each blank with ONE word respectively. The second word is found in the passage.

| Setting | in an orphanage |
|---|---|
| Character | Joe, who is a five-year-old living in an orphanage |
| Narration | _____ ⓐ _____ point of view |
| Figurative language | _____ ⓑ _____ symbolizes the main character |

**02** **Read the poem and follow the directions.** [4 points]

Twirling your blue skirts, travelling the sward
Under the towers of your seminary,
Go listen to your teachers old and contrary
Without believing a word.

Tie the white fillets* then about your hair
And think no more of what will come to pass
Than bluebirds that go walking on the grass
And chattering on the air.

Practise your beauty, blue girls, before it fail;
And I will cry with my loud lips and publish
Beauty which all our powers shall never establish,
It is so frail.

For I could tell you a story which is true;
<u>I know a lady with a terrible tongue</u>,
Blear eyes fallen from blue,
All her perfections tarnished—yet it is not long
Since she was lovelier than any of you.

**fillets: ribbons*

**Explain the meaning of the figure of speech used in the underlined part. Second, describe the thematic idea of the poem.**

## 03 Read the excerpt from a play and follow the directions. [4 points]

| | |
|---|---|
| JENNY | I mean, I guess I'm always thinking about how other people see me. Like I'm picturing how I look to them. |
| JENNY | And I'm always worried about··· like I'm always worried about objects and what they're thinking. I'm always worried that they're unhappy. Elias thinks I have OCD*. |
| MERTIS | What kind of objects? |
| JENNY | Well. All of them I guess. But when I was little I was always worried about my dolls. I had this one doll, um, Samantha, and I always felt like she was incredibly angry at me. |
| GENEVIEVE | Of course she was angry. |
| MERTIS | What do you mean, Genevieve? |
| GENEVIEVE | Angry to be a doll! To be a piece of plastic or glass and to be shaped into a human form and trapped! With one expression on your face! <u>Frozen!</u> People man-handling you. And then put in a dress. Put in an itchy little dress! |
| JENNY | Yeah. Exactly. I felt like she was mad that she was a doll and mad at me for not doing a better job making her life as a doll easier. Sometimes I couldn't sleep at night because I could feel her thinking all these horrible thoughts about me. So I would um··· oh my god I still feel bad about this··· I would get up in the middle of the night and lock her in the kitchen cupboard. So I wouldn't feel her watching me. But then the next morning she'd be even more mad cuz she'd spent all night in the cupboard! And then I'd cry and beg her for forgiveness. |
| MERTIS | And would she forgive you? |
| JENNY | Nope. She never forgave me. |

| | |
|---|---|
| MERTIS | I always thought it would be a wonderful thing to be a doll. To be··· To be free of responsibility. To be able to provide joy to people without even moving. Without even saying anything. |
| GENEVIEVE | You're dead wrong, Mertis. It's a terrible fate. |

** OCD: Obsessive Compulsive Disorder*

**Explain the meaning of the underlined "Frozen!". Second, describe Jenny's major frustration with Samantha.**

## 04 Read the excerpt from a fiction and follow the directions. [4 points]

[A] I do not know why they screamed every night at midnight. We were in the harbor and they were all on the pier and at midnight the refuge women started screaming. We used to turn the searchlight on them to quiet them. That always did the trick. We'd run the searchlight up and down over them two or three times and they stopped it.

[B] One time I was senior officer on the pier and a Turkish officer came up to me in a frightful rage because one of our sailors had been most insulting to him. So I told him the fellow would be sent on ship and be most severely punished. I asked him to point him out. So he pointed out a gunner's mate, most inoffensive chap. Said he'd been most frightfully and repeatedly insulting; talking to me through an interpreter. I couldn't imagine how the gunner's mate knew enough Turkish to be insulting. I called him over and said, "And just in case you should have spoken to any Turkish officers."

[C] "I haven't spoken to any of them, sir."

"I'm quite sure of it," I said, "but you'd best go on board ship and not come ashore again for the rest of the day."

Then I told the Turk the man was being sent on board ship and would be most severely dealt with. He felt topping about it. Great friends we were.

[D] They were all out there on the pier and it wasn't at all like an earthquake or that sort of thing because they never knew about the Turk. They never knew what the old Turk would do. You remember when they ordered us not to come in to take off any more? I had the wind up when we came in that morning. He had any amount of batteries and could have blown us clean out of the water. We were going to come in, run close along the pier, let go the front and rear anchors and then shell the Turkish quarter of the town. They would have blown us out of water but we would have blown the town simply to hell. They just fired a few blank charges at us as we came in.

[E] You remember the harbor. There were plenty of nice things floating around in it. That was the only time in my life I got so I dreamed about things. The Greeks were nice chaps too. When they evacuated they had all their baggage animals they couldn't take off with them so they just broke their forelegs and dumped them into the shallow water. All those mules with their forelegs broken pushed over into the shallow water. It was all a pleasant business. My word yes a most pleasant business.

**First, identify the section (A, B, C, D, E) where verbal irony is revealed. Then, explain the irony.**

# 19회 실전모의고사

모범답안 p.52

**01** **Read the poem and follow the directions.** [2 points]

Love set you going like a fat gold watch.
The midwife slapped your footsoles, and your bald cry
Took its place among the elements.

Our voices echo, magnifying your arrival. New statue.
In a drafty museum, your nakedness
Shadows our safety. We stand round blankly as walls.

I'm no more your mother
Than the cloud that distills a mirror to reflect its own slow
Effacement at the wind's hand.

All night your moth-breath
Flickers among the flat pink roses. I wake to listen:
A far sea moves in my ear.

One cry, and I stumble from bed, cow-heavy and floral
In my Victorian nightgown.
Your mouth opens clean as a cat's. The window square

Whitens and swallows its dull stars. And now you try
Your handful of notes;
The clear vowels rise like balloons.

**Complete the commentary by filling in each blank with ONE word from the passage.**

Commentary

The poem reveals the observations of a mother with her baby's ___ⓐ___ to the house. The poem relies primarily on sound imagery along with visual images. It is notable that images of listening to appear in every stanza except one, wherein the mother instead likens herself to a(the) ___ⓑ___.

---

## 02 Read the <A> and <B> and follow the directions. [4 points]

A

WALTER *(quietly)* Sometimes it's like I can see the future stretched out in front of me—just plain as day. The future, Mama. Hanging over there at the edge of my days. Just waiting for me—a big, looming blank space—full of nothing. Just waiting for me. But it don't have to be. *(Pause. Kneeling beside her chair.)* Mama—sometimes when I'm downtown and I pass them cool, quiet-looking restaurants where them white boys are sitting back and talking 'bout things··· sitting there turning deals worth millions of dollars··· sometimes I see guys don't look much older than me.

MAMA Son—how come you talk so much 'bout money?

WALTER *(with immense passion)* Because it is life, Mama!

MAMA (*quietly*) Oh—*(very quietly)* So now it's life. Money is life. Once upon a time freedom used to be life- now it's money. I guess the world really do change···.

WALTER No—it was always money, Mama. We just didn't know about it.

MAMA No··· something has changed. *(She looks at him.)* You something new, boy. In my time we was worried about not being lynched and getting to the North if we could and how to stay alive and still have a pinch of dignity too··· Now here come you and Beneatha—talking 'bout things we never even thought about hardly, me and your daddy. You ain't satisfied or proud of nothing we done. I mean that you had a home; that we kept you out of trouble till you was grown; that you don't have to ride to work on the back of nobody's streetcar—You my children—but how different we done become.

B

| | |
|---|---|
| WALTER | What I am telling you is that we called you over here to tell you that we are very proud and that this—(*signaling to TRAVIS*) Travis, come here. (*Travis crosses and Walter draws him before him facing the man.*) This is my son, and he makes the sixth generation our family in this country. And we have all thought about your offer— |
| LINDNER | Well, good···—good. |
| WALTER | And we have decided to move into our house because my father—my father—he earned it for us brick by brick. (*MAMA has her eyes closed and is rocking back and forth as though she were in church, with her head nodding the Amen yes.*) We don't want to make no trouble for nobody or fight no causes, and we will try to be good neighbors. And that's all we got to say about that. (*He looks the man absolutely in the eyes.*) We don't want your money. (*He turns and walks away.*) |

Read the two excerpted passages from a play closely. As the narrative progresses, *the character arc*—the transformation of personality and growth over the story's length—of Walter can be observed. Compare the two passages and explain the notable character development made by Walter in terms of race and money.

**03** **Read the passage and follow the directions.** [4 points]

In the woods, the boy stepped from sunlight to sunlight, in and out of shadow. His father showed him a tangle of bramble, hard with thorns, its leaves just beginning to color into autumn. Clusters of purple fruit hung in the branches. His father reached up and chose a blackberry for him. Its skin was plump and shining, each of its purple globes held a point of reflected light.

"You can eat it," his father said.

The boy put the blackberry in his mouth. He rolled it with his tongue and chewed happily. When he laughed his father saw that his mouth was deeply stained. Together they picked and ate the dark berries, until their lips were purple and their hands scratched.

"We should take some for your mother," the man said.

He reached with his stick and pulled down high canes where the choicest berries grew, picking them to take home. They had nothing to carry them in, so the boy put his new cap on the grass and they filled its hollow with berries. He held the cap by its edges and they went home.

"It was a stupid thing to do," his mother said, "utterly stupid. What were you thinking of?"

The young man did not answer.

"If we had the money, it would be different," his mother said, "Where do you think the money comes from?"

"I know where the money comes from," his father said. "I work hard enough for it."

"His new cap," his mother said. "How am I to get him another?"

The cap lay on the table and inside it was wet with the sticky juice of blackberries. Small pieces of blackberry skins were stuck to it. The stains were dark and irregular.

"It will probably dry out all right," his father said.

His mother's face was red and distorted, her voice shrill.

"If you had anything like a job," she shouted, "and could buy caps by the dozen, then-"

She stopped and shook her head. His father turned away, his mouth hard.

"I do what I can," he said.

"That's not much!" his mother said. She was tight with scorn. "You don't do much!"

Appalled, the child watched the quarrel mount and spread. He began to cry quietly, to himself, knowing that it was a different weeping to any he had experienced before, that he was crying for a different pain. And the child began to understand that they were different people; his father, his mother, himself, and that he must learn sometimes to be alone.

**The given story makes use of epiphany. Identify the epiphany of the story, taking care to mention the character who experiences the epiphany and at what point it occurs. Second, explain the contrast between the two parents' point of views in ONE or TWO sentences.**

# 20회 실전모의고사

모범답안 p.53

**01** **Read the poem and follow the directions.** [2 points]

As we come marching, marching in the beauty of the day,
A million darkened kitchens, a thousand mill lofts gray,
Are touched with all the radiance that a sudden sun discloses,
For the people hear us singing: "Bread and roses! Bread and roses!"

As we come marching, marching, we battle too for men,
For they are women's children, and we mother them again.
Our lives shall not be sweated from birth until life closes;
Hearts starve as well as bodies; give us bread, but give us roses!

As we come marching, marching, unnumbered women dead
Go crying through our singing their ancient song of bread.
Small art and love and beauty their drudging spirits knew.
Yes, it is bread we fight for—but we fight for roses, too!

As we come marching, marching, we bring the greater days.
The rising of the women means the rising of the race.
No more the drudge and idler—ten that toil where one reposes,
But a sharing of life's glories: Bread and roses! Bread and roses!

**Complete the commentary by filling in each blank with ONE word from the poem.**

Commentary

In the poem, the speaker employs two main symbols to convey his main point. First, ___ⓐ___ symbolize(s) fair wages while ___ⓑ___ dignity and respect.

## 02 Read the passage and follow the directions. [4 points]

| | |
|---|---|
| Proctor | Abby, that's a wild thing to say— |
| Abigail | A wild thing may say wild things. But not so wild, I think. I have seen you since she put me out; I have seen you nights. |
| Proctor | I have hardly stepped off my farm this sevenmonth. |
| Abigail | I have a sense for heat, John, and yours has drawn me to my window, and I have seen you looking up, burning in your loneliness. Do you tell me you've never looked up at my window? |
| Proctor | I may have looked up. |
| Abigail | *(softening)* And you must. You are no wintry man. I know you, John. I know you. She is weeping. I cannot sleep for dreamin'; I cannot dream but I wake and walk about the house as though I'd find you comin' through some door. She clutches him desperately. |
| Proctor | *(gently pressing her from him)* Child— |
| Abigail | *(with anger)* How do you call me child! |
| Proctor | Abby, I may think of you softly from time to time. But I will cut off my hand before I'll ever reach for you again. Wipe it out of mind. We never touched, Abby. |
| Abigail | Aye, but we did. |
| Proctor | Aye, but we did not. |
| Abigail | *(with a bitter anger)* Oh, I marvel how such a strong man may let such a sickly wife be— |
| Proctor | (*angered*) You'll speak nothin' of Elizabeth! |
| Abigail | She is blackening my name in the village! She is telling lies about me! She is a cold, sniveling woman, and you bend to her! Let her turn you like a— |
| Proctor | (*shaking her*) Do you look for whippin'? |

*A psalm is heard being sung below.*

Abigail *(in tears)* I look for John Proctor that took me from my sleep and put knowledge in my heart! I never knew what pretense Salem was, I never knew the lying lessons I was taught by all these Christian women and their covenanted men! And now you bid me tear the light out of my eyes? I will not, I cannot! You loved me, John Proctor, and whatever sin it is, you love me yet! *(He turns abruptly to go out. She rushes to him).* John, pity me, pity me!

In the above dialogue, Abigail is being detained and questioned over accusations that she has used witchcraft. Explain the apparent connection the two characters have as referenced in their conversation. Also, identify the reason Abigail gives for her increased notoriety in the town.

## 03 Read the passage and follow the directions. [4 points]

Yossarian looked at him soberly and tried another approach. 'Is Orr crazy?'

'He sure is,' Doc Daneeka said.

'Can you ground him?'

'I sure can. But first he has to ask me to. That's part of the rule.'

'Then why doesn't he ask you to?'

'Because he's crazy,' Doc Daneeka said. 'He has to be crazy to keep flying combat missions after all the close calls he's had. Sure, I can ground Orr. But first he has to ask me to.'

'That's all he has to do to be grounded?'

'That's all. Let him ask me.'

'And then you can ground him?' Yossarian asked.

'No. Then I can't ground him.'

'You mean there's a catch?'

'Sure there's a catch,' Doc Daneeka replied. 'Catch-22. Anyone who wants to get out of combat duty isn't really crazy.'

There was only one catch and that was Catch-22, which specified that a concern for one's safety in the face of dangers that were real and immediate was the process of a rational mind. Orr was crazy and could be grounded. All he had to do was ask; and as soon as he did, he would no longer be crazy and would have to fly more missions. Orr would be crazy to fly more missions and sane if he didn't, but if he were sane he had to fly them. If he flew them he was crazy and didn't have to; but if he didn't want to he was sane and had to. Yossarian was moved very deeply by the absolute simplicity of this clause of Catch-22 and let out a respectful whistle.

'That's some catch, that Catch-22,' he observed.

'It's the best there is,' Doc Daneeka agreed.

Yossarian saw it clearly in all its spinning reasonableness. There was an elliptical precision about its perfect pairs of parts that was graceful and shocking, like good modern art, and at times Yossarian wasn't quite sure that he saw it at all, just the way he was never quite sure about good modern art.



**Explain the paradox in the passage. Second, identify what Orr's profession is and what the setting is.**

# 21회 실전모의고사

모범답안 p.54

**01** **Read <A> and <B> and answer the question.** [2 points]

A

Okonkwo wanted him to be a prosperous man, having enough in his barn to feed the ancestors with regular sacrifices. And so he was always happy when he heard him grumbling about women. That showed that in time he would be able to control his women-folk and vindicate his manliness. No matter how prosperous a man was, if he was unable to rule his women and his children (and especially his women) he was not really a man.

So Okonkwo encouraged the boys to sit with him in his obi, and he told them stories of the land—masculine stories of violence and bloodshed. Nwoye knew that it was right to be masculine and to be violent, but somehow he still preferred the stories that his mother used to tell, and which she no doubt still told to her younger children-stories of the tortoise and his wily ways, and of the bird eneke-nti-oba who challenged the whole world to a wrestling contest and was finally thrown by the cat. He remembered the story she often told of the quarrel between Earth and Sky long ago, and how Sky withheld rain for seven years.

That was the kind of story that Nwoye loved. But he now knew that they were for foolish women and children, and he knew that his father wanted him to be a man. And so he feigned that he no longer cared for women's stories. And when he did this he saw that his father was pleased, and no longer rebuked him or beat him. So Nwoye and Ikemefuna would listen to Okonkwo's stories about tribal wars, or how, years ago, he had stalked his victim, overpowered him and obtained his first human head.

In this way the moons and the seasons passed. And then the locusts came. It had not happened for many a long year. They came in the cold harmattan season after the harvests had been gathered, and ate up all the wild grass in the native fields.

B

| | | |
|---|---|---|
| Characterization | Okonkwo | his tragic flaw—the equation of ____ⓐ____ with rashness, pride, and violence |
| Narration | third person point of view | unnamed omniscient figure |
| Symbol | ____ⓑ____ | white colonists descending upon the Africans |

Complete the chart of <B> by filling in each blank with ONE word from the passage.

## 02 Read the excerpt from a play and follow the directions. [4 points]

CATHERINE (*with surging enthusiasm*) Our splendid Bulgarians with their swords and eyes flashing, scattered the wretched Servian dandies like chaff. And you—you kept Sergius waiting a year before you would be betrothed to him. Oh, if you have a drop of Bulgarian blood in your veins, you will worship him when he comes back.

RAINA I am so happy! so proud! (*She rises and walks about excitedly.*) It proves that all our ideas were real after all.

CATHERINE (*indignantly*) Our ideas real! What do you mean?

RAINA Our ideas of what Sergius would do. Our patriotism. Our heroic ideals. I sometimes used to doubt whether they were anything but dreams. Oh, what faithless little creatures girls are! When I buckled on Sergius's sword he looked so noble: it was treason to think of disillusion or humiliation or failure. And yet—and yet—(*She sits down again suddenly.*) Promise me you'll never tell him.

CATHERINE Don't ask me for promises until I know what I'm promising.

RAINA Well, it came into my head just as he was holding me in his arms and looking into my eyes, that perhaps we only had our heroic ideas because we are so fond of reading Byron and Puskhin, and because we were so delighted with the opera that season at Bucharest. Real life is so seldom like that—indeed never, as far as I knew it then. (*Remorsefully*) Only think, mother, I doubted him: I wondered whether all his heroic qualities and his soldiership might not prove mere imagination when he went into a real battle. I had an uneasy fear that he might cut a poor figure there beside all those clever officers from the Tsar's court.

| | |
|---|---|
| CATHERINE | A poor figure! Shame on you! We have beaten them in every battle for all that. |
| RAINA | (*laughing and snuggling against her mother*) Sergius is just as splendid and noble as he looks! |



**Identify ONE word from the passage that corresponds to what Catherine emphasizes in the underlined parts. Then, describe what hesitation about Sergius Raina previously had.**

## 03 Read the poem and follow the directions. [4 points]

A noun's a thing. A verb's the thing it does.
An adjective is what describes the noun.
In "The can of beets is filled with purple fuzz"

of and with are prepositions. The's
an article, a can's a noun,
a noun's a thing. A verb's the thing it does.

A can can roll—or not. What isn't was
or might be, might meaning not yet known.
"Our can of beets is filled with purple fuzz"

is present tense. While words like our and us
are pronouns—i.e. it is moldy, they are icky brown.
A noun's a thing; a verb's the thing it does.

Is is a helping verb. It helps because
filled isn't a full verb. Can's what our owns
in "Our can of beets is filled with purple fuzz."

See? There's almost nothing to it. Just
memorize these rules··· or write them down!
A noun's a thing, a verb's the thing it does.
The can of beets is filled with purple fuzz.

**Describe what the speaker is mainly doing in the poem. Second, the poem is written in a form of villanelle, 9 lines with the traditional rhyme scheme, scattered among five tercets and one quatrain. Identify the rhyme scheme.**

# 22회 실전모의고사

모범답안 p.55

**01** **Read the poem and follow the directions.** [2 points]

I loved him most
when he came home from work,
his fingers still curled from fitting pipe,
his denim shirt ringed with sweat,
and smelling of salt, the drying weeds
of the ocean. I would go to him where he sat
on the edge of the bed, his forehead
anointed with grease, his cracked hands
jammed between his thighs, and unlace
the steel-toed boots, stroke his ankles,
his calves, the pads and bones of his feet.
Then I'd open his clothes and take
the whole day inside me—the ship's
gray sides, the miles of copper pipe,
the voice of the foreman clanging
off the hull's silver ribs, spark of lead
kissing metal, the clamp, the winch,
the white fire of the torch, the whistle,
and the long drive home.

**Complete the commentary by filling in each blank with ONE word from the poem. If necessary, change its word form.**

Commentary

In the poem, the speaker depicts the coming home of her blue-collar husband. He works as a(n) ___ⓐ___ fitter. In the underlined part, the speaker expresses her ___ⓑ___ for him.

## 02 Read the excerpt from a play and answer the question. [4 points]

| | |
|---|---|
| Lady Snob | Me, sir! What has it to do with me? You can hardly imagine that I and Lord Snob would dream of allowing our only daughter—a girl brought up with the utmost care—to marry into a cloakroom, and form an alliance with a parcel? Good morning, Mr. Worthing! (*Lady Snob sweeps out in majestic indignation.*) |
| Jack | Good morning! (*Algy, from the other room, strikes up the Wedding March. Jack looks perfectly furious, and goes to the door.*) For goodness' sake don't play that ghastly tune, Algy! How idiotic you are! (*The music stops, and Algy enters cheerily.*) |
| Algy | Didn't it go off all right, old boy? You don't mean to say Gwendolen refused you? I know it is a way she has. She is always refusing people. I think it is most ill-natured of her. |
| Jack | Oh, Gwendolen is as right as a trivet. As far as she is concerned, we are engaged. Her mother is perfectly unbearable. Never met such a gorgon··· I don't really know what a gorgon is like, but I am quite sure that Lady Snob is one. In any case, she is a monster, without being a myth, which is rather unfair··· I beg your pardon, Algy, I suppose I shouldn't talk about your own aunt in that way before you. |
| Algy | My dear boy, I love hearing my relations abused. It is the only thing that makes me put up with them at all. Relations are simply a tedious pack of people who haven't got the remotest knowledge of how to live, nor the smallest instinct about when to die. |

| | |
|---|---|
| Jack | Upon my word, if I thought that, I'd shoot myself···. (*A pause*) You don't think there is any chance of Gwendolen becoming like her mother in about a hundred and fifty years, do you, Algy? |
| Algy | All women become like their mothers. That is their tragedy. <u>No man does. That's his.</u> |

**Describe why Jack is angry at Lady Snob and explain the meaning of the underlined words in the last line.**

## 03 Read the excerpt from a short story and follow the directions. [4 points]

The Cricks lived at Toad-Water; and in the same upland spot Fate* had pitched the home of the Saunderses. ⓐ For miles around these two dwellings there was never a neighbour or a chimney or even a burying-ground to bring a sense of cheerful communion or social intercourse. Nothing but fields and spinneys and barns, lanes and wastelands. Such was Toad-Water; and, even so, Toad-Water had its history.

Thrust away in the benighted hinterland of a scattered market district, it might have been supposed that these two detached items of the Great Human Family would have leaned towards one another in a fellowship begotten of kindred circumstances and a common isolation from the outer world. And perhaps it had been so once, but the way of things had brought it ⓑ otherwise. Fate, which had linked the two families in such unavoidable association of habitat, had ordained that the Crick household should nourish and maintain among its earthly possessions sundry head of domestic fowls, while to the Saunderses was given a disposition towards the cultivation of garden crops. Herein lay the material, ready to hand, for the coming of feud and bad blood. For the grudge between the man of herbs and the man of live stock is no new thing; you will find traces of it in the fourth chapter of *Genesis*.

And one sunny afternoon in late spring-time the feud came—came, as such things mostly do come, with seeming aimlessness and triviality. One of the Crick hens, in obedience to the nomadic instincts of her kind, wearied of her legitimate scratching-ground, and flew over the low wall that divided the holdings of the neighbours. And there, on the yonder side, with a hurried consciousness that her time and opportunities might be limited, the misguided bird scratched and scraped and beaked and delved in the soft yielding bed that had been prepared for the solace and well-being of a colony of seedling onions.

Mrs. Saunders, sauntering at this luckless moment down the garden path, in order to fill her soul with reproaches at the iniquity of the weeds, stopped in mute discomfiture* before the presence of ⓒ a more magnificent grievance.

** Fate: god of fate*
** discomfiture: embarrassment*

**Write ONE word from the second paragraph that best depicts the situation revealed in the underlined words in ⓐ. Then, describe what the underlined "otherwise" means. Third, identify what the underlined words in ⓒ refer to.**

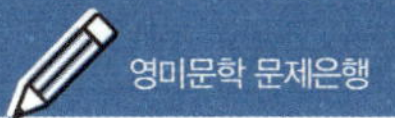


# 23회 실전모의고사

모범답안 p.56

**01** **Read the poem and follow the directions.** [2 points]

No man is an island,
Entire of itself.
Each is a piece of the continent,
A part of the main.
If a clod be washed away by the sea,
Europe is the less.
As well as if a promontory were.
As well as if a manor of thine own
Or of thine friend's were.
Each man's death diminishes me,
For I am involved in mankind.
Therefore, send not to know
For whom the bell tolls,
It tolls for thee.

**What is the thematic idea of the poem? Write your answer by filling in the blank below with ONE word from the poem.**

Any person's __________ is a loss to all of us since we are all part of mankind.

___

## 02 Read the excerpt from a play and follow the directions. [4 points]

MISS MORAY Well··· well, even Margaurita. She had fallen in love with the mice. All three hundred of them. She seemed shocked when she found out Dr. Crocus was··· using··· them at the rate of twenty or so a day in connection with electrode implanting. She noticed them missing after a while and when I told her they'd been decapitated, she seemed terribly upset. It made one wonder if she'd thought we'd been sending them away on vacations or something. But, I'm sure you understood—you have such in sight. (*She is at the tank.*) It's funny, isn't it? To look at these mammals, you'd never suspect they were such rapacious carnivores···

HELEN What do they want with it?

(*The* Let Me Call You Sweetheart *record commences playing but Miss Moray talks over it.*)

MISS MORAY Well, they may have an intelligence equal to our own. And if we can teach them our language—or learn theirs—we'll be able to communicate. (*Raising her voice higher over the record*) Wouldn't that be wonderful. Helen? To be able to communicate?

HELEN I can't understand you.

MISS MORAY (*Louder*) Communicate! Wouldn't it be wonderful?

HELEN Oh, yeah.

MISS MORAY (*With a cutting device*) When Margaurita found out they were using this··· on the mice, she almost fainted. No end of trouble.

HELEN They chopped the heads off three hundred mice?

| | |
|---|---|
| MISS MORAY | Now, Helen, you wanted progress, remember? |
| HELEN | That's horrible. |
| MISS MORAY | Helen, over a thousand individual laboratories did the same study last year. |
| HELEN | A thousand labs chopping off three hundred mice heads. Three hundred thousand mice heads chopped off? That's a lot of mouse heads. Couldn't one lab cut off a couple and then spread the word? |
| MISS MORAY | Now, Helen, this is exactly what I mean. You will do best not to become fond of the subject animals. When you're here a little longer you'll learn—well, there are some things in this world you have to accept on faith. |

**Describe the difference between the perspectives of Miss Moray and Helen towards the research being done in ONE sentence. Second, explain the reason Helen's predecessor Margaurita no longer works for the laboratory, as can be inferred from Miss Moray's words.**

## 03 Read the excerpt from a short story and follow the directions. [4 points]

And it's true: somehow, you've always found me. When I was a child, the postcards came to the house, of course; but later, when I went to college, and then to the first of several apartments. and finally to this house of my own, with husband and daughter of my own, they still kept coming. How you did this I don't know, but you did. You pursued me, and no matter how far away, you always found me. In your way, I guess, <u>you've been faithful</u>.

I put this postcard in a box with all the others you've sent over the years—postcards from Sioux City, Jackson Falls, Horseshoe Bend, Truckee, Elm City, Spivey. Then I pull out the same atlas I've had since a child and look up Manning, North Dakota, and yes, there you are, between Dickinson and Kildeer, a blip on the Read Highway line.

She's in Manning, North Dakota, I tell my husband, just as I used to tell my friends, as if that were explanation enough for your absence. I'd point out where you were in the atlas, and they'd nod.

But in all those postcards, Mother, I imagined you: you were down among the trees in the mountain panorama, or just out of frame on that street in downtown Tupelo, or already through too, hoping to find you and say to you. Come back, come back, there's only one street, one door, we didn't mean it, we didn't know, whatever was wrong will be different.

Several times I decided you were dead, even wished you were dead, but then another postcard would come, with another message to ponder. And I've always read them, even when my husband said not to, even if they've driven me to tears or rage or a blankness when I've no longer cared if you were dead or anyone were dead, including myself. <u>I've been faithful,</u> too, you see. I've always looked up where you were in the atlas, and put your postcards in the box. Sixty-three postcards, four hundred—odd lines of scrawl: our life together.

Why are you standing there like that? my daughter asks me.
I must have been away somewhere, I say. But I'm back.
Yes.
You see, Mother, I always come back. That's the distance that separates us.

03

In the given story, explain the similarity and difference the narrator draws between herself and her mother in the underlined parts. Second, identify a symbol used by the writer which represents their relationship. Do not use more than FIVE consecutive words from the text in your answer.

# 24회 실전모의고사

모범답안 p.57

**01** **Read <A> and <B> and answer the question.** [2 points]

A

Piggy wore the remainders of a pair of shorts, his fat body was golden brown, and the glasses still flashed when he looked at anything. He was the only boy on the island whose hair never seemed to grow. The rest were shock-headed, but Piggy's hair still lay in wisps over his head as though baldness were his natural state and this imperfect covering would soon go, like the velvet on a young stag's antlers. Piggy began again in a reasonable tone.

"You didn't ought to have let that fire out. You said you'd keep the smoke going— "

This from Piggy, and the wails of agreement from some of the hunters, drove Jack to violence. The bolting look came into his blue eyes. He took a step, and able at last to hit someone, stuck his fist into Piggy's stomach. Piggy sat down with a grunt. Jack stood over him. His voice was vicious with humiliation. "You would, would you? Fatty!"

Ralph made a step forward and Jack smacked Piggy's head. Piggy's glasses flew off and tinkled on the rocks. Piggy cried out in terror: "My specs!"

went crouching and feeling over the rocks.

"One side's broken."

Piggy grabbed and put on the glasses. He looked malevolently at Jack. "I got to have them specs. Now I only got one eye. Jus' you wait— " Jack made a move toward Piggy who scrambled away till a great rock lay between them. [deleted...]

"All right. Light the fire."

With some positive action before them, a little of the tension died. Ralph said no more, did nothing, stood looking down at the ashes round his feet. Jack was loud and active. He gave orders, sang, whistled, threw remarks at the silent Ralph—remarks that did not need an answer, and therefore could not invite a snub; and still Ralph was silent.

When they had dealt with the fire another crisis arose. Jack had no means of lighting it. Then to his surprise, Ralph went to Piggy and took the glasses from him. Not even Ralph knew how a link between him and Jack had been snapped and fastened elsewhere. "I'll bring 'em back." Piggy stood behind him, islanded in a sea of meaningless color, while Ralph knelt and focused the glossy spot. Instantly the fire was alight.

B

| | | |
|---|---|---|
| Character | ______ ⓐ ______ | violent and cruel |
| Narration | third person point of view | omniscient |
| Symbol | ______ ⓑ ______ | the power of science and intellectual endeavor |

**Fill in each blank in <B> with ONE or TWO word(s) from passage <A>.**

---

## 02 Read the poem and follow the directions. [4 points]

October. Here in this dank, unfamiliar kitchen
I study my father's embarrassed young man's face.
Sheepish grin, he holds in one hand a string
of spiny yellow perch*, in the other
a bottle of Carlsbad Beer.

In jeans and denim shirt, he leans
against the front fender of a 1934 Ford.
He would like to pose bluff and hearty for his posterity,
Wear his old hat cocked over his ear.
All his life my father wanted to be bold.

But the eyes give him away, and the hands
that limply offer the string of dead perch
and the bottle of beer. Father, I love you,
yet how can I say thank you, <u>I who can't hold my liquor either</u>,
and don't even know the places to fish?

** perch: fish*

**In the poem the speaker sees two sides of this father: the person who he attempts to be and the person he truly is. Explain this dualistic imagery using specific examples from the poem. Second, in the underlined part, what can we as readers infer about the speaker's current problem similar to his father?**

03

## 03 Read the excerpt from a play and follow the directions. [4 points]

*An island off the West of Ireland. Cottage kitchen, with nets, oil-skins, spinning wheel, some new boards. Standing by the wall, etc. Cathleen, a girl of about twenty, finishes kneading cake, and puts it down in the pot-oven by the fire; then wipes her hands, and begins to spin at the wheel. NORA, a young girl, puts her head in at the door.*

NORA (*In a low voice*) Where is mother?

CATHLEEN She's lying down, God help her, and may be sleeping, if she's able.

*Nora comes in softly, and takes a bundle from under her shawl.*

CATHLEEN (*Spinning the wheel rapidly*) What is it you have?

NORA The young priest is after bringing them. It's a shirt and a plain stocking were got off a drowned man in Donegal. (*Cathleen stops her wheel with a sudden movement, and leans out to listen.*) We're to find out if they are Michael's, and she might be for some time down looking by the sea.

CATHLEEN How would they be Michael's, Nora. How would he go the length of that way to the far north?

NORA The young priest says he's known the like of it. "If it's Michael's they are," says he, "you can tell herself he's got a clean burial by the grace of God, and if they're not his, let no one say a word about them, for she'll be getting her death," says he, "with crying."

*The door which Nora half closed is blown open by a gust of wind.*

CATHLEEN (*Looking out in anxiety*) Did you ask him would he stop Bartley going this day with the horses to the Galway fair?

NORA "I won't stop him," says he, "but let you not be afraid. She has been saying her prayers half the night, and the Almighty God won't leave her destitute," says he, "with no son living."

| | |
|---|---|
| CATHLEEN | Is the sea bad by the white rocks, Nora? |
| NORA | Middling bad, God help us. There's a great roaring in the west, and it's worse it'll be getting when the tide's turned to the wind. (*She goes over to the table with the bundle.*) Shall I open it now? |

**In the excerpt there is a conflict between the man and nature. Explain it. Then, identify what the bundle that Nora carries is. Next, identity ONE word revealed in stage directions that corresponds to the overall mood of the story above.**

# 25회 실전모의고사

모범답안 p.59

**01** **Read the excerpt from a play and follow the directions.** [2 points]

SIMONE Oh. merciful God, Nazi are coming up the steps.

MADAME My good Simone, that is what the steps were put there for.

SIMONE But they will ring the bell and I shall have to—

MADAME And you will answer it and behave as if you had been trained by a butler and ten upper servants instead of being the charcoal-burner's daughter from over at Les Chénes. (*This is said encouragingly, not in unkindness.*) You will be very calm and correct—

SIMONE Calm! Madame! With my inside turning over and over like a wheel at a fair!

MADAME A good servant does not have an inside, merely an exterior. (*Comforting*) Be assured, my child. You have your place here; that is more than <u>those creatures</u> on our doorstep have. Let that hearten you—

SIMONE Madame! They are not going to ring. They are coming straight in.

MADAME (*Bitterly*) Yes. They have forgotten long ago what bells are for.

*Door opens. Enter from main entrance a young man in his thirties, dressed in civilian clothes, closely followed by a German corporal.*

STRANGER (*In a bright, confident, casual tone*) Ah, there you are, my dear aunt. I am so glad. Come in, my friend, come in. My dear aunt, this gentleman wants you identify me.

| | |
|---|---|
| MADAME | Identify you? |
| CORPORAL | We found this man wandering in the woods. |
| STRANGER | The corporal found it inexplicable that anyone should wander in a wood. |
| CORPORAL | And he had no papers on him. |

**Fill in each blank in the provided commentary below with ONE word found in the passage respectively.**

Commentary

In the play, the underlined *those creatures* refer to ___ⓐ___. Second, the Corporal has entered the house of Madame and Simone in a rude manner in order to ___ⓑ___ the suspicious individual he has found.

---

## 02 Read the excerpt from a short story and follow the directions. [4 points]

Just after Victor lost his job at the Bureau of Indian Affairs, he also found out that his father had died of a heart attack in Phoenix, Arizona. Victor hadn't seen his father in a few years, only talked to him on the telephone once or twice, but ⓐ there still was a genetic pain, which was soon to be pain as real and immediate as a broken bone.

Victor didn't have any money. Who does have money on a reservation, except the cigarette and fireworks salespeople? His father had a savings account waiting to be claimed, but Victor needed to find a way to get to Phoenix. Victor's mother was just as poor as he was, and the rest of his family didn't have any use at all for him. So Victor called the Tribal Council.

"Listen," Victor said. "My father just died. I need some money to get to Phoenix to make arrangements."

"Now, Victor," the council said. "You know we're having a difficult time financially."

"Well," Victor said. "He had to be cremated. Things were kind of ugly. He died of a heart attack in his trailer and nobody found him for a week. It was really hot, too. You get the picture."

"Now, Victor, we're sorry for your loss and the circumstances. But we can really only afford to give you one hundred dollars."

While Victor stood in line, he watched Thomas Builds-the-Fire standing near the magazine rack, talking to himself. Like he always did. Thomas was a storyteller that nobody wanted to listen to. ⓑ That's like being a dentist in a town where everybody has false teeth.

"Oh," Victor said and looked around the Trading Post. All the other Indians stared, surprised that Victor was even talking to Thomas. Nobody talked to Thomas because he told the same damn stories over and over again.

What does the reader know about the relationship between Victor and his father in the first underlined part. Then, explain the meaning of the underlined words in ⓑ by including identification of the figure of speech used.

**03** **Read the poem and follow the directions.** [4 points]

One that is ever kind said yesterday:
"Your well-belovéd's hair has threads of grey,
And little shadows come about her eyes;
Time can but make it easier to be wise
Though now it seems impossible, and so
All that you need is patience."
Heart cries, "No,
I have not a crumb of comfort, not a grain.
Time can but make her beauty over again:
Because of that great nobleness of hers
The fire that stirs about her, when she stirs,
Burns but more clearly. O she had not these ways
When all the wild summer was in her gaze."

O heart! O heart! If she'd but turn her head,
You'd know the folly of being comforted.

**How can the friend's pointing out that the woman shows signs of aging be considered an attempt to "comfort" the speaker? Write your answer in ONE sentence. Second, the personification of "Heart"(7, 14) is contrasted to the friend's attempt to make the speaker "wise." Explain what the outburst from "Heart" means.**

# 26회 실전모의고사

모범답안 p.60

**01** **Read the story excerpt and follow the directions.** [2 points]

The Widow Douglas she took me for her son, and allowed she would civilize me; but it was rough living in the house all the time, considering how dismal regular and decent the widow was in all her ways; and so when I couldn't stand it no longer I lit out. I got into my old rags and my sugar-hogshead again, and was free and satisfied. But I went back.

The widow she cried over me, and called me a poor lost lamb. She put me in new clothes again, and I couldn't do nothing but sweat and sweat, and feel all cramped up. Well, then, the old thing commenced again. The widow rung a bell for supper, and you had to come to time. When you got to the table you couldn't go right to eating, but you had to wait for the widow to tuck down her head and grumble a little over the victuals.

After supper she got out her book and learned me about Moses and I was in a sweat to find out all about him; but by and by she let it out that Moses had been dead a considerable long time; so then I didn't care no more about him, because I don't take no stock in dead people.

Pretty soon I wanted to smoke, and asked the widow to let me. But she wouldn't. She said it was a mean practice and wasn't clean, and I must try to not do it any more. That is just the way with some people. They get down on a thing when they don't know nothing about it. Here she was a-bothering about Moses, which was no kin to her, and no use to anybody, being gone, you see, yet finding a power of fault with me for doing a thing that had some good in it. And she took snuff, too; of course that was all right, because she done it herself.

Fill in each blank with appropriate ONE word. The word for the second blank is found in the passage above.

| | |
|---|---|
| Narration | the ____ⓐ____ point of view |
| Tone | light-hearted |
| Language | frequently makes use of Southern dialects of the time. |
| Major conflict | Huck struggles against society and its attempts to ____ⓑ____ him. |

## 02 Read the excerpt from a play and follow the directions. [4 points]

| | |
|---|---|
| LEXY | (*saddened*) I had no idea you had any feeling against Mrs. Morell. |
| PROSERPINE | (*indignantly*) I have no feeling against her. She is very nice, very good-hearted: I'm very fond of her and can appreciate her real qualities far better than any man can. (*He shakes his head sadly. She rises and comes at him with intense pepperiness*). You don't believe me? You think I'm jealous? Oh, what a knowledge of the human heart you have, Mr. Lexy Mill! How well you know the weaknesses of Woman, don't You? It must be so nice to be a man and have a fine penetrating intellect instead of mere emotions like us, and to know that the reason we don't share your amorous delusions is that we're all jealous of one another! |
| LEXY | Ah, if your women only had the same clue to Man's strength that you have to his weakness, Miss Prossy, there would be no Woman Question. |
| PROSERPINE | Where did you hear Morell say that? You didn't invent it yourself: you're not clever enough. |
| LEXY | That's quite true, I am not ashamed of owing him that, as I owe him so many other spiritual truths. He said it at the annual conference of the Women's Liberal Federation. Allow me to add that though they didn't appreciate it, I, a mere man, did. (*He turns to the bookcase again, hoping that this may leave her crushed.*) |
| PROSERPINE | Well, when you talk to me, give me your own ideas, such as they are, and not his. <u>You never cut a poorer figure than when you are trying to imitate him.</u> |
| LEXY | (*stung*) I try to follow his example, not to imitate him. |

PROSERPINE (*coming at him again on her way back to her work*) Yes, you do: you imitate him. Why do you tuck your umbrella under your left arm instead of carrying it in your hand like anyone else? Why do you walk with your chin stuck out before you, hurrying along with that eager look in your eyes—you, who never get up before half past nine in the morning.

**Describe the criticism of Lexy that Proserpine gives in the underlined sentence. Next, explain the misconception about women's behavior Proserpine sarcastically identifies in her discussion with Lexy.**

## 03 Read the poem and follow the directions. [4 points]

If but some vengeful god would call to me
From up the sky, and laugh: "Thou suffering thing,
Know that thy sorrow is my ecstasy,
That thy love's loss is my hate's profiting!"

Then would I bear it, clench myself, and die,
Steeled by the sense of ire* unmerited*;
Half-eased in that a Powerfuller than I
Had willed and meted* me the tears I shed.

But not so. How arrives it joy lies slain,
And why unblooms the best hope ever sown*?
—Crass Casualty* obstructs the sun and rain,
And dicing* Time for gladness casts a moan….
These purblind* Doomsters had as readily strown*
Blisses about <u>my pilgrimage</u> as pain.

** ire: anger* ** unmerited: not deserved* ** mete: allot*
** sown: planted* ** Crass Casualty: fate* ** dicing: chopped up*
** purblind: partly blind* ** strown: scattered*

**In the poem above, what is the speaker's perspective toward "god" as presented in the first and second stanzas? Second, to what does "my pilgrimage" in the final line refer?**

# 27회 실전모의고사

모범답안 p.61

**01** **Read the poem and follow the directions.** [2 points]

The dead are always looking down on us, they say.
while we are putting on our shoes or making a sandwich,
they are looking down through the glass bottom boats of heaven
as they row themselves slowly through eternity.

They watch the tops of our heads moving below on earth,
and when we lie down in a field or on a couch,
drugged perhaps by the hum of a long afternoon,
they think we are looking back at them,

which makes them lift their oars and fall silent
and wait, like parents, for us to close our eyes.

**Complete the commentary by filling in each blank with ONE word. The word for the first blank is found in the poem.**

Commentary

Unlike the common images of the afterlife where the dead are serious, this poem playfully depicts the afterlife as a sort of tourism, as they ___ⓐ___ and watch the living curiously. The poet likewise infuses this poem with a reassuring sense. The last two lines express sadness and compassion, invoking a simile to liken the living to ___ⓑ___ who are watched over protectively while falling asleep.

**02** **Read the excerpt from a short story and follow the directions.** [4 points]

Theodoric Voler had been brought up, from infancy to the confines of middle age, by a fond mother whose chief solicitude had been to keep him screened from what she called the coarser realities of life. When she died she left Theodoric alone in a world that was as real as ever, and a good deal coarser than he considered it had any need to be. To a man of his temperament and upbringing even a simple railway journey was crammed with petty annoyances and minor discords, and as he settled himself down in a second-class compartment one September morning he was conscious of ruffled feelings and general mental discomposure. He had been staying at a country vicarage. The pony carriage that was to take him to the station had never been properly ordered, and in this emergency Theodoric, to his mute but very intense disgust, found himself obliged to collaborate with the vicar's daughter in the task of harnessing the pony, which necessitated groping about in an ill-lighted outbuilding called a stable, and smelling very like one—except in patches where it smelled of mice. Without being actually afraid of mice, Theodoric classed them among the coarser incidents of life, and considered that Providence*, with a little exercise of moral courage, might long ago have recognized that they were not indispensable, and have withdrawn them from circulation.

As the train glided out of the station Theodoric's nervous imagination accused himself of exhaling a weak odor of stable yard, and possibly of displaying a moldy straw or two on his unusually well-brushed garments. Fortunately the only other occupation of the compartment, a lady of about the same age as himself, seemed inclined for slumber rather than scrutiny; the train was not due to stop till the terminus was reached, in about an hour's time, and the carriage was of the old-fashioned sort that held no communication with a corridor, therefore no further traveling companions were likely to intrude on Theodoric's semiprivacy. And yet the train had scarcely attained its normal speed before he became reluctantly but vividly aware that he was not alone with the slumbering lady; he was not even alone in his own clothes. A warm, creeping movement over his flesh betrayed the unwelcome and highly resented presence, unseen but poignant, of a strayed mouse.

** Providence: God*

**Explain the reason Theodoric is more vexed by travelling than other people. Second, describe the meaning of the underlined "he was not even alone in his own clothes".**

## 03 Read the dramatic excerpt and follow the instructions. [4 points]

*Living room scene, CHARLES, the husband, is discussing recent fights with his wife, RUTH*

CHARLES You've behaved very well for the last few days, Ruth. You're not going to start making scenes again, are you?

RUTH I resent that air of patronage, Charles. I have behaved well, as you call it, because there was nothing else to do, but I think it only fair to warn you that I offer no guarantee for the future. My patience is being stretched to its uttermost.

CHARLES (*crossing to the armchair and sitting*) As far as I can see the position is just as difficult for Elvira as it is for you—if not more so. The poor little thing comes back trustingly after all those years in the other world, and what is she faced with? Nothing but brawling and hostility!

RUTH What did she expect?

CHARLES Surely even an ectoplasmic* manifestation has the right to expect a little of the milk of human kindness?

RUTH (*rising and going to the fireplace*) Milk of human fiddlesticks*!

CHARLES That just doesn't make sense, dear.

RUTH (*leaning over him*) Elvira is about as trusting as a puff-adder*.

CHARLES You're granite, Ruth—sheer unyielding granite.

RUTH And a good deal more dangerous into the bargain.

CHARLES Dangerous? I never heard anything so ridiculous. How could a poor lonely wistful little spirit like Elvira be dangerous?

RUTH Quite easily—and she is. She's beginning to show her hand.

CHARLES How do you mean—in what way?

RUTH This is a fight, Charles—a bloody battle—a duel to the death between Elvira and me. Don't you realize that?

| | |
|---|---|
| CHARLES | Melodramatic hysteria. |
| RUTH | It isn't melodramatic hysteria; it's true. Can't you see? |
| CHARLES | No, I can't. You're imagining things. Jealousy causes people to have the most curious delusions. |
| RUTH | (*pausing*) I am making every effort not to lose my temper with you, Charles; but I must say you are making it increasingly difficult for me. |
| CHARLES | All this talk of battles and duels··· |

** ectoplasmic: ghost-like*
** fiddlestick: bullshit*
** puff-adder: a venomous viper(snake)*

**Identify one metaphor used by Charles that reveals his sympathy towards Elvira, his ex-wife. Then, explain the major concern Ruth expresses in the conversation.**

# 28회 실전모의고사

모범답안 p.62

**01** **Read the poem and follow the directions.** [2 points]

This living hand, now warm and capable
Of earnest grasping, would, if it were cold
And in the icy silence of the tomb,
So haunt thy days and chill thy dreaming nights
That thou would wish thine own heart dry of blood
So in my veins red life might stream again,
And thou be conscience-calm'd,—see here it is—
I hold <u>it</u> towards you.

**Complete the commentary below by filling in each blank with one word found in the "it" poem.**

Commentary

In the "now" of the poem, the speaker addresses the "you" of the poem about overwhelming sadness should he be in the ______ⓐ______. Then, the underlined "it" refers to a(n) ______ⓑ______.

03

**02** **Read the excerpt from a short story and follow the directions.** [4 points]

There was a ball in the webbing of his mitt when we turned him over. His mitt had been pinned under his body and was coated with an almost luminescent gray film. There was the same gray on his black, hightop gym shoes, as if he'd been running though lime, and along the bill* of his baseball cap—the blue felt one with the red C which he always denied stood for the Chicago Cubs. He may have been a loner, but he didn't want to be identified with a loser. He lacked the sense of humor for that, lacked the perverse pride that sticking up for losers season after season breeds, and the love. He was just an ordinary guy, .250 at the plate, and we stood above him not knowing what to do next. By then the guys from the other outfield positions had trotted over. Someone, the shortstop probably, suggested team prayer. But no one could think of a team prayer. So we all just stood there silently bowing our heads, pretending to pray while the shadows moved darkly across the outfield grass. After a while the entire diamond was swallowed and the field lights came on.

In the bluish squint of those lights he didn't look like someone we'd once known—nothing looked quite right—and we hurriedly scratched a shallow grave, covered him over, and stamped it down as much as possible so that the next right fielder, whoever he'd be, wouldn't trip. It could be just such a juvenile, seemingly trivial stumble that would ruin a great career before it had begun, or hamper it years later the way Mantle's was hampered by bum knees. One can never be sure the kid beside him isn't another Roberto Clemente; and who can ever know how many potential Great Ones have gone down in the obscurity of their neighborhoods? And so, in the catcher's phrase, we "buried the grave" rather than contribute to any further tragedy. In all likelihood the next right fielder, whoever he'd be, would be clumsy too, and if there was a mound to trip over he'd find it and break his neck, and soon right field would get the reputation as haunted, a kind of sandlot Bermuda Triangle, inhabited by phantoms calling for ghostly fly balls, where no one but the most desperate outcasts, already on the verge of suicide, would be willing to play.

** bill: a part of a cap*

**Describe the central event of the given excerpt. Be sure to include mention of the setting in your explanation. Second, identify the speaker's worry regarding the next right fielder.**

**03** **Read the excerpt from a play and follow the directions.** [4 points]

*Actors on a stage are rehearsing a play…*

BELINDA She'll just carry on. Won't you, my love?

FREDERICK But can she see anything without them?

LLOYD Can she hear anything without them?

BROOKE *(suddenly realizing that she is being addressed)* Sorry?

*She straightens up sharply. Her head comes into abrupt contact with Poppy's face.*

POPPY Ugh!

BROOKE Oh. Sorry.

*Brooke jumps up to see what damage she has done to Poppy, and steps backward on to Garry's hand.*

GARRY Ugh!

BROOKE Sorry.

*Dotty hurries to his aid.*

DOTTY Oh my poor darling! *(To Brooke)* You stood on his hand!

FREDERICK Oh dear. *(He hurriedly clasps a handkerchief to his nose.)*

BELINDA Oh, look at Freddie, the poor love!

LLOYD What's the matter with him?

BELINDA He's just got a little nosebleed, my sweet.

LLOYD A nosebleed? No one touched him!

BELINDA No, he's got a thing about violence. It always makes his nose bleed.

FREDERICK *(from behind his handkerchief)* I'm so sorry.

LLOYD Brooke, sweetheart…

BROOKE I thought you said something to me.

LLOYD Yes. *(He picks up a vase and hands it to her.)* <u>Just go and hit the box-office manager with this vase, and you'll have finished off* live theatre in Weston-super-Mare*.</u>

**finished off: destroy*

** Weston-super-Mare: a seaside town in Somerset, England*

Describe the unusual justification Belinda gives for Frederick's bleeding. Then, explain the sarcastic meaning of the underlined expression given by Lloyd.

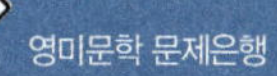


# 29회 실전모의고사

모범답안 p.63

**01** **Read the excerpt from a play and follow the directions.** [2 points]

MR. WEBB Very ordinary town, if you ask me. Little better behaved than most. But our young people here seem to like it well enough. Ninety per cent of 'em graduating from high school settle down right here to live…even when they've been away to college.

STAGE MANAGER Now, is there anyone in the audience who would like to ask Editor Webb anything about the town?

LADY IN A BOX Oh, Mr. Webb? Mr. Webb, is there any culture or love of beauty in Grover's Corners?

MR. WEBB Well, ma'am, there ain't much; not in the sense you mean. Come to think of it, there's some girls that play the piano at High School Commencement; but they ain't happy about it. No, ma'am, there isn't much culture; but maybe this is the place to tell you that we've got a lot of pleasures of a kind here. We like the sun comin' up over the mountain in the morning and we all notice a good deal about the birds. We pay a lot of attention to them. And we watch the change of the seasons; yes, everybody knows about them.

*Mr. Webb exits.*

| | |
|---|---|
| STAGE MANAGER | Thank you, Mr. Webb. Now, we'll go back to the town. It's early afternoon. All 2,642 dinners have been eaten and all the dishes have been washed. There's an early-afternoon calm in our town. For example, a buzzin' and a hummin' from the school buildings… only a few buggies on Main Street… the horses dozing at the hitching posts. You all remember what it's like. Doc Gibbs is in his office, tapping people and making them say "ah." Mr. Webb's cuttin' his lawn over there. |

**Complete the commentary by filling in each blank with ONE word from the excerpt above.**

Commentary

In the town of Grover's Corners, the values placed high are family, comfort, and home. In lieu of ____ⓐ____, they celebrate nature and its manifestations. Also, the STAGE MANAGER emphasizes the ____ⓑ____ atmosphere of the town.

---

**02** **Read the poem and follow the directions.** [4 points]

I tied a paper mask onto my face,
my lips almost inside its small red mouth.
Turning my head to the left, to the right,
I looked like someone I once knew, or was,
with straight white teeth and boyish bangs.
My ordinary life had come, as far as it would,
like a silver arrow hitting cypress.
Know your place or you'll rue it, I sighed
to the mirror. To succeed, I'd done things
I hated; to be loved, I'd competed promiscuously:
my essence seemed to boil down to only this.
Then I saw my own hazel irises float up,
like eggs clinging to a water plant,
seamless and clear, in an empty, pondlike face.

**Explain the significance of the "mask" in the poem as it relates to the speaker's success. Second, select ONE word the poet uses as a comparison for eyes.**

## 03 Read the excerpt from a short story and follow the directions. [4 points]

"He's a marvelous writer, brilliant, one of the very best."

"Why?"

"Well, for one thing he's so simple. Look how few words he uses, and how strong his stories are."

"I see. Do you know him? Does he live in London?"

"Oh now, he's dead."

"Oh. Then why did you—I thought he was alive, the way you talked."

"I'm sorry, I suppose I wasn't thinking of him as dead."

"When did he die?"

"He was murdered. About twenty years ago, I suppose?"

"Twenty years." Her hand began the movement of pushing the book over to me, but then relaxed. "I'll be fourteen in November," she stated, sounding threatened, while her eyes challenged me.

I found it hard to express my need to apologize, but before I could speak, she said, patiently attentive again: "You said he was murdered?"

"Yes."

"I expect the person who murdered him felt sorry when he discovered he had murdered a famous writer."

"Yes, I expect so."

"Was he old when he was murdered?"

"No, quite young really."

"Well, that was bad luck, wasn't it?"

"Yes, I suppose it was bad luck."

"Which do you think is the very best story here? I mean, in your honest opinion, the very very best one."

I chose the story about killing the goose. She read it slowly, while I sat waiting, wishing to take it from her, wishing to protect this charming little person from Isaac Babel.

When she had finished, she said: "Well, some of it I don't understand. He's got a funny way of looking at things. Why should a man's legs in boots look like girls?" She finally pushed the book over at me, and said: "I think it's all morbid."

"But you have to understand the kind of life he had. First, he was a Jew in Russia. That was bad enough. Then his experience was all revolution and civil war and···"

But I could see these words bouncing off the clear glass of her fiercely denying gaze and I said: "Look, Catherine, why don't you try again when you're older? Perhaps you'll like him better then?"

She said gratefully: "Yes, perhaps that would be best."

**Explain the meaning of the underlined section, identifying the figure of speech used there. Also, explain Catherine's opinion of the deceased writer's work.**

# 30회 실전모의고사

모범답안 p.64

**01** **Read the excerpt from a novel and follow the directions.** [4 points]

*Note: The protagonist begins extremely overweight, disgusted with herself, and distant from her husband.*

One night my husband says it won't last, what about the freezer full of low-cal dinners and that treadmill in the basement. I'm not doing it for losing weight and he doesn't believe me either.

But this time there is another part. There are other men in the swimming pool, I tell him. Fish, he says. Fish in the sea. Good luck.

Ma you've lost weight says my daughter-in-law, the one who didn't want me in the wedding pictures. Ones with the whole family. She said she couldn't help that. I learned how to swim, I tell her now, you should try it, it might help your ugly disposition.

They closed the pool for two weeks and I went crazy. Repairing the tiles. I went there anyway, drove by in the car. I drank water all day.

Then they opened again and I went every day, sometimes four times until the green paint and new stripes looked familiar as a face. At first the water was heavy as blood but I kept on until it was thinner and thinner, just enough to hold me up. That was when <u>I stopped with the goggles and cap and plugs</u>, things that kept the water out of me. There was a time I went the day before a holiday and no one was there. It was echoey silence just me and the soundless empty pool and a lifeguard behind the glass. I lowered myself so slow it hurt every muscle.

Explain why the narrator's daughter-in-law did not want the narrator in her wedding pictures. Second, what can the reader infer about the narrator from the underlined words.

## 02 Read the poem and follow the directions. [4 points]

My Life had stood—a Loaded Gun—
In Corners—till a Day
The Owner passed and identified
And carried Me away—

And now We roam in Sovereign Woods—
And now We hunt the Doe—
And every time I speak for Him—
The Mountains straight reply—

And do I smile*, such cordial light
Upon the Valley glow
It is as a Vesuvian* face
Had let its pleasure through

And when at Night—Our good Day done
I guard My Master's Head
'Tis better than the eider-duck's
Deep Pillow—to have shared

To foe of His—I'm deadly foe
None stir the second time
On whom I lay a Yellow Eye
Or an emphatic Thumb

Though I than He—may longer live
He longer must—than I
For I have but the power to kill,
Without the power to die—

** do I smile: if I do smile*
** as a Vesuvian: as if a Vesuvian*
** Vesuvius: the volcano whose eruption (in the year 79 AD) horribly wiped out Pompeii.*

**Identify the major extended metaphor used through the poem. Second, explain why the speaker says she/he may live longer than her/his owner.**

## 03 Read the excerpt from a play and follow the directions. [4 points]

STEPHANO What's this song?
TRINCULO That's the melody, played by Nobody.
STEPHANO (*to the invisible musician*) If you're a man, then let us see what you look like. If you're a devil, then go to hell.
TRINCULO O, forgive me my sins!
STEPHANO Dead men have to pay their debts.—I challenge you!—God help us.
CALIBAN Be not afeard*: the isle is full of noises,
Sounds, and sweet airs, that give delight, and hurt not.
Sometimes a thousand twangling instruments
Will hum about mine ears; and sometimes voices,
That, if I then had wak'd* after long sleep,
Will make me sleep again: and then, in dreaming,
The clouds methought* would open and show riches
Ready to drop upon me; that, when I wak'd,
I cried to dream again.
STEPHANO This will prove a brave kingdom to me, where I shall have my music for nothing.
CALIBAN When Prospero is destroyed.
STEPHANO That shall be by and by. I remember the story.
TRINCULO The sound is going away, let's follow it, and after* do <u>our work</u>.
STEPHANO Lead, monster Caliban, we'll follow.—I would I could see this taborer*! he lays it on*. Wilt come?
TRINCULO I'll follow, Stephano.

** afeard: scared * wak'd: waked * methoght: I thought*
** and after: and then * taborer: drummer * lays it on: plays well*

Caliban describes a unique quality of the island. What is that? Second, to what does the underlined "our work" refer?

# 31 회 실전모의고사

모범답안 p.66

**01** **Read the poem and follow the directions.** [2 points]

When I look behind,
as I am compelled to look
before I can gather strength
to proceed on my journey,
I see the milestones dwindling
toward the horizon
and the slow fires trailing
from the abandoned camp-sites,
over which scavenger angels
wheel on heavy wings.
Oh, I have made myself a tribe
out of my true affections,
and my tribe is scattered!
How shall the heart be reconciled
to its feast of losses?
In a rising wind
the manic dust of my friends,
those who fell along the way,
bitterly stings my face.
Yet I turn, I turn,
exulting somewhat,
with my will intact to go
wherever I need to go,
and every stone on the road
precious to me.

**Complete the statement by filling in the blank with the ONE most appropriate word from the poem.**

| While the major motif of this poem is the sadness of loss, the tone of the poem shifts at the moment the speaker moves to __________ both literally and figuratively. |
|---|

---

## 02 Read the passages <A> and <B> and follow the directions. [4 points]

A

His arms had begun to tremble from the steady strain of clinging to this narrow perch, and he did not know what to do now and was terribly frightened. Clinging to the window stripping with one hand, he again searched his pockets. But now—he had left his wallet on his dresser when he'd changed clothes—there was nothing left but the yellow sheet. It occurred to him irrelevantly that his death on the sidewalk below would be an eternal mystery; the window closed—why, how, and from where could he have fallen? No one would be able to identify his body for a time, either—the thought was somehow unbearable and increased his fear. All they'd find in his pockets would be the yellow sheet. Contents of the dead man's pockets, he thought, one sheet of paper bearing penciled notations—incomprehensible.

He understood fully that he might actually be going to die; his arms, maintaining his balance on the ledge, were trembling steadily now. And it occurred to him then with all the force of a revelation that, if he fell, all he was ever going to have out of life he would then, abruptly, have had. Nothing, then, could ever be changed; and nothing more—no least experience or pleasure—could ever be added to his life. He wished, then, that he had not allowed his wife to go off by herself tonight—and on similar nights. He thought of all the evenings he had spent away from her, working; and he regretted them. He thought wonderingly of his fierce ambition and of the direction his life had taken; he thought of the hours he'd spent by himself, filling the yellow sheet that had brought him out here. Contents of the dead man's pockets, he thought with sudden fierce anger, a wasted life.

B

He was simply not going to cling here till he slipped and fell; he told himself that now. There was one last thing he could try; he had been aware of it for some moments, refusing to think about it, but now he faced it. Kneeling here on the ledge, the fingertips of one hand pressed to the narrow strip of wood, he could, he knew, draw his other hand back a yard perhaps, fist clenched tight, doing it very slowly till he sensed the outer limit of balance, then, as hard as he was able from the distance, he could drive his fist forward against the glass. If it broke, his fist smashing through, he was safe; he might cut himself badly, and probably would, but with his arm inside the room, he would be secure. But if the glass did not break, the rebound, flinging his arm back, would topple him off the ledge. He was certain of that.

**Oftentimes, the external conflict of a story runs in parallel to internal struggles of the protagonist and other characters. Considering this, explain the meaning of the underlined "He was simply not going to cling here till he slipped and fell" in <B>. Support your explanation using citation of ONE specific example from <A> that demonstrates the weakness the character is feeling in contrast to his mindset later in <B>. Do NOT copy more than FIVE consecutive words from the excerpt.**

## 03 Read the excerpt from a play and follow the directions. [4 points]

| | |
|---|---|
| Prince | This isn't a story really. You see. I'm attendant on Prince Simon who is visiting here. |
| Princess | Oh? I'm attendant on Her Royal Highness. |
| Prince | Then you know what he's here for. |
| Princess | Yes. |
| Prince | She's very beautiful, I hear. |
| Princess | Did you hear that? Where have you been lately? |
| Prince | Travelling in distant lands—with Prince Simon. |
| Princess | Ah! All the same, I don't understand. Is Prince Simon in the Palace now? The drawbridge can't be down yet! |
| Prince | I don't suppose it is. And what a noise it makes coming down! |
| Princess | Isn't it terrible? |
| Prince | I couldn't stand it any more. I just had to get away. That's why I'm here. |
| Princess | But how? |
| Prince | Well, there's only one way, isn't there? That beech tree, and then a swing and a grab for the battlements, and don't ask me to remember it all—(*He shudders.*) |
| Princess | You mean you came across the moat by that beech tree? |
| Prince | Yes. I got so tired of hanging about. |
| Princess | But it's terribly dangerous! |
| Prince | That's why I'm so exhausted. Nervous shock. (*He lies back and breathes loudly.*) |
| Princess | Of course, the climb is different for me. |
| Prince | (*Sitting up*) Say that again. I must have got it wrong. |
| Princess | It's different for me, because I'm used to it. Besides, I'm so much lighter. |

| | |
|---|---|
| Prince | You don't mean that you— |
| Princess | Oh yes, often. |
| Prince | And I thought I was a brave man! At least, <u>I didn't until five minutes ago</u>, and now I don't again. |

**In the scene presented above, describe how the Prince arrives inside the Palace. Then, explain the meaning of the underlined part regarding his pride. Do NOT copy more than FIVE consecutive words from the passage.**

# 32회 실전모의고사

모범답안 p.67

## 01 Read the poem and follow the directions. [2 points]

I woke and remembered
nothing of what I was dreaming.

The day grew light, then dark again—
In all its rich hours, what happened?

A few weeds pulled, a few cold flowers
carried inside for the vase.
A little reading. A little tidying and sweeping.

I had vowed to do nothing I did not wish
to do that day, and kept my promise.

Once, a certain hope came close
and then departed. Passed by me in its familiar
shawl, scented with iodine woodsmoke.

I did not speak to it, nor it to me.
Yet still the habit of warmth traveled
between us, like an apple shared by old friends.

One takes a bite, then the other.
They do this until it is gone.

**Complete the statement by filling in each blank with ONE appropriate word. The word for the first blank can be found in the poem.**

> The main theme of the poem is that what we give and take with "hope" is like a(n) ___ⓐ___ which we share with our friend. In order to convey the theme, the poet employs an extended figure of speech, ___ⓑ___, that takes place in stanzas five to seven.

---

## 02 Read the excerpt from a short story and follow the directions. [4 points]

It was as if Angela had foreseen her death. Yet she had been in perfect health when she left the house that morning, six weeks ago; when she stepped off the kerb in Piccadilly and the car had killed her.

Every friend had been left some little token of her affection. To Gilbert, her husband, she had left nothing in particular, unless it were her diary. Fifteen little volumes, bound in green leather, stood behind him on her writing table. Ever since they were married, she had kept a diary. When he came in and found her writing, she always shut it or put her hand over it. "No, no, no," he could hear her say, "After I'm dead—perhaps." So she had left it him, as her legacy. It was the only thing they had not shared when she was alive. [deleted...]

The diary was full of references. His own name occurred less frequently. <u>His interest slackened</u>. Some of the entries conveyed nothing to him. For example: "Had a heated argument about socialism with B. M." Who was B. M.? He could not fill in the initials; some woman, he supposed, that she had met on one of her committees. "B. M. made a violent attack upon the upper classes. I walked back after the meeting with B. M. and tried to convince him." So B. M. was a man—no doubt one of those "intellectuals," as they call themselves, who are so violent and so narrowminded. She had invited him to come and see her apparently. "B. M. came to dinner. He shook hands with Minnie!" That note of exclamation gave another twist to his mental picture. B. M., it seemed, wasn't used to parlourmaids; he had shaken hands with Minnie. Presumably he was one of those tame working men who air their views in ladies' drawing-rooms. Gilbert knew the type, and had no liking for this particular specimen, whoever B. M. might be.

**What can we infer about the character Gilbert from the underlined part? Write your answer in ONE sentence. Then, identify one thing that symbolizes the wife's secret life away from her husband.**

---

03 **Read the excerpt from a play and follow the directions.** [4 points]

A

KATE Helen's waiting for you, too. There's been such a bustle in the house, she expects something, heaven knows what. I expected—a desiccated spinster. You're very young.

ANNIE (*Resolutely*) Oh, you should have seen me when I left Boston. I got much older on this trip.

KATE I mean, to teach anyone as difficult as Helen.

ANNIE I mean to try. They can't put you in jail for trying!

KATE Is it possible, even? To teach a deaf-blind child half of what an ordinary child learns—has that ever been done?

ANNIE Half?

ANNIE (*Reluctantly*) No. (*KATE'S face loses its remaining hope, still appraising her youth.*) Dr. Howe did wonders, but—an ordinary child? No, never. But then I thought when I was going over his reports—(*She indicates the one in her hand.*)—he never treated them like ordinary children. More like—eggs everyone was afraid would break.

KATE (*A pause*) May I ask how old you are?

ANNIE Well, I'm not in my teens, you know! I'm twenty.

KATE All of twenty.

B

KATE Other children are not—impaired.

ANNIE Ho, there's nothing impaired in that head, it works like a mousetrap!

KATE (*Smiles*) But after a child hears how many words, Miss Annie, a million?

ANNIE I guess no mother's ever minded enough to count.

*She drops her eyes to spell into HELEN'S hand, again indicating the card; HELEN spells back, and ANNIE is amused.*

KATE (*Too quickly*) What did she spell?

ANNIE I spelt card. She spelt cake! (*She takes in KATE's quickness, and shakes head, gently.*) No, it's only a finger-game to her, Mrs. Keller. What she has to learn first is that things have names.

KATE And when will she learn?

ANNIE Maybe after a million and one words.

*They hold each other's gaze; KATE then speaks quietly.*

KATE I should like to learn those letters, Miss Annie.

ANNIE (*Pleased*) I'll teach you tomorrow morning. That makes only half a million each!

KATE (*Then*) It's her bedtime. I'm sorry. Miss Annie.

**Explain the meaning intended by Annie in the underlined words. Second, describe the change in perspective that occurs in Kate from Sections A to B, both in regard to Annie and Helen.**

# 33회 실전모의고사

모범답안 p.68

**01** **Read the excerpt from a short story and follow the directions.** [2 points]

Laploshka was one of the meanest men I have ever met, and quite one of the most entertaining. He said horrid things about other people in such a charming way that one forgave him for the equally horrid things he said about oneself behind one's back.

Naturally Laploshka had a large circle of acquaintances, and as he exercised some care in their selection it followed that an appreciable proportion were men whose bank balances enabled them to acquiesce indulgently in his rather one-sided views on hospitality. Thus, although possessed of only moderate means, he was able to live comfortably within his income, and still more comfortably within those of various tolerantly disposed associates.

But towards the poor or to those of the same limited resources as himself his attitude was one of watchful anxiety; he seemed to be haunted by a besetting fear lest some fraction of a shilling or franc, or whatever the prevailing coinage might be, should be diverted from his pocket or service into that of a hard-up companion. A two-franc cigar would be cheerfully offered to a wealthy patron, on the principle of doing evil that good may come, but I have known him indulge in agonies of perjury rather than admit the incriminating possession of a copper coin when change was needed to tip a waiter.

The knowledge of this amiable weakness offered a perpetual temptation to play upon Laploshka's fears of involuntary generosity. To offer him a lift in a cab and pretend not to have enough money to pay the fair, to fluster him with a request for a sixpence when his hand was full of silver just received in change.

**Complete the commentary by filling in the blank below with TWO consecutive words from the passage.**

Commentary

The character of Laploshka functions as a lens through which the reader can view issues of class. Included in this excerpt is the concept of cold double standards employed by the middle class towards the rich and the poor. The habit of distancing himself from "failures" of those around himself is noticed as "______________" by his peers, in regards to his miserly habits with money around them.

**02** **Read the extract from an American modern play and follow the directions.** [4 points]

ROSE He ain't eating right. Miss Pearl say she can't get him to eat nothing.

TROY What you want me to do about it, Rose? I done did everything I can for the man. I can't make him get well. Man got half his head blown away… what you expect?

ROSE Seem like something ought to be done to help him.

TROY Man don't bother nobody. He just mixed up from that metal plate he got in his head. Ain't no sense for him to go back into the hospital.

ROSE Least he be eating right. They can help him take care of himself.

TROY Don't nobody wanna be locked up, Rose. What you wanna lock him up for? Man go over there and fight the war… messin' around with them Japs, get half his head blown off… and they give him a lousy three thousand dollars. And I had to swoop down on that.

ROSE Is you fixing to go into that again?

TROY That's the only way I got a roof over my head… cause of that metal plate.

ROSE Ain't no sense you blaming yourself for nothing. Gabe wasn't in no condition to manage that money. You done what was right by him. Can't nobody say you ain't done what was right by him. Look how long you took care of him… till he wanted to have his own place and moved over there with Miss Pearl.

TROY That ain't what I'm saying, woman! I'm just stating the facts. If my brother didn't have that metal plate in his head… I wouldn't have a pot to piss in or a window to throw it out of. And I'm fifty-three years old. Now see if you can understand that!

> *TROY gets up from the porch and starts to exit the yard.*
>
> ROSE Where you going off to? You been running out of here every Saturday for weeks. I thought you was gonna work on this fence?
>
> TROY I'm gonna walk down to Taylors'. Listen to the ball game. I'll be back in a bit. I'll work on it when I get back.

**Identify the tragedy that has befallen Gabe that the two characters discuss in the excerpt above. Then write the reason Troy feels guilty about his brother's situation. Do not copy more than FIVE consecutive words from the excerpt.**

**03** **Read the poem and follow the directions.** [4 points]

My sister spent a whole life in the earth.
She was born, she died.
In between,
not one alert look, not one sentence.

She did what babies do,
she cried. But she didn't want to be fed.
Still, my mother held her, trying to change
first fate, then history.

Something did change: when my sister died,
my mother's heart became
very cold, very rigid,
like a tiny pendant of iron.

Then it seemed to me my sister's body
was a magnet. I could feel it draw
my mother's heart into the earth,
so it would grow.

**The title of the poem is "Lost Love". Describe the images of "iron" and "magnet" in the last two stanzas. Explain how they contribute to the tone of the poem.**

# 34회 실전모의고사

모범답안 p.70

**01** **Read the poem and follow the directions.** [2 points]

A Bird, came down the Walk—
He did not know I saw—
He bit an Angleworm in halves
And ate the fellow, raw,

And then he drank a Dew
From a convenient Grass—
And then hopped sidewise to the Wall
To let a Beetle pass—

He glanced with rapid eyes
That hurried all around—
They looked like frightened <u>Beads</u>, I thought—
He stirred his Velvet Head

Like one in danger, Cautious,
I offered him a Crumb
And he unrolled his feathers
And rowed him softer home—

Than Oars divide the Ocean,
Too silver for a seam—
Or Butterflies, off Banks of Noon
Leap, plashless* as they swim.

* *plash: splash*

**Complete the commentary below by filling in each blank with ONE word from the poem. If necessary, change the word form.**

Commentary

The speaker describes a natural creature as it eats a worm, hops by a beetle, and glances around. In the third stanza, the speaker uses a figure of speech comparing ___ⓐ___ to "beads" to illustrate the creature's fear. Also, in the last two stanzas, the poet, by offering two comparisons of flight and by using aquatic motion such as ___ⓑ___ and swimming, evokes the delicacy and fluidity of moving through air.

---

## 02 Read the excerpt from a drama and follow the directions. [4 points]

| | |
|---|---|
| Girl | (*admiringly*) What would I do? If I was a good-looking fellow like yourself? Why—I'd just enjoy myself—every minute of the time. I'd sit back and relax, and if I saw a good—looking girl along the side of the road.… (*sharply*) Hey! Look out! |
| Adams | (*breathlessly*) Did you see him too? |
| Girl | See who? |
| Adams | That man. Standing beside the barbed wire fence. |
| Girl | I didn't see—anybody. There wasn't nothing but a bunch of steers —and the barbed wire fence. What did you think you was doing? Trying to run into the barbed wire fence? |
| Adams | There was a man there, I tell you… a thin, gray man with an overnight bag in his hand. And I was trying to—run him down. |
| Girl | Run him down? You mean—kill him? |
| Adams | He's a sort of—phantom. I'm trying to get rid of him—or else prove that he's real. But (*desperately*) you say you didn't see him back there? You're sure? |
| Girl | (*queerly*) I didn't see a soul. And as far as that's concerned, mister… |
| Adams | Watch for him the next time, then. Keep watching. Keep your eyes peeled on the road. He'll turn up again—maybe any minute now. (*excitedly*) There. Look there — |

*Sound: Auto sharply veering and skidding. Girl screams.*

*Sound: crash of car going into barbed wire fence; frightened lowing of steer*

| | |
|---|---|
| Girl | How does this door work? I—I'm getting' outta here. |
| Adams | Did you see him that time? |
| Girl | (*sharply*) No. I didn't see him that time. And personally, mister, I don't expect never to see him. All I want to do is to go on living—and I don't see how I will very long, driving with you— |

| | |
|---|---|
| Adams | I'm sorry. I—I don't know what came over me. Please—don't go··· |
| Girl | So if you'll excuse me, mister— |
| Adams | You can't go. Listen, how would you like to go to California? I'll drive you to California. |
| Girl | Seeing <u>pink elephants</u> all the way? No thanks. |



**Pick one word from the passage that best identifies the mood of the Girl in this scene. Explain what the underlined "pink elephants" means in this context.**

______________________________________________________________

______________________________________________________________

______________________________________________________________

______________________________________________________________

______________________________________________________________

## 03 Read the passage and follow the directions. [4 points]

Early that day the weather turned and the snow was melting into dirty water. Streaks of it ran down from the little shoulder-high window that faced the backyard. Cars slushed by on the street outside, where it was getting dark. But it was getting dark on the inside too.

He was in the bedroom pushing clothes into a suitcase when she came to the door.

I'm glad you're leaving! I'm glad you're leaving! she said. Do you hear?

He kept on putting his things into the suitcase.

Son of a bitch! I'm so glad you're leaving! She began to cry. You can't even look me in the face, can you?

Then she noticed the baby's picture on the bed and picked it up.

He looked at her and she wiped her eyes and stared at him before turning and going back to the living room.

Bring that back, he said.

Just get your things and get out, she said.

He did not answer. He fastened the suitcase, put on his coat, looked around the bedroom before turning off the light. Then he went out to the living room.

She stood in the doorway of the little kitchen, holding the baby.

I want the baby, he said.

Are you crazy?

No, but I want the baby. I'll get someone to come by for his things.

You're not touching this baby, she said.

The baby had begun to cry and she uncovered the blanket from around his head.

Oh, oh, she said, looking at the baby.

He moved toward her.

For God's sake! she said. She took a step back into the kitchen.

I want the baby.

Get out of here!

She turned and tried to hold the baby over in a corner behind the stove.

But he came up. He reached across the stove and tightened his hands on the baby.

Let go of him, he said.

Get away, get away! she cried.

The baby was red-faced and screaming. In the scuffle they knocked down a flowerpot that hung behind the stove.

He crowded her into the wall then, trying to break her grip. He held on to the baby and pushed with all his weight.

Let go of him, he said.

Don't, she said. You're hurting the baby, she said.

I'm not hurting the baby, he said.

The kitchen window gave no light. In the near-dark he worked on her fisted fingers with one hand and with the other hand he gripped the screaming baby up under an arm near the shoulder.

She felt her fingers being forced open. She felt the baby going from her.

No! she screamed just as her hands came loose.

She would have it, this baby. She grabbed for the baby's other arm. She caught the baby around the wrist and leaned back.

But he would not let go. He felt the baby slipping out of his hands and he pulled back very hard.

In this manner, the issue was decided.

**The title of the short story above is "Popular Mechanics". To what aspect of the story does the title refer? Write your answer in ONE sentence. Then, summarize the passage. As you summarize, include the implication of the last sentence.**

# 35회 실전모의고사

모범답안 p.71

**01** **Read the excerpt from a short story and follow the directions.** [2 points]

Pym was a self-made man; that is, he had started his adult life without a nickel or a connection, other than the general friendliness of man to man, and had risen to a vice-presidency in a rayon-blanket firm. He made a large annual contribution to the Baltimore settlement house that had set his feet upon the right path, and he had a few anecdotes to tell about working as a farmhand long, long ago, but his appearance and demeanor were those of a well-established member of the upper middle class, with hardly a trace —hardly a trace of the anxieties of a man who had been through a grueling struggle to put some money into the bank. It is true that beggars, old men in rags, thinly dressed men and women eating bad food in the penitential lights of a cafeteria, slums and squalid mill towns, the faces in rooming-house windows—even a hole in his daughter's socks—could remind him of his youth and make him uneasy. He did not ever like to see the signs of poverty. He took a deep pleasure in the Dutch Colonial house where he lived—in its many lighted windows, in the soundness of his roof and his heating plant—in the warmth of his children's clothing, and in the fact that he had been able to make something plausible and coherent in spite of his mean beginnings. He was always conscious and sometimes mildly resentful of the fact that most of his business associates and all of his friends and neighbors had been skylarking on the turf at Groton or Deerfield or some such school while he was taking books on how to improve your grammar and vocabulary out of the public library. But he recognized this dim __________ of people whose development had been along easier lines than his own as some meanness in his character. Considering merely his physical bulk, it was astonishing that he should have preserved an image of himself as a hungry youth standing outside a lighted window in the rain.

Fill in the blank with ONE word from the excerpt that shows the emotional state of the main character. If necessary, change the word form.

---

## 02 Read the excerpt from a drama and follow the directions. [4 points]

| | |
|---|---|
| Judge | Is defense ready to present its case? |
| Armstrong | (*rising*) Yes, your honor··· |
| Clerk | (*calling out*) Mrs. Margaret Reston··· Please take the stand··· |

*Mrs. Reston rises, comes forward.*

*Dissolve to: Witness Stand*

| | |
|---|---|
| Armstrong | You have a daughter, Mrs. Reston? |
| Mrs. Reston | Aye··· Isabel···. She's 9 years old. |
| Armstrong | Mrs. Reston, would you please tell the Court what happened to your daughter on the night the William Brown was struck by the iceberg···. |
| Mrs. Reston | Well, she was left behind on the sinking ship··· |
| Armstrong | What did you do when you discovered this? |
| Mrs. Reston | Well, I was like out of my mind···. I cried out for help···. And, praise God, one of the seamen, he climbed back on the ship just as she was keeling over and rescued my daughter. Oh, I'll never forget it. That seaman didn't even know me, yet he risked his life. |
| Armstrong | Who was that seaman, Mrs. Reston? |
| Mrs. Reston | David Holmes··· |
| Armstrong | Thank you, Mrs. Reston. Your witness. |
| Dallas | Mrs. Reston, I'm sure there was a great deal of bravery displayed···. The question is: Did he voluntarily and feloniously deprive a fellow creature of his life?··· I therefore ask you: While you were on the longboat, did you see him cause any of the passengers to be thrown into the sea? |

| | |
|---|---|
| Mrs. Reston | I··· I··· |
| Dallas | (*glowering*) Well, Mrs. Reston···? |
| Mrs. Reston | I··· I··· Please···. Please don't ask me··· (*She sobs. Armstrong is on his feet.*) |
| Armstrong | Objection. Is it Necessary to brow-beat the witness, Your Honor? |
| Dallas | Your Honor, I would like to reserve the right to re-examine this witness later when she is more capable of answering questions. |

**Contrast Mrs. Reston and Dallas' opinions of David Holmes in 2-3 sentences. Also, explain why Dallas seeks to hold up further questioning until later.**

# 36회 실전모의고사

모범답안 p.72

**01** **Read the poem and follow the directions.** [2 points]

When the voices of children are heard on the green
And laughing is heard on the hill
My heart is at rest within my breast
And every thing else is still

Then come home my children, the sun is gone down
And the dews of night arise
Come come leave off play, and let us away
Till the morning appears in the skies

No no let us play, for it is yet day
And we cannot go to sleep
Besides in the sky, the little birds fly
And the hills are all cover'd with sheep

Well well go and play till the light fades away
And then go home to bed
The little ones leaped and shouted and laugh'd
And all the hills echoed

Complete the commentary by filling in each blank with appropriate word(s) or letters.

Commentary

The poem is composed of four 4-line stanzas with a(n) ____ⓐ____ rhyme scheme that is consistent throughout each stanza. The theme of the poem is the children's innocent and simple joy. The children can be thought of as a part of ____ⓑ____ symbolized as sheep and birds because they share the innocence and unselfconscious spontaneity of its creatures.

## 02 Read the excerpt from a novel and follow the directions. [4 points]

The fairy palaces burst into illumination, before pale morning showed the monstrous serpents of smoke trailing themselves over Coketown. A clattering of clogs upon the pavement; a rapid ringing of bells; and ⓐ all the melancholy mad elephants, polished and oiled up for the day's monotony, were at their heavy exercise again.

Stephen bent over his loom, quiet, watchful, and steady. A special contrast, as every man was in the forest of looms where Stephen worked, to the crashing, smashing, tearing piece of mechanism at which he laboured. Never fear, good people of an anxious turn of mind, that Art will consign Nature to oblivion. Set anywhere, side by side, the work of God and the work of man; and the former, even though it be a troop of hands of very small account, will gain in dignity from the comparison.

So many hundred hands in this mill; so many hundred horse steam power. It is known, to the force of a single pound weight, what the engine will do; but, not all the calculators of the National Debt can tell me the capacity for good or evil, for love or hatred, for patriotism or discontent, for the decomposition of virtue into vice, or the reverse, at any single moment in the soul of one of these its ⓑ quiet servants, with the composed faces and the regulated actions. There is no mystery in it; there is an unfathomable mystery in the meanest of them, for ever. Supposing we were to reverse our arithmetic for material objects, and to govern these awful unknown quantities by other means!

**Explain the meaning of the metaphor employed in the underlined words in ⓐ. Then identify what the underlined "quiet servants" in ⓑ refers to.**

03

## 03 Read the passage and follow the directions. [4 points]

EIGHT Do you mind if I try it? According to you, it'll only take fifteen seconds. We can spare that. (*He walks over to the two chairs now and lies down on them.*) Who's got a watch with a second hand?

TWO I have.

EIGHT When you want me to start, stamp your foot. That'll be the body falling. Time me from there. (*He lies down on the chairs.*) Let's say he keeps his canes right at his bedside. Right?

TWO Right!

EIGHT Okay. I'm ready.

*They all watch carefully.* TWO *stares at his watch, waiting for the second hand to reach sixty. Then, as it does, he* ______ⓐ______ *his foot loudly.* EIGHT *begins to get up. Slowly he swings his leg over the edges of the chairs, reaches for imaginary canes, and struggles to his feet.* TWO *stares at the watch.* EIGHT *walks as a crippled old man would walk, toward the chair which is serving as the bedroom door. He gets to it and pretends to open it.* [deleted...]

EIGHT What's the time?

TWO Fifteen··· twenty··· thirty··· thirty-one seconds exactly.

ELEVEN Thirty-one seconds.

*Some of the Jurors adlib their surprise to each other.*

EIGHT It's my guess that the old man was trying to get to the door, heard someone racing down the stairs, and assumed it was the boy.

SIX I think that's possible.

THREE (*infuriated*) Assumed? Now, listen to me you people. I've seen all kinds of dishonesty in my day··· but this little display takes the cake. (*To* FOUR) Tell him, will you? The kid was clearly heard threatening to kill the old man!

FOUR sits silently. THREE looks at him and then he strides over to EIGHT.

THREE You come in here with your heart bleeding all over the floor about slum kids and injustice but you make up these wild stories, and you've got some soft-hearted old ladies listening to you. Well I'm not. I'm getting real sick of it. What's the matter with you people? This kid is guilty! He's got to burn! We're letting him slip through our fingers here.

EIGHT (*calmly*) Our fingers? Are you his executioner?

THREE (*raging*) I'm one of them.

EIGHT Perhaps ⓑ <u>you'd like to pull the switch</u>.

THREE (*shouting*) For this kid? You'd bet I'd like to pull the switch!

EIGHT I'm sorry for you.

THREE (*shouting*) Don't start with me.

EIGHT What it must feel like to want to pull the switch!

THREE Shut up!

EIGHT You're a sadist.

THREE (*louder*) Shut up!

EIGHT (*strong*) You want to see this black boy die because you personally want it—not because of the facts.

THREE (*shouting*) Shut up!

*He lunges at* EIGHT, *but is caught by two of the* JURORS *and held. He struggles as* EIGHT *watches calmly.*

**Fill in blank ⓐ with ONE word from the passage. If necessary, change the word form. Additionally, explain what is implied in the underlined words in ⓑ.**

---

# 37회 실전모의고사

모범답안 p.74

**01** **Read the poem and follow the directions.** [2 points]

Music, when soft voices die,
Vibrates in the memory—
Odours, when sweet violets sicken,
Live within the sense they quicken.

Rose leaves, when the rose is dead,
Are heaped for the beloved's bed;
And so thy thoughts, when thou art gone,
Love itself shall slumber on.

**Complete the commentary by filling in each blank with ONE word from the poem. If necessary, change each word form.**

Commentary

The main theme of the poem is that we cannot forget our ___ⓐ___ ones even though they are not with us any longer. To illustrate the theme vividly, the speaker uses several images. For example, even after we stop listening to good music, this soft music lingers on in our memories for a long time to come. Also, even after a(n) ___ⓑ___ withers away its petals are scattered in order to make the room sweet-scented.

## 02 Read the excerpt from a play and follow the directions. [4 points]

| | |
|---|---|
| TEVYA | So, my biggest girl, my silliest, biggest girl, tell me··· |
| TZEITL | Papa, I'm so unhappy. |
| TEVYA | Why? Your father is asking why. |
| TZEITL | I don't want to marry him. |
| TEVYA | And the reason? |
| TZEITL | I don't love him, Papa. |
| TEVYA | Love, I'll tell you about. Love doesn't always happen in the morning. Sometimes it takes all afternoon and part of the evening. |
| TZEITL | I'll carry stones. I'll dig holes. I'll be a servant for the Gentiles*. |
| TEVYA | What terrible life am I sending you to? I'm rescuing you. No more three-in-a-bed. No more without supper. Look at the dress you're wearing. |
| TZEITL | I couldn't, Papa. Never. |
| TEVYA | You enjoy it so much, being the daughter in a house where the wind runs through everything? |
| TZEITL | How can I tell you? I'd be fed and warm—but I that house, Papa, I would die. |
| TEVYA | So much you don't want to? |
| TZEITL | Please, Papa, have pity on me. |
| TEVYA | Tevya's daughters will never be unhappy. Hungry, maybe; but never unhappy. You don't want to marry him, that's all there is to it. After all, today is not yesterday. |
| TZEITL | Thank you, Papa. |
| TEVYA | Not me; thank the Lord in heaven, who opened my eyes. Did you think I was going to force you? Never. Even if in some circles a rich man is not a calamity. |
| TZEITL | Papa, you're wonderful. |

TEVYA Listen, what Tevya thought was preordained was not ordained. So be it. Done and done. Wipe your eyes; you've done enough crying for one day. (*He helps her blow her nose.*) So—I'll return his goblet in the morning. I'll make my explanations to the Rabbi. As the good book tells us. Period.

** A Gentile: a person who is not Jewish*

**What can we infer about Tevya's social status from the passage? Write your answer in ONE sentence. Second, explain the meaning of the underlined part, as it relates to Tevya's intention for the future of his daughter.**

## 03 Read the excerpt from a short story and follow the directions. [4 points]

A group of the townspeople stood on the station siding of a little Kansas town, awaiting the coming of the night train, which was already twenty minutes overdue. The snow had fallen thick over everything. The men on the siding stood first on one foot and then on the other. They conversed in low tones and moved about restlessly, seeming uncertain as to what was expected of them. There was but one of the company who looked as though he knew exactly why he was there, and he kept conspicuously apart, walking to the far end of the platform. Presently he was approached by a tall, spare, grizzled man clad in a faded Grand Army suit, who shuffled out from the group and advanced with a certain deference, craning his neck forward until his back made the angle of a jack-knife three-quarters open.

"I reckon she's a-goin' to be pretty late agin to-night, Jim," he remarked in a squeaky falsetto. "S'pose it's the snow?"

"I don't know," responded the other man with a shade of annoyance, speaking from out an astonishing cataract of red beard which grew fiercely and thickly in all directions.

The spare man shifted the quill toothpick he was chewing to the other side of his mouth. "It ain't likely that anybody from the East will come with the corpse, I s'pose?" he went on reflectively.

"I don't know," responded the other, more curtly than before.

"It's too bad he didn't belong to some lodge or other." The spare man continued, with an ingratiating concession in his shrill voice.

Just then a distant whistle sounded, and there was a shuffling of feet on the platform. A number of lanky boys of all ages appeared as suddenly and slimily as eels wakened by the crack of thunder.

The burly man with the disheveled red beard walked swiftly up the platform toward the approaching train, uncovering his head as he went. The group of men behind him hesitated, glanced questioningly at one another, and awkwardly followed his example. The train stopped.

The coffin was got out of its rough box and down on the snowy platform. The townspeople drew back enough to make room for it and then formed a close semicircle about it, looking curiously at the palm-leaf which lay across the black cover. No one said anything.

The young Bostonian, one of the dead world-renowned sculptor's pupils, who had come with the body, looked about him helplessly. "None of Mr. Merrick's brothers are here?" he asked uncertainly.

The man with the red beard for the first time stepped up and joined the group. "No, they have not come yet; the family is scattered. The body will be taken directly to the house."

**Describe the main event of the passage. Additionally, explain what can be inferred about the sculptor's repute in his hometown in contrast to where he worked.**

# 38회 실전모의고사

모범답안 p.76

**01** **Read the poem and follow the directions.** [2 points]

> The art of losing isn't hard to master;
> so many things seem filled with the intent
> to be lost that their loss is no disaster.
>
> Lose something every day. Accept the fluster
> of lost door keys, the hour badly spent.
> The art of losing isn't hard to master.
>
> Then practice losing farther, losing faster:
> places, and names, and where it was you meant
> to travel. None of these will bring disaster.
>
> I lost my mother's watch. And look! my last, or
> next-to-last, of three loved houses went.
> The art of losing isn't hard to master.
>
> I lost two cities, lovely ones. And, vaster,
> some realms I owned, two rivers, a continent.
> I miss them, but it wasn't a disaster.
>
> —Even losing you (the joking voice, a gesture
> I love) I shan't have lied. It's evident
> the art of losing's not too hard to master
> though it may look like (Write it!) like disaster.

**Fill in each blank in the commentary with ONE word from the poem. If necessary, change each word form.**

Commentary

In the poem, the speaker says that we get used to loss by ___ⓐ___ with little things. However, the word "loss" is employed both metaphorically and literally, undercutting the statement that all losses are equal. The loss that really bothers the speaker is that of a(n) ___ⓑ___ person.

---

**02** **Read the excerpt from a play and fill in each blank with ONE word from the excerpt.** [2 points]

| | |
|---|---|
| DOOLITTLE | Well, the truth is, I've taken a sort of fancy to you, Governor; and if you want the girl, I'm not so set on having her back home again but what I might be open to an arrangement. Regarded in the light of a young woman, she's a fine handsome girl. As a daughter shes not worth her keep; and so I tell you straight. All I ask is my rights as a father; and you're the last man alive to expect me to let her go for nothing; for I can see you're one of the straight sort, Governor. Well, what's a five pound note to you? And what's Eliza to me? |
| PICKERING | I think you ought to know, Doolittle, that Mr. Higgins's intentions are entirely honorable. |
| DOOLITTLE | Course they are, Governor. If I thought they wasn't, I'd ask fifty. |
| HIGGINS | (*revolted*) Do you mean to say, you callous rascal, that you would sell your daughter for fifty pounds? |
| DOOLITTLE | Not in a general way I wouldn't; but to oblige a gentleman like you I'd do a good deal, I do assure you. |
| PICKERING | Have you no ______ⓐ______, man? |
| DOOLITTLE | (*unabashed*) Can't afford them, Governor. Neither could you if you was as poor as me. Not that I mean any harm, you know. But if Liza is going to have a bit out of this, why not me too? |
| HIGGINS | (*troubled*) I don't know what to do, Pickering. There can be no question that as a matter of morals it's a positive crime to give this chap a farthing. And yet I feel a sort of rough justice in his claim. |
| DOOLITTLE | That's it, Governor. That's all I say. A father's heart, as it were. |

| | |
|---|---|
| PICKERING | Well, I know the feeling; but really it seems hardly right— |
| DOOLITTLE | Don't say that, Governor. Don't look at it that way. What am I, Governors both? I ask you, what am I? I'm one of the undeserving poor: that's what I am. Think of what that means to a man. It means that he's up against middle class morality all the time. If there's anything going, and I put in for a bit of it, it's always the same story: "You're undeserving; so you can't have it." [……] What is middle class morality? Just an excuse for never giving me anything. Therefore, I ask you, as two gentlemen, not to play that game on me. I'm playing straight with you. I ain't pretending to be deserving. I'm undeserving. Will you take advantage of a man's nature to do him out of the price of his own daughter what he's brought up and fed and clothed by the sweat of his brow until shes growed big enough to be interesting to you two gentlemen? Is _____ⓑ_____ pounds unreasonable? |

---

## 03 Read the story and follow the directions. [4 points]

"And I know it's kind of a bad time to be telling you. Of course I'll give you money and see you're looked after. But there needn't really be any fuss. It wouldn't be very good for my job."

"I'll get the supper," she managed to whisper.

When she walked across the room she couldn't feel her feet touching the floor. She couldn't feel anything at all except a slight nausea and a desire to vomit. Everything was automatic now—down the steps to the cellar, the light switch, the deep freeze, the hand inside the cabinet taking hold of the first object it met. She lifted it out, and looked at it. It was wrapped in paper, so she took off the paper and looked at it again.

A leg of lamb.

Mary Maloney simply walked up behind him and without any pause she swung the big frozen leg of lamb high in the air and brought it down as hard as she could on the back of his head. [deleted...]

After she fabricated an alibi concerning her whereabouts during this time frame, she got up and went to the phone. She knew the number of the police station, and when the man at the other end answered, she cried to him, "Quick! Come quick! Patrick's dead!"

"Who's speaking?"

"Mrs. Maloney. Mrs. Patrick Maloney."

"You mean Patrick Maloney's dead?"

"I think so," she sobbed. "He's lying on the floor and I think he's dead."

"Be right over," the man said. [deleted...]

"Look, Mrs. Maloney. You know that oven of yours is still on, and the meat still inside."

"Oh dear me!" she cried. "So it is!"

"I better turn it off for you, hadn't I?"

"Will you do that, Jack. Thank you so much."

When the sergeant returned the second time, she looked at him with her large, dark tearful eyes. "Jack Noonan," she said.

"Yes?"

"Would you do me a small favor—you and these others?"

"We can try, Mrs. Maloney."

"Well," she said. "Here you all are, and good friends of dear Patrick's too, and helping to catch the man who killed him. You must be terrible hungry by now because it's long past your suppertime, and I know Patrick would never forgive me, God bless his soul, if I allowed you to remain in his house without offering you decent hospitality. Why don't you eat up that lamb that's in the oven. It'll be cooked just right by now."

There was a good deal of hesitating among the four policemen, but they were clearly hungry, and in the end they were persuaded to go into the kitchen and help themselves. The woman stayed where she was, listening to them speaking among themselves, their voices thick and sloppy because their mouths were full of meat. [deleted...]

"That's the hell of a big club the gut must've used to hit poor Patrick," one of them was saying. "The doc says his skull was smashed all to pieces just like from a sledgehammer."

"That's why it ought to be easy to find."

"Exactly what I say."

**The writer, in the story above, employs dramatic irony. Explain the irony by using the underlined parts.**

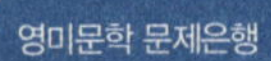



# 39회 실전모의고사

모범답안 p.77

**01** **Read the excerpt from a play and follow the directions.** [2 points]

| | |
|---|---|
| Henry | I simply don't wish to put you to the trouble of changing a large note. |
| Tod | As long as rebukes are going around, I might say that it wasn't quite your affair to infer that we couldn't change any note that you might happen to be carrying around. On the contrary, we can. |
| Henry | Oh, very well. I apologize. Here you are. |
| Tod | Thank you. *(A complete change. He stutters and fumbles.)* Ah—it's—ah—that is—we—ah—you see—It's—(*quickly*) Take it back, please. (*raising voice*) Mr. Smedley! Mr.Smedley! Help! Oh, Mr. Smedley! |
| Smedley | (*coming in; a fussy man*) What is it, Tod, what is it? Stop shouting! |
| Tod | Oh, but Mr. Smedley, I can't control myself. |
| Smedley | What's up? What's the trouble? What's wanting? Who's this? |
| Henry | I am a customer, and I am waiting for my change. |
| Smedley | Change, change! Tod, give him his change. Get it for him. |
| Tod | Get him his change! It's easy for you to say that, Mr. Smedley, but look at the bill yourself. |
| Smedley | Bill, bill! Let me see it! (*pause*) Tod, you ass, selling an eccentric millionaire such an unspeakable suit as that. Tod, you're a fool—a born fool! Drives every millionaire away from a tailor's shop, because he can't tell a millionaire from a tramp. Here, sir, are some suits more in keeping with your position. |
| Henry | Thank you, but this one will do. |

| | |
|---|---|
| Smedley | Of course it won't do! I shall burn it. Tod, burn this suit at once. |
| Tod | Yes, Mr. Smedley. |
| Smedley | We shall be honored to outfit you completely, sir··· morning clothes, evening dress, sack suits, tweeds, Shetlands—everything you need. Come, Tod, book and pen. Now—length of leg, 32 inches; sleeve— |
| Henry | But look here. I can't give you an order for suits unless you can wait indefinitely or change this bill. |
| Smedley | Indefinitely, sir. It's a weak word, a weak word. *Eternally*, that's the word, sir. Tod, rush these things through. Let the minor customers wait. Set down the gentleman's address and— |
| Henry | I'm changing my quarters. I'll drop in and leave the new address. |
| Smedley | Quite right, sir, quite right. One moment—allow me to show you out, sir. And don't worry about paying us. (*fading*) Your credit is the highest. Good day, sir, good day. Your honor us greatly, sir. |

**Fill in each blank in the chart below using ONE or TWO word(s) from the above excerpt.**

| | |
|---|---|
| Setting | ______ⓐ______ |
| Characters | Henry is a protagonist of the play who has been loaned a million-pound note. Tod works for Smedley as his assistant. |
| Conflict | Henry is trying to take a low-quality, spare suit but Smedley is pushing free high quality suits on him because he has falsely mistaken his ______ⓑ______. |
| Plot | Rising action |

## 02 Read the poem and follow the directions. [2 points]

I don't know
if the sunflowers
are angels always
but surely sometimes.

Who, even in heaven
wouldn't want to wear,
for awhile,
such a seed face

and brave spine,
a coat of leaves
with so many pockets—
and who wouldn't want

to stand for a summer day,
in the hot fields,
in the only country
of the wild-haired corn?

This much I know
when I see the bright
stars of their faces,
when I'm strolling nearby,

I grow soft in my speech,
and soft in my thoughts,
and I remember how everything will be
everything else,
by and by.

**Complete the statement by filling in each blank with ONE word from the poem. If necessary, change each word form.**

> The speaker in the poem above is expressing her spiritual awakening when she sees ____ⓐ____ in the countryside. In the fifth stanza of the poem, the speaker employs metaphor, comparing ____ⓑ____ to "stars."

---

## 03 Read the excerpt from a novel and follow the directions. [4 points]

The people felt so betrayed. They stood by helplessly—they really don't know how to fight, and rarely think of it since the old days of tribal wars—as their crops and then their very homes were destroyed. Yes. The roadbuilders didn't deviate an inch from the plan the headman was following. Every hut that lay in the proposed roadpath was leveled. And our church, our school, my hut, all went down in a matter of hours. Fortunately, we were able to save all of our things, but with a tarmac road running straight through the middle of it, the village itself seems gutted.

Immediately after understanding the roadbuilders' intentions, the chief set off toward the coast, seeking explanations and reparations. Two weeks later he returned with even more disturbing news. The whole territory, including the Olinkas' village, now belongs to a rubber manufacturer in England. As he neared the coast, he was stunned to see hundreds and hundreds of villagers clearing the forests on each side of the road, and planting rubber trees. The ancient, giant mahogany trees, all the trees, the game, everything of the forest was being destroyed, and the land was forced to lie flat and ⓐ <u>bare as the palm of his hand</u>.

At first he thought the people who told him about English rubber company were mistaken, if only about its territory including the Olinka village. But eventually he was directed to the governor's mansion, a huge white building, with flags flying in its yard, and there had an audience with the white man in charge. It was this man who gave the roadbuilders their orders, this man who knew about the Olinka only from a map. He spoke in English, which our chief tried to speak also. He never learned English beyond occasional odd phrase he picked up from Joseph, who pronounces "English" "Yanglish." ⓑ <u>It was a pathetic exchange</u>.

Identify the figure of speech used in the underlined ⓐ and explain how it helps the reader to interpret the underlined part as it is intended by the narrator. Then, explain the implication of the underlined words in ⓑ.

# 40회 실전모의고사

모범답안 p.78

**01** **Read the excerpt from a play and follow the directions.** [2 points]

| | |
|---|---|
| AARONOW | How many leads have we got? |
| MOSS | The Glengarry··· the premium leads···? I'd say we got five thousand. Five. Five thousand leads. |
| AARONOW | And you're saying a fella could take and sell these leads to Jerry Graff. |
| MOSS | Yes. |
| AARONOW | How do you know he'd buy them? |
| MOSS | Graff? Because I worked for him. |
| AARONOW | You haven't talked to him. |
| MOSS | No. What do you mean? Have I talked to him about *this*? (*Pause*) |
| AARONOW | Yes. I mean are you actually talking about this, or are we just··· |
| MOSS | No, we're just··· |
| AARONOW | We're just "talking" about it. |
| MOSS | We're just speaking about it. (*Pause*) As an idea. |
| AARONOW | As an idea. |
| MOSS | Yes. |
| AARONOW | We're not actually talking about it. |
| MOSS | No. |
| AARONOW | Talking about it as a··· |
| MOSS | No. |
| AARONOW | As a robbery. |
| MOSS | As a "robbery"?! No. |
| AARONOW | Well. Well··· |

| | |
|---|---|
| MOSS | Hey. (*Pause*) |
| AARONOW | So all this, um, you didn't, actually, you didn't actually go talk to Graff. |
| MOSS | Not actually, no. (*Pause*) |
| AARONOW | You didn't? |
| MOSS | No. Not actually. |
| AARONOW | Did you? |
| MOSS | What did I say? |
| AARONOW | What did you say? |
| MOSS | Yes. (*Pause*) I said, "Not actually." The fuck you care, George? We're just talking… |
| AARONOW | We are? |
| MOSS | Yes. (*Pause*) |
| AARONOW | Because, because, you know, it's illegal. |
| MOSS | That's right. It's illegal. It's also very safe. |
| AARONOW | You're actually talking about this? |
| MOSS | That's right. (*Pause*) |
| AARONOW | You're going to steal the leads? |

**Fill in each blank in the commentary below using a different word from the passage. If necessary, you may change the form.**

Commentary

In this scene, the interaction of Aaronow and Moss focuses primarily on the clarification of motives. Both characters are probing the other's intention. Aaronow seeks to know whether Moss is presenting just a(n) ______ⓐ______, or planning actual ______ⓑ______.

## 02 Read the excerpt from a poem and follow the directions. [2 points]

Two girls discover
the secret of life
in a sudden line of
poetry.

I who don't know the
secret wrote
the line. They
told me

(through a third person)
they had found it
but not what it was
not even

what line it was. No doubt
by now, more than a week
later, they have forgotten
the secret,

the line, the name of
the poem. I love them
for finding what
I can't find,

and for loving me
for the line I wrote,
and for forgetting it
so that

a thousand times, till death
finds them, they may
discover it again, in other
lines

in other
happenings. And for
wanting to know it,
for

assuming there is
such a secret, yes,
for that
most of all.

**Complete the statement by filling in the blank with ONE word from the poem. If necessary, change the word form.**

In the poem, the speaker says that it does not matter if the secret is forgotten. The poet is saying that the search for meaning in ________ is more important than the actual finding of the meaning. The meaning itself can change from time to time as a person grows and changes situations.

---

## 03 Read the passage and follow the directions. [4 points]

"If I am going to be drowned—if I am going to be drowned—if I am going to be drowned, why, in the name of the seven mad gods, who rule the sea, was I allowed to come thus far and contemplate sand and trees?"

During this dismal night, it may be remarked that a man would conclude that it was really the intention of the seven mad gods to drown him, despite the abominable injustice of it. For it was certainly an abominable injustice to drown a man who had worked so hard, so hard. The man felt it would be a crime most unnatural. Other people had drowned at sea since galleys swarmed with painted sails, but still—

When it occurs to a man that nature does not regard him as important, and that she feels she would not maim the universe by disposing of him, he at first wishes to throw bricks at the temple, and he hates deeply the fact that there are no bricks and no temples. Any visible expression of nature would surely be pelleted with his jeers.

Then, if there be no tangible thing to hoot he feels, perhaps, the desire to confront a personification and indulge in pleas, bowed to one knee, and with hands supplicant, saying: "Yes, but I love myself."

A high cold star on a winter's night is the word he feels that she says to him. Thereafter he knows the pathos of his situation.

The men in the dingey had not discussed these matters, but each had, no doubt, reflected upon them in silence and according to his mind. There was seldom any expression upon their faces save the general one of complete weariness. Speech was devoted to the business of the boat.

To chime the notes of his emotion, a verse mysteriously entered the correspondent's head. He had even forgotten that he had forgotten this verse, but it suddenly was in his mind.

*A soldier of the Legion lay dying in Algiers;*
*There was lack of woman's nursing, there was dearth of woman's tears;*
*But a comrade stood beside him, and he took that comrade's hand*
*And he said: "I shall never see my own, my native land."*

In his childhood, the correspondent had been made acquainted with the fact that a soldier of the Legion lay dying in Algiers, but he had never regarded the fact as important. Myriads of his school-fellows had informed him of the soldier's plight, but the dinning had naturally ended by making him perfectly indifferent. He had never considered it his affair that a soldier of the Legion lay dying in Algiers, nor had it appeared to him as a matter for sorrow. It was less to him than breaking of a pencil's point.

**Describe the setting of the story above in one sentence. And, explain what the correspondent realizes about the poem.**

# 41회 실전모의고사

모범답안 p.79

**01** **Read the excerpt from a fiction and follow the directions.** [2 points]

The story of Doctor Reefy and his courtship of the tall dark girl who became his wife and left her money to him is a very curious story. It is delicious, like the twisted little apples that grow in the orchards of Winesburg. In the fall one walks in the orchards and the ground is hard with frost underfoot. The apples have been taken from the trees by the pickers. They have been put in barrels and shipped to the cities where they will be eaten in apartments that are filled with books, magazines, furniture, and people. On the trees are only a few gnarled apples that the pickers have rejected. They look like the knuckles of Doctor Reefy's hands. One nibbles at them and they are delicious. Only the few know their sweetness.

The tall dark girl and Doctor Reefy began their courtship on a summer afternoon. He was forty-five then and already he had begun the practice of filling his pockets with the scraps of paper that became hard balls and were thrown away. The girl came to see Doctor Reefy because she was in the family way* and had become frightened. She was in that condition because of a series of circumstances also curious. The death of her father and mother and the rich acres of land that had come down to her had set a train of suitors on her heels. For two years she saw suitors almost every evening.

For several weeks the tall dark girl and the doctor were together almost every day. The condition that had brought her to him passed in an illness, but she was like one who has discovered the sweetness of the gnarled apples, she could not get her mind fixed again upon the round perfect fruit that is eaten in the city apartments. In the fall after the beginning of her acquaintanceship with him she married Doctor Reefy and in the following spring she died.

* *in the family way: pregnant*

**Complete the commentary below by filling in the blank with the TWO consecutive words from the excerpt.**

Commentary

The __________ symbolize(s) the protagonist, who is a lonely old man.

______________________________

**02** **Read the poem and follow the directions.** [4 points]

The shattered water made a misty din.
Great waves looked over others coming in,
And thought of doing something to the shore
That water never did to land before.
The clouds were low and hairy in the skies,
Like locks blown forward in the gleam of eyes.
You could not tell, and yet it looked as if
The shore was lucky in being backed by cliff,
The cliff in being backed by continent;
It looked as if a night of dark intent
Was coming, and not only a night, an age.
Someone had better be prepared for rage.
There would be more than ocean-water broken
Before God's last Put out the light* was spoken.

** Put out the light: the end of the world*

**Describe the rhyme scheme of the poem. Second, identify what the poet mainly describe.**

**03** **Read the excerpt from a play and follow the directions.** [4 points]

| | |
|---|---|
| WARREN | So do I. But I still don't know if I would really ascribe all that to the theory that people's personalities undergo some kind of fundamental alteration when they get older. |
| JESSICA | Well, they do. And it's a big factor. |
| WARREN | I mean they obviously do to a degree— |
| JESSICA | Yeah! |
| WARREN | And things definitely happen to alter your general trajectory— |
| JESSICA | Yeah! And no matter— |
| WARREN | (*On "And"*) But I think that··· you basically get a set of characteristics, and then they pretty much just develop in different ways. Like— |
| JESSICA | But can I just— |
| WARREN | (*On "can"*) Like the last year of high school, I suddenly realized that all these weird kids I grew up with were like well on their way to becoming really weird adults. And it was pretty scary, you know? Like you see a crazy kid, and you realize, he's never gonna grow out of it. He's a fucked-up crazy kid and he's just gonna be fucked-up crazy adult with like a ruined life. |
| JESSICA | Well can I please say something? |
| WARREN | Go ahead. |
| JESSICA | Thank you: I'm not saying anything about whether you're quote unquote "fucked up" or not. I don't mean it as a moral issue— |
| WARREN | Neither do I. |
| JESSICA | I just— |

| | |
|---|---|
| WARREN | I think that personality components are like protons and electrons. Like in science. Every molecule is made of the same basic components. Like the difference between a hydrogen molecule and a calcium molecule is like one protons or something··· |
| JESSICA | Yeah? That's wrong, but yeah? |
| WARREN | So my theory is that people's personalities are basically constructed the same way. None of them are exactly the same, but they're all made of the same thing. |
| JESSICA | That's interesting. |
| WARREN | Thank you. |
| JESSICA | Unfortunately it has nothing to do with what I'm talking about. |

**In the given conversation, identify the simile used by Warren to support his point of view. Then, explain Jessica's point of view as it contrasts Warren's.**

03

**04** **Read the excerpt from a fiction and follow the directions.** [4 points]

Though when we are young we seldom think much about it, there is now and again a golden day when we feel a sudden, arrogant pride in our youth; in the lightness of our feet and the strength of our arms, in the warm fluid that courses so surely within us; when we are conscious of something powerful and mercurial in our breasts, which comes up wave after wave and leaves us irresponsible and free. All the next morning I felt this flow of life, which continually impelled me toward Mrs. Ebbling. After the merest greeting, however, I kept away. I found it pleasant to thwart myself, to measure myself against a current that was sure to carry me with it in the end. I was content to let her watch the sea—the sea that seemed now to have come into me, warm and soft, still and strong. I played shuffleboard with the Commodore, who was anxious to keep down his figure, and ran about the deck with the stout legs of the little pumpkin-colored Carin about my neck. It was not until the child was having her afternoon nap below that I at last came up and stood beside her mother.

"You are better today," I exclaimed, looking down at her white gown. She colored unreasonably, and I laughed with a familiarity which she must have accepted as the mere foolish noise of happiness, or it would have seemed impertinent.

We talked at first of a hundred trivial things, and we watched the sea. The coast of Sardinia* had lain to our port for some hours and would lie there for hours to come, now advancing in rocky promontories, now retreating behind blue bays. It was the naked south coast of the island, and though our course held very near the shore, not a village or habitation was visible. A narrow strip of beach glistened like white paint between the purple sea and the umber rocks, and the whole island lay gleaming in the yellow sunshine and translucent air. Not a wave broke on that fringe of white sand, not the shadow of a cloud played across the bare hills. In the air about us, there was no sound but that of a vessel moving rapidly through absolutely still water. She seemed like some great sea-animal, swimming silently, her head well up.

** Sardinia: the second-largest island in the Mediterranean Sea*

**Describe the setting of the story above. Next, explain what can be inferred to have occurred the day before.**

# 42회 실전모의고사

모범답안 p.80

**01** **Read the excerpt from a story and follow the directions.** [2 points]

There was no hope for him this time: it was the third stroke. Night after night I had passed the house (it was vacation time) and studied the lighted square of window: and night after night I had found it lighted in the same way, faintly and evenly. If he was dead, I thought, I would see the reflection of candles on the darkened blind for I knew that two candles must be set at the head of a corpse. He had often said to me: "I am not long for this world," and I had thought his words idle. Now I knew they were true. Every night as I gazed up at the window I said softly to myself the word paralysis. It had always sounded strangely in my ears, like the word gnomon in the Euclid and the word simony in the Catechism. But now it sounded to me like the name of some maleficent and sinful being. It filled me with fear, and yet I longed to be nearer to it and to look upon its deadly work.

Old Cotter was sitting at the fire, smoking, when I came downstairs to supper. While my aunt was ladling out my stirabout he said, as if returning to some former remark of his:

"No, I wouldn't say he was exactly… but there was something queer… there was something uncanny about him. I'll tell you my opinion…."

He began to puff at his pipe, no doubt arranging his opinion in his mind. "I have my own theory about it," he said. "I think it was one of those… peculiar cases… But it's hard to say…."

He began to puff again at his pipe without giving us his theory. My uncle saw me staring and said to me:

"Well, so your old friend is gone, you'll be sorry to hear."
"Who?" said I.
"Father Flynn."
"Is he dead?"
"Mr. Cotter here has just told us. He was passing by the house."

**Below is the analysis of the given story. Fill in each blank with the ONE most appropriate word respectively from the excerpt.**

| | |
|---|---|
| Character | The dead Father and the narrator were a good ___ⓐ___. |
| Key event | Father Flynn's death |
| Atmosphere | loss and hopelessness |
| Critical key word | ___ⓑ___: a world where people have turned to stone and seems to be the existential condition. |

03

## 02 Read the poem and follow the directions. [4 points]

[A] Just off the highway to Rochester, Minnesota,
Twilight bounds softly forth on the grass.
And the eyes of those two Indian ponies
Darken with kindness.
They have come gladly out of the willows
To welcome my friend and me.

[B] We step over the barbed wire into the pasture
Where they have been grazing all day, alone.
They ripple tensely, they can hardly contain their happiness
That we have come.

[C] They bow shyly as wet swans. They love each other.
There is no loneliness like theirs.
At home once more,
They begin munching the young tufts of spring in the darkness.

[D] I would like to hold the slenderer one in my arms,
For she has walked over to me
And nuzzled my left hand.
She is black and white,
Her mane falls wild on her forehead,
And the light breeze moves me to caress her long ear

[E] That is delicate as the skin over a girl's wrist.
Suddenly I realize
That if I stepped out of my body I would break
Into blossom.

**Identify the Section (A, B, C, D, E) where epiphany is revealed and explain the epiphany.**

## 03 Read the excerpt from a play and follow the directions. [4 points]

| | |
|---|---|
| MISS HARDCASTLE | I understand you, sir. There must be some, who, wanting a relish for refined pleasures, ⓐ <u>pretend to despise what they are incapable of tasting</u>. |
| MARLOW | My meaning, madam, but infinitely better expressed. And I can't help observing—a— |
| MISS HARDCASTLE | (*Aside*) Who could ever suppose this fellow impudent upon some occasions? (*To him*) You were going to observe, sir— |
| MARLOW | I was observing, madam—I protest, madam, I forget what I was going to observe. |
| MISS HARDCASTLE | (*Aside*) I vow and so do I. (*To him*) You were observing, sir, that in this age of hypocrisy—something about hypocrisy, sir. |
| MARLOW | Yes, madam. In this age of hypocrite there are few who upon strict inquiry do not—a—a—a— |
| MISS HARDCASTLE | I understand you perfectly, sir. |
| MARLOW | (*Aside*) Egad! and that's more than I do myself. |
| MISS HARDCASTLE | You mean that in this hypocritical age there are few that do not condemn in public what they practise in private, and think they pay every debt to virtue when they praise it. |
| MARLOW | True, madam; ⓑ <u>those who have most virtue in their mouths, have least of it in their bosoms</u>. But I'm sure I tire you, madam. |
| MISS HARDCASTLE | Not in the least, sir; there's something so agreeable and spirited in your manner, such life and force—pray, sir, go on. |

| | |
|---|---|
| MARLOW | Yes, madam. I was saying—that there are some occasions, when a total want of courage, madam, destroys all the—and puts us—upon a—a—a— |
| MISS HARDCASTLE | I agree with you entirely. |

**Explain the meaning of underlined selection ⓐ in your own words. Then, select the ONE word in the excerpt that most appropriately matches the underlined words in ⓑ.**

______________________________________________

______________________________________________

______________________________________________

______________________________________________

______________________________________________

## 04 Read the excerpt from a short story and follow the directions. [4 points]

[A] Hermann the Fourteenth was one of the unexpected things that happen in politics. In many ways he was ⓐ <u>the most progressive monarch</u> who had sat on an important British throne; before people knew where they were, they were somewhere else. Even his Ministers, progressive though they were by tradition, found it difficult to keep pace with his legislative suggestions.

"As a matter of fact," admitted the Prime Minister, "we are hampered by these votes-for-women creatures; they disturb our meetings throughout the country, and they try to turn Downing Street into a sort of political picnic-ground."

"They must be dealt with" said Hermann.

"Dealt with," said the Prime Minister; "exactly, just so; but how?"

"I will draft you a Bill," said the King, sitting down at his type-writing machine, "enacting that women shall vote at all future elections. Shall vote, you observe; or, to put it plainer, must. Voting will remain optional, as before, for male electors; but every woman between the ages of twenty-one and seventy will be obliged to vote, not only at elections for Parliament, county councils, district boards, parish-councils, and municipalities, but for swimming-bath instructors, contractors, choir-masters, and other local functionaries whose names I will add as they occur to me. All these offices will become elective, and failure to vote at any election falling within her area of residence will involve the female elector in a penalty of 100 pounds. Absence, unsupported by an adequate medical certificate, will not be accepted as an excuse. Pass this Bill through the two Houses of Parliament and bring it to me for signature the day after tomorrow."

[B] From the very outset the Compulsory Female Franchise produced little or no elation even in ⓑ circles which had been loudest in demanding the vote. The bulk of the women of the country had been indifferent or hostile to the franchise agitation, and the most fanatical Suffragettes began to wonder what they had found so attractive in the prospect of putting ballot-papers into a box. In the country districts the task of carrying out the provisions of the new Act was irksome enough; in the towns and cities it became an incubus*. There seemed no end to the elections. Laundresses and seamstresses had to hurry away from their work to vote, often for a candidate whose name they hadn't heard before.

** incubus: nightmare*

**Explain the reason the king is called "the most progressive monarch". Second, identify the TWO consecutive words from [A] that BEST correspond to the meaning of the underlined words in ⓑ.**

# 43회 실전모의고사

모범답안 p.83

**01** **Read the excerpt from a fiction and follow the directions.** [2 points]

The Burnell children could hardly walk to school fast enough the next morning. They burned to tell everybody, to describe, to—well—to boast about their doll's house before the school bell rang. "I'm to tell," said Isabel, "because I'm the eldest. And you two can join in after. But I'm to tell first."

There was nothing to answer. Isabel was bossy, but she was always right, and Lottie and Kezia knew too well the powers that went with being eldest. They brushed through the thick buttercups at the road edge and said nothing. "And I'm to choose who's to come and see it first. Mother said I might." For it had been arranged that while the doll's house stood in the courtyard they might ask the girls at school, two at a time, to come and look. Not to stay to tea, of course, or to come traipsing* through the house. But just to stand quietly in the courtyard while Isabel pointed out the beauties, and Lottie and Kezia looked pleased….

But hurry as they might, by the time they had reached the tarred palings* of the boys' playground the bell had begun to jangle. They only just had time to whip off their hats and fall into line before the roll was called. Never mind. Isabel tried to make up for it by looking very important and mysterious and by whispering behind her hand to the girls near her, "Got something to tell you at playtime."

Playtime came and Isabel was surrounded. The girls of her class nearly fought to put their arms around her, to walk away with her, to beam flatteringly, to be her special friend. <u>She held quite a court under the huge pine trees at the side of the playground</u>.

** traipse: walk from place to place slowly*
** palings: fence stakes*

**Below is an analysis of the excerpt above. Complete the chart by filling in each blank with the ONE most appropriate word. The first blank can be filled from the passage.**

| | |
|---|---|
| Character | There is hierarchy among the children with the ______ⓐ______ being in charge. |
| Narration | Third person omniscient point of view |
| Setting | house and school |
| Figurative language | In the underlined part ______ⓑ______ is employed. |

## 02 Read the poem and follow the directions. [4 points]

These shriveled seeds we plant,
corn kernel, dried bean,
poke into loosened soil,
cover over with measured fingertips

These T-shirts we fold into
perfect white squares

These tortillas we slice and fry to crisp strips
This rich egg scrambled in a gray clay bowl

This bed whose covers I straighten
smoothing edges till blue quilt fits brown blanket
and nothing hangs out

This envelope I address
so the name balances like a cloud
in the center of sky

This page I type and retype
This table I dust till the scarred wood shines
This bundle of clothes I wash and hang and wash again
like flags we share, a country so close
no one needs to name it

The days are nouns: touch them
The hands are churches that worship the world

In the fifth stanza, the poet employs a simile. Describe what is compared to what. Second, describe the thematic idea of the poem by including the meaning of the last line of the poem.

## 03 Read the excerpt from a play and follow the directions. [4 points]

MICHAEL (*patronizingly*) Let you come up then to the fire. You're looking famished with the cold.

CHRISTY God reward you. Is it often the police do be coming into this place, master of the house?

MICHAEL If you'd come in better hours, you'd have seen "Licensed for the sale of Beer and Spirits, to be consumed on the premises," written in white letters above the door, and what would the polis want spying on me?

CHRISTY (*with relief*)—It's a safe house, so. (*He goes over to the fire. Then he begins gnawing a turnip, too miserable to feel the others staring at him with curiosity.*)

MICHAEL (*going after him*)—Is it yourself fearing the polis? You're wanting, maybe?

CHRISTY There's many wanting.

MICHAEL Many surely, with the broken harvest and the ended wars. (<u>*He picks up some stockings, etc., that are near the fire, and carries them away furtively.*</u>) It should be larceny, I'm thinking?

CHRISTY (*dolefully*) I had it in my mind it was a different word and a bigger.

PEGEEN There's a queer lad. Were you never slapped in school, young fellow, that you don't know the name of your deed?

CHRISTY (*bashfully*) I'm slow at learning, a middling scholar only.

MICHAEL If you're a dunce itself, you'd have a right to know that larceny's robbing and stealing. Is it for the like of that you're wanting?

CHRISTY (*with a flash of family pride*)—And I the son of a strong farmer (*with a sudden qualm*), God rest his soul, could have bought up the whole of your old house a while since, from the butt of his tailpocket, and not have missed the weight of it gone.

| | |
|---|---|
| MICHAEL | (*impressed*) If it's not stealing, it's maybe something big. |
| CHRISTY | (*flattered*) Aye; it's maybe something big. |
| JIMMY | He's a wicked-looking young fellow. Maybe he followed after a young woman on a lonesome night. |
| CHRISTY | (*shocked*) Oh, the saints forbid, mister; I was all times a decent lad. |



**Explain why Michael does as shown in the underlined part. Next, describe the two things the protagonist has not done according to the conversation.**

## 04 Read the excerpt from a fiction and follow the directions. [4 points]

"I bet you ain't even missed Tar Baby, have you?" he asked.

"Missed? No. Where is he?"

Ajax smiled at her delicious indifference. "Jail."

"Since when?"

"Last Saturday."

"Picked up for drunk?"

ⓐ "Little bit more than that," he answered and went ahead to tell her about his own involvement in another of Tar Baby's misfortunes.

On Saturday afternoon Tar Baby had stumbled drunk into traffic on the New River Road. A woman driver swerved to avoid him and hit another car. When the police came, they recognized the woman as the mayor's niece and arrested Tar Baby. Later, after the word got out, Ajax and two other men went to the station to see about him. At first they wouldn't let them in. But they relented after Ajax and the other two just stood around for one hour and a half and repeated their request at regular intervals. When they finally got permission to go in and looked in at him in the cell, he was twisted up in a corner badly beaten and dressed in nothing but extremely soiled underwear. Ajax and the other men asked the officer why Tar Baby couldn't have back his clothes. "It ain't right," they said, "to let a grown man lay around in his own shit."

The policeman, obviously in agreement with Eva, who had always maintained that Tar Baby was white, said that if the prisoner didn't like to live in shit, he should come down out of ⓑ those hills, and live like a decent white man.

More words were exchanged, hot words and dark, and the whole thing ended with the arraignment of the three black men, and an appointment to appear in civil court Thursday next.

Explain the meaning of the underlined words in ⓐ. Second, what is it to be inferred about the underlined “those hills” in ⓑ?

# 44회 실전모의고사

모범답안 p.85

**01 Read the excerpt from a novel and follow the directions.** [2 points]

Even people whose lives have been made various by learning, sometimes find it hard to keep a fast hold on their habitual views of life, on their faith in the Invisible, nay, on the sense that their past joys and sorrows are a real experience, when they are suddenly transported to a new land, where the beings around them know nothing of their history, and share none of their ideas—where their mother earth shows another lap, and human life has other forms than those on which their souls have been nourished. Minds that have been unhinged from their old faith and love, have perhaps sought this Lethean* influence of exile, in which the past becomes dreamy because its symbols have all vanished, and the present too is dreamy because it is linked with no memories. But even their experience may hardly enable them thoroughly to imagine what was the effect on a simple weaver like Silas Marner, when he left his own country and people and came to settle in Raveloe. Nothing could be more unlike his native town, set within sight of the widespread hillsides, than this low, wooded region, where he felt hidden even from the heavens by the screening trees and hedgerows. There was nothing here, when he rose in the deep morning quiet and looked out on the dewy brambles and rank tufted grass, that seemed to have any relation with that life centring in Lantern Yard, which had once been to him the altar-place of high dispensations*.

** Lethean: relating to the river Lethe. Those who drank from it experienced complete forgetfulness.*

** high dispensations: God' special permission*

03

**Complete the commentary by filling in the blank with the ONE most appropriate word from the excerpt. If necessary, change the word form.**

Commentary

Silas' life at Raveloe is so unlike that at Lantern Yard that it seems almost a(n) __________. The countryside is different and even the old Power he has trusted in seems far away here.

---

## 02 Read the poem and follow the directions. [4 points]

The neighbors' dog will not stop barking.
He is barking the same high, rhythmic bark
that he barks every time they leave the house.
They must switch him on on their way out.

The neighbors' dog will not stop barking.
I close all the windows in the house
and put on a Beethoven symphony full blast
but I can still hear him muffled under the music,
barking, barking, barking,

and now I can see him sitting in the orchestra,
his head raised confidently as if Beethoven
had included a part for barking dog.

When the record finally ends he is still barking,
sitting there in the oboe section barking,
his eyes fixed on the conductor who is
entreating* him with his baton

while the other musicians listen in respectful
silence to the famous barking dog solo,
that endless coda* that first established
Beethoven as an innovative genius.

** entreating: seriously asking someone to do something*
** coda: the end piece to a body of music*

The title of the poem is “Another Reason Why I Don’t Keep A Gun In The House”. Explain the meaning of the title, considering the overall context. Second, the speaker uses imagination to help manage his anger and frustration. What does he transform the noisy barking into?

## 03 Read the excerpt from a play and follow the directions. [4 points]

AN ACTOR Soon after, back in England, Blair addresses the Labour Party conference:

BLAIR The state of Africa is a scar on the conscience of the world. But if the world as a community focused on it, we could heal it. And if we don't, it will become deeper and angrier. This is the moment to tackle the problems from the slums of Gaza to the mountain ranges of Afghanistan. This is a moment to seize. The kaleidoscope has been shaken. The pieces are in flux. Soon they will settle again. Before they do, let us reorder this world around us.

AN ACTOR On October 7th the US and Britain begin air and missile strikes against thirty one Al Qaeda and Taliban targets.

*UMSFELD appears for a press conference, flanked by GENERALS.*

RUMSFELD The campaign's going well, couldn't be going better. After two days we are now able to carry out strikes more or less round the clock and we've been hitting 85% of our targets. Some of the targets we hit need to be re-hit. (*Laughter*)

JOURNALIST What are you saying, Mr Secretary? Are you saying you're running out of targets?

RUMSFELD We're not running out of targets. Afghanistan is. (*The press conference becomes a swanky* Washington dinner.*)

AN ACTOR One month later, Rumsfeld is thunderously received when he addresses a black-tie dinner of defence contractors.

RUMSFELD <u>We will not stop for Ramadan*. We will not stop for winter. And after the Taliban and al Qaeda we'll get after the rest. The coalition will not determine the mission. The mission will determine the coalition</u>.

*JACK STRAW steps forward.*

| | |
|---|---|
| AN ACTOR | In Europe, the British Foreign Secretary, Jack Straw, is regularly put forward to control the impact of statements from Rumsfeld and the Pentagon. |
| STRAW | There are always statements coming out of Washington. Washington is a very large place. But this military coalition is about terrorist targets in Afghanistan. |

* *swanky: very expensive*
* *Ramadan: Islamic religious practice*

**Identify TWO metaphors used by Blair. Second, explain the major difference between Rumsfeld and Straw's statements, considering the implication made in the underlined selection by Rumsfeld.**

___

___

___

___

___

## 04 Read the excerpt from a novel and follow the directions. [4 points]

I answered, "I did not think the savages would attack," when the manager asked. For several obvious reasons. The thick fog was one. If they left the bank in their canoes they would get lost in it, as we would be if we attempted to move. Still, I had also judged the jungle of both banks quite impenetrable—and yet eyes were in it, eyes that had seen us. The riverside bushes were certainly very thick; but the undergrowth behind was evidently penetrable. However, during the short lift I had seen no canoes anywhere in the reach—certainly not abreast of the steamer. But what made the idea of attack inconceivable to me was the nature of the noise—of the cries we had heard. They had not the fierce character boding immediate hostile intention. Unexpected, wild, and violent as they had been, they had given me an irresistible impression of sorrow. The glimpse of the steamboat had for some reason filled those savages with unrestrained grief. The danger, if any, I expounded, was from our proximity to a great human passion let loose. Even extreme grief may ultimately vent itself in violence—but more generally takes the form of apathy…

You should have seen the white pilgrims stare! They had no heart to grin, or even to revile me: but I believe they thought me gone mad—with fright, maybe. I delivered a regular lecture. My dear boys, it was no good bothering. Keep a lookout? Well, you may guess I watched the fog for the signs of lifting as a cat watches a mouse; but for anything else our eyes were of no more use to us than if we had been buried miles deep in a heap of cotton-wool. It felt like it, too—choking, warm, stifling.

**Describe the two reasons the narrator thought the savages did not attack. Second, describe in the second paragraph to what the narrator compares "the fog".**

# 45회 실전모의고사

모범답안 p.87

**01** **Read the excerpt from a novel and follow the directions.** [2 points]

[A] The old gentleman, attorney-at-law, is rusty to look at, but is reputed to have made good thrift* out of aristocratic marriage settlements and aristocratic wills. He is surrounded by a mysterious halo of family confidences, of which he is known to be the silent depository. There are noble mausoleums* rooted for centuries in retired glades of parks among the growing timber and the fern, which perhaps hold fewer secrets than walk abroad among men, shut up in the breast of Mr. Tulkinghorn. He is of what is called the old school—a phrase generally meaning any school that seems never to have been young—and wears knee-breeches tied with ribbons, and gaiters or stockings. One peculiarity of his black clothes and of his black stockings, be they silk or worsted, is that they never shine. Irresponsive to any glancing light, his dress is like himself.

[B] He never converses when not professionally consulted. He is found sometimes, speechless but quite at home, at corners of dinner-tables in great country houses and near doors of drawing-rooms, concerning which the fashionable intelligence is eloquent, where everybody knows him and where half the peerage* stops to say "How do you do, Mr. Tulkinghorn?" He receives these salutations with gravity and buries them along with the rest of his knowledge.

* *make good thrift: become rich*
* *mausoleum: a building in which dead people are buried*
* *peerage: aristocracy*

Identify the TWO consecutive words from <A> that BEST correspond to the protagonist's character shown in <B>.

## 02 Read the excerpt from a play and follow the directions. [4 points]

| | |
|---|---|
| DEIRDRE BLAKE | Really nice··· |
| BRIGID BLAKE | It's good, right?—I can set up my music workspace downstairs so I won't drive my boyfriend Richard crazy. |
| DEIRDRE | This is a fancy chair··· Erik, check out this fancy chair··· |
| ERIK BLAKE | I thought all your furniture was on the moving truck. |
| BRIGID | It is—Richard's parents brought us that from their place in Manhattan—a couch, too··· we're not sure if the living area will be up here or—this might become the bedroom··· |
| ERIK | Why would they give something this nice away? |
| BRIGID | Because they got a new one, Dad. |
| MOMO | (*Softly mumbled*)··· fernall all sertrus inner··· |
| DEIRDRE | (*Re: the recliner*) You might want something even bigger up here··· |
| BRIGID | This isn't Scranton, I don't need an oversized recliner in every room in Manhattan. |
| MOMO | (*Mumbled*)··· you can never come back···you can never come back··· |

*Erik is drawn to the windows, studies the surroundings.*

| | |
|---|---|
| BRIGID | Momo···? |
| DEIRDRE | It's her latest phrase-of-the-day··· The doctor says it's normal, the repeating··· |
| BRIGID | And··· how's grandma Momo been? |

*Erik stops staring out the window. Momo's face remains blank and focused on the floor.*

| | |
|---|---|
| ERIK | Uh··· she's still got her good days, you know?··· Yesterday she was pretty with it for most of the morning, but now she's all over the place··· I dunno where she goes··· |
| DEIRDRE | I tried to do her hair, I want her to look good, you know? |

**Explain what can be inferred about Momo's condition. Second, describe from where Brigid is and where she now lives.**

## 03 Read the poem and follow the directions. [4 points]

I walk to town with my father
to buy a newspaper. He walks slower
than I do so I must slow up.
The street is filled with children.
We argue about the price of pomegranates. I convince
him it is the fruit of scholars.
He has taken me on this journey
and it's been lifelong.
He's sure I'll be healthy
so long as I eat more oranges,
and tells me the orange
has seeds and so is perpetual;
and we too will come back
like the orange trees.
I ask him what he thinks
about death and he says
he will gladly face it when
it comes but won't jump
out in front of a car.
I'd gladly give my life
for this man with a sixth
grade education, whose kindness
and patience are true…
The truth of it is, he's the scholar,
and when the bitter-hard reality
comes at me like a punishing
evil stranger, I can always
remember that here was a man
who was a worker and provider,

who learned the simple facts
in life and lived by them,
who held no pretense.
And when he leaves without
benefit of fanfare or applause
I shall have learned what little
there is about greatness.

Describe the thematic idea of the poem, considering the meaning of the "greatness". Second, to what does the underlined "the bitter-hard reality" refer? Write your answer with ONE word shown in the poem.

03

**04** **Read the excerpt from a novel and follow the directions.** [4 points]

[A] The tide was coming in and there was only a narrow strip of firm beach between the water and the white, stumbling stuff near the palm terrace. Ralph chose the firm strip as a path because he needed to think; and only here could he allow his feet to move without having to watch them. Suddenly, pacing by the water, he was overcome with astonishment. He found himself understanding the wearisomeness of his life, where every path was an improvisation and a considerable part of one's waking life was spent watching one's feet.

The time had come for the assembly and as he walked into the concealing splendours of the sunlight he went carefully over the points of the assembly, no chasing imaginary··· This meeting must not be fun, but business. At that he walked faster, aware all at once of urgency and the declining sun and a little wind created by his speed that breathed about his face.

[B] With a convulsion of the mind, Ralph discovered dirt and decay; understood how much he disliked perpetually flicking the tangled hair out of his eyes, and at last, when the sun was gone, rolling noisily to rest among dry leaves. At that, he began to trot. The wind pressed his grey shirt against his chest.

The beach near the bathing-pool was dotted with groups of boys waiting for the assembly. They made way for him silently, conscious of his grim mood and the fault at the fire.

The place of assembly in which he stood was roughly a triangle; but irregular and sketchy, like everything they made. The palm trunk lay parallel to the beach, so that when Ralph sat he faced the island but to the boys was a darkish figure against the shimmer of the lagoon.

Ralph moved impatiently. The trouble was, if you were a chief you had to think, you had to be wise. And then the occasion slipped by so that you had to grab at a decision. This made you think; because thought was a valuable thing, that got results.

**Identify ONE sentence including a concrete image from <B> that corresponds to the underlined part in <A>. Second, describe what the main character's primary concern is.**

# 46회 실전모의고사

모범답안 p.89

**01** **Read the passage and follow the directions.** [2 points]

I have been watching the 2018 World Cup in France, mainly in the bars and cafes of the lower end of the 14th arrondissement* in Paris. This is a mixed neighbourhood that is partly gentrified but also home to council estates with a large immigrant population and the usual low-level social tensions—drugs, gangs, run-ins with the police. So far, however, watching the game has been relatively trouble-free. Each step by the French team towards victory has been followed by good-humoured delirium—much tooting of horns and showering of beer. Watching all of this on the news, what was most striking about the fans was not their racial mix, although numerous ethnicities were represented, but how __________ they were. This is the new generation of millennials for whom the last great French victory in the 1998 World Cup is an event from history. A cartoon in *Le Parisien* said it all: "You've got to stop telling us stories from the last century," young fans tell a portly* middle-aged white male (not unlike myself). The message is clear: this is our World Cup and this is our own triumph to celebrate.

In a sense, they are right. This French team are an extremely young team, largely indifferent to the past and not weighed down by history. Some of them, such as the superstar-in-waiting Kylian Mbappé, weren't even born when France last won the World Cup.

** arrondissement: administrative divisions of France*
** portly: fat*

**Fill in the blank with the ONE most appropriate word from the passage.**

______________________________

## 02 Read the poem and follow the directions. [4 points]

I've seasoned the pork like I imagine
My mother would—sesame oil, ginger,
pepper, scallions chopped imperfectly.
Sheets of doughy skin,
<u>I only have the skill</u>
<u>to buy</u>.

Thumb and forefinger peel
each tender white scrap
of noodle from the clinging
stack. I pat the centers pink
with fragrant spoonfuls
the color of the fat sun in October

Mimicking from memory:
A twist, a tuck, a folding over—
a finger lick of water
to seal my misshapen flowers.

My hands powderdusted;
acquainted with each
new blossom. I line them up
like newborns huddled
together, waiting to be fed
to their distant fathers.

The soup bubbles to overflowing:
I slide the dumplings
in and stir them dizzy.
Freshly drowned,
swollen and glistening, steam hidden
for an instant—

I set them on the table
and decide how many
I will save
for tomorrow.

**Explain the meaning of the underlined part. Second, identify all THREE things that won tons are compared to in the poem.**

## 03 Read the excerpt from a play and follow the directions. [4 points]

| | |
|---|---|
| ROBERT | How old are you? |
| ARK | Seventeen: so they tell me. It might be nineteen. I don't remember. |
| ROBERT | What did you mean when you said that St Catherine and St Margaret talked to you every day? |
| ARK | They do. |
| ROBERT | What are they like? |
| ARK | (*suddenly obstinate*) I will tell you nothing about that: they have not given me leave. |
| ROBERT | But you actually see them; and they talk to you just as I am talking to you? |
| ARK | No: it is quite different. I cannot tell you: you must not talk to me about my voices. |
| ROBERT | How do you mean? voices? |
| ARK | I hear voices telling me what to do. They come from God. |
| ROBERT | They come from your imagination. |
| ARK | Of course. That is how the messages of God come to us. |
| ROBERT | So God says you are to raise the siege of Orleans? |
| ARK | And to crown the Dauphin in Rheims Cathedral. |
| ROBERT | (*gasping*) Crown the D—! Gosh! |
| ARK | And to make the English leave France. |
| ROBERT | (*sarcastic*) Anything else? |
| ARK | (*charming*) Not just at present, thank you, squire. |
| ROBERT | I suppose you think raising a siege is as easy as chasing a cow out of a meadow. You think <u>soldiering is anybody's job?</u> |
| ARK | I do not think it can be very difficult if God is on your side, and you are willing to put your life in His hand. But many soldiers are very simple. |

| | |
|---|---|
| ROBERT | (*grimly*) Simple! Did you ever see English soldiers fighting? |
| ARK | They are only men. God made them just like us; but He gave them their own country and their own language; and it is not His will that they should come into our country and try to speak our language. |



**Identify the source of Ark's grand plan. Then, describe Ark's answer for the underlined question of Robert's.**

## 04 Read the excerpt from a fiction and follow the directions. [4 points]

Henri Deplis was by birth a native of the Grand Duchy of Luxemburg. On maturer reflection he became a commercial traveller. His business activities frequently took him beyond the limits of the Grand Duchy, and he was stopping in a small town of Northern Italy when news reached him from home that a legacy from a distant and deceased relative had fallen to his share.

It was not a large legacy, even from the modest standpoint of Henri Deplis, but it impelled him towards some seemingly harmless extravagances. In particular it led him to patronize local art as represented by the tattoo-needles of Signor Andreas Pincini. Signor Pincini was, perhaps, the most brilliant master of tattoo craft that Italy had ever known, but his circumstances were decidedly impoverished, and for the sum of six hundred francs he gladly undertook to cover his client's back, from the collar-bone down to the waist-line, with a glowing representation of <u>the Fall of Icarus</u>. The design, when finally developed, was a slight disappointment to Deplis, but he was more than satisfied with the execution of the work, which was acclaimed by all who had the privilege of seeing it as Pincini's masterpiece.

It was his greatest effort, and his last. Without even waiting to be paid, the illustrious craftsman departed this life, and was buried under an ornate tombstone. There remained, however, the widow Pincini, to whom the six hundred francs were due. And thereupon arose the great crisis in the life of Henri Deplis, traveller of commerce. The legacy, under the stress of numerous little calls on its substance, had dwindled to very insignificant proportions, and when a pressing wine bill and sundry other current accounts had been paid, there remained little more than 430 francs to offer to the widow. The lady was properly indignant on account of the suggested writing-off of 170 francs, but also at the attempt to depreciate the value of her late husband's acknowledged masterpiece. In a week's time Deplis was obliged to reduce his offer to 405 francs, which circumstance fanned the widow's indignation into a fury. She cancelled the sale of the work of art, and a few days later Deplis learned with a sense of consternation* that she had presented it to the municipality of Bergamo, which had gratefully accepted it.

** consternation: a feeling of shock*



**Describe what the underlined "the Fall of Icarus" is. Second, explain why the widow Pincini presents her husband's masterpiece to Bergamo.**

# 47회 실전모의고사

모범답안 p.91

**01** **Read the excerpt from a novel and follow the directions.** [2 points]

I first met Dean not long after my wife and I split up. I had just gotten over a serious illness that I won't bother to talk about, except that it had something to do with the miserably weary split-up and my feeling that everything was dead. With the coming of Dean Moriarty began the part of my life you could call my life on the road. Before that I'd often dreamed of going West to see the country, always vaguely planning and never taking off. Dean is the perfect guy for the road because he actually was born on the road, when his parents were passing through Salt Lake City in 1926, in a jalopy, on their way to Los Angeles. First reports of him came to me through Chad King, who'd shown me a few letters from him written in a New Mexico reform school. I was tremendously interested in the letters because they so naively and sweetly asked Chad to teach him all about Nietzsche and all the wonderful intellectual things that Chad knew. At one point Carlo and I talked about the letters and wondered if we would ever meet the strange Dean Moriarty. This is all far back, when Dean was not the way he is today, when he was a young jailkid shrouded in mystery. Then news came that Dean was out of reform school and was coming to New York for the first time; also there was talk that he had just married a girl called Marylou.

**Complete the commentary below by filling in the blank with the THREE most appropriate consecutive words from the excerpt.**

Commentary

The narrator starts off by talking about one of major characters Dean Moriarty and how they went ______________ together. Dean just married a woman named Marylou and is coming to New York.

---

## 02 Read the poem and follow the directions. [4 points]

When she comes slip-footing through the door,
she kindles us
like lump coal lighted,
and we wake up glowing.

<u>She puts a spark even in Papa's eyes</u>
<u>and turns out all our darkness</u>.

When she comes sweet-talking in the room,
she warms us
like grits and gravy,
and we rise up shining.

Even at nighttime Mama is a sunrise
that promises tomorrow and tomorrow.

**Describe the extended metaphor throughout the poem. Second, explain the meaning of the underlined part.**

**03** **Read the excerpt from a novel and follow the directions.** [4 points]

She was fast asleep. Gabriel listens to her deep-drawn breath. So she had had that romance in her life: a man had died for her sake. It hardly pained him now to think how poor a part he, her husband, had played in her life. He watched her while she slept, as though he and she had never lived together as man and wife. His curious eyes rested long upon her face and on her hair: and, as he thought of what she must have been then, in that time of her first girlish beauty, a strange, friendly pity for her entered his soul.

Perhaps she had not told him all the story. His eyes moved to the chair over which she had thrown some of her clothes. He wondered at his riot of emotions of an hour before. From what had it proceeded? From his aunt's supper, from his own foolish speech, from the wine and dancing, the merry-making when saying good-night in the hall, the pleasure of the walk along the river in the snow.

The air of the room chilled his shoulders. He stretched himself cautiously along under the sheets and lay down beside his wife. One by one, they were all becoming shades. Better pass boldly into that other world, in the full glory of some passion, than fade and wither dismally with age. He thought of how she who lay beside him had locked in her heart for so many years that image of her lover's eyes when he had told her that he did not wish to live.

Generous tears filled Gabriel's eyes. He had never felt like that himself towards any woman, but he knew that such a feeling must be love. The tears gathered more thickly in his eyes and in the partial darkness he imagined he saw the form of a young man standing under a dripping tree. Other forms were near. His soul had approached that region where dwell the vast hosts of the dead. He was conscious of, but could not apprehend, their wayward and flickering existence. His own identity was fading out into a grey impalpable world: the solid world itself, which these dead had one time reared and lived in, was dissolving and dwindling.

A few light taps upon the pane made him turn to the window. It had begun to snow again. He watched sleepily the flakes, silver and dark, falling obliquely against the lamplight. The time had come for him to set out on his journey westward.

**The excerpt reveals the epiphany the major character experiences in discovering his partner's real life. Explain it. Second, he comes face to face with his own self, with the past and with the future. Describe ONE sentence that BEST indicates an awareness of his new responsibility of the future.**

03

**04** Read the excerpt from a play and follow the directions. [4 points]

| | |
|---|---|
| LORD SIMPLEX | All right. Anywhere you like. We can go on for tea to Richmond afterwards. |
| MISS EVADNE CARRILLON | (*turning to him, rather more seriously*) Real slumming, mind*. My old nurse's neighbours are just awful. |
| LORD SIMPLEX | Oh, I say, slumming, that's a bit thick—for you, I mean. |
| LADY CARFON | (*with a peal of laughter*) You were always an exceptional girl, Evadne. Think of taking your fiancé slumming within half an hour— |
| EVADNE | (*sturdily*) Why not? |
| MRS. CARRILLON | (*rather hopeless and distressed*) Oh, in reason, in reason. It is very charming, but really to-day, my darling, the nurse won't expect you. |
| EVADNE | Yes, she does. I have never broken my promise to her when I am in town, and I am going to-day. |
| LORD SIMPLEX | Well the old nurse and nobody else; no promiscuous slumming, mind; too great a risk. |
| EVADNE | A risk? |
| LORD SIMPLEX | Germs! Small-pox! Measles! Microbes! |
| LADY CARFON | (*following quickly*) Mad ideas. |
| LORD SIMPLEX | Yes, if you like, mad ideas. |
| EVADNE | Don't you want me to have ideas? |
| LORD SIMPLEX | You have plenty; you are perfect as it is. |
| EVADNE | (*laughing*) Seriously, don't you like the ideas you get in the slums? |
| LORD SIMPLEX | (*shuddering*) I don't. I have no use for* them at all. |

| | |
|---|---|
| EVADNE | Well, I often think the ideas you get down there are a great deal more real than the ideas you get in the Park. |
| MRS. CARRILLON | My darling, we are yielding to you to-day, but do not upset us all. |
| EVADNE | Why should it upset mother if now and then I peep in at what people are suffering every day? |
| LORD SIMPLEX | It's not good for you. |
| LADY CARFON | My dear. You are a social butterfly. |
| EVADNE | (*stamping her foot*) "I don't want to be a butterfly; I want to be a worm!" |
| LORD SIMPLEX | (*half laughing, but really rather annoyed*) I won't have my future wife described as a worm even by herself. *(He turns rather swiftly.)* Goodbye, Mrs. Carrillon, see you this evening. Goodbye, Lady Carfon. Come along, Evadne. |
| EVADNE | Well, the sapphires have not settled everything, you know. I see we'll have to fight this out. |

** mind: keep in mind*
** have no use for: hate*

**Explain the "worm" metaphor Evadne mentions. From the above excerpt, what can be inferred to most likely be the engagement present given by Lord Simplex before the excerpt's start?**

# 48회 실전모의고사

모범답안 p.93

**01** **Read the excerpt from a fiction and follow the directions.** [2 points]

Between Elizabeth and her one son George there was a deep unexpressed bond of sympathy, based on a girlhood dream that had long ago died. In the son's presence she was timid and reserved, but sometimes while he hurried about town intent upon his duties as a reporter, she went into his room and closing the door knelt by a little desk, made of a kitchen table, that sat near a window. In the room by the desk she went through a ceremony that was half a prayer, half a demand, addressed to the skies. In the boyish figure she yearned to see something half forgotten that had once been a part of herself re-created. The prayer concerned that. "Even though I die, I will in some way keep defeat from you," she cried, and so deep was her determination that her whole body shook. Her eyes glowed and she clenched her fists. "If I am dead and see him becoming a meaningless drab figure like myself, I will come back," she declared. "I ask God now to give me that privilege. I demand it. I will pay for it. God may beat me with his fists. I will take any blow that may befall if but this my boy be allowed to express something for us both."

Once when she was alone, and after watching a prolonged and meaningless outburst on the part of the baker, who hurled sticks and bits of broken glass to a cat, Elizabeth put her head down on her long white hands and wept. After that she did not look along the alleyway any more, but tried to forget the contest between the bearded man and the cat. It seemed like a rehearsal of her own life, terrible in its vividness.

**Complete the commentary below by filling in the blank with the ONE most appropriate word from the excerpt. If necessary, change the word form.**

Commentary

The protagonist's unhappiness and helplessness is portrayed when she watches from her bedroom window a feud between the town baker and a stray cat. She is frustrated by the __________ of her life.

---

**02** Read the poem and follow the directions. [4 points]

The world is not a pleasant place
to be without
someone to hold and be held by.

A river would stop
its flow if only
a stream were there
to receive it.

An ocean would never laugh
if clouds weren't there
to kiss her tears.

The world is
not a pleasant place to be without
someone.

**In the third stanza, the poet employs a figure of speech to convey the message of the poem. Identify the figure of speech and then describe the thematic idea of the poem.**

______________________________________________

______________________________________________

______________________________________________

______________________________________________

______________________________________________

## 03 Read the play and follow the directions. [4 points]

| | |
|---|---|
| Helen | You pour out, Frank. All of us having a nice cup of tea together. Your mother said she had a visitor today. |
| Frank | Really? Who was that, Mother? Who? |
| Helen | She isn't listening. Her eyes go all funny when she isn't listening. Give her a piece of Cake. |
| Frank | Cake, Mother? |
| Maud | It was the man upstairs. |
| Helen | There isn't a man upstairs. No one upstairs. There isn't an upstairs, unless you count the box room. Haha. No man there. Have this nice bit of cake. |
| Frank | God. She means God. She always used to call Him the man upstairs. I used to get so worried when I was small. |
| Maud | Did you make it, mother? |
| Helen | Helen··· Yes, I made it especially for you. |
| Maud | That's very kind of you. Very kind indeed to go to so much trouble. Double trouble double··· |
| Helen | No bother. |
| Maud | Such strange things dance in my mind. Strange words come··· What will happen to the cat? |
| Frank | We'll take the cat. Don't worry your head about the cat. We'll give her a good home. |
| Maud | She might knock things off the mantelpiece. |
| Frank | Don't you worry about her. |
| Maud | She'll probably die. |
| Frank | I shouldn't think so. Cats are very adaptable beasts. She'll settle in a week or so. |
| Maud | She and I? |
| Frank | You'll settle. You know you'll settle in the new nursing home. |

| | |
|---|---|
| Maud | There's no use buying her Kit-e-kat. She doesn't eat it. She'd stare herself to death rather than eat it. She's funny like that. She'll sniff at it and then walk away. Angry. It makes her really angry if you give her Kit-e-kat. Tell her. |
| Frank | Who? |
| Maud | Your wife. Tell your wife not to waste her money on that stuff. |
| Frank | She's here, mother. This is Helen. |
| Maud | I don't know. I called her mother. |
| Helen | But I told you I was Helen. |
| Maud | You called me mother. |
| Helen | Yes I've always called you mother. |
| Maud | It all comes to the same thing in the end. |

**Identify at least TWO strange details that inform the reader of Maud's situation. Second, explain what the cat symbolizes.**

## 04 Read the excerpt from a fiction and follow the directions. [4 points]

"O, Mr. Thompson!" she cried out, catching her suspended breath, "don't leave me here all alone!"

Though rough in exterior, Joe Thompson, the wheelwright, had a heart, and it was very tender in some places. He liked children, and was pleased to have them come to his shop, where sleds and wagons were made or mended for the village lads without a draft on their hoarded sixpences.

"No, dear," he answered, in a kind voice, going to the bed, and stooping down over the child, "You sha'n't be left here alone." Then he wrapped her with the gentleness almost of a woman, in the clean bedclothes which some neighbor had brought; and, lifting her in his strong arms, bore her out into the air and across the field that lay between the hovel and his home.

Now, Joe Thompson's wife, who happened to be childless, was not a woman of saintly temper, nor much given to self-denial for others' good, and Joe had well-grounded doubts touching the manner of greeting he should receive on his arrival. Mrs. Thompson saw him approaching from the window, and with ruffling feathers met him a few paces from the door, as he opened the garden gate, and came in. He bore a precious burden, and he felt it to be so. As his arms held the sick child to his breast, a sphere of tenderness went out from her, and penetrated his feelings. A bond had already corded itself around them both, and love was springing into life.

"What have you there?" sharply questioned Mrs. Thompson.

Joe, felt the child start and shrink against him. He did not reply, except by a look that was pleading and cautionary, that said, "Wait a moment for explanations, and be gentle;" and, passing in, carried Maggie to the small chamber on the first floor, and laid her on a bed. Then, stepping back, he shut the door, and stood face to face with his vinegar-tempered wife in the passage-way outside.

"You haven't brought home that sick brat!" <u>Her face was in a flame</u>.

"I think women's hearts are sometimes very hard," said Joe. Usually Joe Thompson got out of his wife's way, or kept rigidly silent and non-combative when she fired up on any subject; it was with some surprise, therefore, that she now encountered a firmly-set countenance and a resolute pair of eyes.



**Explain the reason Mrs. Thompson is upset. Then explain the meaning of the metaphorical expression in the underlined part.**

# 49회 실전모의고사

모범답안 p.95

**01** **Read the excerpt from a fiction and follow the directions.** [2 points]

The last time I saw my father was in Grand Central Station. I was going from my grandmother's in the Adirondacks to a cottage on the Cape that my mother had rented. So I wrote my father that I would be in New York between trains for an hour and a half, and asked if we could have lunch together. He was a stranger to me. His secretary wrote to say that he would meet me at the information booth at noon, and at twelve o'clock sharp I saw him coming through the crowd. <u>My mother divorced him three years ago and I hadn't been with him since</u>. However as soon as I saw him I felt that he was my father, my flesh and blood, my future and my doom. I knew that when I was grown I would be something like him; I would have to plan my campaigns within his limitations. He was a big, good-looking man, and I was terribly happy to see him again. He struck me on the back and shook my hand. "Hi, Charlie," he said. "Hi, boy. I'd like to take you up to my club, but it's in the Sixties, and if you have to catch an early train I guess we'd better get something to eat around here." He put his arm around me, and I smelled my father the way my mother sniffs a rose. It was a rich compound of whiskey, after-shave lotion, shoe polish, woolens, and the rankness of a mature male. I hoped that someone would see us together. I wished that we could be photographed. I wanted some record of our having been together.

**Describe ONE sentence from the passage that best corresponds to the meaning of the underlined part.**

______________________________

03

**02** **Read the poem and follow the directions.** [4 points]

They hold hands
as they walk with slow steps.
Careful together they cross the plaza
both slightly stooped, <u>bodies returning to the land</u>,
he in faded khaki and straw hat,
she wrapped in soft clothes, black
rebozo* round her head and shoulders.

Tourists in halter tops and shorts
pose by flame trees and fountains,
but the old couple walks step by step
on the edge.
Even in the heat, only their wrinkled
hands and faces show. They know
of moving through a crowd at their own pace.

I watch him help her
off the curb and I smell love
like dried flowers, old love
of holding hands with one man for fifty years.

** rebozo: Spanish for "shawl"*

**Explain the literal meaning of the underlined figure of speech "bodies returning to the land". Next, in the first two stanzas, what contrast of dress does the speaker draw?**

## 03 Read the excerpt from a play and follow the directions. [4 points]

| | |
|---|---|
| EDDIE | I don't care what the question is. You—don't—know—nothin'. They got stool pigeons* all over this neighborhood they're payin' them every week for information, and you don't know who they are. It could be your best friend. You hear? *(To Beatrice)* Like Vinny Bolzano, remember Vinny? |
| BEATRICE | Oh yeah. God forbid. |
| EDDIE | Tell her about Vinny. *(To Catherine)* You think I'm blowin' steam* here? *(To Beatrice)* Go ahead, tell her. *(To Catherine)* You was a baby then. There was a family lived next door to Beatrice's mother, Vinny was about sixteen— |
| BEATRICE | No, he was not more than fourteen, cause I was to his confirmation* in Saint Agnes. But the family had an uncle that they were hidin' in the house, and Vinny snitched to the Immigration. |
| CATHERINE | The kid squealed? |
| EDDIE | On his own uncle! |
| CATHERINE | What, was he crazy? |
| EDDIE | He was crazy after, I tell you that, boy. |
| BEATRICE | Oh, it was terrible. He had five brothers and the old father. And they grabbed him in the kitchen and pulled him down the stairs—three flights··· his head was bouncin' like a coconut. And they spit on him in the street, his own father and his brothers. The whole neighborhood was cryin'. |
| CATHERINE | Ts! So what happened to him? |
| BEATRICE | I think he went away. *(To Eddie)* I never seen him again, did you? |
| EDDIE | ··· Him? You'll never see him no more, a guy do a thing like that. How's he gonna show his face? *(To Catherine)* Just remember, <u>you can quicker get back a million dollars that was stole than a word that you gave away</u>. |

** stool pigeons: spy*
** blowin' steam: talking useless thing*
** confirmation: a Catholic ritual*

Describe about what the whole dialogue is mainly. Second, explain what kind of lesson Eddie is trying to give to Catherine through the underlined words of the last line.

## 04 Read the excerpt from a novel and follow the directions. [4 points]

It is a most miserable thing to feel ashamed of home. There may be black ingratitude in the thing, and the punishment may be retributive and well deserved; but, that it is a miserable thing, I can testify.

Home had never been a very pleasant place to me, because of my sister's temper. But, Joe had sanctified it, and I had believed in it. I had believed in the best parlour as a most elegant saloon; I had believed in the front door, as a mysterious portal of the Temple of State whose solemn opening was attended with a sacrifice of roast fowls; I had believed in the kitchen as a chaste* though not magnificent apartment*; I had believed in the forge as the glowing road to manhood and independence. Within a single year, all this was changed. Now, it was all coarse and common, and I would not have had my beloved Estella and her adoptive mother Miss Havisham see it on any account.

How much of <u>my ungracious* condition of mind</u> may have been my own fault, how much Miss Havisham's, how much my sister's, is now of no moment to me or to any one. The change was made in me; the thing was done. Well or ill done, excusably or inexcusably, it was done.

Once, it had seemed to me that when I should at last roll up my shirt-sleeves and go into the forge, Joe's apprentice, I should be distinguished and happy. Now the reality was in my hold, I only felt that I was dusty with the dust of small coal, and that I had a weight upon my daily remembrance to which the anvil was a feather.

** chaste: decent or clean* ** apartment: room* ** ungracious: ungrateful*

**The narrator says his life is changed. Explain what makes him change his opinion about his home. Second, describe to what the underlined words refer.**

# 50회 실전모의고사

모범답안 p.97

**01** **Read the excerpt from a novel and follow the directions.** [2 points]

"Marner, you ought to remember your own life's uncertain, and Eppie is at an age now when her lot may soon be fixed in a way very different from what it would be in her father's home. Though I'm sorry to hurt you after what you've done, and what I've left undone, I feel now it's my duty to insist on taking care of my own daughter. I want to do my duty." Godfrey said.

Marner was again stricken in conscience, and alarmed lest Godfrey's accusation should be true—lest he should be raising his own will as <u>an obstacle to Eppie's good</u>. For many moments he was mute, struggling for the self-conquest necessary to the uttering of the difficult words. They came out tremulously.

"I'll say no more. Let it be as you will. Speak to the child, Eppie. I'll hinder nothing."

Nancy, Godfrey's wife, with all the acute sensibility of her own affections, shared her husband's view, that Marner was not justifiable in his wish to retain Eppie, after her real father Godfrey had avowed himself. She felt that it was a very hard trial for the poor weaver, who had raised Eppie with a lot of love since she was very young, but her code allowed no question that a father by blood must have a claim above that of any foster-father. Besides, Nancy, used all her life to plenteous circumstances and the privileges of the upper class, could not enter into the pleasures which early nurture and habit connect with all the little aims and efforts of the poor who are born poor. To her mind, Eppie, in being restored to her birthright, was entering on a too long withheld but unquestionable good. Hence she heard Marner's last words with relief, and thought, as Godfrey did, that their wish was achieved.

Identify the FIVE consecutive words from the excerpt that BEST correspond to the underlined words.

---

03

## 02 Read the poem and follow the directions. [4 points]

Starfish were lovely in the quartz and jasper* sand
As if they had created terrariums* with their bodies
On purpose; adding sprigs of seaweed, seashells,
White feathers, eel bones, miniature
Mussels, a fish jaw. Hundreds; no—
Thousands of baby <u>stars</u>. We touched them,
Surprised to find them soft, pliant*, almost
Living in their attitudes. We would dry them, arrange them,
Form seascapes, geodesics*··· We gathered what we could
In the approaching darkness. Then we left hundreds of
Thousands of flawless five-fingered specimens sprawled
Along the beach as far as we could see, all massed
Together: little martyrs, soldiers, artless* suicides
In lifelong liberation from the sea. So many
Splayed hands, the tide shoveled in.

** jasper: a reddish, yellow type of quartz*
** terrarium: glass container*
** pliant: easily bent*
** geodesics: relating to the shortest possible line between two points*
** artless: simple; innocent*

**Identify to what the underlined "stars" refer. Second, how does the description of the "approaching darkness" change the tone of the poem?**

## 03 Read the excerpt from a play and follow the directions. [4 points]

| | |
|---|---|
| Geroge | Martha's lying. I want you to know that, right now. Martha's lying. *(Martha laughs.)* There are very few things in this world that I am sure of… national boundaries, the level of the ocean, political allegiances, practical morality… none of these would I stake my stick on any more… but the one thing in this whole sinking world that I am sure of is my partnership, my chromosomological partnership in the… creation of our blond-eyed, blue-haired… son. |
| Honey | Oh, I'm so glad! |
| Martha | That was a very pretty speech, George. |
| George | Thank you, Martha. |
| Martha | You rose to the occasion… good. Real good. |
| Honey | Well… real well. |
| Nick | Honey…. |
| George | Martha knows… she knows better. |
| Martha | *(Proudly)* I know better. I been to college like everybody else. |
| George | Martha been to college. Martha been to a convent when she were a little twig of a thing, too. |
| Martha | And I was an atheist. *(Uncertainly)* I still am. |
| George | Not an atheist, Martha… a pagan. *(To Honey and Nick)* Martha is the only true pagan on the eastern seaboard. *(Martha laughs.)* |
| Honey | Oh, that's nice. Isn't that nice, dear? |
| Nick | *(Humoring her)* Yes… wonderful. |
| George | And Martha paints blue circles around her things. |
| Nick | You do? |
| Martha | *(Defensively, for the joke's sake)* Sometimes. *(Beckoning)* You wanna see? |
| George | *(Admonishing)* Tut, tut, tut. |
| Martha | Tut, tut yourself… you old floozie! |
| Honey | He's not a floozie… he can't be a floozie*… you're a whore. *(Giggles)* |

Martha *(Shaking a finger at Honey)* Now you watch yourself!
Honey *(Cheerfully)* All right. I'd like a nipper of brandy, please.
Nick Honey, I think you've had enough, now…
George Nonsense! Everybody's ready, I think. *(Takes glasses, etc.)*
Honey *(Echoing George)* Nonesense.
Nick *(Shrugging)* O.K.

* *floozy: whore*

**According to the excerpt, describe what one "pagan" quality of Martha they joke about is. Next, what is the relationship between George and Martha?**

**04** **Read the excerpt from a novel set in the early 20th century USA and follow the directions.** [4 points]

"You have to be pure in heart, and you have to be disciplined in body and mind. Brother, you understand what I mean?"

"Yes, I think I do," I said. "Some folks feel that way about their religion."

"Religion?" He blinked his eyes. "Folks like me and you is full of distrust," he said. "We been corrupted 'til it's hard for some of us to believe in Brotherhood. And some even want revenge! That's what I'm talking about. We have to root it out! We have to learn to trust our other brothers. After all, didn't they start the Brotherhood? Didn't they come and stretch out their hand to us black men and say, 'We want y'all for our brothers?' Didn't they do it? Didn't they, now? Didn't they set out to organize us, and help fight our battle and all like that? Sho they did, and we have to remember ____ⓐ____ twenty-four hours a day. That's the word we got to keep right in front of our eyes every second. Now this brings me to why I come to see you, Brother."

He sat back, his huge hands grasping his knees. "I got a plan I want to talk over with you."

"What is it, Brother?" I said.

"Well, it's like this. I think we ought to have some way of showing what we are. We ought to have some banners and things like that. Specially for us black brothers."

"I see," I said, becoming interested. "But why do you think this is important?"

"Because it helps the Brotherhood, that's why. First, if you remember, when you watch our people when there's a parade or a funeral, or a dance or anything like that, they always have some kind of flags and banners even if they don't mean anything. It kind of makes the occasion seem more important like. It makes people stop look and listen. 'What's coming off here?' But you know and I know that they ain't none of 'em got no true flag—"

"Yes, I think I do," I said, remembering that there was always that sense in me of being apart when the national flag went by. It had been a reminder, until I'd found the Brotherhood, that ⓑ <u>my star was not yet there.</u>

* *Sho: Sure*

**Fill in the blank ⓐ with the ONE most appropriate word from the excerpt. Second, explain what the underlined words in ⓑ tell the reader about the man's view of the national flag.**

# 51회 실전모의고사

모범답안 p.99

**01** **Read the fable and follow the directions.** [2 points]

Goat and Fox were quarreling, and Goat told Fox that he intended to get him into trouble so that he would never be able to get out. Fox said, "All right; you do that, and I will return the favor to you."

Goat went for a walk and saw Leopard. Being frightened, Goat asked, "Auntie, what are you doing here?" "My little one is sick," said Leopard. Then Goad, thinking quickly, said, "Fox has medicine that will make your little one well." Leopard said to call Fox, so Goat went to Fox and said, "They are calling you."

"Who is calling me?" replied Fox. "I don't know," said Goat; "I think it is your friend. Go this way and you will run into him." Fox went down the path and at length came upon Leopard. Fox was frightened and inquired, "Did you call me?" "Yes, my son. Goat came just a while ago and told me you had medicine that would make my little one well."

"Yes," said Fox. "I have medicine that will cure your little one, but I must have a little goat horn to put it in. If you get me a goat horn I will let you have the medicine."

"Which way did the Goat go?" asked Leopard. "I left him up there," replied Fox. "You wait here with my little one, and I will bring you the horn," said Leopard, and away she ran. Soon after, Leopard killed Goat and returned with his horns to Fox.

**What is the lesson of the fable above? Write your answer by filling in the blank with the ONE most appropriate word from the fable above.**

| Beware, lest you fall into the __________ you set for someone else. |
|---|

__________________________________________________

## 02 Read the excerpt from a play and follow the directions. [4 points]

Knowlt Hoheimer:

I was the first fruits of the battle of Missionary Ridge.
When I felt the bullet enter my heart
I wished I had staid at home and gone to jail
For stealing the hogs of Curl Trenary,
Instead of running away and joining the army.
Rather a thousand times the country jail
Than to lie under this marble figure with wings,
And this granite pedestal
Bearing the words, "Pro Patria*."
What do they mean, anyway?

Lydia Puckett:

Knowlt Hoheimer ran away to the war
The day before Curl Trenary
Swore out a warrant through Justice Arnett
For stealing hogs.
But that's not the reason he turned a soldier.
He caught me running with Lucius Atherton.
We quarreled and I told him never again
To cross my path.
Then he stole the hogs and went to the war—
Back of every soldier is a woman.

* *Pro Patria: For One's Country*

**The character of Knowlt Hoheimer is an unreliable narrator. Explain the reason. Second, describe where Knowlt Hoheimer is now.**

## 03 Read the poem and follow the directions. [4 points]

The moment when, after many years
of hard work and a long voyage
you stand in the centre of your room,
house, half-acre, square mile, island, country,
knowing at last how you got there,
and say, I own this,

is the same moment when the trees unloose
their soft arms from around you,
the birds take back their language,
the cliffs fissure and collapse,
the air moves back from you like a wave
and you can't breathe.

No, they whisper. You __________ nothing.
You were a visitor, time after time
climbing the hill, planting the flag, proclaiming.
We never belonged to you.
You never found us.
It was always the other way round

**Fill in the blank with the ONE most appropriate word from the poem. Second, explain at what idea nature rebels.**

## 04 Read the excerpt from a novel and follow the directions. [4 points]

"Thassall!" A Mexican official grinned. "You boys all set. Go ahead. Welcome Mexico. Have good time. Is not hard enjoin yourself in Mehico."

"Yes!" shuddered Dean and off we went across the street into Mexico on soft feet happily. We left the car parked, and all three of us abreast went down the Spanish street into the middle of the dull brown lights. Old men sat on chairs in the night and looked like Oriental junkies and oracles. No one was actually looking at us, yet everybody was aware of everything we did. We turned sharp left into the smoky lunchroom and went in to music of campo guitars on an American 'thirties jukebox. We bought three bottles of cold beer—cerveza was the name of beer. We gazed and gazed at our wonderful Mexican money that went so far, and played with it and looked around and smiled at everyone.

Behind us lay the whole of America and everything Dean and I had previously known about life. We had finally found the magic land at the end of the road and we never dreamed the extent of the magic. "Think of these cats staying up all hours of the night," whispered Dean. "And think of this big continent ahead of us with those enormous Sierra Madre mountains we saw in the movies, and the jungles all the way down and a whole desert plateau as big as ours and reaching clear down to Guatemala and God knows where, whoo! What'll we do? What'll we do? Let's move!" We got out and went back to the car.

"What a wild country!" I yelped. Dean and I were completely awake. "Now, we're leaving everything behind us and entering a new and unknown phase of things. All the years and troubles and kicks—and now this! So that we can safely think of nothing else and just go on ahead with our faces stuck out like this you see. Understand the world as, really and genuinely speaking, other Americans haven't done before us. They were here, weren't they? The Mexican war, cutting across here with cannon."

Identify to what the underlined “the magic land” refers. Second, describe ONE sentence that shows the insight of the narrator’s post-colonialism.

# 52회 실전모의고사

모범답안 p.101

## 01 Read the excerpt from a fiction and follow the directions. [2 points]

[A] There are no types, no plurals. There is a rich boy, and this is his and not his brothers' story. All my life I have lived among his brothers but this one has been my friend. Let me tell you about the very rich. They are different from you and me. They possess and enjoy early. And it does something to them, makes them soft where we are hard, and cynical where we are trustful, in a way that, unless you were born rich, it is very difficult to understand. They think, deep in their hearts, that they are better than we are because we had to discover the compensations and refuges of life for ourselves. Even when they enter deep into our world or sink below us, they still think that they are better than we are. The only way I can describe young Anson Hunter is to approach him as if he were a foreigner and cling stubbornly to my point of view. If I accept his for a moment I am lost—I have nothing to show but a preposterous movie.

[B] Anson was the eldest of six children who would some day divide a fortune of fifteen million dollars, and he reached the age of reason—is it seven?—at the beginning of the century when daring young women were already gliding along Fifth Avenue in electric "mobiles*." <u>In those days he and his brother had an English governess who spoke the language very clearly and crisply and well, so that the two boys grew to speak as she did—their words and sentences were all crisp and clear and not run together as ours are</u>. They didn't talk exactly like English children but acquired an accent that is peculiar to fashionable people in the city of New York.

** electric "mobiles": automobiles*

Identify the ONE sentence from <A> that BEST corresponds to the underlined words in <B>.

---

## 02 Read the passage and follow the directions. [4 points]

Once your eyes suspect a liar, next let your ears have a turn. Here are ⓐ cues to listen for. A story in strict chronological order. When a complex lie is to be told, whether to a CIA agent, the parent of a teenager, or Bob Woodward and Carl Bernstein, liars often rehearse their story, which usually is spun from—logically—start to finish. A fun trick? If you think you're hearing a tall tale, ask to hear the story backwards: "So when you just happened to see the car in the ditch—what happened before that again?" and watch the liar squirm.

Way too much linguistic convolution or overcompensation. Does your suspected liar use a hundred words when ten would do? Or use formal language with many clauses? For example, compare these two statements: "In light of the given situation, it can categorically be stated that I have never, and would never, remove your lunch from the shared office refrigerator." Contrast that with "I didn't eat your lunch."

A truth-teller names names, while a liar uses impersonal phrases or pronouns; for example, "that woman" rather than "Miss Lewinsky." In addition, liars avoid saying "I." For example, instead of "I didn't skim off the register," you'll hear, "No one here would ever skim off the register."

Liars work really hard to come across as truthful. They smile at all the right moments and say all the right things. But the result often appears contrived and fake, which it is. If you feel like you're being sold a bag of goods, you probably are. In short, ⓑ a bright toothy smile probably means a shark.

**Identify to what all "cues" refer in the passage. Then explain the meaning of the underlined words in ⓑ.**

________________________________________

________________________________________

________________________________________

03

**03** **Read the excerpt from a play and follow the directions.** [4 points]

| | |
|---|---|
| THE NOBLEMAN | Now this is what I call workmanship. There is nothing on earth more exquisite than a bonny* book, with well-placed columns of rich black writing in beautiful borders, and illuminated pictures cunningly inset. But nowadays, instead of looking at books, people read them. A book might as well be one of those orders for bacon and bran* that you are scribbling. |
| THE CHAPLAIN | I must say, my lord, you take our situation very coolly. Very coolly indeed. |
| THE NOBLEMAN | (*supercilious*) What is the matter? |
| THE CHAPLAIN | The matter, my lord, is that we English have been defeated. |
| THE NOBLEMAN | That happens, you know. It is only in history books and ballads that the enemy is always defeated. |
| THE CHAPLAIN | But we are being defeated over and over again. First, Orleans— |
| THE NOBLEMAN | (*poohpoohing*) Oh, Orleans! |
| THE CHAPLAIN | I know what you are going to say, my lord: that was a clear case of witchcraft and sorcery. But we are still being defeated. (*He throws down his pen, almost in tears.*) I feel it, my lord: I feel it very deeply. I cannot bear to see my countrymen defeated by a parcel of foreigners. |
| THE NOBLEMAN | Oh! you are an Englishman, are you? |
| THE CHAPLAIN | Certainly not, my lord: I am a gentleman. Still, like your lordship, I was born in England; and it makes a difference. |

** bonny: pretty*

** bran: useless outer skin of grain*

Explain the outcome of the Orleans battle as can be inferred from the excerpt above. Next, what does the Nobleman prefer to do with books?

**04** **Read the poem and follow the directions.** [4 points]

You may write me down in history
With your bitter, twisted lies,
You may trod me in the very dirt
But still, like dust, I'll rise.

Does my sassiness* upset you?
Why are you beset with gloom?
'Cause I walk like I've got oil wells
Pumping in my living room.

Just like moons and like suns,
With the certainty of tides,
Just like hopes springing high,
Still I'll rise.

Did you want to see me broken?
Bowed head and lowered eyes?
Shoulders falling down like teardrops,
Weakened by my soulful cries?

You may shoot me with your words,
You may cut me with your eyes,
You may kill me with your hatefulness,
But still, like air, I'll rise.

Does my sexiness upset you?
Does it come as a surprise
That I dance like I've got diamonds
At the meeting of my thighs?

Out of the huts of history's shame
I rise
Up from a past that's rooted in pain
I rise
I'm a black ocean, leaping and wide,
Welling and swelling I bear in the tide.

Leaving behind nights of terror and fear
I rise
Into a daybreak that's wondrously clear
I rise
Bringing the gifts that my ancestors gave,
I am the dream and the hope of the slave.
I rise
I rise
I rise.

** sassiness: the state of being impudently self-confident*

**Who is the "You" in the poem? Second, explain why the speaker states "I rise" repeatedly through the poem.**

**05** **Read the excerpt from a novel and follow the directions.** [4 points]

So there you have all of it that's important. Or at least you almost have it. I'm an invisible man and it placed me in a hole—or showed me the hole I was in, and I reluctantly accepted the fact. What else could I have done? Once you get used to it, reality is as irresistible as a club*, and I was clubbed into the cellar before I caught the hint. Perhaps that's the way it had to be; I don't know. Nor do I know whether accepting the lesson has placed me in the rear or in the avant-garde. That, perhaps, is a lesson for history.

Let me be honest with you. In fact being honest is a feat* which, by the way, I find of the utmost difficulty. When one is invisible, he finds such problems as good and evil, honesty and dishonesty, of such shifting shapes that he confuses one with the other, depending upon who happens to be looking through him at the time. Well, now I've been trying to look through myself, and there's a risk in it. I was never more hated than when I tried to be __________. No one was satisfied—not even I. On the other hand, I've never been more loved and appreciated than when I tried to "justify" and affirm someone's mistaken beliefs; or when I've tried to give my friends the incorrect, deceitful answers they wished to hear. In my presence they could talk and agree with themselves, the world was nailed down*, and they loved it. They received a feeling of security.

But here was the rub*: Too often, in order to justify them, I had to take myself by the throat and choke myself until my eyes bulged and my tongue hung out and wagged like the door of an empty house in a high wind. Oh, yes, it made them happy and it made me sick. So I became ill of affirmation, of saying "yes" against the nay-saying of my stomach—not to mention my brain.

** club: hamme* ** feat: achievement*
** nail down: fix or fasten* ** the rub: difficulty*

**Fill in the blank with the ONE most appropriate word from the passage. Second, describe what the disease of affirmation is.**

---

# 53회 실전모의고사

모범답안 p.104

**01** **Read the excerpt from a novel passage and follow the directions.** [2 points]

Young Goodman Brown came forth, at sunset, into the street of Salem village, but put his head back, after crossing the threshold, to exchange a parting kiss with his young wife. And Faith, as the wife was aptly named, thrust her own pretty head into the street, letting the wind play with the pink ribbons of her cap, while she called to Goodman Brown.

"Dearest heart," whispered she, softly and rather sadly, when her lips were close to his ear, "pr'y thee, put off your journey until sunrise, and sleep in your own bed to-night. A lone woman is troubled with such dreams and such thoughts, that she's afeard of herself, sometimes. Pray, tarry with me this night, dear husband, of all nights in the year!"

"My love and my Faith," replied young Goodman Brown, "of all nights in the year, this one night must I tarry away from thee. My journey, as thou callest it, forth and back again, must needs be done 'twixt now and sunrise. What, my sweet, pretty wife, cost thou doubt me already, and we but three months married!"

"Then, God bless you!" said Faith, with the pink ribbons, "and may you find all well, when you come back."

"Amen!" cried Goodman Brown.

So they parted; and the young man pursued his way, until, being about to turn the corner by the meeting-house, he looked back, and saw the head of Faith still peeping after him, with a melancholy air, in spite of her pink ribbons. [···*deleted*]

Goodman Brown passed on through the forest, where no church had ever been gathered, nor solitary Christian prayed. He caught hold of a tree, for support, being ready to sink down on the ground, faint and overburdened with the heavy sickness of his heart. He looked up to the sky, doubting whether there really was a Heaven above him. "With Heaven above, and Faith below, I will yet stand firm against the devil!" cried Goodman Brown. [···*deleted*]

The next moment, there was one voice, of a young woman, uttering lamentations, yet with an uncertain sorrow, and entreating for some favor, which, perhaps, it would grieve her to obtain. And all the unseen multitude, both saints and sinners, seemed to encourage her onward.

"Faith!" shouted Goodman Brown, in a voice of agony and desperation; and the echoes of the forest mocked him, crying—"Faith! Faith!" as if bewildered wretches were seeking her, all through the wilderness.

The cry of grief, rage, and terror, was yet piercing the night, when the unhappy husband held his breath for a response. There was a scream, drowned immediately in a louder murmur of voices, fading into far-off laughter, as the dark cloud swept away, leaving the clear and silent sky above Goodman Brown. But something fluttered lightly down through the air, and caught on the branch of a tree. The young man seized it, and beheld a pink ribbon.

"My Faith is gone!" cried he, after one stupefied moment. "There is no good on earth."

**Below is an analysis of the excerpt above. Fill in each blank ⓐ and ⓑ with appropriate words.**

| Setting | nearby the protagonist's house and in a forest |
|---|---|
| Characters | a husband and a wife |
| Point of view | ____ⓐ____ limited omniscient narration |
| Symbol | ____ⓑ____ symbolize(s) Faith's purity. |

## 02 Read the essay and follow the directions. [2 points]

> Our age is retrospective. It builds the sepulchres of the fathers. It writes biographies, histories, and criticism. The foregoing generations beheld God and nature face to face; we, through their eyes. Why should not we also enjoy an original relation to the universe? Why should not we have a poetry and philosophy of insight and not of tradition, and a religion by revelation to us, and not the history of theirs? Embosomed for a season in nature, whose floods of life stream around and through us, and invite us by the powers they supply, to action proportioned to nature, why should we grope among the dry bones of the past, or put the living generation into masquerade out of its faded wardrobe? The sun shines today also. There is more wool and flax in the fields. There are new lands, new men, new thoughts. Let us demand our own works and laws and worship.
>
> Undoubtedly we have no questions to ask which are unanswerable. We must trust the perfection of the creation so far as to believe that whatever curiosity the order of things has awakened in our minds, the order of things can satisfy. Every man's condition is a solution in hieroglyphic to those inquiries he would put.

**Complete the idea the essayist is conveying by filling in the blank with ONE word from the essay.**

> All our questions about the order of the universe—about the relationships between God, man, and nature—should be answered by our own experience, not by the knowledge and traditions of the ___________.

## 03 Read the poem and follow the directions. [4 points]

She is as in a field a silken tent
At midday when the sunny summer breeze
Has dried the dew and all its ropes relent,
So that in guys* it gently sways at ease,
And its supporting central <u>cedar pole</u>,
That is its pinnacle to heavenward
And signifies the sureness of the soul,
Seems to owe naught to any single cord,
But strictly held by none, is loosely bound
By countless silken ties of love and thought
To every thing on earth the compass round,
And only by one's going slightly taut
In the capriciousness of summer air
Is of the slightest bondage made aware.

** guy: rope to control a spar on a sailboat*

**First, explain the extended metaphor of the poem by focusing on the underlined "cedar pole". Second, describe the specific structure of the poem by mentioning the rhythm and rhyme scheme.**

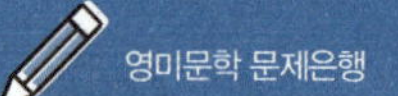



# 54회 실전모의고사

모범답안 p.105

**01** **Read the passage and follow the directions.** [2 points]

I stand here ironing, and what you asked me moves tormented back and forth with the iron. "I wish you would manage the time to come in and talk with me about your daughter. I'm sure you can help me understand her. She's a youngster who needs help and whom I'm deeply interested in helping."

"Who needs help,"—Even if I came, what good would it do? You think because I am her mother I have a key, or that in some way you could use me as a key? She has lived for nineteen years. There is all that life that has happened outside of me, beyond me.

And when is there time to remember, to sift, to weigh, to estimate, to total? I will start and there will be an interruption and I will have to gather it all together again. Or I will become engulfed with all I did or did not do, with what should have been and what cannot be helped.

She was a beautiful baby. The first and only one of our five that was beautiful at birth. You do not guess how new and uneasy her tenancy in her now-loveliness. You did not know her all those years she was thought homely, or see her poring over her baby pictures, making me tell her over and over how beautiful she had been—and would be, I would tell her—and was now, to the seeing eye. But the seeing eyes were few or nonexistent. Including mine.

I nursed her. They feel that's important nowadays. I nursed all the children, but with her, with all the fierce rigidity of first motherhood, I did like the books then said. Though her cries battered me to trembling and my breasts ached with swollenness. I waited till the clock decreed.

**Below is an analysis of the excerpt above. Fill in the blank with ONE word from the excerpt.**

| | |
|---|---|
| Setting | inside the protagonist's house |
| Conflict | The narrator is struggling with herself. She is trying to get to grips with what she sees as her failure as a mother. |
| Point of view | the first-person narration |
| Symbol | ______________ represents the duties and responsibilities as a woman; and the oppressive world of domestic tasks. |

## 02 Read the excerpt from a short story and follow the directions. [4 points]

Sometimes I speculate on the exact nature of the conspiracy which brought me here. At times I believe it was instigated by my wife of former days, whose name was… I am only pretending to forget. I know her name very well, as well as I know the name of my former motor oil (Quaker State) or my old Army serial number (US 54109268). Her name was Brenda, and the conversation I recall best, the one which makes me suspicious now, took place on the day we parted. "You have the soul of a whore," I said on that occasion, stating nothing less than literal, unvarnished fact. "You," she replied, "are a pimp, a poop, and a child. I am leaving you forever and I trust that without me you will perish of your own inadequacies. Which are considerable." [*…deleted*]

It may be that on my first trip through the schools I was too much under the impression that what the authorities (who decides?) had ordained for me was right and proper, that I confused authority with life itself. My path was not particularly of my own choosing. My career stretched out in front of me like a paper chase, and my role was to pick up the clues. When I got out of school, the first time, I felt that this estimate was substantially correct, and eagerly entered the hunt. I found clues abundant: diplomas, membership cards, campaign buttons, a marriage license, insurance forms, discharge papers, tax returns, Certificates of Merit. They seemed to prove, at the very least, that I was in the running. [*…deleted*]

I misread a clue. Do not misunderstand me: it was a tragedy only from the point of view of the authorities. I conceived that it was my duty to obtain satisfaction for the injured, for this elderly lady (not even one of our policyholders, but a claimant against Big Ben Transfer & Storage, Inc.) from the company. The settlement was $165,000; the claim, I still believe, was just. But without my encouragement Mrs. Bichek would never have had the self-love to prize her injury so highly. The company paid, but its faith in me, in my efficacy in the role, was broken. Henry Goodykind, the district manager, expressed this thought in a few not altogether unsympathetic words, and told me at the same time that I was to have a new role. The next thing I knew I was here, at Horace Greeley Elementary, under the lubricious eye of Miss Mandible. [*…deleted*]

We read signs as promises. I myself, in my former existence, read the company motto ("Here to Help in Time of Need") as a description of the duty of the adjuster, drastically mislocating the company's deepest concerns. I believed that because I had obtained a wife who was made up of wife-signs (faithfulness, charm, softness etc.) I had found love. Brenda, reading the same signs. All of us, Miss Mandible, Sue Ann, myself, Brenda, Mr. Goodykind, still believe that the American flag betokens a kind of general righteousness.

But I say, looking about me in this incubator of future citizens, that signs are signs, and that some of them are lies. This is the great discovery of my time here.

**In the excerpt above, the narrator's musing on the unreliability of signs underscores the idea that life and society promise things that are often unattainable. Identify all the examples of the "unreliability of signs" in the excerpt.**

## 03 Read the poem and follow the directions. [4 points]

This ⓐ God of ours, the Great Geometer,
Does something for us here, where He hath put
(if you want to put it that way) things in shape,
Compressing the little lambs into orderly cubes,
Making the roast a decent cylinder,
Fairing the tin ellipsoid of a ham,
Getting the luncheon meat anonymous
In squares and oblongs with all the edges bevelled*
Or rounded (streamlined, maybe, for greater speed).

ⓑ Praise Him, He hath conferred aesthetic distance
Upon our appetites, and on the bloody
Mess of our birthright, our unseemly need,
Imposed significant form. Through Him the brutes
Enter the pure Euclidean kingdom of number,
Free of their bulging and blood-swollen lives
They come to us holy, in cellophane
Transparencies*, in the mystical body,

That we may look unflinchingly on death
As the greatest good, like a philosopher should.

** bevelled: tilted*

** cellophane transparencies: transparent cellophane wrapping*

The title of the poem is "Grace to Be Said at the Supermarket." The terms such as "cubes," "cylinder," "ellipsoid," "squares, and oblongs" are mathematical or geometrical terms. The speaker in the poem deals with how meat is processed and presented to us in a form that looks nothing remotely like the animal from which it came. First, who is ⓐ "God of ours, the Great Geometer"? What kind of figure of speech is used here? Second, write down the thematic idea of the poem focusing on the irony used in the underlined part ⓑ.

# 55회 실전모의고사

모범답안 p.106

**01** **Read the poem and follow the directions.** [2 points]

The sun is blazing and the sky is blue.
Umbrellas clothe the beach in every hue.
Naked, you trot across the avenue.

Oh, never have I seen a dog so bare!
Naked and pink, without a single hair…
Startled, the passersby draw back and stare.

Of course they're mortally afraid of rabies.
You are not mad; you have a case of scabies
but look intelligent. Where are your babies?

(A nursing mother, by those hanging teats.)
In what slum have you hidden them, poor bitch,
while you go begging, living by your wits?

Didn't you know? It's been in all the papers,
to solve this problem, how they deal with beggars?
They take and throw them in the tidal rivers.

Yes, idiots, paralytics, parasites
go bobbing in the ebbing sewage, nights
out in the suburbs, where there are no lights.

If they do this to anyone who begs,
drugged, drunk, or sober, with or without legs,
what would they do to sick, four-legged dogs?

In the cafés and on the sidewalk corners
the joke is going round that all the beggars
who can afford them now wear life preservers.

**Complete the statement by filling in the blank below with ONE word from the poem above.**

The pink dog represents ________________.

## 02 Read the passage and follow the directions. [2 points]

I will wait for her in the yard that Maggie and I made so clean and wavy yesterday afternoon.

Maggie will be nervous until after her sister goes: she will stand hopelessly in corners, homely and ashamed of the burn scars down her arms and legs, eying her sister with a mixture of envy and awe. She thinks her sister has held life always in the palm of one hand, that "no" is a word the world never learned to say to her.

Have you ever seen a lame animal, perhaps a dog run over by some careless person rich enough to own a car, sidle up to someone who is ignorant enough to be kind to him? That is the way my Maggie walks. She has been like this, chin on chest, eyes on ground, feet in shuffle, ever since the fire that burned the other house to the ground.

Dee is lighter than Maggie, with nicer hair and a fuller figure. She's a woman now, though sometimes I forget. How long ago was it that the other house burned? Ten, twelve years? Sometimes I can still hear the flames and feel Maggie's arms sticking to me, her hair smoking and her dress falling off her in little black papery flakes. Her eyes seemed stretched open, blazed open by the flames reflected in them. And Dee. I see her standing off under the sweet gum tree she used to dig gum out of; a look of concentration on her face as she watched the last dingy gray board of the house fall in toward the red-hot brick chimney. Why don't you do a dance around the ashes? I'd wanted to ask her. She had hated the house that much.

I used to think she hated Maggie, too. But that was before we raised money, the church and me, to send her to Augusta to school. She used to read to us without pity; forcing words, lies, other folks' habits, whole lives upon us two, sitting trapped and ignorant underneath her voice. She washed us in a river of make-believe, burned us with a lot of knowledge we didn't necessarily need to know. Pressed us to her with the serious way she read, to shove us away at just the moment, like dimwits, we seemed about to understand.

**Complete the commentary by filling in blank ⓐ with ONE or TWO word(s) and blank ⓑ with ONE word from the passage.**

Commentary

The story above is told by Mama in the ____ⓐ____ point of view. Through this choice of point of view, the reader can see the discontent Mama has towards her daughter, Dee.

In the underlined part above, Mama tells the reader about Dee's formative years, when she would return home from boarding school. Like the fire that destroyed the family's first house, ____ⓑ____ is portrayed as a volatile and unwelcome presence that threatens the home's simplicity and stability.

## 03 Read the excerpt from a play and follow the directions. [2 points]

*A country road. A tree.*

*Evening.*

*Estragon, sitting on a low mound, is trying to take off his boot. He pulls at it with both hands, panting. He gives up, exhausted, rests, tries again. As before.*

*Enter Vladimir.*

ESTRAGON (*giving up again*) Nothing to be done.

VLADIMIR (*advancing with short, stiff strides, legs wide apart*) I'm beginning to come round to that opinion. All my life I've tried to put it from me, saying Vladimir, be reasonable, you haven't yet tried everything. And I resumed the struggle. (*He broods, musing on the struggle. Turning to Estragon.*) So there you are again.

ESTRAGON Am I?

VLADIMIR I'm glad to see you back. I thought you were gone forever.

ESTRAGON Me too.

VLADIMIR Together again at last! We'll have to celebrate this. But how? (*He reflects.*) Get up till I embrace you.

ESTRAGON (*irritably*) Not now, not now.

VLADIMIR (*hurt, coldly*) May one inquire where His Highness spent the night?

ESTRAGON In a ditch.

VLADIMIR (*admiringly*) A ditch! Where?

ESTRAGON (*without gesture*) Over there.

VLADIMIR And they didn't beat you?

ESTRAGON Beat me? Certainly they beat me.

VLADIMIR The same lot as usual?

ESTRAGON The same? I don't know.

VLADIMIR When I think of it··· all these years··· but for me··· where would you be··· (*Decisively*) You'd be nothing more than a little heap of bones at the present minute, no doubt about it.

ESTRAGON And what of it?

| | |
|---|---|
| VLADIMIR | (*gloomily*) It's too much for one man. (*Pause. Cheerfully.*) On the other hand what's the good of losing heart now, that's what I say. We should have thought of it a million years ago, in the nineties. |
| ESTRAGON | Ah stop blathering and help me off with this bloody thing. |
| VLADIMIR | Hand in hand from the top of the Eiffel Tower, among the first. We were respectable in those days. Now it's too late. They wouldn't even let us up. (*Estragon tears at his boot.*) What are you doing? |
| ESTRAGON | Taking off my boot. Did that never happen to you? |
| VLADIMIR | Boots must be taken off every day, I'm tired telling you that. Why don't you listen to me? |
| ESTRAGON | (*feebly*) Help me! |
| VLADIMIR | It hurts? |
| ESTRAGON | (*angrily*) Hurts! He wants to know if it hurts! |
| VLADIMIR | (*angrily*) No one ever suffers but you. I don't count. I'd like to hear what you'd say if you had what I have. |
| ESTRAGON | It hurts? |
| VLADIMIR | (*angrily*) Hurts! He wants to know if it hurts! |

**Complete the commentary by filling in blank ⓐ with ONE word from the excerpt and blank ⓑ with TWO words. If necessary, change the word form in blank ⓐ.**

Commentary

The language in the excerpt goes nowhere. The two main characters misunderstand each other, often responding to a statement with a ridiculous comment. Although the two characters have known each other for years, they misunderstand each other. For instance, tugging at his boot, Estragon says in frustration, "Nothing to be done." Vladimir, interpreting the statement as a view about life in general, alludes he is beginning to accept that point of view but has decided to keep ___ⓐ___ anyway. Then he tells Estragon he is glad to meet him again even though they had been together the day before. On the other hand, in the excerpt above, the ___ⓑ___ adds to the emotions in the lines.

03

**04** **Read the excerpt from a short story and follow the directions.** [4 points]

The store in which the Justice of the Peace's court was sitting smelled of cheese. The boy, crouched on his nail keg at the back of the crowded room, knew he smelled cheese, and more: from where he sat he could see the ranked shelves close-packed with the solid, squat, dynamic shapes of tin cans whose labels his stomach read, not from the lettering which meant nothing to his mind but from the scarlet devils and the silver curve of fish—this, the cheese which he knew he smelled and the hermetic* meat which his intestines believed he smelled coming in intermittent gusts momentary and brief between the other constant one, the smell and sense just a little of fear because mostly of despair and grief, the old fierce pull of blood. He could not see the table where the Justice sat and before which his father and his father's enemy (*our enemy* he thought in that despair; *ourn! mine and hisn both! He's my father!*) stood, but he could hear them, the two of them that is, because his father had said no word yet:

"But what proof have you, Mr. Harris?"

"I told you. The hog got into my corn. I caught it up and sent it back to him. He had no fence that would hold it. I told him so, warned him. The next time I put the hog in my pen. When he came to get it I gave him enough wire to patch up his pen. The next time I put the hog up and kept it. I rode down to his house and saw the wire I gave him still rolled on to the spool in his yard. I told him he could have the hog when he paid me a dollar pound* fee. That evening a nigger came with the dollar and got the hog. He was a strange nigger. He said, 'He say to tell you wood and hay kin burn.' I said, 'What?' 'That whut he say to tell you,' the nigger said. 'Wood and hay kin burn.*' That night my barn burned. I got the stock out but I lost the barn."

"Where is the nigger? Have you got him?"

"He was a strange nigger, I tell you. I don't know what became of him."

"But that's not proof. Don't you see that's not proof?"

"Get that boy up here. He knows."

The boy felt no floor under his bare feet; he seemed to walk beneath the palpable weight of the grim turning faces. His father, stiff in his black Sunday coat donned not for the trial but for the moving, did not even look at him. *He aims for me to lie,* he thought, again with that frantic grief and despair. *And I will have to do hit**.

** hermetic: canned*
** pound: an enclosure in which stray animals are kept*
** wood and hay kin burn: wood and hay can burn*
** hit: it*

**In this excerpt, the setting is in the courthouse. First, explain why the boy and his father are in the courthouse. Second, the writer utilizes olfactory images in order to deal with the conflicts of the protagonist. Identify the two kinds of smells in the excerpt and explain the meanings of those two smells as they are intended by the narrator.**

# 56회 실전모의고사

모범답안 p.109

**01** **Read the excerpt from a poem and follow the directions.** [2 points]

Curiosity may have killed the cat; more likely
the cat was just unlucky, or else curious
to see what death was like, having no cause
to go on licking paws, or fathering
litter on litter of kittens, predictably.

Nevertheless, to be curious
is dangerous enough. To distrust
what is always said, what seems
to ask odd questions, interfere in dreams,
leave home, smell rats, have hunches
do not endear cats to those doggy circles
where well-smelt baskets, suitable wives, good lunches
are the order of things, and where prevails
much wagging of incurious heads and tails.

Face it. Curiosity
will not cause us to die—
only lack of it will.
Never to want to see
the other side of the hill
or that improbable country
where living is an idyll
(although a probable hell)
would kill us all.
Only the curious
have, if they live, a tale
worth telling at all.

**Complete the thematic idea of the poem by filling in the blank with ONE word from the poem.**

Though curiosity leads to suffering and discomfort, one cannot really ________ without it.

03

## 02 Read the excerpt from a short story and follow the directions. [2 points]

I am sitting over coffee and cigarettes at my friend Rita's and I am telling her about it. Here is what I tell her.

It is late of a slow Wednesday when Herb seats the fat man at my station.

This fat man is the fattest person I have ever seen, though he is neat-appearing and well dressed enough. [···*deleted*]

I put the Special food in front of the fat man and a big bowl of vanilla ice cream with chocolate syrup to the side.

Thank you, he says.

You are very welcome, I say—and a feeling comes over me.

Believe it or not, he says, we have not always eaten like this.

Me, I eat and I eat and I can't gain, I say. I'd like to gain, I say.

No, he says. If we had our choice, no. But there is no choice.

Then he picks up his spoon and eats.

What else? Rita says, lighting one of my cigarettes and pulling her chair closer to the table. This story's getting interesting now, Rita says.

That's it. Nothing else. He eats his desserts, and then he leaves and then we go home, Rudy and me.

Some fatty, Rudy says, stretching like he does when he's tired. Then he laughs and goes back to watching the TV.

I pour the water in the pot, arrange the cups, the sugar bowl, carton of half and half, and take the tray in to Rudy. Rudy says, I knew a fat guy once, a couple of fat guys, really fat guys, when I was a kid. They were tubbies, my God. I don't remember their names. Fat, that's the only name this one kid had. We called him Fat, the kid who lived next door to me. He was a neighbor. The other kid came along later. His name was Wobbly. Everybody called him Wobbly except the teachers. Wobbly and Fat. Wish I had their picture, Rudy says.

I can't think of anything to say, so we drink our tea and pretty soon I get up to go to bed. Rudy gets up too, turns off the TV, locks the front door, and begins his unbuttoning.

I get into bed and move clear over to the edge and lie there on my stomach. But right away, as soon as he turns off the light and gets into bed, Rudy begins. I turn on my back and relax some, though it is against my will. But here is the thing. When he gets on me, I suddenly feel I am fat. I feel I am terrifically fat, so fat that Rudy is a tiny thing and hardly there at all.

My life is going to change. I feel it.

**Complete the commentary by filling in the blank with ONE word from the story.**

Commentary

In the story above, the narrator, who works as a waitress in a restaurant, is telling her friend Rita about a customer who came into her diner one day. Whereas the narrator's boyfriend, Rudy, makes crude jokes at the customer's expense and those of other ___________ kids he used to tease, the waitress empathizes with the customer and tries to understand the significance of their encounter.

## 03 Read the excerpt from a play and follow the directions. [2 points]

MARY (*turns smilingly to them, in a merry tone that is a bit forced*) I've been teasing your father about his snoring. (*To James Tyrone*) I'll leave it to the boys, James. They must have heard you. No, not you, Jamie. I could hear you down the hall almost as bad as your father. You're like him. As soon as your head touches the pillow you're off and ten foghorns couldn't wake you. (*She stops abruptly, catching Jamie's eyes regarding her with an uneasy, probing look. Her smile vanishes and her manner becomes self-conscious.*) Why are you staring, Jamie? (*Her hands flutter up to her hair*) Is my hair coming down? It's hard for me to do it up properly now. My eyes are getting so bad and I never can find my glasses.

JAMIE (*looks away guiltily*) Your hair's all right, Mama. I was only thinking how well you look.

TYRONE (*heartily*) Just what I've been telling her, Jamie. She's so fat and sassy, there'll soon be no holding her.

EDMUND Yes, you certainly look grand, Mama. (*She is reassured and smiles at him lovingly. He winks with a kidding grin.*) I'll back you up about Papa's snoring. Gosh, what a racket!

JAMIE I heard him, too. (*He quotes, putting on a ham-actor manner.*) "The Moor, I know his trumpet." (*His mother and brother laugh.*)

TYRONE (*scathingly*) If it takes my snoring to make you remember Shakespeare instead of the dope sheet on the ponies, I hope I'll keep on with it.

MARY Now, James! You mustn't be so touchy. (*Jamie shrugs his shoulders and sits down in the chair on her right.*)

EDMUND (*irritably*) Yes, for Pete's sake, Papa! The first thing after breakfast! Give it a rest, can't you? (*He slumps down in the chair at left of table next to his brother. His father ignores him.*)

| | |
|---|---|
| MARY | (*reprovingly*) Your father wasn't finding fault with you. You don't have to always take Jamie's part. You'd think you were the one ten years older. |
| JAMIE | (*boredly*) What's all the fuss about? Let's forget it. |
| TYRONE | (*contemptuously*) Yes, forget! Forget everything and face nothing! It's a convenient philosophy if you've no ambition in life except to— |
| MARY | James, do be quiet. (*She puts an arm around his shoulder—coaxingly.*) You must have gotten out of the wrong side of the bed this morning. (*To the boys, changing the subject*) What were you two grinning about like Cheshire cats when you came in? What was the joke? |

**Fill in each blank with appropriate word(s) from the excerpt above.**

| | |
|---|---|
| Setting | in a house |
| Stage directions | add to the emotions in the lines |
| Character relations | Mary is the mother of Jamie and Edmund. Mary consistently demonstrates her mastery of the maternal art of peacemaking. |
| Conflict | Tyrone does not take kindly to Jamie's remark and ___ⓐ___, hurt on behalf of Jamie, overreacts. |
| Literary device | Mary's concern for her ___ⓑ___ is the symbolic action of her return to her drug addiction. |

**04** **Read the excerpt from a novel and follow the directions.** [4 points]

The owners of the land came onto the land, or more often a spokesman for the owners came. They came in closed cars, and they felt the dry earth with their fingers, and sometimes they drove big earth augers into the ground for soil tests. The tenants, from their sun-beaten dooryards, watched uneasily when the closed cars drove along the fields. And at last the owner men drove into the dooryards and sat in their cars to talk out of the windows. The tenant men stood beside the cars for a while, and then squatted on their hams and found sticks with which to mark the dust.

In the open doors the women stood looking out, and behind them the children corn-headed children, with wide eyes, one bare foot on top of the other bare foot, and the toes working. The women and the children watched their men talking to the owner men. They were silent.

Some of the owner men were kind because they hated what they had to do, and some of them were angry because they hated to be cruel, and some of them were cold because they had long ago found that one could not be an owner unless one were cold. And all of them were caught in something larger than themselves. Some of them hated the mathematics that drove them, and some were afraid, and some worshiped the mathematics because it provided a refuge from thought and from feeling. If a bank or a finance company owned the land, the owner man said, The Bank or the Company—needs—wants—insists—must have—as though the Bank or the Company were a monster, with thought and feeling, which had ensnared them. These last would take no responsibility for the banks or the companies because they were men and slaves, while the banks were machines and masters all at the same time. The owner men went on leading to their point: You know the land's getting poorer. You know what cotton does to the land; robs it, sucks all the blood out of it.

The squatters nodded they knew, God knew. If they could only rotate the crops they might pump blood back into the land. Well, it's too late. You see, a bank or a company doesn't breathe air, don't eat side-meat. They breathe profits. You all have to leave from the land now.

In the above excerpt, explain what can be inferred about the gender dynamics in the story's setting. Use direct citation to support your point. Additionally, explain the figurative meaning intended in the underlined part.

# 57회 실전모의고사

모범답안 p.111

**01 Read a short story and follow the directions.** [2 points]

Up to this evening, which should have been the most delightful of all, everything had been delightful. "Delightful" was Gopal's new word. "London is delightful," he wrote home. "The college is delightful, Professor William Morgan is delightful and so is Mrs. Morgan and the little Morgans, but perhaps," he added with pain, for he had to admit that the Morgan children were rough and spoiled, "perhaps not so delightful if you see them for a very long time··· The hostel is delightful··· I find my work delightful." He had planned to write home that Paris was delightful. "We went to a famous French restaurant in the rue Perpignan*," he had meant to write, "it is called the Chez Perpignan. It is de-" Now tears made his dark eyes bright; he could not write that; it was not delightful at all.

Gopal's family lived in Bengal; they were Brahmini Hindus and his mother kept the household to orthodox ways in spite of all he and his elder brother could do. Now Gopal saw her orthodox food: and flat brass platters of rice, the pile of luchis—flaky, puffed, pale gold biscuits—the vegetable fritters fried crisp, the great bowl of lentil puree, and the small accompanying bowls of relishes—shredded coconut or fried onion or spinach or chilis in tomato sauce or chutney, all to be put on the rice. He saw fruit piled on banana leaves, the bowl of fresh curd, the milk or orange or bel-fruit juice in the silver drinking tumblers; no meat or fish, not even eggs, were eaten in that house. "We shall not take life," said his mother. Gopal looked down the oyster at his plate in the Perpignan and shuddered.

He had come to Europe with shining intentions, eager, anxious to do as the Romans did, as the English, the French, as Romans everywhere. "There will be things you will not be able to stomach," he had been warned; so far he had stomached everything. His elder brother Jai had been before him and had come back utterly accustomed to everything Western dishes. When Jai and his wife Tooni went out to dinner they had western dishes: they ate meat, even beef, but not in their own home. "Not while I live," said his mother.

** Perpignan: a town in South France*

**Below is an analysis of the story above. Fill in each blank with ONE word respectively.**

| ____ⓐ____ | a French restaurant in Perpignan |
|---|---|
| Main character | a young Indian of the Hindu Brahmin caste, who is studying in Western countries |
| Point of view | ____ⓑ____ narration |
| Climax | an inner conflict between the main character's wish to adapt Western culture and the main character who is terrified at his plate |

**02** **Read the passage and follow the directions.** [4 points]

Laugh, and the world laughs with you;
  Weep, and you weep alone;
For the sad old earth must borrow its mirth,
  But has trouble enough of its own.
Sing, and the hills will answer;
  Sigh, it is lost on the air;
The echoes bound to a joyful sound,
  But shrink from voicing care.

Rejoice, and men will seek you;
  Grieve, and they turn and go;
They want full measure of all your pleasure,
  But they do not need your woe.
Be glad, and your friends are many;
  Be sad, and you lose them all,—
There are none to decline your nectared wine,
  But alone you must drink life's gall.

<u>Feast, and your halls are crowded;</u>
  <u>Fast, and the world goes by.</u>
Succeed and give, and it helps you live,
  But no man can help you die.
There is room in the halls of pleasure
  For a large and lordly train,
But one by one we must all file on
  Through the narrow aisles of pain.

This poem reveals a powerful and undeniable reality of human nature. Describe the thematic idea of the poem and explain how the underlined part is related to the thematic idea.

## 03 Read the short story and follow the directions. [4 points]

There was a merchant in Bagdad who sent his servant to market to buy provisions and in a little while the servant came back, white and trembling and said, Master, just now when I was in the market-place I was jostled by a woman in the crowd and when I turned I saw it was Death that jostled me. She looked at me and made a threatening gesture; now, lend me your horse, and I will ride away from this city and avoid my fate. I will go to Samarra and there Death will not find me. The merchant lent him his horse, and the servant mounted it, and he dug his spurs in its flanks and as fast as the horse could gallop he went. Then the merchant went down to the market-place and he saw me standing in the crowd and he came to me and said, Why did you make a threatening gesture to my servant when you saw him this morning? That was not a threatening gesture, I said, it was only a start of surprise. I was astonished to see him in Bagdad, for I had an appointment with him tonight in Samarra.

**Identify the speaker of the story and explain the reason Death was surprised. Also, describe the underlying message of the short story.**

# 58회 실전모의고사

모범답안 p.113

**01 Read the passage and follow the directions.** [2 points]

A miser was able to get hold of all the laughter in the world, and he packed it tightly and locked it up in his house and hid the key.

The trouble was that nobody missed it. He had to tell them what they were missing. Nobody knew what he was talking about. Nobody believed him. Nobody thought that what he was talking about was real. Who could believe that, after all? Would anyone believe it if someone came up and said that they had all the laughter in the world locked up somewhere? Would anyone believe it, even if neither of them laughed?

He tried to describe laughter to them. He showed them how it was done. He showed different ways in which different people could laugh. He told them all the things that made people do it, everything he could remember or invent. People falling down. Filth. People making terrible mistakes. People unable to control themselves. Misfortunes of all kinds. People with something the matter with them. No interest.

He told them that it would be good for their health, and that he would not make it expensive for them. No interest. There were many things about it that he didn't even know, he said. No interest. It had been called divine, he said. No interest.

But the man kept on trying. Because at least at night he could always go home and take out the key and open up some and have a good laugh to himself. But then one night he started to laugh at himself and that made him lonely.

He tried to invite somebody else in to laugh. But it was very hard. He even said he would give the laughter away. At that somebody else laughed. So that person remembered how to laugh. So that person was on his side. They were laughing together. Somebody else was laughing with him. But that meant that somebody else had some of the laugher in the world. So he started making plans to steal it. But the other kept giving it away.

**Below is an analysis of the story above. Fill in each blank with ONE word from the story respectively.**

| | |
|---|---|
| Setting | a surreal area and time |
| Conflict | While his new companion gives away the laughter freely, the miser wants to steal it back. |
| Satire | A valuable thing disappears, but people do not care at all. |
| The moral | the effects of greed on relationships: the miser becomes ___ⓐ___ when he hoards the ___ⓑ___, until he shares by accident. |

## 02 Read the critical essay and follow the directions. [4 points]

Islam was a real provocation in many ways. It lay uneasily close to Christianity, geographically and culturally. It drew on the Judeo-Hellenic traditions, it borrowed creatively from Christianity, it could boast of unrivaled military and political successes. Nor was this all. The Islamic lands sit adjacent to and even on top of the Biblical lands; moreover, the heart of the Islamic domain has always been the region closest to Europe, what has been called the Near Orient or Near East. Arabic and Hebrew are Semitic languages, and together they dispose and redispose of material that is urgently important to Christianity. From the end of the seventh century until the battle of Lepanto in 1571, Islam in either its Arab, Ottoman, or North African and Spanish form dominated or effectively threatened European Christianity. That Islam outstripped and outshone Rome cannot have been absent from the mind of any European past or present.

Islam excepted, the Orient for Europe was until the nineteenth century a domain with a continuous history of unchallenged Western dominance. This is patently true of the British experience in India, the Portuguese experience in the East Indies, China, and Japan, and the French and Italian experiences in various regions of the Orient. There were occasional instances of native intransigence to disturb the idyll, as when in 1638-1639 a group of Japanese Christians threw the Portuguese out of the area; by and large, however, only the Arab and Islamic Orient presented Europe with an unresolved challenge on the political, intellectual, and for a time, economic levels. For much of its history, then, Orientalism carries within it the stamp of a problematic European attitude towards Islam.

**Explain why only Islam was considered as a problematic group to European Christianity and describe the commonality among such countries as India, the East Indies, China, and Japan.**

## 03 Read the passage and follow the directions. [4 points]

Happy the man, whose wish and care
A few paternal acres bound,
Content to breathe his native air,
In his own ground.

Whose herds with milk, whose fields with bread,
Whose flocks supply him with attire,
Whose trees in summer yield him shade,
In winter fire.

Blest, who can unconcernedly find
Hours, days, and years slide soft away,
In health of body, peace of mind,
Quiet by day,

Sound sleep by night; study and ease,
Together mixed; sweet recreation;
And innocence, which most does please,
With meditation.

Thus let me live, unseen, unknown;
Thus unlamented let me die;
Steal from the world, and not a stone
Tell where I lie.

**Describe the main theme of the poem and explain how the second stanza is related to the theme. When you answer, identify all products of the farm in the second stanza.**

# 59회 실전모의고사

모범답안 p.114

**01** **Read the essay and follow the directions.** [2 points]

There is something in the very season of the year that gives a charm to the festivity of Christmas. At other times we derive a great portion of our pleasures from the mere beauties of nature. Our feelings sally forth and dissipate themselves over the sunny landscape, and we live abroad and everywhere. The song of the bird, the murmur of the stream, the breathing fragrance of spring, the soft voluptuousness of summer, the golden pomp of autumn; earth with its mantle of refreshing green, and heaven with its deep delicious blue and its cloudy magnificence, all fill us with mute but exquisite delight, and we revel in the luxury of mere sensation. But in the depth of winter, when nature lies despoiled of every charm, and wrapped in her shroud of sheeted snow, we turn for our gratifications to moral foundations. The dreariness and desolation of the landscape, the short gloomy days and darksome nights, while they circumscribe our wanderings, shut in our feelings also from rambling abroad, and make us more keenly disposed for the pleasures of the social circle. Our thoughts are more concentrated; our friendly sympathies more aroused. We feel more sensibly the charm of each other's society, and are brought more closely together by dependence on each other for enjoyment. Heart calls unto heart; and we draw our pleasures from the deep wells of living kindness, which lie in the quiet recesses of our bosoms; and which, when resorted to, furnish forth the pure element of domestic felicity.

Describe the main idea that the writer is conveying by filling in each blank with ONE word from the essay respectively.

| As opposed to other seasons that draws people's attention to beautiful nature, in ____ⓐ____ people find pleasure in ____ⓑ____ sources, relying on each other. |
|---|

---

## 02 Read the excerpt from a short story and follow the directions. [2 points]

The small locomotive engine, Number 4, came clanking, stumbling down from Selston—with seven full wagons. It appeared round the corner with loud threats of speed, but the colt that it startled from among the gorse*, which still flickered indistinctly in the raw afternoon, outdistanced it at a canter. A woman, walking up the railway line to Underwood, drew back into the hedge, held her basket aside, and watched the footplate of the engine advancing. The trucks thumped heavily past, one by one, with slow inevitable movement, as she stood insignificantly trapped between the jolting black wagons and the hedge. In the open, the smoke from the engine sank and cleaved to the rough grass. The fields were dreary and forsaken, and in the marshy strip that led to the whimsey, a reedy pit-pond, the fowls had already abandoned their run among the alders, to roost in the tarred fowl-house. The pit-bank* loomed up beyond the pond, flames like red sores licking its ashy sides, in the afternoon's stagnant light. The miners were being turned up.

The engine whistled as it came into the wide bay of railway lines beside the colliery, where rows of trucks stood in harbour.

<u>Miners, single, trailing and in groups, passed like shadows diverging home.</u> At the edge of the ribbed level of sidings squat a low cottage, three steps down from the cinder track. A large bony vine clutched at the house, as if to claw down the tiled roof. Beside the path hung dishevelled pink chrysanthemums, like pink cloths hung on bushes. A woman came stooping out of the felt-covered fowl-house, half-way down the garden. She closed and padlocked the door, then drew herself erect, having brushed some bits from her white apron.

** gorse: a dark green bush that grows in Europe*

** pit-bank: In mining, the raised ground upon which the coals are sorted and screened at the surface*

**Complete the commentary below by filling in each blank with appropriate ONE word.**

Commentary

The excerpt describes a mining village at the end of the mine's afternoon shift. The setting is full of an atmosphere of bleakness and despair. Overall, humanity and nature do not harmonize with the its environment. The narrator, in the underlined part, makes use of simile comparing ___ⓐ___ to ___ⓑ___ so as to convey the idea that workers appear insignificant under the regime of ___ⓒ___.

## 03 Read the poem and follow the directions. [4 points]

Still, citizen sparrow, this vulture which you call
Unnatural, let him but lumber again to air
Over the rotten office, let him bear
The carrion ballast up, and at the tall

Tip of the sky lie cruising. Then you'll see
That no more beautiful bird is in heaven's height,
No wider more placid wings, no watchfuller flight;
He shoulders nature there, the frightfully free,

The naked-headed one. Pardon him, ⓐ <u>you</u>
Who dart in the orchard aisles, for it is ⓑ <u>he</u>
Devours death, mocks mutability,
Has heart to make an end, keeps nature new.

Thinking of Noah*, childheart, try to forget
How for so many bedlam* hours his saw
Soured the song of birds with its wheezy gnaw,
And the slam of his hammer all the day beset

The people's ears. Forget that he could bear
To see the towns like coral under the keel,
And the fields so dismal deep. Try rather to feel
How high and weary it was, on the waters where

He rocked his only world, and everyone's.
Forgive ⓒ <u>the hero</u>, you who would have died
Gladly with all you knew; he rode that tide
To Ararat*; all men are Noah's sons.

** Noah: the hero of the Flood, and the father of mankind. He was regarded mad by people before the Flood.*
** bedlam: a great deal of noise and disorder*
** Ararat: a mountain said to be the resting place of Noah's Ark after the Flood according to the Bible*

This poem is a satire of the modern civilized human beings. First, describe the thematic idea of the poem including the symbolic meanings of the "vulture" and the "sparrow" respectively. Second, identify what the underlined ⓐ, ⓑ, and ⓒ refer to respectively.

# 60회 실전모의고사

모범답안 p.115

**01** **After reading the short story <A> and criticism <B>, follow the directions.** [2 points]

A

At last we went out and stood on the lawn and watched the sun go down, and my father said, "If it weren't for art, we'd have vanished from the face of the earth long ago."

What art really is, though, or what human being really is, and what the world really is. I just don't know, that's all.

Standing there, watching the sun go down the sea, my father said, "In every house there ought to be an art table on which, one by one, things are placed, so that everybody in that house might look at the things very carefully, and see them."

"What would you put on a table like that?"

"A leaf. A coin. A button. A stone. A small piece of torn newspaper. An apple. An egg. A pebble. A flower. A dead insect. A shoe."

"Everybody's seen those things."

"Of course. But nobody looks at them, and that's what art is. To look at familiar things as if they had never before been seen. A plain sheet of paper with typing on it. A necktie. A pocketknife. A key. A fork. A cup. A bottle. A bowl. A walnut."

"What about a baseball? A baseball is a beautiful thing."

"It certainly is. You should play something on the table and look at it. The next morning you would take it away, and put something else there—anything, for there is nothing made by nature or by man that doesn't deserve to be looked at particularly."

Now, the sun was gone all the way into the sea. There was a lot of orange light on the water, and in the sky above the water. Legion of Honor Hill grew dark, and my father brought out a cigarette and lighted it and inhaled and then let the smoke out of his nose and mouth, and he said, "Well, boy, there's another day of the wonderful world go forever."

"New day tomorrow, though."

"What do you say we drive to the Embarcadero and look at the ships from all over the world?"

B

The purpose of art is to impart the sensation of things as they are perceived and not as they are known. To achieve the goal, the artist needs to employ the technique of presenting to audiences common things in a strange way. This technique is a central concept in 20th century art and theory, ranging over movements including Dada, postmodernism, epic theatre, and science fiction.

**Fill in the blank ⓐ with ONE word from the story <A>. When you answer, you may find some clue from the criticism <B> and if necessary, you may change the form of the word.**

In the story <A>, the father advises his son to see the things in a(n) ____ⓐ____ way.

**02** **Read the excerpt from a play and follow the directions.** [2 points]

*A basement room. Two beds, flat against the back wall. A serving hatch, closed, between the beds. A door to the kitchen and lavatory, left. A door to a passage, right.*

*BEN is lying on a bed, left, reading a paper. GUS is sitting on a bed, right, tying his shoelaces, with difficulty. Both are dressed in shirts, trousers and braces.*

*Silence.*

*GUS ties his laces, rises, yawns and begins to walk slowly to the door, left. He stops, looks down, and shakes his foot.*

*BEN lowers his paper and watches him. GUS kneels and unties his shoe-lace and slowly takes off the shoe. He looks inside it and brings out a flattened matchbox. He shakes it and examines it. Their eyes meet. BEN rattles his paper and reads. GUS puts the matchbox in his pocket and bends down to put on his shoe. He ties his lace, with difficulty. BEN lowers his paper and watches him. GUS walks to the door. GUS puts the packet in his pocket, bends down, puts on his shoe and tie the lace.*

*He wanders off, left.*

*BEN slams the paper down on the bed and glares after him. He picks up the paper and lies on his back, reading.*

*Silence.*

*A lavatory chain is pulled twice off, left, but the lavatory does not flush.*

*Silence.*

*GUS re-enters, left, and halts at the door, scratching his head.*

*BEN slams down the paper.*

BEN Kaw! (*He picks up the paper.*) What about this? Listen to this! (*He refers to the paper.*) A man of eighty-seven wanted to cross the road. But there was a lot of traffic, see? He couldn't see how he was going to squeeze through. So he crawled under a lorry.

GUS He what?

BEN He crawled under a lorry. A stationary lorry.

GUS No?

BEN The lorry started and ran over him.

GUS Go on!

BEN That's what it says here.

GUS Get away.

**Complete the commentary by filling in each blank with (an) appropriate word(s).**

The setting of the play is a ____ⓐ____. In the play the writer uses repetition as a literary device to convey the absurdity of life. In other words, Ben repeatedly reads a newspaper. Gus laborously tries to ____ⓑ____ repeatedly. Also, the plot structure in a play is divided into five parts. The excerpt above belongs to the part of ____ⓒ____, which introduces all of the main characters in the play.

## 03 Read the poem and follow the directions. [4 points]

Turning and turning in the widening gyre*
The falcon* cannot hear the falconer;
Things fall apart; the centre cannot hold;
Mere anarchy is loosed upon the world,
The blood-dimmed tide is loosed, and everywhere
The ceremony of innocence is drowned;
The best lack all conviction, while the worst
Are full of passionate intensity.

Surely some revelation is at hand;
Surely the Second Coming is at hand.
The Second Coming! Hardly are those words out
When a vast image out of Spiritus* Mundi
Troubles my sight: a waste of desert sand;
<u>A shape with lion body and the head of a man</u>,
A gaze blank and pitiless as the sun,
Is moving its slow thighs, while all about it
Wind shadows of the indignant desert birds.
The darkness drops again but now I know
That twenty centuries of stony sleep
Were vexed to nightmare by a rocking cradle,
And what rough beast, its hour come round at last,
Slouches towards Bethlehem* to be born?

** gyre: a spiral movement or path*
** falcon: hawk*
** Spiritus Mundi: world spirit*
** Bethlehem: birthplace of Jesus Christ*

The poem is divided into two sections. In the first stanza, the poet depicts the conditions present in the world. How does he describe the state of things? Make specific reference to the poem in order to support your answer. Also, what does the underlined "A shape with lion body and the head of a man" (line 14) refer to?

## 04 Read the essay and follow the directions. [4 points]

**Limbo**

My parents' divorce was final. The house had been sold and the day had come to move. Thirty years of the family's life was now crammed into the garage. The two-by-fours that ran the length of the walls were the only uniformity among the clutter of boxes, furniture and memories. All was frozen in limbo* between the life just passed and the one to come. The sunlight pushing its way through the window splattered against a barricade of boxes. Like a fluorescent river, it streamed down the sides and flooded the cracks of the cold, cement floor. I stood in the doorway between the house and garage and wondered if the sunlight would ever again penetrate the memories packed inside those boxes. For an instant, the cardboard boxes appeared as tombstones, monuments to those memories. The furnace in the corner, with its huge tubular fingers reaching out and disappearing into the wall, was unaware of the futility of trying to warm the empty house. The rhythmical whir of its effort hummed the elegy for the memories boxed in front of me. I closed the door, sat down on the step, and listened reverently. The feeling of loss transformed the bad memories into not-so-bad, the not-so-bad memories into good, and committed the good ones to my mind. Still, I felt as vacant as the house inside. A workbench to my right stood disgustingly empty. Not so much as a mail had been left behind. I noticed, for the first time, what a dull, lifeless green it was. Lacking the disarray of tools that used to cover it, now it seemed as out of place as a bathtub in the kitchen. In fact, as I scanned the room, the only things that did seem to belong were the cobwebs in the corners. A group of boxes had been set aside from the others and stacked in front of the workbench. Scrawled like graffiti on the walls of dilapidated buildings were the words "Salvation Army." Those words caught my eyes as effectively as a flashing neon sign. They reeked of irony. I suddenly became aware of the coldness of the garage, but I didn't want to go back inside the house, so I made my way through the boxes to the couch. I cleared a space to lie down and curled up, covering myself with my jacket. I hoped my father would return soon with the truck so we could empty the garage and leave the cryptic silence of parting lives behind.

** limbo: a intermediate place between heaven and hell*

**The narrator of the essay is a woman. First, explain the reason the title of the passage is "Limbo." Second, why are the boxes marked "Salvation Army" ironic? Do NOT copy more than SEVEN consecutive words from the passage.**

# 61회 실전모의고사

모범답안 p.117

**01 Read the excerpt from a short story and follow the directions.** [4 points]

In walks these three girls in nothing but bathing suits.

Lengel comes in from haggling with a truck full of cabbages on the lot and is about to scuttle into that door marked MANAGER behind which he hides all day when the girls touch his eye. Lengel's pretty dreary, teaches Sunday school and the rest, but he doesn't miss that much. He comes over and says, "Girls, this isn't the beach."

Queenie blushes, though maybe it's just a brush of sunburn I was noticing for the first time, now that she was so close. "My mother asked me to pick up a jar of herring snacks." Her voice kind of startled me, the way voices do when you see the people first, coming out so flat and dumb yet kind of tony, too, the way it ticked over "pick up" and "snacks." All of a sudden I slid right down her voice into her living room. Her father and the other men were standing around in ice-cream coats and bow ties and the women were in sandals picking up herring snacks on toothpicks off a big plate and they were all holding drinks the color of water with olives and sprigs of mint in them.

"That's all right," Lengel said. "But this isn't the beach." His repeating this struck me as funny, as if it had just occurred to him, and he had been thinking all these years the A&P* was a great big dune and he was the head lifeguard. He didn't like my smiling—as I say he doesn't miss much—but he concentrates on giving the girls that sad Sunday-school-superintendent stare.

Queenie's blush is no sunburn now. "We weren't doing any shopping. We just came in for the one thing."

"That makes no difference," Lengel tells her, and I could see from the way his eyes went that he hadn't noticed she was wearing a two-piece before. "We want you decently dressed when you come in here."

"We are decent," Queenie says suddenly, her lower lip pushing, getting sore now that she remembers her place, a place from which the crowd that runs the A&P must look pretty crummy. Fancy Herring Snacks flashed in her very blue eyes.

"Girls, I don't want to argue with you. After this come in here with your shoulders covered. It's our policy." He turns his back. That's policy for you. Policy is what the kingpins want. What the others want is juvenile delinquency.

All this while, the customers had been showing up with their carts but, you know, sheep, seeing a scene, they had all bunched up on Stokesie, who shook open a paper bag as gently as peeling a peach.

The girls and the customers, sheep, are in a hurry to get out, so I say "I quit" to Lengel.

"Did you say something, Sammy?"

"I said I quit."

"You'll feel this for the rest of your life," Lengel says, and I know that's true, too.

** A&P: supermarket chain*

**The excerpt describes a distinct battle for power. Identify the person who has the most power in the excerpt and explain the reason. Second, why does the narrator call customers "sheep"? Write your answer by mentioning the difference between "sheep" and the narrator.**

## 02 Read the poem and follow the directions. [4 points]

All the while
I was teaching
in the state of Virginia
I wanted to see
gray fox.
Finally I found him.
He was in the highway.
He was singing
His death song.
I picked him up
And carried him
Into a field
While the cars kept coming.
He showed me
How he could ripple
How he could bleed.
Goodbye I said
To the light of his eye
As the cars went by.
Two mornings later
I found the other.
She was in the highway.
She was singing
Her death song.
I picked her up
And carried her
Into the field
Where she rippled
Half of her gray
Half of her red
While the cars kept coming.
While the cars kept coming.
Gray fox and gray fox.
Red, red, red.

Describe the main theme of the poem and explain how such symbols as "gray fox" and "cars" are related to the theme.

# 62회 실전모의고사

모범답안 p.118

**01** **Read the critical essay written by a novelist and follow the directions.** [2 points]

In the world of daily life, the world which we perforce inhabit, there is much talk about order, particularly from statesmen and politicians. They tend, however, to confuse order with orders, just as they confuse creation with regulations. Order is something evolved from within, not something imposed from without; it is an internal stability, a vital harmony, and in the social and political category, it has never existed except for the convenience of historians. Viewed realistically, the past is really a series of ___ⓐ___ succeeding one another by discoverable laws, no doubt, and certainly marked by an increasing growth of human interference, but disorders all the same. So that what I hope for today is a disorder which will be more favourable to artists than is the present one, and which will provide them with fuller inspirations and better material conditions. It will not last—nothing lasts—but there were some advantageous disorders in the past, and we may do something to accelerate the next one.

We cannot reach social and political ___ⓑ___ for the reason that we continue to make scientific discoveries and to apply them, and thus to destroy the arrangements which were based on more elementary discoveries. If Science would discover rather than apply—if, in other words, men were more interested in knowledge than in power—mankind would be in a far safer position. In that case, the stability statesmen talk about would be a possibility and there could be a new order based on vital harmony. But Science shows no signs of doing this.

**Fill in each blank with ONE word from the passage. If necessary, you may change the form(s) of each word.**

---

03

## 02 Read the excerpt from a novel and follow the directions. [4 points]

With much interest I sat watching him. Savage though he was, and hideously marred about the face—at least to my taste—his countenance yet had a something in it which was by no means disagreeable.

I began to be sensible of strange feelings. I felt a melting in me. No more my splintered heart and maddened hand were turned against the wolfish world. This soothing savage had redeemed it. There he sat, his very indifference speaking a nature in which there lurked no civilized hypocrisies and bland deceits. Wild he was; a very sight of sights to see; yet I began to feel myself mysteriously drawn towards him.

After supper, and another social chat and smoke, we went to our room together. He made me a present of his embalmed head.

I was a good Christian; born and bred in the bosom of the infallible Presbyterian Church. How then could I unite with this wild idolator in worshipping his piece of wood? But what is worship? thought I. Do you suppose now, Ishmael, that the magnanimous God of heaven and earth—pagans and all included—can possibly be jealous of an insignificant bit of black wood? Impossible! But what is worship?—to do the will of God—that is worship. And what is the will of God?—to do to my fellow man what I would have my fellow man to do to me—that is the will of God. Now, Queequeg is my fellow man. And what do I wish that this Queequeg would do to me? Why, unite with me in my particular Presbyterian form of worship. Consequently, I must then unite with him in his; ergo, I must turn idolater. So I kindled the shavings; helped prop up the innocent little idol; offered him burnt biscuit with Queequeg; salaamed before him twice or thrice; kissed his nose; and that done, we undressed and went to bed, at peace with our own consciences and all the world. But we did not go to sleep without some little chat.

In the excerpt above, the narrator understands a central religious truth about Christianity as he interprets it. Explain how he understands the religion.

## 03 Read the poem and follow the directions. [4 points]

At first <u>it</u> will seem tame,
willing to be domesticated.

It will nest
in your pocket
or curl up in a corner
reciting softly to itself
the names of the presidents.

It will delight your friends,
shake hands with men
like a dog and lick
the legs of women.

But like an amoeba
it makes love
in secret
only to itself.

Fold it frequently;
it needs exercise.

Water it every three days
and it will repay you
with displays of affection.

Then one day when you think
you are its master
it will turn its head
as if for a kiss
and bite you gently
on the hand.

There will be no pain
but in thirty seconds
the poison will reach your heart.

The poem consists of eight stanzas. Describe the thematic idea of the poem. When you answer, identify what "it" is, and explain the meaning of the figure of speech used in the third line of the third stanza.

# 63회 실전모의고사

모범답안 p.119

**01** **Read the essay written by a novelist and follow the directions.** [2 points]

Our tragedy today is a general and universal physical fear so long sustained by now that we can even bear it. There are no longer problems of the spirit. There is only the question: When will I be blown up? Because of this, the young man or woman writing today has forgotten the problems of the human heart in conflict with itself which alone can make good writing because only that is worth writing about, worth the agony and the sweat.

He must learn them again. He must teach himself that the basest of all things is to be afraid; and, teaching himself that, forget it forever, leaving no room in his workshop for anything but the old verities and truths of the heart, the old universal truths lacking which any story is ephemeral and doomed—love and honor and pity and pride and compassion and sacrifice. Until he does so, he labors under a curse. He writes not of love but of lust, of defeats in which nobody loses anything of value, of victories without hope and, worst of all, without pity or compassion. His griefs grieve on no universal bones, leaving no scars. He writes not of the heart but of the glands.

Until he relearns these things, he will write as though he stood among and watched the end of man. I decline to accept the end of man. It is easy enough to say that man is immortal simply because he will endure: that when the last dingdong of doom has clanged and faded from the last worthless rock hanging tideless in the last red and dying evening, that even then there will still be one more sound: that of his puny inexhaustible voice, still talking.

I refuse to accept this. I believe that man will not merely endure: he will prevail. He is immortal, not because he alone among creatures has an inexhaustible voice, but because he has a soul, a spirit capable of compassion and sacrifice and endurance.

**Describe the main assertion the writer makes by filling in the blank with TWO words from the passage.**

| The writer is a booster of the ___________. |
|---|

---

## 02 Read the poem and follow the directions. [4 points]

There was a time when meadow, grove, and stream,
The earth, and every common sight,
To me did seem
Apparell'd in celestial light,
The glory and the freshness of a dream.
It is not now as it hath been of yore;—
Turn wheresoe'er I may,
By night or day,
The things which I have seen I now can see no more.

The rainbow comes and goes,
And lovely is the rose;
The moon doth with delight
Look round her when the heavens are bare;
Waters on a starry night
Are beautiful and fair;
The sunshine is a glorious birth;
But yet I know, where'er I go,
That there hath pass'd away a glory from the earth.

**Describe what the speaker laments in the first stanza. Second, for the second stanza, identify the rhyme scheme and summarize the stanza in about 15 words.**

## 03 Read the story and the poem and follow the directions. [4 points]

A

The best thing in the Museum of Natural History was that everything always stayed right where it was. Nobody'd move. You could go there a hundred thousand times, and that Eskimo would still be just finished catching those two fish, the birds would still be on their way south, the deers would still be drinking out of that water hole, with their pretty antlers and their pretty, skinny legs, and that squaw* with the naked bosom would still be weaving that same blanket. Nobody'd be different. The only thing that would be different would be you. Not that you'd be so much older or anything. It wouldn't be that, exactly. You'd just be different, that's all. You'd have an overcoat on this time. Or the kid that was your partner in line the last time had got scarlet fever and you'd have a new partner. Or you'd have a substitute taking the class, instead of Miss Aigletinger.

** squaw: Native American Indian woman or indigenous woman of North America*

B

Heard melodies are sweet, but those unheard
  Are sweeter; therefore, ye soft pipes, play on;
Not to the sensual ear, but, more endear'd,
  Pipe to the spirit ditties of no tone:
Fair youth, beneath the trees, thou canst not leave
  Thy song, nor ever can those trees be bare;
    Bold Lover, never, never canst thou kiss,
Though winning near the goal—yet, do not grieve;
  She cannot fade, though thou hast not thy bliss,
    For ever wilt thou love, and she be fair!

The narrator of the story <A> is seeing Eskimos in the display case in the Museum of Natural History while the speaker of the poem <B> is seeing an urn in a museum. The narrator of <A> likes the location very much and the speaker of the poem admires the picture on the urn. Explain the reason the narrator of <A> likes the museum as well as why the speaker of <B> says that the boy should not feel sad about not catching his lover to give her a kiss.

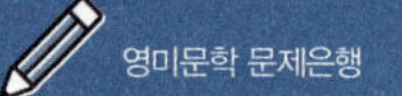


# 64회 실전모의고사

모범답안 p.120

**01 Read the criticism and follow the directions.** [2 points]

Since the 1940s, literary criticism in the United States has divided into two streams: into literary theory, which has been pursued by the New Critics and formalists, by Marxists, by maverick systematizers, by structuralists, and more recently by poststructuralist comparatists; and into generalist criticism, represented by such figures as Trilling and Leavis. The gap between these two tendencies has steadily widened, to the point where we now can see evidence, in reviews of new books, of two distinct approaches. On the one side are theorists who display "expert" knowledge; in the United States they tend to dominate only in the universities (they dominate more widely in France, where literary theory has a public), and they usually promote a favorite doctrine. On the other side are the wide ranging, generalist critics. In their reviews, the theoretical critics have usually gone in for philosophical, historical, aesthetic, and linguistic analysis. The generalists have usually been more concerned with contemporary experience and with values and judgments. In addition, the generalists have been more eclectic in their critical approach and more casual in their reviewing style, producing literary essays accessible to lay people, rather than highly rhetorical or closely argued technical disquisitions. The theoretical critics have filled the academic journals, while the generalists have typically written for the broader interest quarterlies. This split is disturbing because it indicates something is wrong. Theorists' criticism has become more technical, and generalists' criticism has become more impressionistic and journalistic. The academy and the marketplace have moved further apart.

The following chart is the summary of the criticism above. Fill in each blank with appropriate word(s) from the passage.

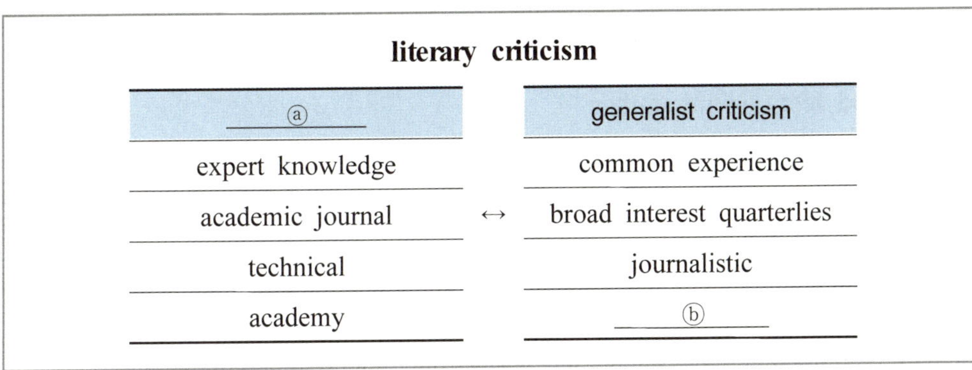

**literary criticism**

| ⓐ ______ | | generalist criticism |
|---|---|---|
| expert knowledge | ↔ | common experience |
| academic journal | | broad interest quarterlies |
| technical | | journalistic |
| academy | | ______ ⓑ ______ |

## 02 Read the poem and follow the directions. [4 points]

The cardiologist prescribed
a new medication
and lectured my father
that he had to stop working.
And my father said: I can't.
The landlord won't let me.
ⓐ The heart pills are dice
in my father's hand,
gambler who needs cash
by the first of the month.

On the night his mother died
in far away Puerto Rico
my father lurched upright in bed,
heart hammering
like the fist of a man at the door
with an eviction notice.
Minutes later,
the telephone sputtered
with news of the dead.

Sometimes ⓑ I dream
my father is a guitar,
with a whole in his chest
where the music throbs
between my fingers.

First, explain the metaphorical meaning of the underlined ⓐ. Second, explain the speaker's attitude toward his father by focusing on the figure of speech used in the underlined ⓑ.

## 03 Read the excerpt from a novel and follow the directions. [4 points]

"Negroes don't control this school or much of anything else—haven't you learned even that? No, sir, they don't control this school, nor white folk either. True they support it, but I control it. I's big and black and I say 'Yes, suh' as loudly as any burrhead when it's convenient, but I'm still the king down here. I don't care how much it appears otherwise. Power doesn't have to show off. Power is confident, self-assuring, self-starting and self-stopping, self-warming and self-justifying. When you have it, you know it. Let the Negroes snicker and the crackers laugh! Those are the facts, son. The only ones I even pretend to please are big white folk, and even those I control more than they control me. This is a power set-up, son, and I'm at the controls. You think about that. When you buck against me, you're bucking against power, rich white folk's power, the nation's power—which means government power!"

Dr. Bledsoe paused to let it sink in and I waited, feeling a numb, violent outrage.

"And I will tell you something your sociology teachers are afraid to tell you," he said. "If there weren't men like me running schools like this, there'd be no South. Nor North, either. No, and there'd be no country—not as it is today. You think about that, son." He laughed. "With all your speechmaking and studying I thought you understood something. But you··· All right, go ahead. See Norton ··· You're a black educated fool, son. These white folk have newspapers, magazines, radios, spokesmen to get their ideas across. If they want to tell the world a lie, they can tell it so well that it becomes the truth; and if I tell that you're lying, they'll tell the world even if you prove you're telling the truth···"

I heard the high thin laugh again. "You're nobody, son. You don't exist—Can't you see that? The white folk tell everybody what to think—except men like me. I tell them; that' my life, telling white folk how to think about the things I know about. Shocks you, doesn't it? Well, that's the way it is. It's a nasty deal and I don't always like it myself··· But I've made my place in it and I'll have every Negro in the country hanging on tree limbs by morning if it means staying where I am."

In the above excerpt, Dr. Bledsoe reveals his real thoughts on the politics of race and power. How does he, as an African-American, position himself inside the power structure? When you answer, you can use specific citation from the excerpt.

모범답안 p.122

**01** **Read the poem and follow the directions.** [2 points]

"Forward, the Light Brigade!"
Was there a man dismayed?
Not though the soldier knew
  Someone had blundered.
  Theirs not to make reply,
  Theirs not to reason why,
  Theirs but to do and die.
  Into the valley of Death
  Rode the six hundred.

Cannon to right of them,
Cannon to left of them,
Cannon in front of them
  Volleyed and thundered;
Stormed at with shot and shell,
Boldly they rode and well,
Into the jaws of Death,
Into the mouth of hell
  Rode the six hundred.

**Compete the commentary by filling in each blank appropriate word(s) from the poem.**

Commentary

The poem above is depicting a group of soldiers, called ___ⓐ___, who are charging into certain ___ⓑ___ because they were commanded to do so.

---

## 02 Read the excerpt from a play and answer the question. [2 points]

A *private dining room in a first rate restaurant in Paris. The present. At stage right is a dining table, set for six. Against the wall at stage left is a long serving table with large silver tureens of food with bottles of champagne, a few already open. In the center of the room is a small sofa for two and a chair on each side of the sofa. Everything in the room, from furniture to the wall decorations are French and softly attractive.*

*At Rise:*

*Claude Pichon, early forties, in black tie, stands alone in the room, looks at his watch and sips champagne. He looks a little lost. He looks at the dining table, then crosses to the buffet table, lifts tureen covers, sniffs food, then over to the hors d'oeuvres and samples a few. Turns and looks lost again. There is a double door almost at rear center stage. Another door, smaller, on the side wall. The large door opens and another man enters, about the same age, in black tie as well. This is Albert Donay.*

ALBERT Hello. Am I in the right place? The Gerard party?

CLAUDE Yes. Well, I think so. I'm the first one here. (*Albert comes in, closes the door.*)

ALBERT I'm Albert Donay.

CLAUDE Claude Pichon. (*They shake hands. Albert winces in pain, pulls his hand away and tries to shake off pain.*)

ALBERT AHHH··· Ooooh.

CLAUDE I'm sorry. Did I do that?

ALBERT No, I did. Hurt my finger putting my tie on.

CLAUDE Yes, bow ties are a bother. Did you make it yourself?

ALBERT No, it's my father's. He snapped it while my finger was up. (*Holds his finger to his throat*) This is very nice, isn't it?

| | |
|---|---|
| CLAUDE | Well, it is La Cassette… They say that Josephine lived here once…. Napoleon used to visit her secretly through that door. (*He points to the small door.*) |
| ALBERT | Really? How convenient to have a restaurant in your own home. |
| CLAUDE | I er, don't think it was a restaurant then. |

**Complete the commentary by filling in each blank with appropriate literary term(s).**

Commentary

Claude Pichon and Albert Donay are the first to arrive at the party held in a present-day Paris restaurant. The opening paragraphs of this excerpt (the text in *italics*) is an example of ___ⓐ___, which is an instruction in the text of a play, especially one indicating the movement, position, or tone of an actor, or the sound effects and lighting. The ___ⓑ___ between the two characters is funny, as they banter back and forth about relatively silly topics.

---

## 03 Read the short story and follow the directions. [4 points]

One winter Pauline, an African American woman, discovered she was pregnant. When she told Cholly, he surprised her by being pleased. He began to drink less and come home more often. They eased back into a relationship more like the early days of their marriage, when he asked if she were tired or wanted him to bring her something from the store. In this state of ease, Pauline stopped doing day work and returned to her own housekeeping. But the loneliness in those two rooms had not gone away. When the winter sun hit the peeling green paint of the kitchen chairs, when the smoked hocks were boiling in the pot, when all she could hear was the truck delivering furniture downstairs, she thought about back home, about how she had been all alone most of the time then too, but this lonesomeness was different. Then she stopped staring at the green chairs, at the delivery truck; she went to the movies instead. There in the dark her memory was refreshed, and she succumbed to her earlier dreams. Along with the idea of romantic love, she was introduced to another—physical beauty. Probably the most destructive ideas in the history of human thought. Both originated in envy, thrived in insecurity, and ended in disillusion.

In equating physical beauty with virtue, she stripped her mind, bound it, and collected self contempt by the heap. She forgot lust and simple caring for. She regarded love as possessive mating, and romance as the goal of the spirit. It would be for her a well-spring from which she would draw the most destructive emotions, deceiving the lover and seeking to imprison the beloved, curtailing freedom in every way.

She was never able, after her education in the movies, to look at a face and not assign it some category in the scale of absolute beauty, and the scale was one she absorbed in full from the silver screen.

The excerpt above suggests that going to the movies will only make Pauline more unhappy with her life. Explain why Pauline wants to go to the movies and why going to the movies will make Pauline more unhappy. Do not copy more than SIX consecutive words from the excerpt.

03

# 66회 실전모의고사

모범답안 p.124

**01** **Read the poem and follow the directions.** [2 points]

A scent of ripeness from over a wall.
And come to leave the routine road
And look for what has made me stall,
There sure enough was an apple tree
That had eased itself of its summer load,
And of all but its trivial foliage free,
Now breathed as light as a lady's fan.
For there had been an apple fall
As complete as the apple had given man.
The ground was one circle of solid red.

May something go always unharvested!
May much stay out of our stated plan,
Apples or something forgotten and left,
So smelling their sweetness would be no theft.

**Complete the commentary by filling in the blank with ONE word from the poem.**

Commentary

The poem illustrates that there is more value to things than their direct industrial value. The apples are gathered for harvest but the speaker wishes that some were left on the ground because their __________ is pleasing.

## 02 Read an excerpt from a play and follow the directions. [2 points]

JUAN Life needs a brain, this irresistible force, lest in its ignorance it should resist itself. What a piece of work is man!

THE DEVIL Did I not say, when I was arranging that affair of Faust's, that all Man's reason has done for him is to make him beastlier than any beast. One splendid body is worth the brains of a hundred dyspeptic, flatulent philosophers.

JUAN You forget that brainless magnificence of body has been tried. Things immeasurably greater than man in every respect but brain have existed and perished. The megatherium, the icthyosaurus have paced the earth with seven-league steps and hidden the day with cloud vast wings. Where are they now? Fossils in museums. These things lived and wanted to live; but for lack of brains they did not know how to carry out their purpose, and so destroyed themselves.

THE DEVIL And is man any the less destructive for all this boasted brain of his? Have you walked up and down upon the earth lately? I have; and I have examined Man's wonderful inventions. And I tell you that in the arts of life man invents nothing; but in the arts of death he outdoes Nature herself, and produces by chemistry and machinery all the slaughter of plague, pestilence, and famine. The peasant I tempt today eats and drinks what was eaten and drunk by the peasants of ten thousand years ago. But when he goes out to slay, he carries a marvel of mechanism that lets loose at the touch of his finger all the hidden molecular energies. In the arts of peace Man is a bungler. His heart is in his weapons. This marvellous force of Life of which you boast is a force of Death: Man measures his strength by his destructiveness. What is his religion? An excuse for hating me. What is his law? An excuse for hanging you. What is his morality? Gentility! An excuse for consuming without producing. What are his politics? Either the worship of a despot because a despot can kill, or parliamentary cockfighting.

**Complete the commentary with ONE word from the excerpt above.**

Commentary

While Juan has abiding faith in humanity's potential as the highest miracle of organization, The Devil decries a human being as a __________ creature, one who is a bungler in the arts of peace.

---

## 03 Read an excerpt from a short fiction and follow the directions. [4 points]



James Kruma's hopes were fulfilled much earlier than he had expected. He was appointed headmaster of Ndume Central School, a backward school. He had many wonderful ideas and this was an opportunity to put them into practice··· [deleted]

One evening as Kruma was admiring his work he was scandalized to see an old woman from the village hobble right across the compound, through a marigold flower bed and the hedges··· [deleted]

"The path," said a teacher apologetically, "appears to be very important to village people. Although it is hardly used, it connects the village shrine with their place of burial."

"And what has that got to do with the school?" asked the headmaster.

"Well, I don't know," replied the other with a shrug of the shoulders. "But I remember there was a big row some time ago when we attempted to close it."

"That was some time ago. But it will not be used now," said Kruma as he walked away. "What will the Government Education Officer think of this when he comes to inspect the school next week?" Heavy sticks were planted closely across the path.

Three days later the village priest of Ani called on the headmaster. He was an old man and walked with a slight stoop.

"I have heard," he said after the usual exchange of cordialities, "that our ancestral footpath has recently been closed···"

"Yes," replied Mr. Kruma. "We cannot allow people to make a highway of our school compound."

"Look, here, my son," said the priest bringing down his walking stick, "this path was here before you were born and before your father was born. The whole life of this village depends on it. Our dead relatives depart by it and our ancestors visit us by it. But most important, it is the path of children coming in to be born···"

Mr. Kruma listened with a satisfied smile on his face.

"The whole purpose of our school," he said finally, "is to eradicate just such beliefs as that. Dead men do not require footpaths. The whole idea is just fantastic. Our duty is to teach your children to laugh at such ideas."

"I have no more words to say," said the old priest, already outside.

Two days later a young woman in the village died in childbed. A diviner was immediately consulted and he prescribed heavy sacrifices to propitiate ancestors insulted by the fence.

Kruma woke up the next morning among the ruins of his work. The beautiful hedges were torn up. That day, the white Supervisor came to inspect the school and wrote a nasty report on the state of the premises but more seriously about the "tribal-war situation developing between the school and the village, arising in part from the misguided zeal of the new headmaster."

**In the ending of the excerpt, there is an instance of irony. Identify what kind of irony this is and explain it. Second, the "path" in the excerpt works as a symbol. What does the path symbolize?**

**04** **Read the poem and follow the directions.** [4 points]

The mower stalled, twice; kneeling, I found
A hedgehog jammed up against the blades,
Killed. It had been in the long grass.

I had seen it before, and even fed it, once.
Now I had mauled its unobtrusive world
Unmendably. Burial was no help:

Next morning I got up and it did not.
The first day after a death, the new absence
Is always the same; we should be careful

Of each other, we should be kind
While there is still time.

**What does the poem describe? Write your answer in about 15 words. Second, describe the thematic idea of the poem in ONE sentence.**

유희태 영미문학 ❹

# 영미문학 문제은행


**1판 1쇄** 2014년 5월 10일
**2쇄** 2015년 4월 10일
**2판 1쇄** 2017년 1월 3일
**2쇄** 2017년 12월 20일
**3쇄** 2018년 5월 10일
**4쇄** 2019년 4월 30일
**3판 1쇄** 2020년 10월 23일
**2쇄** 2022년 4월 15일
**3쇄** 2023년 2월 1일
**4판 1쇄** 2024년 1월 10일

저자와의 협의하에 인지생략

**저자** 유희태 **발행인** 박 용
**발행처** (주)박문각출판
**표지디자인** 박문각 디자인팀
**등록** 2015. 4. 29. 제2015-000104호
**주소** 06654 서울시 서초구 효령로 283 서경 B/D
**팩스** (02) 584-2927
**전화** 교재 주문 (02) 6466-7202 동영상 문의 (02) 6466-7201





정 가 37,000원
ISBN 979-11-6987-622-3

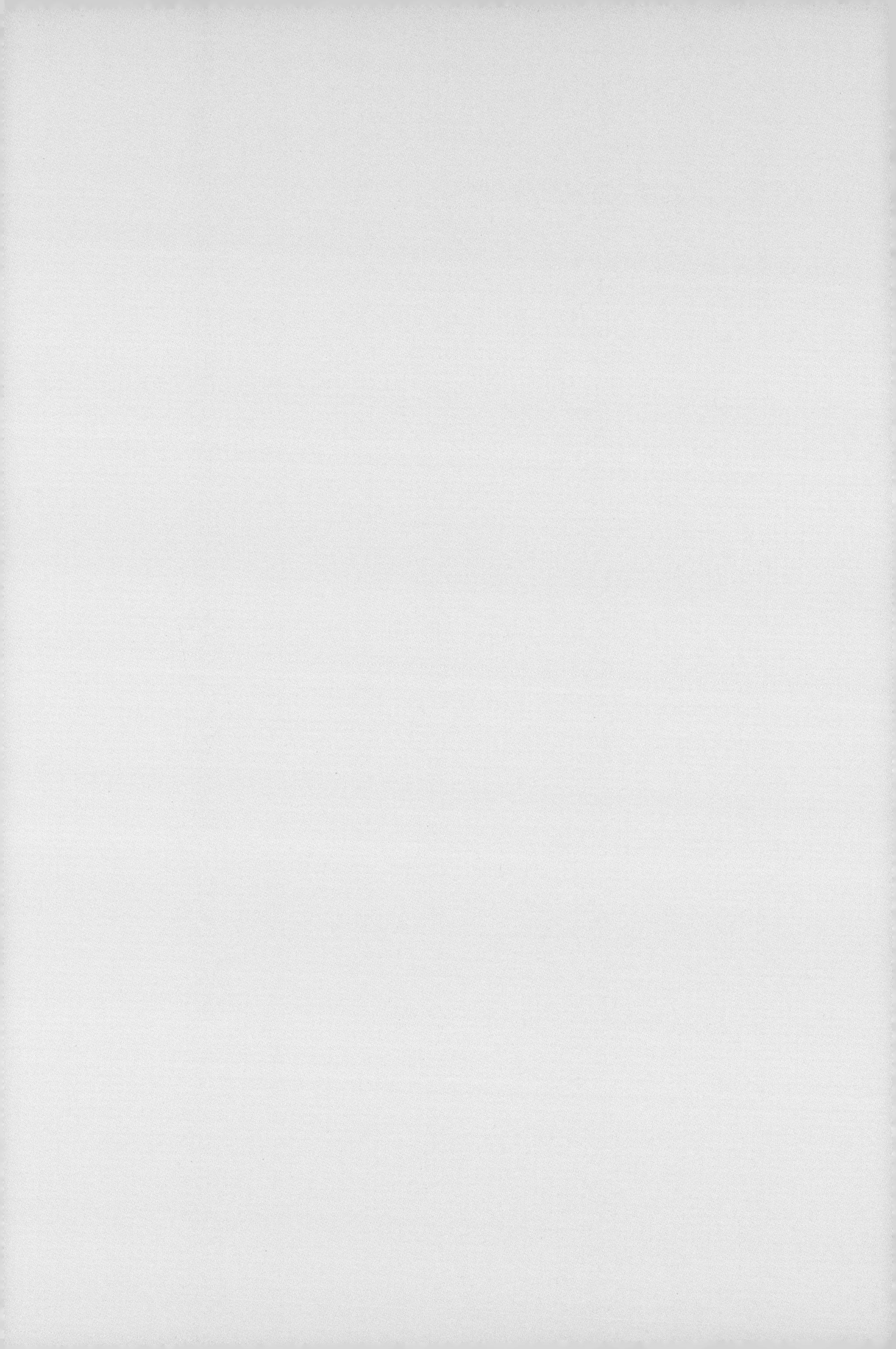

유희태 영미문학 ❹

# 영미문학 문제은행

literature

제4판

교원임용고시
영미문학 필독서

## 유희태 영미문학 4

# 영미문학 문제은행

임용영어수험생 대다수가 선택하는 전공영어의 보통명사

LSI 영어연구소 유희태 박사 저

모범답안

박문각 임용 동영상강의 www.pmg.co.kr

박문각

유희태 영미문학 ④

# 영미문학 문제은행

제4판

교원임용고시
영미문학 필독서

## 유희태 영미문학 ④

# 영미문학 문제은행

임용영어수험생 대다수가 선택하는 전공영어의 보통명사

LSI 영어연구소 유희태 박사 저

박문각 임용 동영상강의 www.pmg.co.kr

박문각

모범답안

유희태 영미문학 ④

# 영미문학 문제은행

차례

# Contents

# Part 01 기본이론문제 1

## 01 회

본책 p.8

**01** In the excerpt above, metaphors as figurative language are employed. Oath is compared to straw and fire to impulse.

OR The above excerpt of the poem is figurative, wherein metaphors are used. An oath is called straw, which is burned by "fire i' the blood", which is another metaphor for passion. The comparison drawn is meant to suggest that passions will dissolve the strength of oaths, which are founded in reason.

**02** In the line above, metaphor is employed. Desert is compared to an animal like lion.

OR The excerpt above includes figurative language in the form of a metaphor. The desert is described as a tawny-colored animal, such as a lion, due to the similar coloration between lions and the tan color of desert.

**03** literal

**04** In the line above, metaphor is used. Tomorrow is compared to day of death.

OR The sentence above is figurative. A metaphor is used, as the literal truth is not that the listeners will die the next day, but the speaker means the day of death does exist in their future, so they should enjoy themselves.

**05** literal

**06**
- Literal or figurative: figurative
- Literal term: Orange County ladies' souls
- Figurative term: furnished homes
- Meaning: This comparison criticizes the minds of these women, suggesting that they have no thoughts of their own, that someone else has already furnished their thoughts and values.

**07**
- Literal or figurative: figurative
- Literal term: Tom
- Figurative term: a snake
- Meaning: The snake comparison suggests that Tom is deceitful, devious, somewhat evil to the poor.

**08** In the underlined part ⓐ, a simile is used comparing the evening to a patient (anesthetized with ether, lying on the table of a hospital operating room). This use of simile suggests that the evening is lifeless and listless.

**09** In the underlined part ⓐ, the speaker employs the poetic technique of personification when s/he uses a word "hands" instead of such words as claws or talons. By doing so, the speaker lets us know that the story of the eagle is not just a study of an animal in its natural environment, but that s/he is telling us about human beings.

**10** In the final line, the speaker employs a simile to create an image of the bird's swift and powerful descent on his prey.

## 02회

본책 p.13

**01** In the excerpt above, figures of speech such as personification and metaphors are used. Here, a day is compared to a haughty person; and sky a blue urn; and sun is liken to fire.

**02** In the excerpt above, a simile is used. Words are liken to sunbeams.

**03** A metaphor describing Beatrice as an apple is used above. The metaphor suggests that the most appealing thing is Beatrice, as it is the object tantalizing him and gaining his attention.

**04** Metaphor appears above, wherein the letter is described as a keystone. This shows that the most crucial part of the application is the letter, as a keystone holds all other stones in place in an archway.

**05** The figure of speech of personification is used to describe the car's actions. The car is described as a person belching smoke, revealing the disgusting and obnoxious nature of the car's exhaust problem.

**06** The simile comparing the salesman to a shark is used here to suggest the vicious and ravenous nature of the salesman, and that one should not be careless around him.

**07** An metaphor here describing the smoke as an animal that flies and rests at the guests' feet shows the movement of the smoke. This description gives a tone of warmth, comfort and familiarity, like a family dog joining its master.

**08** The figure used here is personification, wherein the pigeons are addressed as if talking amongst themselves as a means to show the soft sound they are making coo-ing.

**09** In the underlined part, a hyperbole and a similes are used. "Bent double" is an example of hyperbole because a person might be bent over, but not really bent in two. Also, the soldiers are compared first to "old beggars" who are typically burdened with large sacks which strain them drastically. They also are compared to "old hags", coughing in a way that seems aged and weak. By using these three figures of speech, the speaker conveys the feeling of exhaustion and decrepitude felt by the soldiers vividly.

## 03회

본책 p.17

**01** The students are compared to knives as a simile. The term "sharp" is used to mean "intelligent," so by being extremely sharp it is suggested they are very intelligent.

**02** In the preceeding excerpt, simile is used to draw comparison and illustrate the scene. The first such simile is the description of the dying man "floundering" as if burning alive, which demonstrates the horrific and intense pain he underwent as he died. The simile used in the underlined part ⓑ describes the setting as if "under a green sea", because the speaker is observing through an eerie cloud of the deadly gas.

**03** In the above excerpt several figures of speech appear. First, the symbol of an "invisible worm" is used to indicate an unseen threat to the rose, such as decay or destruction, because worms in nature devour plants and flowers. The subsequent figure of speech is the metaphor of the "howling storm," which is a terrifying description as howling is an intense action, indicating a loud, tumultuous storm. The final figure is the personification of "bed of crimson joy," which describes the crimson rose bud. This metaphor of a bed suggests a comfortable, pure home space, with sexual overtones, of the rose that is being invaded by the threat of the worm.

## 04회

본책 p.19

**01** In the second and third stanzas, similes are utilized. Here, a poem is compared to large medals and the stone ledge of a casement window respectively. These two similes objectify poetry in the form of being soundless, which means there should not be a clear "message," but a quiet and persevering beauty, such as with a relic or old, well-worn stone.

**02** In the above paradox, the speaker shows the contradictions of a poem "motionless in time" while time moves in the form of the "climbing" moon. The speaker here is insisting that poetry should express something universal to all times and cultures.

OR In the above paradox, the speaker shows the contradictions of a moon that is both "motionless" and "climbing." The speaker here suggests that poetry should express something universal to all times and cultures.

**03** In the above fragment, personification is used to describe summer as a person who enters into agreement(contract) of a lease. The "short" "lease" is a complaint on how quickly summer ends. Here, it reveals that summer is short-lived despite the speaker's wish that it last longer.

## 05회

본책 p.22

**01** They enable the poet to achieve greater economy.

**02** The sound of a poem has to contribute to the meaning of the poem(its meaning). To illustrate this principle, the speaker gives several examples in lines 5-14. When the poem is about soft and smooth effects("Zephyr"), the speaker employs an abundance of alliteration such as s in soft, strain, smooth stream, smoother. When harshness and loudness are the subject, the lines become cacophonous. For example, heavy labor is expressed in cacophony("Ajax strives some rock's vast weight to throw"), while lightness and speed are expressed with euphonious short i sounds ("swift Camilla … skims").

**03** The speaker and the poet have differing senses of understanding the same situation, revealing dramatic irony. The former seems to accept his lot in life. He doesn't know anything else, this is what he has been doing his whole life. In lines 7-8, the speaker says, "Hush, Tom! never mind it, for when your head's bare, You know that the soot cannot spoil your white hair." Here, while the speaker tries to make the best of his and his friend's situation, the poet is implying that such a comfort cannot comfort his friend. Here, the dramatic irony occurs because there is a discrepancy(or incongruity) between what the child says and what the poet actually is implying. Also, in line 24, the speaker says that if the young chimney sweepers keep working hard, they would make the best of their situation and enjoy a happy future for themselves. The poet, on the contrary, is implying that by doing their "duty", the young chimney sweepers would be harmed and killed. Here, the dramatic irony occurs because there is a discrepancy(or incongruity) between what the child says and what the poet actually is implying.

## 06 회

본책 p.26

**01** In the above couplet, the speaker uses metaphor to describe an aged man as a tattered coat. This figurative element of the coat shows the age and wear of the man and his somewhat decrepit state.

**02** In the poem above, the speaker uses metaphor to describe the lips of the girls as if they were roses. The figurative image shows the youthful freshness and coloration of the girls and alludes to classical romance associated with roses.

**03** In the line of poem above, personification is used as the guns are given human characteristics. The image of monstrous anger illustrates the terror the guns create in the speaker, and the harm they suggest.

**04** In the poem above, the speaker uses simile to compare a yellow leaf to a frog. The leaf is skipping in an animated way, in the same motion as a frog.

**05** In the above poem synecdoche is used to describe the sculptor, by way of addressing him as "the hand" instead of naming him as a whole person. The heart is that of the long-gone king, Ozymandias.

**06** Ozymandias is a symbol for hubris, or absurd arrogance of vanity and power.

**07** The main theme is that all works and empires disappear eventually, no matter how great they are for a moment.

**08** The speaker recalls having met a traveler "from an antique land," who told him a story about the ruins of a statue in the desert of his native country. Two vast legs of stone stand without a body, and near them a massive, crumbling stone head lies "half sunk" in the sand. The traveler told the speaker that the frown and "sneer of cold command" on the statue's face indicate that the sculptor understood well the emotions(or "passions") of the statue's subject. The memory of those emotions survives "stamped" on the lifeless statue, even though both the sculptor and his subject are both now dead. On the pedestal of the statue appear the words, "My name is Ozymandias, king of kings: / Look on my works, ye Mighty, and despair!" But around the ruin of the statue, nothing remains, only the "lone and level sands," which stretch out around it.

## 07회

본책 p.30

**01** In the poem above, the speaker uses personification to describe the sea as if it were a person waking up from sleep. This personification shows a shift in the sea's condition, as the sea becomes busier suddenly and catches the attention of the speaker.

**02** In the poem above, the speaker uses a metaphor to talk about the second person "you" of the poem as if they were a piece of laundry. The figurative expression is meant to show the way the second person has become deeply important and intertwined with the life of the speaker in an intimate way.

**03** In the underlined part above, the speaker uses personification to give the saw the traits of a person. This description illustrates the severity of the accident in nefarious way, as the saw, described here as it were hungry for supper, sought to devour the boy.

**04** In the underlined part above, the speaker uses a metaphor, describing the grave as if it were a house. The metaphor emphasizes the notion that there is a person who occupies a grave, alluding to how we expect houses to have living dwellers.

**05** In the underlined part above, the speaker uses metaphor to describe sleep as if it were an object. The literal subject, the "you" of the poem, is described as having grey hair and acting lethargic or sleepy as a result of age's effect.

**06** The above poem features three types of images: tactile, olfactory and visual. The tactile images are of the soft-lifted hair as well as the oozing. Secondly, the olfactory image is that of the fumes of poppies. The third category of imagery is visual which occurs in several instances, such as twined flowers.

**07** In the above poem, personification is used to describe autumn as a real woman. The images of nature are described as if they were anatomy or personal, such as the scents of the poppies and fields of hair.

## 08회

본책 p.34

**01** The poem uses its three stanzas to delineate three stages in the life of the speaker: during boyhood, young manhood and maturity. First, the speaker is a child imaging himself to be tough while reading comic/adventure books. Next he imagines himself to be like a menacing monster or vampire, sleeping with many women, akin to a vampire's fictional powers of seduction. Finally he becomes a coward, "yellow", and lives as the man who disappoints the lead female before a hero arrives, managing a store.

**02** There was a time when reading was one way I could avoid almost all my troubles—except for school. It seemed worth the danger of ruining my eyes to read stories in which I could imagine myself maintaining my poise in the face of threats and having the boxing skill and experience needed to defeat bullies who were twice my size.

**03** Later, already having to wear thick glasses because my eye-sight had become so poor, I found my delight in stories of sex and evil: imagining myself with Dracula cloak and fangs, I relished vicious nocturnal adventures. I identified myself with sexual marauders whose inexhaustible potency was like a weapon wielded against women who were sweet and fragile.

**04** I don't read much any more because now I can identify myself only with the flawed secondary characters, such as the flashy dresser who wins the heroine's confidence and then betrays her in a moment of crisis before the cowboy here comes to her rescue, or the cowardly storekeeper who cringes behind the counter at the first sign of danger. Getting drunk is better than reading— books are just full of useless lies.

## 09회

본책 p.37

**01** The speaker above uses simile to compare himself to a lost memory, which indicates how inconsequential he has become to their friends.

**02** The speaker above uses metaphor to describe fog moving on "cat feet", indicating the gentle nature of the fog's arrival.

**03** The above poem uses personification in two instances. First, the landscape is described as "listening", and the shadows are "holding" breath, both images serve to emphasize the literal figure of the silence the speaker experiences.

**04** The detonations of cross here can be the religious "cross", or crucifix as well as the "Cross" of mixed race children, as well as "cross" as in "angry." The connotations of mixed race can indicate the differing cultures and strife of such (feeling alienated slightly to both sides of one's heritage). Crucifix indicates religious imagery such as right or wrong, sin, and curses. The "Cross" of anger connotes rage or bitterness.

**05** The language is important because it can help suggest the possible "mixed class" of the speaker who might not be entirely well schooled due to his mixed race, which is a problem in that time. Also, this is colloquial language of the south, which American readers will know is where these problems can be most severe.

## 10 회

본책 p.40

**01** The above speaker uses a simile to describe their "heart" as if a figurative, laden apple tree. This comparison is meant to show the fullness of the emotion they feel and implies the stress that brings, as a bent branch is close to breaking.

**02** The speaker uses personification to describe a soul as if it were a real person. The intended literally meaning is that a person chooses the people who matter most and ignores most others.

**03** In the above poem, two categories are compared to each other to make a point about the power of a book. The figurative element, modes of transportation, in the forms of: "frigate", "coursers", and a "chariot" are compared to the literary objects of "a book", "a page", and "poetry." The figurative group, which is modes of transport, is described as being unequal to literature. The speaker writes of literature: "the poorest take / Without oppress of toll." That is to say, by reading about things, they can engage in experiences outside of themselves or foreign to their ordinary environment without paying the cost of any travel.

## 11 회

본책 p.42

**01** At the foot of the Catskill Mountains, which was magnificent and mysterious, near the Hudson was a picturesque village founded by Dutch colonists. Approaching it, one would see gabled houses (and shingle roofs reflecting the sunlight). A simple, easygoing man named Rip Van Winkle, who was of Dutch descent, lived in this village, in a weather-beaten house, at the time when New York was an English colony.

**02** The above poem describes the death of a young soldier, as described by himself. The youth of the speaker is indicated by his "falling" out of his mother's sleep. Later, he is woken by anti-aircraft guns while flying. His death is spoken explicitly and shown to be gruesome, as he is washed out of his turret "with a hose."

## 12 회

본책 p.44

**01** The tone of the passage is humorous.

**02** The above passage uses simile to compare the landlord to a sundial. This is meant to convey the regularity how he moved his chair throughout each day to avoid the sunlight.

**03** Nicolas Vedder is comically described as quiet and powerful. He stays in the same place through most of every day, only shifting his seat a bit to find shade. To communicate his opinions he doesn't speak them aloud, but shows his reactions, either good or bad, through the way he smokes his pipe.

**04** humorous

**05** The problem implied by this passage is that Turkey is an alcoholic and gets inebriated everyday starting at noon which adversely affects his work.

**06** The passage employs simile to compare Turkey's face to burning coals(or burning grate). This shows the reader the vivid red color his face takes on as he drinks each day.

**07** This refers to Turkey.

**08** 니퍼즈의 과민함과 그것에서 기인하는 신경질은, 주로 소화불량에 그 원인이 있었기 때문에, 대개 아침에 관찰할 수 있었고, 오후엔 상대적으로 온화하다는 점은 나에겐 다행스러운 일이었다. 반면에 터키의 주기적 발작은 약 12시경에만 찾아오기 때문에, 그 둘의 기이함을 한꺼번에 당해야 하는 불행한 사태는 일어나지 않았다. 그들의 발작은 경비병처럼 서로서로의 문제를 완화해주었다(교대를 했다). 니퍼즈가 보초를 설 때면 터키는 비번이었고 그 반대도 마찬가지였다. 이런 상황 아래서는 참 다행스러운 자연의 배열이었다.

**09** humorous

## 13 회

본책 p.50

**01** the uncertainty and unpredictability of life, which may end accidentally at any moment, and the tragic waste of human potentiality that takes place when such premature deaths occur.

**02** pessimistic and despair

**03** metonymy

**04** Metaphor is used here; life is compared to a tale; there is no meaning or purpose in life.

**05** By using the allusion, the poet not only reinforces emotion but also helps to define his theme: the tragic brevity and uncertainty of life or premature death.

**06** In the poem, the speaker, who is 20 years old, is contemplating the remainder of his life. The theme is "carpe diem," Latin for "seize the day." The first clue that reveals this to the reader are the statement, "Twenty will not come again", meaning he has no chance to change the events of 20 years as he has already lived them. Also, such remarks as "only leaves me fifty more" and "Fifty springs are little room" show the reader that the speaker is reacting to the urgent need to live and enjoy as much of the world as possible before his one short life ends like that of the cherry blossoms on the branch.

# Part 02 기본이론문제 2

## 01 회

본책 p.56

### [01-03]

한글 번역

나의 배는 망각의 짐을 싣고
겨울 밤 바위 사이의 거친 바다를 지나가오.
또한 나의 원수. 아아.
나의 애인은 무정하게 키를 잡으오.

그리고 젓는 노마다 이럴 땐 죽음도,
하찮은 것인 양 손쉽게 생각하오.
거짓 한숨으로 두려움도 마음 든든하다는 듯이
쉴 새 없이 부는 바람은 재빨리 돛을 찢고.

눈물의 비와 경멸의 검은 구름은,
닳아버린 돛 줄을 크게 손상케 하니,
이는 망상과 무지의 뒤얽힘.

이 고역으로 나를 인도한 별이여 꺼져라,
나를 동반해야 할 이성이 물에 빠지니,
기항의 가망도 없이 나는 떠도네.

**01** (Petrarchan or Italian) Sonnet

**02** abba abba cddcee

**03** extended metaphor

### [04-06]

한글 번역

어느 날 백사장에 그녀 이름을 적었더니,
파도가 밀려와서 씻어 버렸네:
다시 그 이름 적어 봤지만,
물결은 밀려와 내 수고를 삼켜 버렸네.
그녀 말하길 "덧없는 날 불멸케 하려
그토록 공연히 애쓰는 부질없는 그대여;
나도 이 파도처럼 꺼지고,
내 이름 또한 그처럼 소멸하리라"
나 대답하길 "천만에, 천한 것들이야 죽어
흙이 된들 어떠랴마는 그대 이름 영원히 살아남으리;
나의 시는 그대의 귀한 덕을 영원케 하고,
하늘에 그대의 빛나는 이름 기록하리라:
죽음이 온 세상을 정복할지라도,
우리의 사랑 하늘에 살고 삶은 다시 새로워지리."

**04** iambic pentameter

**05** abab bcbc cdcd ee

**06** (It symbolizes) the earthly things subject to decay and death.

## [07-10]

한글 번역

탐식하는 세월이여, 사자의 발톱을 무디게 하고,
대지로 하여 귀여운 새끼들을 탐식케 하고;
사나운 범의 턱에서 날카로운 이빨을 뽑아 버리고,
활기에 찬 장생할 불사조를 불살라 죽이고,
질주하면서 서글픈 계절을 즐겁게 하여도 좋다.
날쌘 발걸음인 세월이여, 그대 마음대로 해 봐라,
넓은 세계와 곧 사라질 그 모든 아름다움에 대해.
하지만 한 가지 극악한 죄만은 금하노라;

오! 내 연인의 아름다운 이마에 너의 시간 새기지 말라.
너의 그 낡은 붓으로 그 이마에 주름을 긋지 말라;
길이 후손들에게 미의 모범이 되도록
너의 행로에서 그를 더럽혀서는 안 된다.
늙은 세월이여, 네 아무리 몹쓸 죄를 저지를지라도,
내 사랑은 내 시 속에 영원히 젊음 잃지 않으리라.

**07** abab cdcd efef gg

**08** ⓐ apostrophe
ⓑ metaphor (Time is compared to a sculptor.)

**09** (The main theme is) the ravages of time and immortality of art.

**10** Oh, don't carve wrinkles into my love's beautiful forehead, and don't draw lines there with your old pen. Let him pass through time untainted, to serve as the paradigm of beauty for men to come.

OR Time, do not make my love's face grow old and wrinkly; Allow him to remain beautiful, to serve as a model of beauty for future generations.

# 02 회

본책 p.62

## [01-04]

한글 번역

고결한 사람들은 조용히 죽어가면서,
그들의 영혼에게 가자고 속삭인다.
슬퍼하는 몇몇 친구들이 지금 숨이
떨어진다고 말하면, 또 한편에선 그렇지 않다 말하는 동안;

그렇게 우리도 사그라들어, 아무 소음도 내지 말자.
눈물의 홍수도, 탄식의 폭풍우도 일으키지 말자.
일반인들에게 우리의 사랑을 알리는 것은
우리의 기쁨을 모독하는 것이니.

지진은 재해와 공포를 일으키고
사람들은 그 피해와 의미를 헤아린다.
그러나 천체의 진동은
훨씬 더 크지만, 해가 없다.

우둔한 달 아래 연인들의 사랑은
(그 사랑의 정수는 감각인데) 이별을
인정할 수가 없다, 왜냐하면 이별이 그 사랑의 기본
요소들을 없애버리기에.

그러나 사랑에 의해 너무도 순화되어
우리 자신도 그 이별이 무엇인지를 모르는 우리는,
서로의 마음을 믿어,
눈과 입술과 손이 없는 것을 별로 상관치 않는다.

우리의 두 영혼은 하나여서,
비록 나는 가야 하지만,
단절이 아니라 확장을 감내한다,
공기처럼 얇게 쳐 늘인 금처럼

만일 우리의 영혼이 둘이라면, 그들은 둘이요,
마치 뻣뻣한 콤파스 두 다리가 둘인 것처럼;
당신의 영혼은 고정된 다리여서, 움직일 기색도
안 보이지만, 다른 다리가 움직이면, 움직이게 된다.

**01** In the first stanza, the separation between lovers is compared to souls parting their bodies.

**02** earthquake

**03** Dull sublunary lovers' love

**04** The paradox expressed in "Our two souls, therefore, which are one" declares the lovers as two living bodies but sharing one heart and one soul. Also, the expansion of their souls is compared to that of beaten gold. Gold can be expanded and condensed over and over again, but it will never break. The strength of gold is also the strength of the love between the couple. Like gold, it cannot be severed or torn by expansion.

## [05-07]

**한글 번역**

오직 그대의 눈으로만, 내게 축배를 들어다오.
그러면 나는 내 눈으로 축배를 들으리;
혹은 오직 술잔에만 키스를 남겨다오
그러면 나는 술을 찾지 않으리.
영혼에서 우러나는 갈증은
신의 술을 요구하네:
허나 혹 내가 제우스의 넥타를 마실 수 있다 한들,
나는 그대의 것과는 바꾸지 않으리.

얼마 전 나는 그대에게 장미 꽃다발을 보냈소,
그대를 영광스럽게 하기 위해서라기보단
거기선 그 장미가 시들 수 없으리란
한 가닥 희망을 안고서;
그런데 그대는 단지 장미향을 맡기만 하고선
내게 다시 돌려 보냈소;
그 후로 그것은 자라면서 향기를 풍겼소 (맹세하오)
장미가 아니라 그대의 체취를.

**05** The speaker is a lover, the man who loves Celia dearly.

**06** a rosy wreath

**07** ⓐ sight ⓑ touch ⓒ taste ⓓ smell

## [08]

**한글 번역**

가라, 사랑스러운 장미여!
나와 그녀의 시간을 낭비하는 그녀에게 말하라,
이제야 아느냐고,
내가 그녀를 너와 견줄 때
그녀가 얼마나 사랑스럽고 아름답게 보이는가를.

젊음과 우아함을 보이기를 꺼리는
그녀에게 말하라,
만일 네가 사람 하나 살지 않는
사막에서 피었더라면
너는 틀림없이 칭찬 받지 못한 채 죽었으리라는 것을.

빛으로부터 물러난
미의 가치는 적나니:
그녀에게 나오라고,
사랑받도록 허락하고,
찬미 받는 것에 대해 얼굴 붉히지 말도록 말하라.

그리고 나서 죽어라! 그래서 그녀가
너에게서 희귀한 모든 것의 공통된
운명을 읽을 수 있도록:
놀랍도록 사랑스럽고 아름다운 것이 차지하는
시간의 몫이 얼마나 짧은가를.

**08** carpe diem (seize the day)

## [09-10]

한글 번역

죽음이여, 잘난 척 마오, 혹자는 당신이 무적이며
무섭다고 하지만, 사실 당신은 그렇지 않기 때문이오.
당신이 멸망시킨다고 생각하는 사람들은
죽는 것이 아니오. 불쌍한 죽음이여, 또한 당신은
나 역시 죽이지 못하기 때문이오.
다만 당신의 형태에 불과한 휴식이나 잠의 상태는
큰 기쁨일 뿐이오; 그러하니 당신에게서는 더 많은
기쁨이 흘러나올 것이 분명하오.
가장 훌륭한 사람들이 가장 먼저 당신과 가 버린다오,
자신들 유골의 안식과 영혼의 인도를 받으며.
당신은 필연과 우연, 제후들과 보잘것없는 사람들의
노예라오.
그리고 독약과 전쟁, 질병과 함께 하는 존재라오.
한편 양귀비나 마술이 당신의 손길만큼이나 우리를
편히 자게 할 수 있으니;
당신은 왜 그리 잔뜩 뽐내느냐 말이오?
한 번의 짧은 잠이 지나면, 우리는 영원히 깨어나게 되니.
죽음은 더 이상 존재하지 않을 것이오; 죽음이여,
바로 당신이 죽게 될 것이오.

**09** This metaphor compares "rest" and "sleep" to "pictures," like a painting or drawing. The point is that the rest and sleep are pale imitations, and Death is the real thing. On the other hand, Death is only a much stronger version of sleep, and not something scary and different.

**10** apostrophe

# 03회

본책 p.68

## [01-03]

한글 번역

일어나요! 창피한 줄 알고 일어나요, 꽃피는 아침이
그녀의 날개에게 긴 머리카락의 신을 보여주고 있소.
보시오 오로라가 공중에
그녀의 아름다운, 새로이 누빈 색깔을 던지는 모습을:
일어나요, 예쁜 잠꾸러기, 보시오
이슬의 반짝거리는 풀과 나무를.
모든 꽃들이 이슬을 떨구는 동쪽으로 고개 숙인 지
한 시간 이상 지났는데도, 당신은 아직 옷도 안 입었소;
아니, 침대에서 나오기조차 하지 않았소?
모든 새들이 아침 기도를 드리고,
찬미가를 노래했을 때, 그건 죄요,
아니, 신성모독이요, 방안에 있는 것은.
수많은 처녀들이 아가위 꽃을 따오기 위해
종달이보다 일찍 펄쩍 뛰어 일어나는 이 날.

나오시오, 우리 인생의 전성기에 있는 이때, 우리
같이 갑시다;
그리고 시간의 무해한 어리석음에 취해봅시다.
우리는 금세 늙어 죽을 것이오
우리의 자유를 알기도 전에.
우리의 인생은 짧고, 우리의 날들은
해처럼 빨리 달려가오;
그리고, 증기나 빗방울처럼,
한번 잃으면, 결코 다시는 찾을 길 없소;
그러니 당신이나 내가
이야기, 노래, 혹은 사라지는 유령이 될 때면,
모든 사랑, 모든 애호, 모든 환희는
우리와 함께 끝없는 밤 속에 익사하여 누워 있게 되오.
그러니 시간이 있는 동안, 우리가 썩고 있는 동안,
자, 코리나, 자, 우리 오월제 놀이 갑시다.

**01** carpe diem

**02** simile

**03** simile

## [04-05]

한글 번역

어머니는 남쪽 황야에서 나를 낳으셨다.
그래서 나는 까맣다, 그러나 오! 내 영혼은 희다;
천사처럼 흰 영국 아이,
그러나 나는 까맣다, 마치 빛을 빼앗긴 듯.

어머니는 나무 아래에서 나를 가르치셨다,
그리고 날이 뜨거워 지기 전에 앉아서
나를 무릎 위에 얹고 키스해 주셨다,
그리고 동쪽을 가리키면서 말하기 시작했다:

저 봐 떠오르는 해를: 저 곳에 하나님이 사시고,
빛을 주시고 열을 내보내신단다;
그리고 꽃들과 나무들, 짐승들과 사람들이
아침이면 위로를, 정오엔 즐거움을 받는단다.

그리고 우리는 이 세상에 잠시 있으면서,
사랑의 빛을 견디어내는 법을 배워야 한단다;
그리고 이 검은 몸뚱이와 햇볕에 탄 얼굴은,
다만 구름에 지나지 않고, 그늘진 숲과 같아.

왜냐하면 우리들의 영혼이 열을 견디는 법을 배웠을 때,
구름은 사라질 것이니; 우리는 하나님의 목소리를
들을 거야,
숲에서 나와라, 내 사랑아,
내 황금빛 집 주위에서 양들처럼 즐거워해라.'

이렇게 어머니는 말하시며 나에게 키스했다;
그리고 나는 이렇게 말했다. 꼬마 영국 아이에게.
내가 검은 구름에서, 그 아이가 흰 구름에서 나와
자유로울 때,
그리고 양처럼 하나님의 천막을 둘러싸고 우리는
기뻐할 거야:

그 아이가 견딜 수 있을 때까지 더위로부터 그를 그
늘지게 할 것이야,
우리 아버지의 무릎에 기쁨으로 기댄 채.
그러고 나서 나는 서서 그의 은빛 머리카락을 쓰다
듬을 것이다,
그리고 그와 같이 되면 그는 나를 사랑할 것이야.

**04** ⓐ race ⓑ his mother's lesson ⓒ pride

**05** abab cdcd

**06** I am as much in love with you as you are beautiful.

**07** hyperbole (or overstatement)

## [08-10]

한글 번역

이것은 보기에 거룩한 광경인가?
기름지고 풍성한 나라에서,
어린 아기들은 비참한 신세되어,
강탈하는 매몰찬 손길에 한술 얻어먹네.

저 떨리는 울음이 노래인가?
환희의 노래일 수 있는가?
숱한 어린이들 가난한데?
빈곤의 나라로다!

그들의 태양은 결코 빛나지 않고,
그들의 들판은 검고 황량해라,
그들의 길은 온통 가시로 가득차고,
그곳은 영원한 겨울이로다.

태양이 빛나는 곳이라면,
비가 내리는 곳이라면,
그런 곳이라면 어린 아기가 배고픈 일 있을 수 없고,
가난으로 마음조차 졸이는 일 없을 것이기에.

**08** It is to question social and moral injustice.

**09** By using the contrast, the speaker continues his questioning of the virtue of a society where resources are abundant but young children are still "reduced to misery". (The "cold and usurous hand" that feeds them is motivated more by self-interest than by love and pity.)

**10** They symbolize the wasting of a nation's resources and the public's neglect of the future.

## 04회

본책 p.76

### [01-04]

한글 번역

나의 존재가 그칠지도 모른다는 두려움을 느낄 때
나의 펜이 충만한 두뇌에서 이삭을 다 줍기도 전에,
문자로 높이 쌓인 책들이,
풍성한 곡식처럼 원숙한 곡식알을 간직하기도 전에;
내가, 밤의 별이 총총한 얼굴에서
로맨틱한 거대한 구름의 상징들을 쳐다보고
그 상징들의 그림자를, 행운의 마술적인 손으로,
추적할 만큼 결코 살 수 없으리란 생각이 들 때;
그리고 내가, 덧없는 아름다운 것이여,
내가 다시는 그대를 더 바라볼 수 없다고 느낄 때
분별없는 사랑이
없다고 생각할 적에; 그때 광막한 세계의
해변에 나는 홀로 서서 생각한다
사랑과 명성이 무로 가라앉을 때까지.

**01** ⓐ fame ⓑ love

**02** personification (Chance is compared to a human being.)

**03** (If I die) before I have written lots of books which hold my words like a grain silo.

**04** ⓐ repetition ⓑ personifying

### [05-06]

한글 번역

우리 둘이 헤어지던 날
말없이 눈물 흘리며
여러 해 떨어질 생각에
가슴이 찢어졌었다.
너의 뺨이 파랗게 질려 차가웠고
너의 입맞춤은 더욱 차가웠다.
정녕 그때 이미
오늘의 슬픔은 예고됐었다.

아침의 이슬은
내 눈썹에 차갑게 내려
마치 내가 지금 느끼는 감정을
예고해주는 듯하였다.
너의 맹세는 다 깨지고
너의 평판은 좋지 않구나.
나는 네 이름을 남들이 말하는 걸 듣고
같이 부끄러움을 느낀다.

사람들이 내 앞에서 네 이름을 부르면
내 귀엔 조종이 울리고
온몸은 몸서리쳐진다.
왜 네가 이처럼 사랑스러웠던가?
그들은 내가 너를 알았던 것을 모른다.
하지만 너를 너무도 잘 알고 있었다, 나는.
오래오래 나는 너를 슬퍼하리라
이루 말할 수 없이 깊게.

남몰래 만났던 우리.
이제 난 말없이 슬퍼하네
잊기 잘하는 그대 마음
속이기 잘하는 그대 영혼을
오랜 세월 지난 뒤
그대 다시 만나면
어떻게 인사를 해야 할까?
말없이 눈물 흘리며.

**05** It denotes the speaker's inability to leave his moment of pain behind.

**06** The speaker uses metaphor, comparing hearing her name spoken by outsiders to the "knell" of a heavy bell—like a church bell tolling a funeral. By using the figure of speech, the speaker conveys his sorrow vividly.

**07** ⓒ six lines ⓓ ababab

**08** woes

**09** The speaker uses simile, which tells the reader that he used to be remembered by his friends, but has now been forgotten. This makes the speaker's loneliness more poignant because it involves a moment of loss and betrayal rather than perpetual lack.

**10** It is about an exploration of the meaning and value of life in light of an isolated existence.

## 05회

본책 p.82

### [01-04]

**한글 번역**

오늘 밤 바다는 잔잔하오.
조수는 가득차고 달빛은 아스라이
해협을 비추니 – 프랑스 해안에선
불빛이 깜박이다 사위고 영국의 해변들은
고요한 후미에서 우람한 모습으로 가물거리오.
창가로 오시오, 밤 공기가 감미롭소!
다만, 바다와 달빛에 하얀 뭍이 맞닿는
물보라 이는 긴 해안선에서,
들어보오. 조약돌 파도쳐 구르는 소리를.
물결이 물러났다 되돌아오면서 높은
해안에 내리칠 때에, 다시, 물결이 밀리다
또 멈추고, 또 되풀이하면서
떨리는 듯 느린 선율로, 그건
영원한 비애의 가락을 빚고 있소.

신념의 바다도
예전에 만조였다오, 그래서 지구의 해안 둘레에
눈부신 코르셋의 주름마냥 접혀서 놓여 있었다오.
그러나 지금 나는 다만 들을 뿐이오
그 애수에 잠긴, 후퇴하는 긴 표효 소리만을,
밤바람의 숨결에 맞추어
광막하고 황량한 물가로,
노출된 세계의 자갈 깔린 해변으로 퇴각하는 소리를.

아, 님이여, 우리 서로 진실합시다!
그처럼 다정하고, 아름다우며, 새로운
꿈나라처럼, 우리 눈앞에 펼쳐진 듯한 세계는
실상 아무런 기쁨도, 사랑도, 빛도,
확실성도, 평화도, 고통의 해소도 없소,
우리는 상대방을 분간 못하는 군대들이 야간 전투하며
공격과 퇴각 나팔소리 뒤섞여 휩쓰는
황혼이 깃든 전장 같은 곳에 있으니.

**01** The speaker is on Dover Beach—the cliffs lie in the distance and the speaker can view both them and the French coast. And he is speaking to his lover. The time is late night, late enough for the moon to be out.

**02** Metaphor and simile are used here. The speaker uses metaphor, comparing the sea to religion. The "Sea of Faith" is a time when religion could be experienced by people without doubt that modernity caused. When religion was strong and real, it securely and peacefully surrounded the world like "folds of a bright girdle furled," protecting us from doubt and despair, as the sea wraps itself around the continents and islands of the world.

**03** In the last three lines, the speaker illustrates that the world is growing gloomier and gloomier. The people of the world are confused and are ignorant, hopelessly warring day and night. The "armies" are both figurative and literal. It is literal because it refers to actual wars going on at the time. It is also figurative in the sense that the common people of the world are becoming ignorant and doing foolish things.

**04** lamentable; melancholic; sad

## [05-08]

**한글 번역**

나의 사랑하는 포플러, 공중의 새장들을 달래던
날뛰는 태양을 나뭇잎들 속에서 달래고 어르던 포플러가
모두 베어졌다, 베어졌다, 모두 베어졌다.
생기 넘치고 울창한 나무들이
남김없이, 하나도 남김없이
풀밭과 강둑, 바람 헤매는
잡초가 굽이치는 강둑에서
헤엄치거나 가라앉았던 샌들을 신은 그림자가 흔들거렸던 나무들.

오 우리가 무얼하고 있는지 안다면
우리가 땅을 파거나 나무를 벨 때—
자라나는 녹색 초목을 난도질하고 고문할 때!
전원은 건드리기에는
너무도 연하고, 가냘퍼서,
이 윤기나는 눈알처럼
단 한 번 찌르기만 해도 눈이 멀게 된다,
우리가, 우리가 정원을 고치려고
하는 일이 정원을 끝장내 버린다,
우리가 나무를 베거나 땅을 팔 때.
나중에 오는 사람들은 지난날의 아름다움을 짐작할 수 없다.

**05** The speaker compares the line of trees to a rank of soldiers. The military image implies that the industrial development of the countryside equals a kind of warfare. (The natural curves and winding of the river bank contrast with the rigid linearity of man-made arrangements of objects, a rigidity implied by the soldiers marching in formation.)

**06** mournful or tragic

**07** ⓒ sprung rhythm ⓓ onomatopoeic

**08** The pricked eyeball is a startling and painful image, used deliberately to emphasize the speaker's acute pain and sorrow over the felled poplars.

## [09-10]

한글 번역

그곳은 늙은이들의 나라가 되지 못한다.
젊은이들은 서로 껴안고, 새들은 나무에서
—저 죽어가는 세대들—노래하고 ,
연어가 오르는 폭포, 고등어가 몰려드는 바다는
물고기와 짐승과 새들이 여름 내내
잉태되고 태어나며 죽는 모든 것들을 찬미한다.
관능의 음악에 사로잡혀 모두가
늙지 않는 지성의 위업을 소홀히 한다.

늙은 사람은 하찮은 존재일 뿐.
막대에 꽂힌 누더기 걸친 허수아비인 것.
영혼이 손뼉치며 노래하지 않는다면, 닳아 없어질
옷의 조각들을 위해 더욱 드높이 노래하지 않는다면,
또한 거기엔 노래하는 학교만이 있어서
영혼의 장엄한 기념비를 탐구하는 곳이기에;
난 바다를 건너
성스러운 도시 비잔티움에 왔노라.

**09** ⓔ

**10** An old man is a paltry thing, merely a tattered coat upon a stick, unless his soul can clap its hands and sing; and the only way for the soul to learn how to sing is to study monuments of its own magnificence. Therefore, I have come to the holy city of Byzantium.

# 06 회

본책 p.88

## [01-03]

한글 번역

저기 붉은 옷을 입은 들판의 시골뜨기는
산정에서 내려다 보는 그대를 모르고 있다.
고지의 농장에서 우는 암소의
먼 울음소리는 그대 귀를 즐겁게 하려는 것은 아니다.
정오에 종을 치는 교회의 일꾼은
위대한 나폴레옹이 말을 세워
즐거운 마음으로 귀 기울이고 있음을 모르고 있다.
대열이 저기 알프스산을 휘돌아가는 동안,
그대의 생애가 이웃사람들의 신조에
무슨 보탬이 되었는가는 알 수 없는 일이다.
전체는 각자가 필요로 하는 것,
홀로 아름답거나 좋은 것은 없다.
나는 새벽녘 오리나무 가지 위에서 노래하는
참새소리를 천상의 것으로 생각하였다.
저녁 때 둥우리째 집으로 데려왔다.
노래는 부르되 재미가 없다.
강과 하늘을 집으로 가져오지 않은 까닭;
그는 내 귀에 노래해 주었으나 그들은 내 눈에 노래해 주었다.
기묘한 조개들이 해안에 놓여 있었다.
마지막 파도의 거품이
패각에 맑은 진주를 뿌려 주었다.
야만스러운 바다는 그들의 도피를
포효로 맞아 주었다.
나는 해초와 거품을 씻어내고
바다에서 난 보물을 집으로 가져왔다.
그러나 보기 싫고 떠들썩한 이 물건들은
해안에 아름다움을 두고 온 것이다.
해와 모래와 시끄러운 소리 속에.

**01** have been removed from their natural place in the universe and have therefore lost some of their natural beauty

**02** To truly appreciate them, we have to go outside and see them in their natural places. When the sparrow in the tree and the seashells on the seashore are taken away from where they belong, they lose some of their natural glimmer.

**03** the shells

## [04-07]

**한글 번역**

내 사랑이여, 잠이 오는 당신의 머리를
나의 신의 없는 팔 위에 눕히시오;
생각이 깊은 아이들에게서
시간과 열정은 아름다움을
불살라버리고, 무덤은
아이들의 덧없음을 증명하네;
그러나 날을 지샐 때까지
내 품에 그대 숨결이 안기게 해다오.
그대 덧없고 죄 많은 숨결이어도
내겐 더할 나위 없이 아름다우니.

정신과 육체는 경계가 없는 것.
연인들 여느 때처럼 황홀하여
비너스의 너그러운 마력의 둔덕에 누우니
여신은 그들에게 초연한 동정과
만물의 사랑, 희망의
엄숙한 환영을 비춘다.
빙하와 암석 사이에서
관념적 직관이
은둔자의 육체적 황홀감을 깨우쳐 주나니.

확신과 신의는
자정이 지나자
종소리처럼 사라지고
시류를 탄 미치광이들은
현학적 구호를 지루하게 외쳐대는구나.
두려운 점괘는 하나같이 말한다.
한 푼도 공짜는 없는 것이라고. 하지만 이 밤부터는
한 마디의 속삭임, 한 가닥의 생각도
한 번의 키스와 눈짓도 남아있을 것이라고.

**04** No one lives forever; even children end up in the grave eventually. (Every dead adult was once a beautiful child.)

**05** Souls and bodies have no boundaries as lovers lie together. (The lovers share bodies and souls with each other as they are tangled up in each other's arms.)

**06** Venus

**07** pessimistic and critical

## [08-10]

**한글 번역**

내게 말하지 마시오, 슬픈 시구로,
인생은 한낱 공허한 꿈이라고.
잠든 영혼은 죽은 것이니,
사물은 겉모습 그대로가 아니라오.

인생은 실재요 진지한 것.
무덤은 인생의 목표가 아니라오.
흙으로부터 와 흙으로 돌아갈 것이니
하는 말은 영혼에겐 해당되지 않는 것.

기쁨도 슬픔도 다같이
우리의 운명적 종말이나 길이 아니오.
오로지 행동, 그리하여 다가오는 내일이
오늘보다 더 발전하는 계기가 되도록.

예술은 길고 시간은 덧없이 지나가며
우리의 마음, 비록 굳세고 씩씩해도
검은 천에 가린 북처럼
무덤으로 향하는 장송곡을 울리나니.

이 세상 드넓은 싸움,
인생의 노숙에서
말 못하고 쫓기는 가축이 되지 말고
싸움에서 영웅이 되시오.

위인들의 생애는 모두
우리도 숭고한 삶을 이룩할 수 있고
떠날 때는 시간의 모래밭에
발자국 남길 수 있을 것임을 상기시켜주니.

**08** trochaic tetrameter

**09** The speaker employs metaphor, comparing life to a battle field (or living in the world to fighting on a battlefield). Using the metaphor, the speaker tells readers that (from the day people are born until the day they die,) people are leading and participating in wars and battles. In those wars, people should lead heroic and courageous lives and not sit idle and remain ineffectual.

**10** In the stanza, the speaker tells the reader that people should take as example all the great men that have come before. People should strive to be like them and leave footprints on the world.

## 07 회

본책 p.94

### [01-02]

한글 번역

나는 즐겨보네 그것이 수십 리를 핥고
계곡을 핥아
물탱크에서 배를 채우고
다시 큰 걸음을 디뎌

이 산 저 산을 돌아
오만한 눈빛으로
길가의 오두막집들을 들여다 보는 것을;
그리곤 제 옆구리에 맞도록

바위를 뚫고는 그 틈을 비집고 기어나오면서
소름끼치는 괴성으로
줄곧 끙끙거리는 것을;
그리고 산을 좇아내려 오더니만

「보아너게」 마냥 울어제치는 것을;
그리고, 별처럼 시간을 맞춰
— 유순하고 전능한 모습으로 —
자신의 마구간 문 앞에서 걸음을 멈추는 것을.

**01** a train (or an iron horse)

**02** (The poem describes a train in metaphors that suggest an animal that is both "docile" and "omnipotent".) The train "laps the miles" and "licks up the valleys," then stops to "feed itself" at tanks along the way. It passes mountains with a "prodigious step", "peers" arrogantly into shanties, and moves through a narrow passage in a quarry. After descending a hill, it stops at the terminal like a horse before its barn door.

### [03]

한글 번역

난 하잘것없다오! 당신은 누군가요?
그대 또한 하잘것없다고요?
그럼 우린 한 패인가요—말하지 말아요!
그들이 우리를 쫓아낼 거예요!

중요한 사람이 된다는 건 얼마나 끔찍한가요!
개구리마냥, 긴긴 유월 내내
자신을 추종하는 늪을 향해 개골개골 자신의 이름을 외쳐댐이
그 얼마나 세속적인 일이냐 말이에요!

**03** The speaker satirizes glory seekers, or people who wants to be somebody. For the speaker, to be somebody is horrible because they are too busy keeping their names in circulation, croaking like frogs in a swamp.

**[04-07]**

**한글 번역**

커다란 여송연을 마는 자,
그중 힘센 자를 불러서는 부엌 컵 속에 든
탐욕스러운 응유를 휘젓도록 해라.
계집들에겐 그들이 입는 데 익숙한
옷을 입고 빈둥거리게 하고, 사내들에게는
지난달의 신문으로 꽃을 싸서 가져오도록 해라.
현존이 가상의 종국이 되게 하라.
유일한 황제는 아이스크림의 황제이다.

세 개의 유리손잡이가 모자란, 소나무 널빤지로
만든 화장대에서 그녀가 한때는 공작비둘기를
수놓았던 그 시트를 꺼내어
그녀의 얼굴을 뒤덮도록 펼쳐라.
그녀의 뿔 같은 발이 튀어나온다면, 이는 그녀가
얼마나 차갑고 말이 없는가를 보여주기 위함이다.
남포등이 그 빛을 발하게 하라.
유일한 황제는 아이스크림의 황제이다.

**04** ephemeral sensual or physical pleasure

**05** Let being(or life) be the end of superficial appearance; Let's be exactly what we are.

**06** death

**07** the light of life; enlightenment

**08** ⓒ walks down dark streets
ⓓ supermarket
ⓔ Garcia Lorca
ⓕ the grocery clerks
ⓖ a store detective
ⓗ where they are headed

**09** He makes a comment on American consumer culture (or commodification).

**10** Walt Whitman

# Part 03 실전모의고사

## 01 회

본책 p.104

### 01

하위내용영역 문학(소설) B형 단답형 배점 4점 예상정답률 35%

**모범답안** Bartholomew means that earlier the soldiers yelling up at their sign made a big interesting show. Second, Edith has been partying to make herself feel like "the World's Worst butterfly".

**채점기준**

+ 2점 : 밑줄 친 ⓐ의 의미를 "earlier the soldiers yelling up at their sign made a big (interesting) show"라 서술하였거나 유사하였다.
+ 2점 : Edith가 자기 자신을 "세상에서 가장 나쁜 사교적 인물"이라 느끼도록 만든 행위가 무엇이냐는 질문에 "Edith has been partying 또는 Edith has been enjoying the party"라 서술하였거나 유사하였다.

### 02

하위내용영역 문학(시) B형 서술형 배점 4점 예상정답률 40%

**모범답안** The one thing is ⓓ. Second, the advice is not to stop enjoying oneself even if the world around oneself is trying to silence one from doing so.

**채점기준**

+ 2점 : ⓐ－ⓔ 중 시 전체의 맥락의 의미에서 나머지들과 다른 하나를 "ⓓ"라 정확히 썼다. 이것 외에는 답이 될 수 없다.
+ 2점 : 화자가 주는 조언(advice)을 "not to stop enjoying oneself even if the world around oneself is trying to silence(or stop) one from doing so"라 서술하였거나 유사하였다.
  ▷ 다음과 같은 내용이 들어가도 2점을 준다.
  - "아이처럼 그 어떤 일이 일어나도 playful 한 삶을 살아 나가라는 것"
  - "세상이 막아도(실패해도) 굴하지 않고 즐겁게 자기 일을 해 나가라는 것"

### 03

하위내용영역 문학(드라마) B형 단답형 배점 4점 예상정답률 45%

**모범답안** Clitheroe missed the news of his promotion and orders to go to battle. Second, Nora's emotions change from nervous to angry in the stage directions.

**채점기준**

+ 2점 : Clitheroe가 놓친 것을 "the news of his promotion(1점) and orders to go to battle(1점)"라 서술하였거나 유사하였다.
+ 2점 : 지문(stage directions)에서 드러난 Nora의 정서적 상태의 변화를 "from nervous(or anxious) to angry" 또는 "from nervousness to anger"라 서술하였거나 유사하였다.

# 02회

본책 p.110

## 01

하위내용영역 문학(소설) B형 서술형 배점 4점 예상정답률 45%

**모범답안** It can be inferred that Myers enjoys his isolated life. Second, it was his son jumping on him and hitting him while he threatened his son's life.

**채점기준**

+ 2점 : 밑줄 친 부분에서 알 수 있는 Myers의 성격을 "Myers enjoys his isolated life"라 서술하였거나 유사하였다.
+ 2점 : Myers가 아들과의 재회에 대해 숙고하게 만든 마지막 (둘 사이의) 직접적 상호작용을 "his son jumping on him and hitting him (while he threatened his son's life)"라 서술하였거나 유사하였다.

## 02

하위내용영역 문학(시) B형 서술형 배점 4점 예상정답률 45%

**모범답안** The nails are needed to close up coffins for those who have died in the war. Next, the word is "bright".

**채점기준**

+ 2점 : 못의 용도를 "to close up coffins for those who have died in the war"라 서술하였거나 유사하였다.
+ 2점 : 빈칸에 들어갈 단어를 "bright"라 정확히 기입하였다.

## 03

하위내용영역 문학(드라마) B형 서술형 배점 4점 예상정답률 40%

**모범답안** The person is President Diem. Second, Toulon feels frightened of eavesdropping. Third, Toulon is separating his personal opinion of advocating the coup from those that he would share professionally.

**채점기준**

+ 1점 : 밑줄 친 ⓐ의 "him"을 "President Diem"이라 정확히 서술하였다. 이것 외에는 답이 될 수 없다.
+ 1점 : 지문에서 반복되는 "Toulon freezes"에서 알 수 있는 것을 "Toulon feels fear(frightened) of being eavesdropped(=overheard) upon"라 서술하였거나 유사하였다.
+ 2점 : 밑줄 친 ⓑ의 의미를 "Toulon is separating his personal opinion of advocating the coup from those that he would share (professionally)"라 서술하였거나 유사하였다.

## 03회

본책 p.115

### 01

하위내용영역 문학(시) B형 서술형 배점 4점 예상정답률 35%

모범답안 The poet says that subtraction, which usually means reduction, is addiction because loss in one place means gain wherever the lost thing arrives. Second, the words are "three remaining".

채점기준

+ 2점: 4연에 사용된 paradox를 "The poet says that subtraction, (which usually means reduction), is addiction because loss in one place means gain wherever the lost thing arrives"라 서술하였다.
+ 2점: 밑줄 친 부분("나머지 홀수")과 상응하는 두 단어를 "three remaining"라 서술하였다. 이것 외에는 답이 될 수 없다.

### 02

하위내용영역 문학(소설) B형 서술형 배점 4점 예상정답률 50%

모범답안 The interview is the meeting between the dog and the child. Second, the dog is trying to hide its movement guiltily more because the child beats it when he notices it following but it still wants to be around the boy.

채점기준

+ 2점: 밑줄 친 "interview"의 의미를 "the meeting between the dog and the child"라 서술하였거나 유사하였다.
+ 2점: 마지막 문장에 사용된 비유적 언어의 의미를 "the dog is trying to hide its movement guiltily more because the child beats it when he notices it following but it still wants to be around the boy"라 서술하였거나 유사하였다.

### 03

하위내용영역 문학(드라마) B형 서술형 배점 4점 예상정답률 45%

모범답안 Valerie criticizes Hellena's new lover for falling in love with every face. Second, Hellena was previously in a nunnery.

채점기준

+ 2점: Valerie가 Hellena의 새로운 남자를 비판하는 내용을 "Valerie criticizes Hellena's new lover for falling in love with every face"라 서술하였거나 유사하였다.
+ 2점: Hellena가 전에 있었던 곳을 "nunnery"라 서술하였다.

# 04회

본책 p.121

## 01

하위내용영역 문학(소설) B형 서술형 배점 4점 예상정답률 40%

모범답안 The most distinct difference is that in that time a child being scolded would be looked on with seriousness by others, while today it would not be. Second, the crowd would feel no compassion or sympathy to the person being punished.

채점기준

+ 2점 : 과거의 혼나던 아이와 현재의 아이 사이에서 나타나는 가장 큰 차이를 "in that time a child being scolded would be looked on with seriousness(severity) by others, while today(now) it would not be (looked on like that)"라 서술하였거나 유사하였다.
+ 2점 : 밑줄 친 부분의 의미를 "the crowd (bystanders) would feel no compassion or sympathy to the person being punished"라 서술하였거나 유사하였다.

한글 번역

지금부터 적어도 2세기 전 어느 여름날 아침, 프리즌 레인에 있는 감옥 앞 풀밭에는 보스턴 주민이 꽤 많이 모여 무쇠 못을 박아 고정해 놓은 참나무 문을 하나같이 뚫어지게 바라보고 있었다. 만일 이런 일이 다른 지방 사람들 사이에서 일어났다거나 뉴잉글랜드 역사에서 좀 더 뒷날에 일어났더라면, 턱수염을 기른 이 착한 주민들 얼굴에 돌처럼 딱딱하게 굳은 표정이 감돌고 있는 것을 보고 아마 무슨 끔찍한 일이라도 한창 벌어지고 있는 것으로 짐작했을 것이다. 모르긴 몰라도 아마 어느 악명 높은 죄수의 형을 예상대로 집행하는 것인지 모른다. 그 죄수에 대한 법정의 평결은 일반인들의 판단을 확인해 주는 것에 지나지 않았던 것이다. 하지만 초기 청교도들의 엄격한 성격에 비추어 볼 때 이와 같은 추측을 그렇게 자신 있게 내릴 수는 없을 것이다. 그것은 게으름 피우는 종이나 부모가 관원의 손에 넘긴 불효자식이 태형 기둥에서 처벌을 받는 장면이었을지도 모른다. 또는 퀘이커 교도나 그 밖의 이단적 신도가 채찍을 맞으면서 마을 밖으로 쫓겨나거나 집 없이 떠돌아다니는 게으름뱅이 인디언이 백인의 화주를 마시고 취한 채 길거리에서 야단법석을 떨다가 회초리를 맞으며 어두운 숲속으로 쫓기는 것이었을지도 모른다. 그것도 아니라면 어느 마녀가 히빈스 노파처럼 처형대의 이슬로 사라지고 있는 장면이었을지도 모른다. 그 어떤 경우든 구경꾼들의 태도는 이 무렵의 사람들과 어울리게 하나같이 아주 엄숙했다. 그들 사이에서는 종교와 법이 거의 동일했고, 그들의 성격에는 이 두 가지가 하나로 잘 융합되어 있었기 때문에 가벼운 것이든 무거운 것이든 공적인 처벌행위는 존경의 대상인 동시에 공포의 대상이었다. 그러므로 처형대에 오른 죄수가 그런 구경꾼들에게서 바랄 수 있는 동정이란 참으로 보잘것없고 눈물겹도록 냉혹한 것이었다. 한편 요즘 같으면 한낱 수치거리나 조롱거리에 지나지 않을 처벌도 이 무렵에는 사형 못지않게 준열한 위엄을 지녔을지도 모른다.

## 02

하위내용영역 문학(시) B형 서술형 배점 4점 예상정답률 35%

모범답안 The simile of "a door someone was rushing into" tells the reader that the conversation moved into unusual new topics that were surprising or varied. Second, the word for ⓐ is "friends" and the word for ⓑ is "cord".

채점기준

+ 2점: 직유를 통해 시적 화자가 하려는 말을 "The simile of 'a door someone was rushing into' tells the reader that the conversation moved into unusual new topics that were surprising or varied"라 기입하였다.
+ 1점: ⓐ에 들어갈 단어를 "friends"라 정확히 기입하였다. 이것 외에는 답이 될 수 없다.
+ 2점: ⓑ에 들어갈 단어를 "cord"라 정확히 기입하였다. 이것 외에는 답이 될 수 없다.

## 03

하위내용영역 문학(드라마) B형 서술형 배점 4점 예상정답률 35%

모범답안 The cardinal is using hyperbole, saying that constant women are so rare that you would have to look into space for one. Second, they are having an affair.

채점기준

+ 1점: 밑줄 친 부분에 사용된 비유적 언어를 "hyperbole" 또는 "overstatement"라 서술하였다. 이것 외에는 답이 될 수 없다.
+ 1점: hyperbole를 통해서 Cardinal이 주장하는 바를 "constant(faithful) women are so rare that you would have to look into space for one"라 서술하였거나 유사하였다.
+ 2점: Julia와 Cardinal의 관계를 "they (Julia and the Cardinal) are having an affair" 또는 "they are having an extramarital relationship"라 서술하였거나 유사하였다.

# 05회

본책 p.127

## 01

하위내용영역 문학 A형 서술형 배점 4점 예상정답률 45%

모범답안 The lesson is that the speaker should have cared better for the old apple tree rather than neglecting it to take care of new pear trees. Second, the speaker did it for "two decades"

채점기준

+ 2점: 밑줄 친 교훈을 "the speaker should have cared better for the old apple tree rather than neglecting it (to take care of new pear trees)"라 서술하였거나 유사하였다.
  ▷ 또는 "if something valuable is neglected much, it will eventually disappear"라 했어도 맞는 것으로 한다.
+ 2점: 화자가 사과나무를 감상한 기간을 "two decades"라 서술하였다. 이것 외에는 답이 될 수 없다.

## 02

하위내용영역 문학 A형 서술형 배점 4점 예상정답률 45%

모범답안 "She" is Thomasina Coverly. Second, ignorance should be innocent and waiting for pure knowledge instead of being exposed to vulgar things.

채점기준

+ 2점: 밑줄 친 "she"를 "Thomasina Coverly"라 서술하였다. 이것 외에는 답이 될 수 없다.
+ 2점: 밑줄 친 부분에서 비유적 언어의 의미를 "ignorance should be innocent and waiting for pure knowledge(truth) instead of being exposed(or taught) to vulgar(or obscene) things"라 서술하였거나 유사하였다.

## 03

하위내용영역 문학(소설) B형 서술형 배점 4점 예상정답률 40%

모범답안 She believes the funeral to be unfittingly small, obscure, a mockery and bleak. Second it is implied the two men had affairs with Mrs. Crasthorpe. Third, the words are windscreen wipers.

채점기준

+ 2점 : Mrs. Crasthorpe의 남편 장례식에 대한 가장 주요한 의견을 "to be unfittingly small, obscure, (a mockery) and bleak"라 서술하였거나 유사하였다.
+ 1점 : Kildare와 Donald에 관해 지문에서 추론할 수 있는 것을 "the two men had affairs with Mrs. Crasthorpe"라 서술하였거나 유사하였다.
+ 1점 : 빈칸에 들어갈 단어를 "windscreen wipers"라 정확하게 기입하였다. 이것 외에는 답이 될 수 없다.

# 06회

본책 p.133

## 01

하위내용영역 문학(시) B형 서술형 배점 4점 예상정답률 45%

모범답안 It is shown that the speaker's brother graduated, drove trucks, sold real estate, married and had a child. Second, the death of the brother in a motorcycle accident is alluded to.

채점기준

+ 2점 : 나열된 자동차들을 통해 알 수 있는 시적 화자 동생의 중요한 개인 신상을 "the speaker's brother (graduated, drove trucks, sold real estate,) married and had a child."라 서술하였거나 유사하였다.
+ 2점 : 마지막 연에서 추론할 수 있는 주요 사건을 "the death of the brother in a motorcycle accident"라 서술하였거나 유사하였다.

## 02

하위내용영역 문학(소설) B형 서술형 배점 4점 예상정답률 45%

모범답안 She is more likely to assume the cosmopolitan standard. Second the person is "Caroline" because of her naivety, ambition and interest in exploring the city.

채점기준

+ 2점: 밑줄 친 ⓐ로 판단해볼 때 주인공이 선택할 것 같은 것을 "She is more likely to assume(=take) the cosmopolitan standard"라 서술하였거나 유사하였다.

+ 1점: (무장도 제대로 하지 못한 채 어떤 멀고도 높은 곳에 대한 막연한 꿈에 사로잡혀 그 대도시의 신비를 정찰해 보겠다고 나선) ⓑ의 "어설픈 어린 기사"를 "Caroline"이라 서술하였다.

+ 1점: 위처럼 말한 이유를 "because of her naivety(=ill-informed nature), ambition and interest in exploring the city"라 서술하였거나 유사하였다.

한글 번역

[A] 콜롬비아시는 시카고에서 그리 먼 곳은 아니기 때문에 그녀도 언젠가 시카고에 가본 적이 있었다. 하기야 몇 시간 또는 기껏해야 몇 백 마일이 무슨 대수랴. 그녀는 언니의 주소를 적은 작은 쪽지를 꺼내보며 생각했다. 빠르게 거꾸로 스쳐 지나가는 초록색 풍경을 응시하다 갑자기 앞으로 전개될 시카고에서의 생활을 상상해 보았다. 열여덟 소녀가 집을 나설 때에는 대개 다음과 같은 두 가지 경우 중 하나의 길을 걷게 된다. 즉, 누군가의 손에 구조되어 전보다 나은 처지가 되든지, 아니면 코스모폴리탄적 가치관을 재빨리 몸에 익혀 타락하게 되는 것이다. 이런 상황에서는 둘 사이에서 균형을 잡는 것은 불가능하다. 대도시는 언제나 그 특유의 교활한 농간을 부리기도 하고 때론 크고 작은 좀더 인간적인 유혹의 손길을 무수히 내민다. (대도시는) 매우 세련된 교양인들에게 있을 법한 은근한 설득력을 가지고 사람의 마음을 유혹하는 커다란 힘이 있다. 무수히 반짝이는 현란한 불빛은 여자의 마음을 녹여버리는 남자의 매혹적인 눈초리 못지않은 위력을 가진다. 때묻지 않은 순수한 처녀의 마음은 도시의 초자연적인 힘에 의해 반쯤은 파멸되어 버린다. 요란한 소리, 복잡한 생활양식, 즐비하게 늘어선 건물들이 내뿜은 뜻 모를 호소력은 사람을 당황하게 한다. 자상한 설명을 들려줄 조언자도 없기에, 도시라는 이 괴물은 무방비 상태의 시골소녀의 귓속에 어떠한 유혹과 속임수를 속삭일지 모를 일이다. 이렇듯 달콤한 속삭임은 자신의 정체를 알아차릴 틈도 주지 않은 채 음악처럼 스며들어 한 소박한 마음을 산란하게 하고 약화시켜 마침내는 타락하게 만드는 예는 얼마든지 있다.

[B] 캐롤라인은 사물을 관찰하고 분석할 만한 힘은 거의 없었다. 이기심은 높았지만 그렇다고 그렇게 강하지도 않았다. 그럼에도 그것이 그녀의 핵심적인 성격이었다. 처녀 시절의 환상에 부풀어 있는 그녀는 아직 설익은 미모를 지녔으나 잘만 가꾸면 웬만한 미인을 능가할 만한 바탕과 몸매를 지녔으며, 선천적으로 지성적인 인상을 풍기는 눈초리를 가진 그녀의 전체적인 모습은 한 눈으로 보아 미국에 이민 온 지 3대쯤 되는 전형적인 중류 계급의 표본처럼 보였다. 책에는 애당초 관심이 없었고, 지식이란 그녀에겐 봉인된 책(수수께끼 같은 것)일 따름이었다. 직관적 우아함에 있어서는 아직도 조잡했다. 두 손은 볼품없이 생겼고, 발은 예쁘장하게 작지만 아직 촌티가 흘렀다. 하지만 그녀는 여자로서의 자신의 매력에 매우 관심을 가지고 있었으며, 생의 여러 잔재미에 민감하여 물질에 대한 소유욕도 만만치 않았다. 말하자면 그녀는 무장도 제대로 하지 못한 채 어떤 멀고도 높은 곳에 대한 막연한 꿈에 사로잡혀 그 대도시의 신비를 정찰하겠다고 나선 어설픈 어린 기사와 같았다. 그리하여 그 안에 숨어있을 행복을 노획하여 자신의 발밑에 무릎 꿇게 하려는 것이다.

## 03

하위내용영역 문학(드라마) B형 서술형 배점 4점 예상정답률 45%

모범답안 It can be interred that John's wife is in the grave. Second, his friends' children made John and Mari feel left behind.

채점기준

+ 2점: John의 부인이 있는 곳을 "in the grave"라 서술하였거나 유사하였다.

+ 2점: John과 그의 부인 Mari가 소외감을 느끼게 만드는 것을 "his friends' children"라 서술하였거나 유사하였다.

# 07회

본책 p.139

## 01

하위내용영역 문학(시) A형 서술형 배점 4점 예상정답률 45%

**모범답안** The figure of speech is "personification" and the speaker compares the clean blue pool to a human being, who is gentle and polite to the speaker and her friend(s) and approaches the speaker as the slide into it. Second, the detail is "sunburned shoulders".

채점기준

+ 1점: 첫 번째 행에 사용된 비유적 언어를 "personification"라 정확하게 서술하였다. 이것 외에는 답이 될 수 없다.
+ 1점: 비유적 언어의 의미를 "the speaker compares the clean blue pool to a human being, who is gentle and polite to the speaker and her friend(s) (and approaches the speaker as the slide into it)"라 서술하였거나 유사하였다.
+ 2점: 파라다이스의 한계를 나타내는 세부사항을 "sunburned shoulders" 또는 "chain link (at an improbable world)"라 서술하였다.

## 02

하위내용영역 문학(드라마) B형 서술형 배점 4점 예상정답률 50%

**모범답안** The word is "marry". Second, the boy is anxious the mother won't accept him because of his skin color.

채점기준

+ 2점: 빈칸에 들어갈 단어를 "marry"라 정확하게 기입하였다. 이것 외에는 답이 될 수 없다.
+ 2점: "the mother won't accept him because of his skin color (or his race/ his dark skin)"라 서술하였거나 유사하였다.
  - ▷ 또는 "it is because he is colored"라 서술하였어도 2점을 준다.

## 03

하위내용영역 문학(소설) B형 서술형 배점 4점 예상정답률 50%

**모범답안** The content is that Finn and the narrator have been kicked out of their living space. Second, the "metamorphosis" was that Magdalen had changed to wanting to be married.

채점기준

+ 2점: "무엇인가가 잘못되었다는 것"의 내용을 "Finn and the narrator have been kicked out of their living space"라 서술하였거나 유사하였다.
  - ▷ 또는 "They have to find a new place to stay"라 서술하였어도 2점을 준다.
+ 2점: "변신"을 "Magdalen had changed to wanting to be married"라 서술하였거나 유사하였다.

## 08회

본책 p.145

### 01

**하위내용영역** 문학(소설) B형 서술형 **배점** 4점 **예상정답률** 55%

**모범답안** Shreve and the narrator are college classmates. The word is "watch".

**채점기준**

+ 2점 : narrator와 Shreve의 관계를 "college classmates 또는 schoolmates"라 서술하였거나 유사하였다.
+ 2점 : 빈칸에 들어갈 단어를 "watch"라 서술하였다. 이것 외에는 답이 될 수 없다.

**한글 번역**

커튼에 창틀 그림자가 보이니 일곱 시에서 여덟 시 사이일 것이며 시계 소리를 듣고 있는 난 또다시 시간 안에 있는 것이다. 시계는 할아버지의 것이었으며 아버지가 내게 주며 말하길 "내 너에게 모든 희망과 욕망의 능묘를 주니 네가 이것을 사용해 인간의 모든 경험이 결국은 부조리함을 알 것이며, 이는 네 개인적인 필요에 맞되 네 할아버지나 할아버지의 아버지에게 그랬던 것보다 나을 바 없을 것 같은 생각이 드니 마음이 아프구나. 내 너에게 이것을 주는 건 시간을 기억하라 함이 아니라, 이따금 잠시라도 시간을 잊으라는 것이요, 시간을 정복하려고 인생 전부를 들이지 않도록 하기 위함이다. 그것은 시간과의 싸움에서 이긴 자 없기 때문이다. 싸움은 성립조차 안 된다. 그 전쟁터는 인간의 우매와 절망을 드러낼 뿐, 승리는 철학자들과 바보들의 망상일 따름이다.
벽 너머에서 쉬리브의 침대 스프링 소리에 이어 직직 슬리퍼 끄는 소리가 들렸다. 나는 일어나 서랍장으로 갔다. 서랍장을 따라 가로로 손을 미끄러뜨려 가다가 손에 잡힌 시계를 엎어 놓고 다시 침대로 돌아갔다. 하지만 창틀 그림자는 여전히 그 자리에 있었다. 나는 거의 일 분도 틀리지 않고 몇 시인지 익히 알 수 있기에 창틀을 등지고 돌아누워야 할 것이다. 그것이 위에 있을 때 동물의 눈이 머리 뒤에 있었다면 느꼈을 근질거림을 느끼면서. *빈둥거리는 습관을 들이면 나중에 반드시 후회한다.* 아버지가 한 말이다. *예수는 십자가에 못 박히지 않고 작은 톱니바퀴들의 미세한 째깍거림에 마모되었다고 했다.* 아버지는 교화하고도 엄중히 말씀하셨지. *하버드에 다니는 일 년 동안 보트 경주도 보지 않으면 환불을 받아야지.* 제이슨을 보내세요. 제이슨을 하버드에 다니게 하세요.
쉬리브가 셔츠 칼라를 달며 문간에 서 있었다. 그의 얼굴색으로 덧칠된 안경알이 장밋빛으로 반짝였다.
"오늘 아침 빠질 거야?"
"그렇게나 늦었어?"
쉬리브가 시계를 보았다. "2분만 있으면 종이 울릴 거야."
"그렇게 늦은 줄 몰랐어." 그가 계속 시계를 보는데 입이 어떤 모양을 이루었다. "나 서둘러 가야 해. 또 빠지면 감당 못해. 학장이 지난주에 나한테…" 그가 시계를 호주머니에 다시 집어 넣었다. 그제야 나는 말을 멈췄다.
"빨리 바지 걸치고 뛰는 게 좋을 거야." 그가 말하고는 방에서 나갔다.
나는 일어나 그가 있는 벽 너머로 귀를 기울이며 서성였다. 그가 거실로 나와 문쪽으로 갔다.
"아직 준비 안 됐냐?"
"응 아직, 먼저 가. 나도 따라갈게."
그가 갔다. 문이 닫혔다. 복도를 걸어나가는 그의 발소리가 났다.

## 02

하위내용영역 문학(시) B형 서술형 배점 4점 예상정답률 45%

**모범답안** It means without any leaves. Second, the niece is alone because she is so competitive and outstanding that no boy is willing to match her.

채점기준

+ 2점: "bald(벗겨진)"의 의미를 "without any leaves(=foliage)"라 서술하였거나 유사하였다.
+ 2점: 화자의 조카가 홀로인 이유를 "the niece is alone because she is so competitive and outstanding that no boy is willing to match her"라 서술하였거나 유사하였다.

## 03

하위내용영역 문학(드라마) B형 서술형 배점 4점 예상정답률 45%

**모범답안** Harry is an explorer. Second, Joshua warns of an uprising among the stable boys and Clive proposes replacing them and hiding.

채점기준

+ 2점: Harry가 하는 일을 "an explorer"라 서술하였거나 유사하였다.
  ▷ 또는 "a person who scouts", "a person who explores unknown areas"라 했어도 맞는 것으로 한다.
+ 1점: Joshua가 묘사하는 문제를 "an uprising among the stable boys" 또는 "a risk of violence from the stable boys"라 서술하였다.
+ 1점: Clive가 제안한 해결책을 "replacing (or firing) them(=the stable boys) and hiding"이라 서술하였거나 유사하였다.

# 09회

본책 p.150

## 01

하위내용영역 문학(시) B형 서술형 배점 4점 예상정답률 40%

**모범답안** The tone changes(=shifts) in the final line of the third stanza: "all silenced by cold rain". Second, the word is "cease".

채점기준

+ 2점: 주요하게 어조(tone)의 변화가 일어나는 곳을 "the final line of the third stanza" 또는 "all silenced by cold rain"라 정확하게 서술하였다.
+ 2점: 빈칸에 들어갈 단어를 "cease"라 정확하게 기입하였다.

## 02

하위내용영역 문학(소설) B형 서술형 배점 4점 예상정답률 50%

**모범답안** The metaphor means that life is unpleasant like a prison endured during a life sentence. Second, the words are "raging sea".

채점기준

+ 2점: 밑줄 친 ⓐ의 은유의 의미를 "life is unpleasant like a prison endured during a life sentence"라 서술하였거나 유사하였다.
+ 2점: "가정의 파괴자"에 상응하는 두 단어를 "raging sea"라 정확하게 서술하였다.

한글 번역

[A] 그를 처음 만난 건 피레에우스(라는 항구도시)에서였다. 날이 밝기 직전이었는데 밖에는 비가 내렸고 나는 항구에서 크레타섬으로 가는 배를 기다리고 있는 중이었다. 유리문을 닫았는데도 북아프리카에서 불어오는 시로코 바람이 파도의 하얀 포말을 카페 안으로 몰아왔다. 카페 안은 발효한 샐비어 술과 사람 냄새로 가득 차 있었고 유리창은 추운 날씨 때문에 사람들이 내뿜는 숨에 뽀얗게 김이 서렸다. 밤을 그곳에서 보낸 뱃사람 대여섯 명이 갈색 염소 가죽 지퍼 재킷 차림으로 앉아 커피나 샐비어 술을 마시며 부옇게 밝아오는 창 너머 바다를 바라보았다. 거친 물결에 놀란 물고기들이 아예 바다 깊숙이 들어가 수명이 잠잠해지길 기다릴 때였다. 어부들은 사나운 바다가 잠잠해져 물고기들이 미끼를 쫓아 수면으로 올라올 때를 기다리며 카페에서 북적댔다. 서대기, 놀래기, 홍어가 밤의 여행에서 돌아올 시각을 기다리는 것이다. 날이 점점 밝아왔다.

[B] 건장한 덩치에 옷 곳곳에 진흙이 튄 늙수그레한 부두 노동자 하나가 모자도 없이 맨발로 유리문을 밀고 들어섰다.

"어이, 코스탄디! 요즘 재미가 어때?" 하늘색 외투 차림의 늙은 뱃사람 하나가 소리쳤다.

"그래, 어떨 것 같나? 아침 인사는 술집에서 하고 저녁 인사는 하숙집에서 하지! 사는 게 이 모양이라네. 일거리가 있어야 말이지." 코스탄디라고 불린 사내가 침을 뱉으며 말을 받았다. 몇 사람은 웃고 몇 사람은 고개를 가로저으며 불경스러운 소리를 했다.

"세상은 종신형이지" 카라괴즈에서 개똥철학을 주워들은 콧수염을 기른 자가 말했다. "암, 종신형이지. 빌어먹을."

창백하고 푸르스름한 빛 한 줄기가 카페의 지저분한 창문을 거쳐 손이며 콧잔등, 이마를 비추고 내친김에 카운터 위 술병을 휘감았다. 밤새 술을 파느라 잠을 설친 주인이 빛을 보고 손을 뻗어 전등 스위치를 꺼버렸다.

잠시 가게 안이 조용해졌다. 사람들은 일제히 희끄무레하게 밝아오는 창밖의 하늘을 바라보았다. 파도 소리가 카페 안으로 들어와 물 담배 빠는 소리와 한데 어울렸다. 늙은 뱃사람이 한숨을 쉬었다. "레모니 선장 어떻게 된 거 아닐까? 아이고 하느님, 그 분을 좀 도와주십쇼." 그는 이렇게 말하고는 바다를 보며 호통을 쳤다. "남의 가정을 파괴시키는 너, 바다의 신의 저주가 있을 지어다!" 말이 끝나자 그는 자신의 잿빛 수염을 깨물었다.

## 03

하위내용영역 문학(드라마) B형 서술형 배점 4점 예상정답률 45%

**모범답안** Amanda is concerned that Laura will have a bad future because she has made no plans. Second, the word is "father's".

**채점기준**

+ 2점 : Amanda가 걱정하는 것을 "Laura will have a bad future because she has made no plans"라 서술하였거나 유사하였다.
+ 2점 : 빈칸에 들어갈 단어를 "father's"라 서술하였다. 이것 외에는 답이 될 수 없다.

## 10 회

본책 p.156

### 01

하위내용영역 문학(소설) B형 서술형 배점 4점 예상정답률 45%

**모범답안** The meaning is that the connection the woman has to God is practiced through her dedication to cleanliness and duty. Second, the instance is "the whole house dancing".

**채점기준**

+ 2점: 밑줄 친 부분의 의미를 "the connection the woman has to God is practiced through her dedication to cleanliness (and duty)"이라 정확하게 기입하였다.
  ▷ 또한 "A good Christian should keep up her house and herself to be clean"이라 하였어도 2점을 준다.
+ 2점: 화자의 즐거운 감정을 보여주는 의인화의 예를 "the whole house dancing"이라 서술하였거나 유사하였다.

### 02

하위내용영역 문학(소설) B형 서술형 배점 4점 예상정답률 35%

**모범답안** Roth is being trained to prepare a corpse for sending to a funeral home. Second, the tone shift occurs when the daughter of the dead man arrives and is sad about the loss, which hasn't been an issue of emotion for the workers whose job is to handle him.

**채점기준**

+ 2점: Roth가 받고 있는 훈련을 "to prepare a corpse for sending to a funeral home"이라 서술하였거나 유사하였다.
+ 2점: 글의 마지막 부분에 있는 어조의 변화를 "when the daughter of the dead man arrives and is sad about the loss, which hasn't been an issue of emotion for the workers whose job is to handle him"라 서술하였거나 유사하였다.

### 03

하위내용영역 문학(드라마) B형 서술형 배점 4점 예상정답률 50%

**모범답안** Candy references her parents as an example of love, as they have a successful relationship. Second, she brings up the bloody face cloth to criticize Bernie's violence.

**채점기준**

+ 2점: Candy가 자신의 부모를 언급하는 이유를 "as an example of love, as they have a successful relationship"이라 정확하게 기입하였다. 이것 외에는 답이 될 수 없다.
+ 2점: Candy가 Bernie를 비난하기 위해 소환한 구체적인 예를 "she brings up the bloody face cloth to criticize Bernie's fighting(violence)"라 서술하였거나 유사하였다.

## 11 회

본책 p.162

### 01

하위내용영역 문학(소설) B형 서술형 배점 4점 예상정답률 45%

**모범답안** Black people would care for their elderly, while White people would put them into care homes. Second, the word is "community". Third, Bottom became a mostly White area, as more white people moved in and living there became too costly for black people.

**채점기준**

+ 1점: 양로원에 대한 백인과 흑인의 차이를 "Black people would care for their elderly, while White people would put them into care homes(= old people's homes; nursing homes)"라 서술하였거나 유사하였다.
+ 1점: 이 차이의 이유를 "community"라 서술하였다. 이것 외에는 답이 될 수 없다.
+ 2점: 바텀 마을의 주민 구성의 변화를 "Bottom became a mostly White area, as more white people moved in and living there became too costly(= unaffordable) for black people"라 서술하였거나 유사하였다.

**한글 번역**

[A] 아, 세월은 얼마나 빠르게 흐르는가. 넬은 이제 이 읍내에 아는 사람이 거의 없었다. 이제 노인들을 위한 또 다른 양로원이 생겼다. 이 메달리온 읍내는 계속해서 노인들을 위한 집들을 짓는 것 같았다. 길을 하나 건설할 때마다 그들은 양로원을 지었다. 사람들은 더 오래 살고 있는 것으로 생각할지 모르나 실상을 더 빠른 속도로 그들의 생명의 불빛이 꺼져가고 있는 것이다. 넬은 가장 최근에 지은 것의 내부 시설을 본 일이 없었으나, 제5순방회에서 그녀가 그 곳에 사는 노인 몇몇을 방문해야 할 차례였다. 목사가 정규적으로 그들을 방문했지만, 그 순방회에서는 개별적인 방문도 효과가 클 것이라고 생각했다. 다른 곳에 있었던 흑인 여성들은 아홉 명이었는데, 바로 그곳에도 아홉 명의 흑인 여성들이 있었다. 그러나 백인들은 많이 있었다. 백인들은 그들의 노인들을 내보내는 일에 주저하지 않았다. 하지만 흑인들은 그들이 가도록 하게 하는 데에 상당한 어려움이 있었는데, 혹 어떤 이가 늙고 홀로됐다 하더라도 다른 사람들이 가서 마루를 닦아주거나 요리를 해주었다. 그들이 미치거나 다룰 수 없게 되었을 때에만 그들은 요양소로 떠나도록 돼있었다.
넬은 단지 1년 정도만 교회에서 정말 적극적으로 활동해 오고 있었는데, 그것은 아이들이 다 자라서 그녀의 마음속에서 시간도 덜 차지하고 있었고, 그녀 마음의 공간도 덜 차지하고 있었기 때문이었다. 주드가 나가 버린 이래 25년이 넘도록 그녀는 생활을 줄여 근근이 살아왔다. 재혼해 보려고 약간의 시간도 보내본 적이 있었으나 세 아이와 함께 그녀를 도맡기를 원하는 이는 한 명도 없었고, 남자친구와의 관계를 유지해 나갈만한 여유가 없었다.

[B] 그러는 동안 바텀 마을은 몰락해 버렸다. 전쟁 동안에 돈을 번 이들이 이 계곡에 근접할 수 있는 한 되도록 가까이 이사해 왔고, 백인들 역시 강기슭, 강 건너 할 것 없이 마치 강 두 양쪽에 그어진 두 줄처럼 메달리온을 확장시키며 땅을 사들이고 있었다. 이 바텀 마을에 사는 흑인들은 더이상 없었다. 백인들은 그 위에 텔레비전 방송국을 짓기 위해 탑을 세우고 있었고, 골프장이나 그 밖의 것에 대한 소문도 나돌고 있었다. 하여간 이 언덕 땅은 이제 더 값비싼 곳이 되었고, 전쟁 후, 그리고 1950년대에 그 언덕 아래로 이사해 온 흑인들은 그들이 되돌아가고 싶어도 그럴 만한 여유가 없었다.
이처럼 백인들은 그들의 마음을 바꾸어 계곡의 편편한 곳을 가지는 대신 이제는 강을 내려다볼 수 있고 느릅나무들이 언덕 주변을 둘러싸고 있는 그 언덕 꼭대기를 원하였다. 흑인들은 그들의 새로운 모습에도 불구하고 계곡 쪽으로 내려가거나 읍내를 떠나거나 누구든 흥미를

느끼는 사람에게 넘기기 위해 언덕을 포기하는 일을 몹시 갈망하는 것 같이 보였다. 이 바텀 마을은 정말 살 만한 곳이었기 때문에 이는 슬픈 현상이었다. 이 젊은이들은 공동체에 관해 거듭 이야기하고 있었으나, 그들은 이 언덕을 가난한 이들, 늙은이들, 고집 센 이들, 그리곤 그 부유한 백인들에게 남겨두고 떠나버렸다. 아마, 이곳은 공동체가 아니라 하나의 장소였을 것이다. 이젠 어떤 장소조차 남겨져 있지 않고, 각자의 텔레비전과 전화를 가지고, 남의 집들에는 점점 덜 들르는 각각의 집들만 있게 되어 버렸다. 이런 생각은 그녀가 읍내에 갈 때면 언제나 가졌던 똑같은 생각들이었다.

## 02

**하위내용영역** 문학(시) B형 서술형 **배점** 4점 **예상정답률** 50%

**모범답안** It refers to afterlife. Second, the word is “visitor”.

**채점기준**

+ 2점 : 밑줄 친 “그 어둠의 오두막”이 가리키는 것을 “afterlife” 또는 “death”라 서술하였다.
+ 2점 : 빈칸에 들어갈 단어를 “visitor”라 서술하였거나 유사하였다.

**한글 번역**

죽음이 오면  
가을에 굶주린 곰처럼  
죽음이 오면 빛나는 동전을 죄다 꺼내어

나를 사려고 죽음이 와서 지갑을 달칵 닫으면  
홍역과 마마처럼  
죽음이 오면

어깨뼈 사이로 빙산처럼  
죽음이 오면

나는 호기심에 가득 차 그 문으로 걸어 나가보고 싶다.  
그 어둠의 오두막은 어떻게 생겼을까 궁금해 하며

그래서 나는 모든 것을  
형제애로, 자매애로 바라본다.  
나는 시간을 하나의 관념으로 보며  
영원을 또 하나의 가능성으로 본다.

그리고 각 생명이 하나의 꽃이라고 생각한다.  
들판의 데이지처럼 흔하면서도 단 하나뿐인

모든 이름들은 입 안에서 자연스러운 음악과 같고  
모든 음악이 그러하듯 침묵을 향해 가며

하나하나의 육체는 용맹한 사자이고  
대지에 귀중한 것.

삶이 끝나면 나는 말하고 싶다. 평생  
나는 경이로움과 결혼한 신부였노라고  
세계를 두 팔에 껴안은 신랑이었노라고

삶이 끝나면 나는 내가 내 삶을  
특별하고 진정하게 살았는지 궁금해 하고 싶지 않다.

한숨지으며 두려워하는 모습을 보고 싶지 않다  
싸우려는 내 모습도

나는 이 세상을 그저 방문한 것으로 끝내고 싶지 않다.

## 03

**하위내용영역** 문학(드라마) B형 서술형 **배점** 4점 **예상정답률** 45%

**모범답안** The words are “green industry.” Second, Skilling wants to develop energy in other forms than oil and gas but Roe wants to continue with oil and natural gas.

**채점기준**

+ 2점 : 풍력발전지역이나 수력발전시설과 상응하는 단어를 “green industry”라 정확하게 기입하였다. 이 것외에는 답이 될 수 없다.
+ 2점 : Skilling과 Roe 사이의 주요한 차이를 “Skilling wants to develop energy in other forms than oil and gas but Roe wants to continue with oil and natural gas”라 서술하였거나 유사하였다.

## 12 회

본책 p.168

### 01

하위내용영역 문학(소설) B형 서술형 배점 4점 예상정답률 50%

모범답안 It is "By using her bones like the sails of a ship". Second, the butcher is stunned, nervous and only reluctantly fills her order.

채점기준

+ 2점: 주요 인물의 육체적 상황을 드러내는 비유적 언어가 있는 문장을 "By using her bones like the sails of a ship"이라 정확하게 기입하였다. 이것 외에는 답이 될 수 없다.
+ 2점: 의미를 "the butcher is stunned, nervous and only reluctantly fills her order"라 서술하였거나 유사하였다.

### 02

하위내용영역 문학(시) A형 서술형 배점 4점 예상정답률 45%

모범답안 The students believed that the weather was too enjoyable in Florida to stay focused on writing poetry, unlike the cold north. Second, the word is "stillness". Third, the word is "classroom".

채점기준

+ 2점: 플로리다에 위대한 시인들이 거의 없는 이유에 대한 학생들의 의견을 "the weather was too enjoyable in Florida to stay focused on writing poetry, unlike the cold north"라 서술하였거나 유사하였다.
+ 1점: 밑줄 친 부분과 상응하는 단어를 "stillness"라 서술하였다. 이것 외에는 답이 될 수 없다.
+ 1점: 빈칸에 들어갈 단어를 "classroom"라 정확하게 기입하였다. 이것 외에는 답이 될 수 없다.

### 03

하위내용영역 문학(드라마) B형 서술형 배점 4점 예상정답률 50%

모범답안 Joyce is angry with Marlene for leaving their hometown and family to pursue her career. Second, it is implied Jeanine will not get hired because it is expected she will put her family ahead of work.

채점기준

+ 2점: Joyce가 Marlene에게 화가 난 주요한 이유를 "for leaving(=because she left) their hometown and family (in order) to pursue her career"라 서술하였거나 유사하였다.
+ 2점: Jeanine이 자신의 결혼 계획을 회사에 알렸다면 일어날 수 있는 일을 "Jeanine will not get hired because it is expected she will put her family ahead of work"라 서술하였거나 유사하였다.

# 13회

본책 p.174

## 01

하위내용영역 문학(소설) B형 서술형 배점 4점 예상정답률 40%

모범답안 The personification that reflects the narrator's inner life is that the rain is described as being "like it's angry with someone". Second, this reflects the speaker's inner life in that he/she is expecting conflict because he/she is speaking in a way which might offend the woman he/she speaks with. Third, "museum" best fills in the blank.

채점기준

+ 1점: 화자가 사용한 personification을 "the rain is described as being like it is angry with someone"라 서술하였거나 유사하였다.
  ▷ 다음과 같이 서술하였어도 1점을 준다.
  - "the rain is coming down like it's angry with someone"
  - "the rain is compared to a person who is angry with someone"
+ 1점: 위의 personification을 화자가 사용할 때, 화자의 내적 상태를 "he/she is expecting conflict because he/she is speaking in a way which might offend the woman he/she speaks with"라 서술하였거나 유사하였다.
+ 2점: 빈칸에 들어갈 단어를 "museum"이라 정확히 기입하였다. 이것 외에는 답이 될 수 없다.

## 02

하위내용영역 문학(시) B형 서술형 배점 4점 예상정답률 30%

모범답안 The thematic idea of the poem is that inside a grocery store there are many issues affected by consumerism (capitalism/international corporations) that are ignored (such as local farmers, wars, and deaths). Second, "these people" are those harmed by the effects of large grocery corporations such as local farmers, children, the dark-skinned man, Nicaraguan heroes.

채점기준

+ 2점: 시의 중심 주제를 "inside a grocery store there are many issues affected by consumerism (capitalism/international corporations) that are ignored (such as local farmers, wars, and deaths)"라 서술하였거나 유사하였다.
+ 2점: "these people"이 누구냐는 질문에 "those harmed by the effects of large grocery corporations (such as local farmers, children, the dark-skinned man, Nicaraguan heroes)"라 서술하였거나 유사하였다.

## 03

하위내용영역 문학(드라마) B형 서술형 배점 4점 예상정답률 40%

모범답안 In the above excerpt, A can be inferred to be the oldest and C the youngest. Second, B is shown to be practical by declaring it best to tell children they are dying "the minute they're alive".

채점기준

+ 2점: 세 명의 등장인물 중 "A가 가장 나이가 많고 C가 가장 젊다"라 서술하였다.
+ 2점: B의 현실주의적 성격을 보여주는 부분을 "B is shown to be practical by declaring it best to tell children they are dying "the minute they're alive"라 서술하였거나 유사하였다.
  ▷ 다음과 같이 서술하였어도 1점을 준다.
  "Character B's practical personality is demonstrated in the part, "Start in young; make 'em aware they've got only a little time. Make 'em aware they're dying from the minute they're alive."

# 14 회

본책 p.180

## 01

하위내용영역 문학(소설) B형 서술형 배점 4점 예상정답률 30%

모범답안 The simile of the underlined helps the reader understand how omnipresent the mud is, as cheesemites live on the surface of cheese and it forms their whole environment. Second, the other major setting other than the battlefield is the estaminet.

채점기준

+ 2점: 밑줄 친 부분의 직유의 의미를 "how omnipresent the mud is, as cheesemites live on the surface of cheese and it forms their whole environment (or world)"라 서술하였거나 유사하였다.
+ 2점: 전쟁터를 제외한 주요 세팅을 "estaminet"라 정확히 기입하였다. 이것 외에는 답이 될 수 없다.

감점 본문에 나오는 연속되는 5단어 이상을 사용하였으면 0.5점 감점한다.

## 02

하위내용영역 문학(시) B형 서술형 배점 4점 예상정답률 45%

모범답안 The underlined "Black shapes" refer to surfers. Second, the second-to-last stanza uses alliteration in the pairs of: slick/seals, board/bare.

채점기준

+ 2점 : 밑줄 친 "검은 형태"가 가리키는 것을 "surfers" 또는 "surf riders"라 하였다.
+ 1점 : 마지막의 두 번째 연에서 사용된 시적 장치를 "alliteration"이라 하였다.
+ 1점 : "alliteration"의 예를 다음의 4가지 중 2개를 서술하였다.
"① slick/seals ② board/bare ③ foot/ feels ④ suck/shingle"

## 03

하위내용영역 문학(드라마) B형 서술형 배점 4점 예상정답률 45%

모범답안 Hester believes marriages are about feeling and shouldn't be discussed while Robert believes they should be. Second, Hester is frustrated with the interference of her future mother-in-law in their issues and Robert's concern for her(mother-in-law) over her(Hester).

채점기준

+ 2점 : 결혼에 대한 Hester와 Robert의 상이한 관점을 "Hester believes marriages are about feeling and shouldn't be discussed while Robert believes they should be"라 서술하였거나 유사하였다.
+ 2점 : Hester가 지닌 미래의 시어머니에 대한 태도를 "Hester is frustrated with the interference of her future mother-in-law in their issues and Robert's concern for her(mother-in-law) over her(Hester)"라 서술하였거나 유사하였다.

# 15 회

본책 p.186

## 01

하위내용영역 문학(소설) B형 서술형 배점 4점 예상정답률 40%

모범답안 Big Fat represents religion or a religious leader. Second, the song made their tempers and rage rise.

채점기준

+ 2점 : Big Fat이 상징하는 것을 "a religious leader"라 서술하였거나 유사하였다.
+ 2점 : 밑줄 친 부분의 의미를 "the song made their tempers and rage rise"라 서술하였거나 유사하였다.
  ▷ 20세기 초반 미국 작가의 우화적 단편의 한 부분을 읽고, 그 우화 속 등장인물의 상징성을 이해하고 있는지를 평가한다.

감점 본문에 나오는 연속되는 4단어 이상을 사용하였으면 0.5점 감점한다.

한글 번역

"하지만 정말 이상했지. 시간이 지날수록 남은 사람들은 더 뼈빠지게 일하는데도, 우리 바다마을의 먹을 것은 점점 더 적어졌거든."
"하지만 염소와 옥수수, 알뿌리, 어망이 있잖아요?" 어둠이 무서워서 말했다. "그건 어떻게 된 거예요? 사람들이 일을 하는데도 먹을 것이 줄어들었나요?"
"그렇단다." 긴 수염 할아버지가 말했다. "어망을 가진 세 사람은 어망이 생기기 전 온 부족이 잡은 물고기보다 더 많이 잡았지. 고기를 더 많이 잡을수록 우리가 먹을 것은 더 적어졌단다."
"그렇다면 일을 하지 않는 사람들이 그걸 모두 먹었다는 거잖아요?" 노란 머리가 물었다.

긴 수염이 슬픈 얼굴로 고개를 끄덕이며 말했다. "개이빨이 키우는 개들은 고기를 잔뜩 먹었고, 아무 일도 안하고 햇볕에 누워 뒹구는 자들은 살이 뒤룩 뒤룩 쪘지만, 많은 아이들은 배가 고파서 잠을 못 자고 울었단다. 우리가 불평하면, 큰 뚱보가 일어서서, 신이 현명한 자들에게 땅과 어망을 갖게 하며, 그런 현명한 자들이 없으면 우리는 모두 나무에 살던 그 시절처럼 동물보다 나을 게 없다고, 신을 대리하는 목소리로 말했단다."

"그리고 어떤 사람이 나타나서 왕을 위해 노래하는 가수가 되었지. 우리는 그를 벌레라고 불렀지. 아주 작은 데다 얼굴도 사지도 볼품없었고, 일이나 행동에도 뛰어난 점이란 없었거든. 벌레는 기름진 골수와 최고급 생선, 갓 짜낸 염소젖, 햇곡식을 좋아했지. 그래서 왕의 가수가 되면서 아무것도 하지 않고 살찔 수 있는 방법을 찾았지. 사람들의 불만이 갈수록 심해지고, 몇몇은 왕의 초가집에 돌을 던졌을 때, 벌레는 고기잡이 부족으로 사는 것이 얼마나 좋은 것인지를 노래로 불렀어. 그의 노래에서 벌레는 고기잡이 부족은 신으로부터 선택된 자들이고 신이 만든 최고의 인간들이라 말했지. 벌레는 육식부족은 돼지나 까마귀 따위고, 고기잡이족이 육식족과 싸워서 그들을 죽이는 것이 얼마나 좋고 선한 일인지—이게 신의 뜻이라면서—노래했지. 벌레의 노래가사가 우리 가슴에 불을 지폈고, 우리는 육식족과 싸우러 달려 나갔어. 우리는 배고픈 것도 잊고, 왜 우리가 불평했는지도 잊은 채, 호랑이 얼굴이 우리를 이끌고 경계를 넘어가는 모습에 감격했지. 그 경계를 넘어서 우리는 많은 육식족을 죽였고 기뻐했단다."

## 02

**하위내용영역** 문학(시) B형 서술형 **배점** 4점 **예상정답률** 50%

**모범답안** The setting is described in two similes, "ice looked like a photograph", and "outdoors seem like a room". Second, the six words are "why were they on his property".

**채점기준**

+ 2점: 시의 배경을 묘사하는 직유를 "ice looked like a photograph" and "outdoors seem like a room"이라 서술하였다. 이것 외에는 답이 될 수 없다.
  - ▷ 2개중 2개 모두를 정확하게 서술하였으면 2점; 2개중 1개만 정확하게 서술하였으면 1점; 2개중 0개 서술하였으면 0점을 준다.
+ 2점: 빈칸에 들어갈 6단어를 "why were they on his property"라 정확하게 기입하였다. 이것 외에는 답이 될 수 없다.
  - ▷ 20세기 현대시를 읽고 그 안에서 시의 기본적 요소인 "배경"과 "비유적 언어"에 대해 이해하고 있는지를 평가한다.

## 03

**하위내용영역** 문학(드라마) B형 서술형 **배점** 4점 **예상정답률** 40%

**모범답안** Red Carter describes experiencing injustice when he was arrested for having "too much money" and assumed to be a thief. Next, the word is "arrested".

**채점기준**

+ 2점: Red Carter가 말하는 자신이 경험한 부정의를 "he was arrested for having "too much money" and assumed to be a thief"라 서술하였거나 유사하였다.
+ 2점: 빈칸에 들어갈 단어를 "arrested"라 정확하게 기입하였다. 이것 외에는 답이 될 수 없다.
  - ▷ 드라마에 등장하는 인물들 간의 대화를 통해 각 개인들의 "캐릭터"와 "중요 사건"을 이해하고 있는지를 평가한다.

**감점** 본문에 나오는 연속되는 4단어 이상을 사용하였으면 0.5점 감점한다.

## 16 회

본책 p.192

### 01

하위내용영역 문학(드라마) A형 기입형 배점 2점 예상정답률 45%

모범답안 ⓐ illiterate ⓑ alligator

채점기준

- 2점 : 모범답안과 같다. 이것 외에는 답이 될 수 없다. Spelling 오류는 0점 처리한다.
- 1점 : 둘 중 하나만 맞았다.
- 0점 : 모범답안과 다르다.

[출전] <The Rivals>(1775) by Richard Brinsley Sheridan(1751-1816)

### 02

하위내용영역 문학(시) A형 서술형 배점 4점 예상정답률 35%

모범답안 In the first line, a verbal irony happens*(comes about)* when there is a discrepancy between what the speaker says and what she means. To be specific, the speaker says life is "nice" though she really means life is not nice. The speaker reveals that life is shallow, false, and ultimately meaningless through "sarcastic" tone.

채점기준

+ 4점 : the speaker says life is "nice" though she really means life is not nice(1.5점). The speaker reveals that life is shallow, false, and ultimately meaningless(0.5점) through "sarcastic" tone(2점).
  - ▷ sarcastic 대신에 cynical이라 하였어도 2점을 준다.

[출전] "Life Is a Nice Place" by Louise Gluck (1943-)

### 03

하위내용영역 문학(소설) B형 서술형 배점 4점 예상정답률 45%

모범답안 The landlady's smile faded because the man is leaving suddenly and she thought he would want his advance back. The smile returns because he willingly gives over the week's advance rent.

채점기준

+ 2점 : 여관 주인의 웃음이 사라진 이유를 "because (the man is leaving suddenly and) she thought he would want his advance back"이라 서술하였거나 유사하였다.
+ 2점 : 여관 주인의 웃음이 다시 돌아온 이유를 "because he willingly gives over the week's advance rent"라 서술하였거나 유사하였다.

[출전] <The Dubious Battle>(1936) by John Steinbeck (1902-1968)

### 04

하위내용영역 문학(소설) B형 서술형 배점 4점 예상정답률 40%

모범답안 The dramatic irony is revealed in section [D]. Second, the dramatic irony happens when there is a discrepancy between what the characters — the policemen — know and what the reader knows. Specifically, the policemen believe the murder weapon is such a big club that they can find it easily, but the reader knows such a thing will never happen because they are getting rid of it by eating the leg of lamb.

채점기준

+ 2점 : 극적 아이러니가 드러난 부분이 [D]임을 정확히 기술하였다.
+ 2점 : 글의 전체 맥락에서 극적 아이러니가 일어나는 방식을 "the policemen believe the murder weapon is such a big club that they can find it easily(1점), but the reader knows such a thing will never happen because they are getting rid of it*(this important piece of evidence)* by eating the leg of lamb(1점)."라 서술하였거나 유사하였다.

[출전] "Lamb to the Slaughter"(1953) by Roald Darl(1916-1990)

## 17 회

본책 p.199

### 01

하위내용영역 문학(소설) A형 기입형 배점 2점 예상정답률 55%

모범답안 • stars

채점기준

- 2점 : 모범답안과 같다. 이것 외에는 답이 될 수 없다.
- 0점 : 모범답안과 다르다.

한글 번역

키노는 어스름 속에서 잠이 깼다. 별은 아직도 빛나고 있었으나 동쪽 하늘에서는 아스라이 동이 텄다. 수탉은 얼마 동안 '꼬끼오'하고 울어댔고, 부지런한 돼지는 먹을 것이 떨어져 있나 나뭇가지와 나뭇조각을 쉴 새 없이 휘젓고 있었다. 선장이 덤불로 둘러싸인 초가집 바깥에는 작은 새들이 재잘거리며 날개를 치고 있었다.
키노는 눈을 뜨자 먼저 환하게 밝아 오는 구형의 문쪽으로 눈길을 돌리고 나서 코요티토가 잠들어 있는 그물 침대를 쳐다보았다. 그리고 마지막에는 하늘빛 숄로 코와 가슴과 작은 등을 감싸고 그의 옆 돗자리에 누워있는 쥬아나에게로 고개를 돌렸다. 쥬아나도 깨어있었다. 키노는 자기가 잠에서 깼을 때 아내의 눈이 감겨져 있는 것을 한 번도 본 일이 없었다. 그녀의 검은 눈은 별을 거의 반사하고 있지 않았다. 쥬아나는 그가 잠에서 깼을 때 언제나 쳐다보던 그 눈빛으로 그를 바라보고 있었다.
키노는 해변가에서 밀려오는 아침의 잔물결 소리를 듣고 있었다. 대단히 상쾌한 소리였다—키노는 다시 눈을 감고 그 음악에 귀를 기울이고 있었다. 어쩌면 그만이 그 음악을 듣고 있었는지도 모르고 또 어쩌면 모든 그의 종족이 듣고 있었는지도 모른다. 그의 종족은 한때 노래를 아주 잘 만들어서 그들이 보는 것이나 생각한 것, 하는 것, 듣는 것들 모두가 노래가 되었다. (하지만) 그것도 이미 오래전 일이 되었다.

[출전] "Pearl" by John Steinbeck(1902-1968)

## 02

하위내용영역 문학(시) A형 서술형 배점 4점 예상정답률 35%

모범답안• The sarcasm of the third stanza is that the priest is described as showing "care" when he violently take the child to be burned. Second, the poet disapproves of the power and violence shown by the church against free thinking.

채점기준

+ 2점: 3연에 있는 시인의 빈정대는 내용을 "the priest is described as showing "care" when he violently takes the child to be burned"라 서술하였거나 유사하였다.

+ 2점: 시인이 시에서 주요하게 비난하는 것에 대해 "the poet disapproves of the power and violence shown by the church against free thinking"이라 서술하였거나 유사하였다.

▷ 또는 다음과 같이 서술하였어도 2점을 준다.

- "a religious system that denounces human reason as a means to reach spiritual truth, and suppresses human imagination"
- "the authority of the church that is cruel and dogmatic"
- "the church that lacks compassion"
- "the abusive authority of the church"
- "the restrictive faith promoted by religious institutions, instead defending the use of reason in order to better understand one's faith"
- "the close-mindedness of the church"

▷ priest라고만 하였으면 1.5점을 준다.

[출전] "A Little Boy Lost" by William Blake (1757-1827)

## 03

하위내용영역 문학(소설) B형 서술형 배점 4점 예상정답률 40%

모범답안• The most important symbol is the old negro woman. Second, the most positive thing is that they raise a healthy child.

채점기준

+ 2점: 두 커플의 깨진 관계를 가장 잘 드러내는 상징을 "the old negro woman"라 서술하였다.

▷ 다음과 같이 서술하였어도 2점을 준다.
"the negro woman" 또는 "the old woman" 또는 "a black woman"

+ 2점: 이 커플의 관계에서 가장 긍정적인 부분을 "they raise a healthy child"라 서술하였거나 유사하였다.

▷ "their healthy child"라 하였어도 2점을 준다.

[출전] "Song on Royal Street" by Richard Blessing (1939-1983)

## 04

하위내용영역 문학(드라마) B형 서술형 배점 4점 예상정답률 45%

모범답안• "Dinner money" is the money that the employees steal*(take)* from the income. Next, Toni is the newest member.

채점기준

+ 2점: "Dinner money"를 "the money that the employees steal from the income"라 서술하였거나 유사하였다.

+ 2점: 가장 최근에 들어온 직원이 "Toni"임을 정확하게 기술하였다.

[출전] <The Flick> by Annie Baker(1981-)

## 18 회

본책 p.207

### 01

하위내용영역 문학(소설) A형 서술형 배점 2점 예상정답률 55%

모범답안 ⓐ third-person ⓑ shadow

채점기준

- 2점 : 모범답안과 같다. 이것 외에는 답이 될 수 없다.
- 1점 : 둘 중 하나만 맞았다.
- 0점 : 모범답안과 다르다.

한글 번역

점심때가 조금 지난 한적한 시간에 조용한 빈 복도에서 그림자처럼 수수하고 조용한 조는 다섯 살 먹은 아이치고도 작은 아이였다. 그 복도에 다른 이가 있었다 해도 그가 언제, 어느 문으로, 어느 방으로 사라졌는지 알 수가 없었을 것이다. 하지만 이 시간에 복도에는 아무도 없었다. 그는 그것을 알고 있었다. 영양사가 사용하고 있던 치약을 우연히 발견한 이래 거의 일 년 동안이나 이런 일을 해 왔던 것이다.

방에 들어서자 그는 소리가 나지 않게 맨발로 곧장 세면대로 가서 튜브에 든 치약을 찾아냈다. 그는 분홍빛 벌레와도 같은 치약이 매끄럽게 빠져나와 양피지 빛깔의 자기 손가락에 차갑고 천천히 기어오르는 것을 지켜보다가 갑자기 복도에서 울려오는 발자국 소리를 들었고, 다음 순간 바로 문밖에서 나는 사람의 말소리를 들었다. 손에 치약 튜브를 쥔 채 맨발로 그림자처럼 조용히 방을 가로질러 그 방 한 쪽 구석을 막아 놓은 커튼 밑으로 살짝 숨어 들어갔다. 엉거주춤한 자세로 영양사와 그녀의 동반자가 방으로 들어오는 소리를 들었다.

영양사는 그에겐 이렇다 할 중요한 존재가 아니었는데, 단지 먹는 일, 음식, 식당, 나무의자에서 식사하는 몸가짐 등에 언제나 부수적으로 따라다니는 존재이며 가끔 그의 시야에 그녀가 들어올 때에도 전혀 무슨 의미를 나타내지 못하고, 다만 어쩐지 기분이 좋고 그 모습을 보는 것이 즐거울 뿐이었다. 그는 또한 그녀의 동반자의 목소리도 알았다. 그것은 고아원 전속 의사의 조수이며 공립병원에서 온 젊은 인턴의 목소리였다.

[출전] <Light in August> by William Faulkner (1897-1962)

### 02

하위내용영역 문학(시) A형 서술형 배점 4점 예상정답률 45%

모범답안 Its meaning is that the narrator knows a woman who has a negative way of speaking. Second, the thematic idea of the poem is that beauty swiftly fades.

채점기준

- 2점 : 밑줄 친 부분의 의미를 "<u>the narrator knows a woman who has a negative way of speaking</u>"라 서술하였거나 유사하였다.
- 2점 : 시의 중심 주제를 "<u>beauty swiftly fades</u>"라 하였거나 유사하게 서술하였다.
  - ▷ 다음과 같이 서술하였어도 2점을 준다.
    - "beauty is transitory *(or passing rapidly)*"
    - "Age has rapidly destroyed beauty"

한글 번역

푸른 소녀들

푸른 스커트 자락 펄럭이며
신학교 탑 아래 잔디밭을 지나
늙고 만만치 않은 선생들의 강의를 들으러 가거라
단 그들의 말을 한마디도 믿지는 말고.

풀밭 위를 거닐며
공중에서 재잘대는 파랑새처럼
무슨 일이 벌어질지 생각일랑 말고
하얀 리본으로 머리를 묶으렴.

푸른 소녀들아. 시들기 전에 네 아름다움 발휘해 보렴
그러면 나의 시끄러운 입술로 소리쳐 공표할테니.
아름다움은 아무리 해도 규명할 수 없는
연약한 것이라고.

그건 내가 들려줄 수 있는 경험에서 나온 것이지
혀가 사나운 여인을 알고 있는데
어느덧 그녀의 푸르던 눈은 흐릿해지고
모든 완벽함도 퇴색해버렸지 – 허나 얼마 전만 해도
너희들 가운데 그 어느 누구보다 더 아름다웠지.

[출전] "Blue Girls" by John C. Ransom(1888-1974)

## 03

하위내용영역 문학(드라마) B형 서술형 배점 4점 예상정답률 45%

**모범답안** The meaning of "Frozen!" is completely paralyzed and unable to move. Next, Jenny's frustration with Samantha is that she believes her to be unhappy with her for not making her life as a doll easier.

**채점기준**

+ 2점: 밑줄 친 부분의 의미를 "completely paralyzed and unable to move"라 하였거나 유사하게 서술하였다.
+ 2점: Jenny가 Samantha에게 좌절하는 핵심적 내용을 "she(Jenny) believes her(Samantha) to be unhappy with her for not making her life as a doll easier"라 하였거나 유사하게 서술하였다.

[출전] <John> by Annie Baker(1981-)

## 04

하위내용영역 문학(소설) B형 서술형 배점 4점 예상정답률 45%

**모범답안** The irony is revealed in section [E]. The Greeks are described as "nice" but this doesn't fit the reality of the situation as*(because)* they are massacring the baggage animals.

**채점기준**

+ 2점: verbal irony가 있는 곳이 "[E]"라 정확히 답하였다.
+ 2점: 이 아이러니의 의미를 "The Greeks are described as "nice" but this doesn't fit the reality of the situation as*(because)* they are massacring the baggage animals."라 서술하였다.
  ▷ 다음과 같이 서술하였어도 2점을 준다.
  "The massacring of the animals is described as "pleasant business" but this doesn't fit the reality of the horrible situation."

[출전] "On the Quai at Smyrna" by E. Hemingway (1899-1961)

## 19 회

본책 p.214

### 01

하위내용영역 문학(시) A형 기입형 배점 2점 예상정답률 40%

모범답안 ⓐ arrival ⓑ cloud

채점기준

- 2점: 모범답안과 같다. 이것 외에는 답이 될 수 없다.
- 1점: 둘 중 하나만 맞았다.
- 0점: 모범답안과 다르다.

[출전] "Morning Song" by Sylvia Plath(1932-1963)

### 02

하위내용영역 문학(드라마) A형 서술형 배점 4점 예상정답률 45%

모범답안 Between the two sections, we can see Walter's personality change in terms of his views on race and money. In terms of race, in Section <A>, he shows envy for wealthy white men and no pride in his black family's accomplishments. However in Section <B>, he expresses pride in his father's earning of the house. Regarding money, initially Walter wants money as a chance for "freedom", then later shows to change his mind and wants to keep the family home rather than accept money to move.

채점기준

+2점: "race"의 측면에서 Walter의 변화가 보이는 부분을 "in Section <A>, he shows envy for wealthy white men and no pride in his black family's accomplishments(1점). However in Section <B>, he expresses pride in his father's earning of the house(1점)"라 서술하였다.

+2점: "money"의 측면에서 Walter의 변화가 보이는 부분을 "initially*(in Section <A>)* Walter wants money as a chance(1점), then later*(in Section <B>)* shows to change his mind and wants to keep the family home rather than accept money to move(1점)"라 서술하였다.

[출전] <A Raisin in the Sun> by Lorrain Hansberry (1930-1965)

### 03

하위내용영역 문학(소설) A형 서술형 배점 4점 예상정답률 50%

모범답안 In the story, the epiphany is experienced by the child who realizes that people have different opinions and experiences and sometimes he must be away from other people. Next, the contrast between the parents' views is that the father wants to enjoy himself picking blackberries even at the risk of the child's cap, and the mother thinks that he is irresponsible for dirtying the hat because they can't afford to replace it.

채점기준

+2점: epiphany를 경험하는 등장인물이 "the child(boy)(0.5점)"이고, epiphany를 경험하게 되는 순간이 "people have different opinions and experiences and sometimes he must be away from other people(1.5점)"라 서술하였거나 유사하였다.

+2점: 아이의 어머니와 아버지의 관점의 차이를 "the father wants to enjoy himself picking blackberries even at the risk of the child's cap(1점), and the mother thinks that he is irresponsible for dirtying the hat because they can't afford to replace it(1점)"라 서술하였거나 유사하였다.

[출전] "Blackberries" by Leslie Norris(1921-2006)

## 20회

본책 p.220

### 01

하위내용영역 문학(시) A형 기입형 배점 2점 예상정답률 65%

모범답안 ⓐ bread ⓑ roses

채점기준

- 2점 : 모범답안과 같다.
- 1점 : 둘 중 하나만 맞았다.
- 0점 : 모범답안과 다르다.

[출전] "Bread and Roses" by James Oppenheim (1882-1932)

### 02

하위내용영역 문학(드라마) A형 서술형 배점 4점 예상정답률 50%

모범답안 The connection between the two characters is that they have had an affair, though Proctor denies it emphatically. Next, Abigail explains that she has become notorious or has had her name "blackened" by the efforts of Proctor's wife Elizabeth in spreading rumors.

채점기준

+ 2점 : 두 등장인물이 서로 맺고 있는 관계를 "they have had an affair, *(though Proctor denies it emphatically – 이 부분은 서술하지 않았어도 맞는 것으로 한다)*"라 서술하였거나 유사하였다.
  ▷ 성적 관계란 표현이 들어가면 모두 맞는 것으로 한다.
+ 2점 : Abigail은 자신이 마을에서 오명을 얻게 된 이유를 "by the efforts of Proctor's wife Elizabeth in spreading rumors"라 서술하였거나 유사하였다.

[출전] <The Crucible> by Arthur Miller(1915-2005)

### 03

하위내용영역 문학(소설) A형 서술형 배점 4점 예상정답률 45%

모범답안 The paradox of the passage lies in the "Catch-22", an unfair rule given to combat pilots. The rule states that any pilot who willingly goes into combat duty is crazy and thus that pilot can be "grounded" as such. However, the rule also requires the airman to ask for this, which demonstrates sanity, and thus means that he is mentally fit to fly, so it will be rejected. Thus no one is eligible to be excused from flying by the paradoxical rule. Orr is a combat pilot and the setting is on a combat base during wartime.

채점기준

+ 2점 : 작품에 등장하는 paradox를 "The paradox of the passage lies in the "Catch-22", an unfair rule given to combat pilots. The rule states that when a pilot is crazy, that pilot can be "grounded." However, the rule also requires the pilot to ask for this, which demonstrates sanity, and thus means that he is mentally fit to fly, so it will be rejected"라 서술하였거나 유사하였다.
+ 1점 : Orr의 직업을 "(combat) pilot"라 정확하게 서술하였다.
  ▷ "soldier"라 했으면 0.5점을 준다.
+ 1점 : 작품의 setting을 "combat base*(or battle field)* during wartime"라 정확하게 서술하였다.

[출전] <Catch-22> by Joseph Heller(1923-1999)

# 21 회

본책 p.226

## 01

하위내용영역 문학(소설) A형 기입형 배점 2점 예상정답률 55%

모범답안 ⓐ manliness ⓑ locusts

채점기준

- 2점 : 모범답안과 같다.
- 1점 : 둘 중 하나만 맞았다.
- 0점 : 모범답안과 다르다.

[출전] <Things Fall Apart> by Chinua Achebe (1930-)

## 02

하위내용영역 문학(드라마) A형 서술형 배점 4점 예상정답률 45%

모범답안 The one word is "patriotism". Second, her hesitation about Sergius stems from her wondering if her imagination created her lofty image of him and in reality he might be a "poor figure" in comparison to other officers.

채점기준

+ 2점 : 밑줄 친 부분에서 Catherine이 강조하는 것과 상응하는 한 단어를 "patriotism"이라 답하였다. 이것 외에는 답이 될 수 없다.
+ 2점 : 이전부터 Raina가 Sergius에 가지고 있었던 주저함에 대해 "her hesitation about Sergius stems from her wondering if her imagination created her lofty image of him and in reality he might be a "poor figure" in comparison to other officers"라 답하였다.

[출전] <Arms and the Man> by George Bernard Shaw(1856-1950)

## 03

하위내용영역 문학(소설) A형 서술형 배점 4점 예상정답률 55%

모범답안 The speaker is teaching grammar. Second, the rhyme scheme is "aba aba aba aba aba abaa".

채점기준

+ 2점 : 화자가 "is teaching grammar"하고 있다고 서술하였다. 또는 "is giving a grammar lesson"이라 하였어도 맞는 것으로 한다.
  ▷ 다음과 같이 서술하였으면 1.5점만 준다. "teaches grammar" 또는 "gives a grammar lesson"
+ 2점 : the rhyme scheme을 "aba aba aba aba aba abaa"라 서술하였다.
  ▷ "aba aba aba aba aba cdaa"라 하였어도 맞는 것으로 한다.

[출전] "The Grammar Lesson" by Steve Kowit (1938-2015)

## 22회

본책 p.231

### 01

하위내용영역 문학(시) A형 서술형 배점 2점 예상정답률 60%

모범답안 ⓐ pipe ⓑ love

채점기준

- 2점 : 모범답안과 같다.
- 1점 : 둘 중 하나만 맞았다.
- 0점 : 모범답안과 다르다.

[출전] "The Shipfitter's Wife" by Dorianne Laux(1952-)

### 02

하위내용영역 문학(드라마) A형 서술형 배점 4점 예상정답률 45%

모범답안 Jack is angry at Lady Snob because she is insulting to his poor status and doesn't want him to marry her daughter. Second, the meaning of the underlined words is that men do not grow up to take on the qualities of their mothers that would improve them, which is a tragedy.

채점기준

+ 2점 : Jack이 Lady Snob에게 화를 내는 이유를 "because she is insulting to his working class status(1점) and doesn't want him to marry her daughter(1점)"라 서술하였거나 유사하였다.
+ 2점 : 밑줄 친 부분의 의미를 "men do not grow up to take on the qualities of their mothers that would improve them, which is a tragedy"라 서술하였거나 유사하였다.

[출전] <The Importance of Being Earnest> by Oscar Wilde(1854-1900)

### 03

하위내용영역 문학(서술) B형 서술형 배점 4점 예상정답률 45%

모범답안 The word best describing the underlined is "isolation". Second, the meaning of "otherwise" is that the two families had not been close despite their shared circumstances. Finally, the underlined words in ⓒ refer to the neighbor's fowl*(hen)* Mrs. Saunders finds eating her garden.

채점기준

+ 2점 : 밑줄 친 ⓐ의 상황을 가장 잘 드러내는 한 단어를 "isolation"이라 답하였다. 이것 외에는 답이 될 수 없다.
+ 1점 : "otherwise"의 의미를 "the two families had not been close"라 답하였거나 유사하였다.
  ▷ "서로 잘 지내지 못했다(불화했다)"의 의미로 답하였으면 모두 맞는 것으로 한다.
+ 1점 : 밑줄 친 ⓒ의 "더 엄청난 불만거리"가 가리키는 것이 "the Cricks' hen messing up her garden"이라 답하였거나 유사하였다.

[출전] "The Blood-Feud of Toad-Water" by Hector Hugh Munro(1870-1916)

## 23회

본책 p.237

### 01

하위내용영역 문학(시) A형 기입형 배점 2점 예상정답률 65%

모범답안 death

채점기준

- 2점 : 모범답안과 같다. 이것 외에는 답이 될 수 없다.
- 0점 : 모범답안과 다르다.

[출전] "For Whom The Bell Tolls" (from *Meditation XVII*) by John Donne(1572-1632)

### 02

하위내용영역 문학(드라마) A형 서술형 배점 4점 예상정답률 50%

모범답안 Miss Moray is numb to the way animals are harmed for research, whereas Helen is very upset and shocked by the way mice are destroyed by the lab. Second, it can be inferred that Margaurita does not work at the laboratory due to her dislike of the destruction of test mice.

채점기준

+ 2점 : 연구실에서 행해지고 있는 실험에 대해 Miss Moray와 Helen의 관점의 차이를 "Miss Moray is undisturbed by(=uncaring about) the way animals are harmed for research, whereas Helen is very upset and shocked by the way mice are destroyed by the lab"이라 서술하였거나 유사하였다.
  ▷ "Miss Moray is numb regarding the way animals are harmed for research, whereas Helen is very upset and shocked by the way mice are destroyed by the lab"라 하였어도 맞는 것으로 한다.
+ 2점 : Margaurita가 실험실에서 더 이상 일을 하지 않은 이유를 "it can be inferred that Margaurita does not work at the laboratory due to her dislike of the destruction of test mice"라 서술하였거나 유사하였다.

[출전] <Let Me Hear You Whisper> by Paul Zindel (1936-2003)

### 03

하위내용영역 문학(소설) A형 서술형 배점 4점 예상정답률 45%

모범답안 The similarity of the speaker and her mother is that they both are "faithful" as the mother regularly mails her postcards and the speaker takes care to read and track her mother in an atlas. On the other hand, the speaker differs from her always out-of-reach mother by remaining in the same place with her family. Second, the symbol representing their relationship is the postcards.

채점기준

+ 1.5점 : 화자와 그녀의 엄마의 유사점을 "the similarity of the speaker and her mother is that they both are "faithful" as the mother regularly mails her postcards (0.7점) and the speaker takes care to read and track her mother in an atlas(0.8점)"라 서술하였거나 유사하였다.

+ 1.5점: 화자와 그녀의 엄마의 차이점을 "the speaker differs from her always out-of-reach mother(0.7점) by remaining in the same place with her family"(0.8점)라 서술하였거나 유사하였다.
   ▷ 또는 "unlike the narrator who remains in the same place with her family, the mother does not 'come back' *(to her daughter)*"라고 하였어도 맞는 것으로 한다.
+ 1점: 화자와 그녀의 엄마의 관계를 드러내 주는 상징을 "the postcards"라 서술하였다. 이것 외에는 답이 될 수 없다.

[출전] "Love, Your Only Mother" by David Michael Kaplan(1946-)

## 24회

본책 p.242

### 01

하위내용영역 문학(소설) A형 기입형 배점 2점 예상정답률 50%

**모범답안** ⓐ Jack
ⓑ Piggy's glasses (or Piggy's specs)

**채점기준**
- 2점: 모범답안과 같다.
- 1점: 둘 중 하나만 맞았다.
- 0점: 모범답안과 다르다.

[출전] <Lord of the Flies> by William G. Golding (1911-1993)

### 02

하위내용영역 문학(시) A형 서술형 배점 4점 예상정답률 45%

**모범답안** The father thinks of himself as "bold", posing in front of a car and wearing his hat in a brash way holding beer and fish. In truth, he is "embarrassed" and "sheepish" as can be read in his eyes and hands that are limp. Second, it can be inferred that the speaker also has a problem with alcohol(ism) like his father.

**채점기준**
+ 3점: 화자가 이상적으로 생각하는 아버지의 모습과 실제 아버지의 모습을 "The father thinks of himself as "bold", posing in front of a car and wearing his hat in a brash way holding beer and fish(1.5점). In truth, he is "embarrassed" and "sheepish" as can be read in his eyes and hands that are limp(1.5점)"라 서술하였거나 유사하였다.

+ 1점 : 밑줄 친 부분에서 추론할 수 있는 화자와 화자의 아버지가 유사하게 지니고 있는 문제를 "a problem with alcohol(ism)"라 서술하였거나 유사하였다.

**[출전]** "Photograph of My Father in His Twenty-Second Year" by Raymond Carver(1938-1988)

## 03

하위내용영역 문학(드라마) B형 서술형 배점 4점 예상정답률 45%

**모범답안** The conflict between man and nature occurs as the storm and sea brings heavy wind, a drowning, and other trouble to the characters. Next, the "bundle" Nora carries contains clothes recovered from a *(unidentified)* drowned man *(found in a city to the north)*. The word in the stage directions that best fits the mood is "anxiety".

**채점기준**

+ 2점 : 인간과 자연의 투쟁(갈등)이 "the storm and sea brings heavy wind, a drowning, and other trouble to the characters"라 서술하였거나 유사하였다.
  - ▷ "강력한 자연 앞에서 죽음을 비롯한 고통을 겪고 인간들 *(사이의 갈등)*"이라는 취지의 내용이 들어가도 맞는 것으로 한다.
+ 1점 : Nora가 들고 있는 보따리(bundle)를 "clothes recovered from a *(unidentified)* drowned man"라 서술하였거나 유사하였다.
+ 1점 : 글 전체의 분위기와 상응하는 한 단어를 "anxiety"라 서술하였다.

**한글 번역**

(아일랜드 서쪽 한 섬. 어떤 오두막집의 부엌, 그물, 방수복들, 물레, 벽에 기대어 세워 놓은 몇 개의 새 나무 판자 등. 20살쯤 된 소녀 캐슬린이 케이크 반죽을 막 끝내고는, 불가에 있는 오븐에 집어넣는다. 그러고선 손을 닦고, 물레를 돌리기 시작한다. 어린 소녀인 노라는 머리를 문 안으로 들이민다.)

노라 : (낮은 목소리로) 엄마 어디 있어?

캐슬린 : 잠자리에 누워있지만, 가능하면 잠을 자고 있을지도 몰라.

(노라가 살며시 숄 아래 꾸러미를 숨겨서 들어온다.)

캐슬린 : (물레를 빠르게 돌리며) 가지고 있는 게 뭐니?

노라 : 젊은 신부님이 가져왔어. 도니골에서 익사한 남자에게서 벗겨낸 셔츠와 스타킹이야.

(캐슬린은 빠른 속도로 물레를 돌리던 손길을 갑자기 멈추고는 이야기를 경청한다.)

엄마가 집에서 나가서 바다를 내려다보고 있을 때에 마이클의 것인지 확인해 보자.

캐슬린 : 그게 어떻게 마이클의 것이겠니. 어떻게 그렇게 멀리 물에 떠내려 갈 수 있겠어?

노라 : 젊은 신부님이 그런 경우를 본 적 있다고 말했어. "마이클 것이라면, 하나님의 은총으로 깨끗한 장례식을 치렀다고 그녀에게 얘기할 수 있고, 만약 그의 것이 아니라면 아무 얘기도 마세요. 울고 애도하느라 거의 죽을 지경이 될 거예요."라고 그가 말했어.

(반쯤 닫아두었던 문이 휙 몰아친 바람에 의해서 열린다.)

캐슬린 : (근심 어린 표정으로 밖을 내다보며) 오늘 Galway 장터로 말을 팔러 가는 바틀리를 막아 달라고 그에게 부탁했니?

노라 : "그를 막을 수 없어요." 신부님이 말했어. "하지만 걱정 말아요. 그녀가*(노라와 캐슬린의 엄마)* 밤의 절반 정도는 기도를 하고 있고 전능하신 하느님께서 아들이 하나도 없게 만들어 그녀를 비참하게 만들지는 않으실 거예요."

캐슬린 : 노라, 흰 바위 옆도 바다가 험하니?

노라 : 꽤 험해. 신의 가호가 있기를. 서쪽 바다에서 심하게 파도가 치고 있고, 조수가 바람 반대방향이 되면 상황은 더 나빠질 거야.

(그녀는 꾸러미를 식탁으로 가져간다.)

내가 지금 열어볼까?

**[출전]** <Riders to the Sea>(바다로 달려간 사람들) by John M. Synge(1871-1909)

## 25 회

본책 p.247

### 01

하위내용영역 문학(드라마) A형 서술형 배점 2점 예상정답률 50%

모범답안 ⓐ Nazi ⓑ identify

채점기준

- 2점: 모범답안과 같다. 이것 외에는 답이 될 수 없다.
- 1점: 둘 중 하나만 맞았다.
- 0점: 모범답안과 다르다.

### 02

하위내용영역 문학(소설) A형 서술형 배점 4점 예상정답률 50%

모범답안 The reader knows that the Victor and his father were emotionally distant but he was still very saddened by his father's death. Next, the meaning of the underlined words given through a simile indicates that the storyteller had no use in the town just as a dentist would need customers with real teeth to be useful.

채점기준

+ 2점: Victor와 그의 아버지의 관계를 "the Victor and his father were emotionally distant but he was still very saddened by his father's death"라 서술하였거나 유사하였다.
+ 1.5점: 밑줄 친 ⓑ의 의미를 "the storyteller *(=Thomas)* had no use in the town just as a dentist *(=just like a dentist who)* would need customers with real teeth"라 서술하였거나 유사하였다.

▷ 다음과 같이 서술하였어도 1.5점을 준다. "Thomas was someone who nobody really listened to, which is why the Narrator compares him to a dentist in a town where no one has (real) teeth"

+ 0.5점: 사용된 비유적 언어를 "simile"라 올바르게 서술하였다.

### 03

하위내용영역 문학(시) B형 서술형 배점 4점 예상정답률 35%

모범답안 The "comfort" offered by the friend is intended to make the speaker feel not burdened by his love of the woman because time will age her and make it easier to handle. *(From this, it is implied the speaker has been in love with the woman for some time and this pains him.)* Secondly, the outburst from Heart means that actually the woman *(speaker's beloved)* is becoming more beautiful as time goes by (to the speaker) and will never be easier to cope with.

채점기준

+ 2점: 친구의 지적−그녀가 나이듦의 징후가 드러난다는−이 화자에게 어떻게 위안을 주는지에 대해 "The "comfort" offered by the friend is intended <u>to make the speaker feel not burdened by his love of the woman because time will age her and make it easier to handle</u>"라 서술하였거나 유사하였다.

+ 2점 : 심장의 울부짖음이 의미하는 것을 "actually the woman*(speaker's beloved)* is becoming more beautiful as time goes by (to the speaker) and will never be easier to cope with"이라 서술하였거나 유사하였다.

**한글 번역**

늘 다정한 이가 어제 말했지:
'그대가 사랑하는 이도 잿빛 머리카락을 지니게 되고,
그녀의 두 눈에도 작은 그늘이 생기게 된다네;
비록 지금은 불가능한 것처럼 보이지만
시간이 흐를수록 현명해지기는 쉬운 법, 그러니
그대에게 필요한 것은 인내뿐이라네.'
(나의) 심장이 울부짖네, '아니야,
나에겐 한 톨의 위안도, 한 부스러기의 위안도 되지 않아.
시간은 단지 그녀의 아름다움을 또다시 더해갈 뿐이라네:
그녀의 위대한 고귀함에
그녀 주위에서 흔들리는 그 불길은, 그녀가 흔들수록, 더 뚜렷이 타오른다네. 오 그녀 눈길에 모든 거친 여름이 있었을 때에는 이러할 길이 없었네.'

오 심장이여, 오 심장이여! 그녀가 단지 고개만 돌리면,
그대는 알게 될 걸세, 위로를 받는 것이 어리석은 일이란 것을.

**[출전]** "The Folly of Being Comforted" by W.B. Yeats

## 26 회

본책 p.252

### 01

**하위내용영역** 문학(소설) A형 기입형 **배점** 2점 **예상정답률** 55%

**모범답안** ⓐ first-person ⓑ civilize

**채점기준**

- 2점 : 모범답안과 같다. 이것 외에는 답이 될 수 없다.
- 1점 : 둘 중 하나만 맞았다.
- 0점 : 모범답안과 다르다.

**[출전]** <The Adventure of Huckleberry Finn> by Mark Twain(1835-1910)

### 02

**하위내용영역** 문학(드라마) A형 서술형 **배점** 4점 **예상정답률** 45%

**모범답안** In the underlined sentence, Prosperine criticizes Lexy's parroting of Morell's ideas as making him appear less adequate. Next, the misconception about women's behavior that Prosperine sarcastically identifies is that women do not have intellect and are full of jealousy*(mere emotions)*.

**채점기준**

+ 2점 : Prosperine이 Lexy에 하는 비판을 "Prosperine criticizes Lexy's parroting of Morell's ideas as making him appear less adequate"라 서술하였거나 유사하였다.
+ 2점 : Prosperine이 냉소적으로 여성의 행위라고 잘못 이해하고 있는 것을 "women do not have intellect and are full of jealousy*(mere emotions)*"라 서술하였거나 유사하였다.

**[출전]** <Candida> by George B. Shaw(1856-1950)

## 03

하위내용영역 문학(시) A형 서술형 배점 4점 예상정답률 35%

모범답안 The speaker's perspective in the poem is that if it is "god" that intentionally gives suffering, then he/she will accept it. Second, "my pilgrimage" refers to the speaker's life.

채점기준

+ 2점 : 1~2연에서 제시되는 신에 대한 화자의 입장이 "if it is "god" that intentionally gives suffering, then they *(he/she)* will accept it"라 서술하였거나 유사하였다.
+ 2점 : 마지막 행에 있는 "나의 순례"가 가리키는 것이 "the speaker's life"라 서술하였다.

한글 번역

우연

만일 어느 원한으로 가득한 신이 하늘 위에서,
"너희, 고통 받는 것들아,
알아두거라. 너희들의 슬픔은 나의 환희요,
너희가 사랑하는 것들의 손실은 내 증오의 이익이
란다"라며 날 불러 비웃는다면

그런다면 나는 그 악감정이 부당한 만큼
도리어 강철처럼 견디며 이를 악물고 죽을 텐데
나보다 센 어떤 '권능'이 있어 그의 의지로
내 몫의 눈물 쏟았노라 생각하고 절반은 안도하며.

허나 그렇지 않네. 왜 기쁨은 살해되어 쓰러지고
왜 최고의 희망은 씨를 뿌린 후 꽃 필줄 모르는가?
무관심한 우연이 해와 비를 막고,
잘게 써는 시간은 재미삼아 신음을 던지네…
반 소경인 이 재판관들이 나의 순례길에
고통과 함께 짐짓 축복을 흩뿌려 놓았네.

[출전] "Hap" by Thomas Hardy

# 27 회

본책 p.257

## 01

하위내용영역 문학 A형 기입형 배점 2점 예상정답률 40%

모범답안 ⓐ row
ⓑ infants / children / babies

채점기준

- 2점 : 모범답안과 같다. 이것 외에는 답이 될 수 없다.
- 1점 : 둘 중 하나만 맞았다.
- 0점 : 모범답안과 다르다.

[출전] "The Dead" by Billy Collins

## 02

하위내용영역 문학(소설) A형 서술형 배점 4점 예상정답률 45%

모범답안 The reason Theodoric has trouble traveling is because his mother raised him to be shielded from the "coarser realities of life" which left him unprepared for normal difficulties. Second, the meaning of the underlined words is that in his clothes he had been *(unknowingly)* carrying a mouse *(from the stables)*.

채점기준

+ 2점 : Theodoric이 여행할 때 당황하는 이유를 "his mother raised him to be shielded from the "coarser realities of life" which left him unprepared for normal difficulties"라 서술하였거나 유사하였다.
+ 2점 : 밑줄 친 "심지어 그의 옷 속에는 그 혼자만 있는 게 아니었다"의 의미를 "in his clothes he had been carrying a mouse"라 서술하였거나 유사하였다.

[출전] "The Mouse" by Hector Hugh Munro(1870-1916)

## 03

하위내용영역 문학(드라마) A형 서술형 배점 4점 예상정답률 40%

**모범답안** The metaphor used by Charles to show sympathy toward his ex-wife is "milk of human kindness". Second, the major concern of Ruth is that Elvira is dangerous and trying to harm(kill) her.

**채점기준**

+ 2점: Charles가 전 부인인 Elvira에 대해 동정심을 드러내는 은유를 "milk of human kindness"라 서술하였거나 유사하였다.
+ 2점: Ruth가 가지고 있는 가장 큰 걱정이 "Elvira is dangerous and trying to harm(kill) her"라 서술하였거나 유사하였다.

[출전] <Blithe Spirit> by Noël Coward(1899-1973)

# 28 회

본책 p.262

## 01

하위내용영역 문학(시) A형 기입형 배점 2점 예상정답률 45%

**모범답안** ⓐ tomb ⓑ hand

**채점기준**

- 2점: 모범답안과 같다. 이것 외에는 답이 될 수 없다.
- 1점: 둘 중 하나만 맞았다.
- 0점: 모범답안과 다르다.

[출전] "This Living Hand" by John Keats(1795-1821)

## 02

하위내용영역 문학(소설) A형 서술형 배점 4점 예상정답률 40%

**모범답안** The central event of the given passage is the death and burial of the right fielder that has occurred suddenly on the baseball field. Second, the worry of the speaker is that the next right fielder might trip over*(stumble)* the grave of the previous.

**채점기준**

+ 2.5점: 핵심 사건을 "the death and burial of the right fielder that has occurred suddenly on the baseball field"라 서술하였거나 유사하였다.
  ▷ Setting인 "the baseball field"를 언급하지 않았으면 1점 감점한다.
+ 1.5점: 새로 온 우익수에 대해 화자가 우려하는 것을 "the next right fielder might trip over the grave of the previous *(right fielder)*"라 서술하였거나 유사하였다.

[출전] "Death of the Right Fielder" by Stuart Dybek(1942-)

## 03

하위내용영역 문학(드라마) A형 서술형 배점 4점 예상정답률 30%

모범답안• The reason Belinda gives for Frederick's nosebleed is that his just seeing violence caused it. Second, the sarcastic meaning of the underlined words is that Brooke has been careless by hurting people. The joke Lloyd makes is that Brooke could destroy the whole theatre arts of the city if she just hits one last person, the box-office manager, which is an exaggeration of the number of people she has harmed.

채점기준

+ 2점 : Frederick의 코피에 대한 Belinda의 이상한 정당화를 "his just seeing violence caused it"라 서술하였거나 유사하였다.
+ 2점 : 밑줄 친 Lloyd의 표현에서 의도되는 것을 "Brooke has been careless by hurting people. The joke Lloyd makes is that Brooke could destroy the whole theatre arts of the city if she just hits one last person, the box-office manager, which is an exaggeration of the number of people she has harmed"라 서술하였거나 유사하였다.

[출전] <Noises Off> by Michael Frayn(1933-)

# 29회

본책 p.267

## 01

하위내용영역 문학(드라마) A형 서술형 배점 2점 예상정답률 55%

모범답안• ⓐ culture ⓑ calm

채점기준

- 2점 : 모범답안과 같다.
- 1점 : 둘 중 하나만 맞았다.
- 0점 : 모범답안과 다르다.

[출전] <Our Town> by Thornton Wilder(1897-1975)

## 02

하위내용영역 문학(시) A형 기입형 배점 4점 예상정답률 40%

모범답안• The significance of the mask is as a false identity the speaker used to surpass limitations and be loved in order to succeed. Second, the poet uses "eggs" in comparison for eyes.

채점기준

+ 2점 : 화자의 성공과 관련하여 마스크의 중요성을 "as a false identity the speaker used to surpass limitations in order to succeed"라 답하였다.
+ 2점 : 눈과 비유되는 한 단어를 "eggs"라 답하였다.

[출전] "Mask" by Henri Cole(1956-)

## 03

하위내용영역 문학(소설) A형 서술형 배점 4점 예상정답률 50%

모범답안 The meaning of the underlined words is that Catherine does not accept what she is hearing, as if her expression of intense denial was metaphoric glass holding back the words from reaching her. Second, Catherine does not enjoy the deceased writer's work because, according to her youthful perspective, the style and setting unusual, morbid, and the unappealing.

채점기준

+ 2점: 밑줄 친 부분의 의미를 "Catherine does not accept what she is hearing(1.5점), as if her expression of intense denial was metaphoric(0.5점) glass holding back the words from reaching her"라 서술하였거나 유사하였다.
+ 2점: Catherine이 죽은 작가의 작품에 대해 "Catherine does not enjoy the deceased writer's work because the style and setting unusual, morbid, and the unappealing"라 서술하였거나 유사하였다.

[출전] "Homage for Isaac Babel" by Doris Lessing (1919-2013)

# 30회

본책 p.272

## 01

하위내용영역 문학(소설) A형 서술형 배점 4점 예상정답률 45%

모범답안 The narrator' daughter-in-law did not want the narrator in her wedding pictures because of her overweight appearance. Second, it can be inferred that the speaker no longer needed those items for swimming because her increased confidence and swimming ability.

채점기준

+ 2점: 화자의 며느리가 화자와 함께 결혼 사진을 같이 찍기를 원하지 않았던 이유를 "her overweight appearance"라 서술하였다.
+ 2점: 밑줄 친 부분에서 추론할 수 있는 것을 "the speaker no longer needed those items for swimming because her increased (confidence and) swimming ability"라 서술하였거나 유사하였다.

[출전] "Disappearing" by Monica Wood

## 02

하위내용영역 문학(시) A형 서술형 배점 4점 예상정답률 45%

모범답안 The major extended metaphor is that the speaker('s life) is a gun. Second, because it is a gun, the speaker will not die, or break, until after its owner has died.

채점기준

+ 2점: 중심적인 확장된 은유를 "the speaker is a gun"이라 서술하였다.
+ 2점: 화자가 자신의 주인보다 오래 살 것이라 말하는 이유를 "(because it is a gun,) the speaker will not die, or break, until after its owner has died"라 서술하였거나 유사하였다.

한글 번역

내 삶은 장전된 총
내내 구석에 서 있던 어느 날
주인이 지나가다 알아보고
날 데려갔네

우리는 왕의 숲을 헤매고
우리는 사슴 사냥을 하네
주인을 위해 내가 소리칠 때마다
산들이 곧바로 대답을 하네

내가 웃음 지으면 다정한 빛이
계곡에서 번쩍이네
마치 베수비오 화산이
기쁨을 참지 못한 듯

멋진 하루를 보내고 밤이 되면
나는 주인의 머리맡을 지키네
하루를 함께 지낸 기분이
푹신한 오리털 베개를 베는 것보다 좋지

주인의 적에게 나는 무서운 적
내가 노란 눈길로 노려보거나
엄지손가락을 단호히 놓으면
아무도 두 번 다시 꼼짝 못하지

내가 주인보다 오래 살지 모르나
주인은 나보다 오래 살아야 한다네
왜냐하면 내게는 죽이는 능력뿐
죽는 힘은 없으니까

[출전] "My Life Had Stood - a Loaded Gun" by Emily Dickinson

## 03

하위내용영역 문학(드라마) A형 서술형 배점 4점 예상정답률 45%

모범답안 The unique quality of the island is that magical music appears in places all over it. Second, the "our work" referred to is the killing of Prospero.

채점기준

+ 2점: 섬의 독특한 점을 "magical music appears in places all over the island"라 서술하였거나 유사하였다.
+ 2점: 밑줄 친 "our work"가 가리키는 것이 "the murder of Prospero"라 서술하였거나 유사하였다.

[출전] <The Tempest> by William Shakespeare

## 31 회

본책 p.278

### 01

하위내용영역 문학(시) A형 기입형 배점 2점 예상정답률 50%

모범답안 turn

채점기준

- 2점: 모범답안과 같다. 이것 외에는 답이 될 수 없다.
- 0점: 모범답안과 다르다.

[출전] "The Layers" by Stanley Kunitz(1905-2006)

### 02

하위내용영역 문학(소설) A형 서술형 배점 4점 예상정답률 35%

모범답안 The underlined words in Section <B> indicate the character's renewed and vigorous commitment to life. As the protagonist gathers his strength to attempt to save himself, he envisions the way he needs to move forward to succeed. As he faces the external conflict courageously, he shows a stark change of emotional state from Section <A>, when he was focused on his death and "frightened" and arms were "trembling" in weakness thinking of his "wasted life".

채점기준

+ 2.5점: 밑줄 친 부분이 의미하는 것이 "the character's renewed and vigorous commitment to life"이라 서술하였거나 유사하였다.
  ▷ 다음과 같이 서술하였어도 2.5점을 준다. (죽을지도 모르는) 고통스런 외적 상황에 직면한 주인공의 내적 갈등이 드러나는 부분에서 (나약한 인간의 모습을 보이는 <A>와는 달리) <B>에 있는 밑줄 친 부분("그냥 쉽게 떨어져 죽을 때까지 마냥 기다리지만은 않겠다는 다짐")을 "<u>주인공이 삶에 대한 새롭고도 강한 의지를 보이고 있다</u>"라 서술하였다.
+ 1.5점: <B>에서 보이는 결단력 있는 주인공의 의식 상태와 대조적인 것으로, <A>에서 보이는 주인공의 나약함을 드러내는 구체적인 예를 "when he was focused on his death and 'frightened' and arms were 'trembling'"라 서술하였거나 유사하였다.
  ▷ "frightened"나 "trembling" 중 하나를 서술하였으면 맞는 것으로 한다.

감점 본문에 나오는 연속되는 6단어 이상을 사용하였으면 0.5점 감점한다.

[출전] "Contents of the Dead Man's Pockets" by Jack Finney(1911-1995)

### 03

하위내용영역 문학(드라마) A형 서술형 배점 4점 예상정답률 40%

모범답안 In the scene, the Prince arrived inside the Palace by climbing a beech tree, because he did not like to wait for the slow, loud drawbridge. Second, in the underlined part, the Prince had thought of himself as "brave" because of his climb, but upon learning that the Princess "often" makes the same climb, he becomes humbled.

채점기준

+ 2점: 왕자가 궁에 어떻게 들어왔는지에 대해 "the Prince arrived inside the Palace by climbing a beech tree"라 서술하였거나 유사하게 서술하였다.
+ 2점: 밑줄 친 부분의 의미를 왕자의 자부심과 연결하여 "The Prince had thought of himself as "brave" because of his climb, but upon learning that the Princess "often" makes the same climb, he becomes humbled"라 서술하였거나 유사하였다.

감점 본문에 나오는 연속되는 6단어 이상을 사용하였으면 0.5점 감점한다.

[출전] "The Ugly Duckling" by A. A. Milne (1882-1956)

## 32 회

본책 p.284

### 01

하위내용영역 문학(시) A형 기입형 배점 2점 예상정답률 50%

모범답안 ⓐ apple ⓑ personification

채점기준

- 2점: 모범답안과 같다.
- 1점: 둘 중 하나만 맞았다.
- 0점: 모범답안과 다르다.

[출전] "Apple" by Jane Hirshfield(1953-)

### 02

하위내용영역 문학(소설) A형 서술형 배점 4점 예상정답률 50%

모범답안 From the underlined part, we can infer that Gilbert is self-absorbed, as he is only interested in his deceased wife's writings as it concerns him. Next, the diary symbolizes the wife's secret life away from her husband Gilbert.

채점기준

+ 2점: 밑줄 친 부분에서 Gillbert에 대해 추론할 수 있는 것을 "Gilbert is self-absorbed, as he is only interested in his deceased wife's writings as it concerns him"이라 서술하였거나 유사하였다.
  ▷ "selfish", "self-centered", "egocentric" 등으로 썼어도 맞는 것으로 한다.
+ 2점: 죽은 부인의 비밀스러운 삶을 상징하는 것을 "the diary"라 서술하였다. 이것 외에는 답이 될 수 없다.

감점 첫 번째 답안을 하나의 문장으로 서술하지 않았으면 0.2점 감점한다.

[출전] "Legacy" by Virginia Woolf(1882-1941)

## 03

하위내용영역 문학(드라마) A형 서술형 배점 4점 예상정답률 40%

**모범답안** The meaning of the underlined words is that the learning ability of Helen is strong and quick to hold onto things she is taught like a mouse caught in a trap. Next, Kate first thinks that Annie is too young for the position and that Helen can't be taught. Her perspective changes as she comes to respect Annie's insight and ability and resolves herself to help teach Helen language.

**채점기준**

+ 2점 : 밑줄 친 부분에서 Annie가 의도하는 것이 "the learning ability of Helen is strong and quick to hold onto things she is taught like a mouse caught in a trap"이라 서술하였거나 유사하였다.
+ 2점 : Annie와 Helen에 대한 Kate의 관점의 변화를 "Kate first thinks that Annie is too young for the position(0.5점); Helen can't be taught(0.5점). Kate comes to respect Annie's insight and ability(0.5점); resolves herself to help teach Helen language(0.5점)."라 서술하였거나 유사하였다.
  - ▷ Annie에 대한 태도의 변화 1점 (변화하기 전과 변화된 후 각각 0.5점)
  - ▷ Helen에 대한 태도의 변화 1점 (변화하기 전과 변화된 후 각각 0.5점)

[출전] "The Miracle Worker" by William Gibson (1914-2008)

# 33회

본책 p.289

## 01

하위내용영역 문학(소설) A형 기입형 배점 2점 예상정답률 40%

**모범답안** amiable weakness

**채점기준**

- 2점 : 모범답안과 같다. 이것 외에는 답이 될 수 없다.
- 0점 : 모범답안과 다르다.

[출전] "The Soul of Laploshka" by Saki(본명 Hector Hugh Munro, 1870-1916)

## 02

하위내용영역 문학(드라마) A형 서술형 배점 4점 예상정답률 45%

**모범답안** The tragedy regarding Gabe is the major head injury he received in the war against Japan, leaving him with a "metal plate" in his head (*and "three thousand dollars"*). Troy feels guilt because he used the money given for the injury to purchase a home for himself while his brother still suffers.

**채점기준**

+ 2점 : 두 인물(*Troy와 Rose*)이 말하는 Gabe(*Troy의 동생*)에게 일어난 비극이 무엇인지를 지적하라는 문제에 "The tragedy regarding Gabe is the major head injury he received in the war against Japan(1점), leaving him with a "metal plate" in his head(1점)"라 서술하였다.

+ 2점: Troy가 Gabe에게 죄책감을 가지고 있는 이유를 "Troy feels guilt because he used the money given for the injury to purchase a home for himself(1.5점) while his brother still suffers(0.5점)"라 서술하였다.

[출전] <Fences> by August Wilson(1945-2005)

## 03

하위내용영역 문학(시) A형 기입형 배점 4점 예상정답률 40%

모범답안• The image of the "tiny pendant of iron" indicates that the mother's heart became cold and hard like "iron", while the image of the sister's body in the grave as a "magnet" combines with that image to show that the mother is weighed down by sorrow, as a magnet has a strong physical pull on iron. This combination of images serves to illustrate the sadness of the poem and the effect of loss on the mother vividly.

채점기준

+ 3점: "iron"과 "magnet"의 이미지를 "The image of the "tiny pendant of iron" indicates that the mother's heart became cold and hard like iron(1.5점), while the image of the sister's body in the grave like a "magnet" shows that the mother is weighed down by sorrow, as a magnet has a strong physical pull on iron(1.5점)." 라 각각 설명하였다.

+ 1점: 이 두 이미지가 시 전체의 tone에 어떻게 기여하고 있는가를 "This combination of images serves to illustrate the sadness of the poem and the effect of loss on the mother vividly."라 설명하였다.

▷ "슬픔"과 유사한 어휘가 사용되었으면 맞는 것으로 한다.

[출전] "Lost Love" by Louise Gluck(1943-)

## 34회

본책 p.294

### 01

하위내용영역 문학(시) A형 기입형 배점 2점 예상정답률 55%

모범답안 ⓐ eyes ⓑ rowing

채점기준

- 2점 : 모범답안과 같다. 이것 외에는 답이 될 수 없다.
- 1점 : 둘 중 하나만 맞았다.
- 0점 : 모범답안과 다르다.

[출전] "A Bird, come down the walk" by Emily Dickinson(1830-1886)

### 02

하위내용영역 문학(희곡) A형 서술형 배점 4점 예상정답률 50%

모범답안 The word that best identifies the Girl's mood is "frightened". The underlined "pink elephants" is *(an allusion to)* absurd hallucination, which the Girl has noticed Adams experiencing.

채점기준

+ 2점 : the Girl's mood를 "frightened"라 답하였다. 이것 외에는 답이 될 수 없다.
+ 2점 : 밑줄 친 "pink elephants"가 의미하는 것이 "absurd hallucination, which the Girl has noticed Adams experiencing"라 서술하였다.
  ▷ phantom이라 하였어도 1.5점을 준다.

[출전] <*The Hitchhiker*> by Lucille Fletcher (1912-2000)

### 03

하위내용영역 문학(소설) A형 서술형 배점 4점 예상정답률 40%

모범답안 The title of the story refers to the common, or "popular" use of violence as a means to solve conflicts in families. Second, the summary is as follows: This story recounts a struggle between a man and a woman over whom can retain custody of their child. It begins with a man packing to leave a woman as she curses him. Their angry conversation turns towards the custody of their baby, which they both want. Then, shouting turns to physical conflict as they both tug at the child, both wanting to keep their son and not let the other take him. The implication of the final line is that as the struggle becomes rougher, *(causing damage to the home and driving both to use greater force,)* the matter has come down to physical force, not reason nor discussion.

채점기준

+ 2점 : 제목의 의미를 "The title of the story refers to the common, or "popular" use of violence as a means to solve conflicts in families."라 답하였다.
+ 2점 : This story recounts a struggle between a man and a woman over whom can retain custody of their child(1점; topic sentence). It begins with a man packing to leave a woman as she curses him. Their angry conversation turns towards the custody of their baby, which they both want. Then, shouting turns to physical conflict as they both tug at the child, both wanting to keep their son and not let the other take him(0.5점;본문 요약).

The implication of the final line is that as the struggle becomes rougher, *(causing damage to the home and driving both to use greater force,)* the matter has come down to physical force, not reason nor discussion(0.5점; 마지막 문장의 함의).

[출전] "Popular Mechanics" by Raymond Carver (1938-1988)

## 35 회

본책 p.300

### 01

하위내용영역 문학(소설) A형 서술형 배점 2점 예상정답률 50%

**모범답안** resentment

**채점기준**

- 2점: 모범답안과 같다. 이것 외에는 답이 될 수 없다.
  ▷ resentness; resentful 등 표현이나 어법에 어긋나는 것은 모두 오답 처리한다.
- 0점: 모범답안과 다르다.

**한글 번역**

윌 핌은 자수성가한 남자였다. 즉 그는 일반적인 친분 관계 외에는 땡전 한 푼, 연줄 하나 없이 사회생활을 시작해서 레이온담요 회사의 부사장까지 오른 인물이었다. 그는 자신이 올바른 길로 들어서도록 해 준 볼티모어 복지관에 해마다 많은 돈을 기부했고 아주 오래전 농장 노동자로 일하던 시절에 대한 일화를 몇 가지 가지고 있었다. 하지만 그의 용모와 태도는 제대로 자리 잡은 중상류 계층 사람처럼 보였고, 은행에 돈 몇 푼을 집어넣기 위해 허리띠를 졸라매던 사람의 불안감 같은 것은 여간해서 흔적도 찾아볼 수 없었다. 물론 거지들, 넝마를 걸친 늙은이들, 흐릿한 불빛의 셀프서비스 식당에서 질 낮은 음식을 먹는 차림의 부실한 남자들과 여자들, 빈민가와 지저분한 공장지대, 싸구려 셋집 창문에 비치는 얼굴들 – 심지어 딸들의 양말에 난 구멍까지도 – 은 그에게 젊은 시절을 떠올려 불안감을 줄 수 있는 것은 사실이었다. 그래서 그는 가난의 조짐이 보이는 것이라면 그 어느 것도 좋아하지 않았다. 그는 자기가 살고 있는 네덜란드 식민지풍의 주택에서, 그 집의 불이 밝혀진 많은 창문들에서, 튼튼한 지붕과 난방 시설에서, 아이들의 따뜻한 옷에서, 자신의 시작은 미미했더라도 뭔가 그럴듯하고 내세울 만한 것을 이루었다는 깊은 즐거움을 느꼈다. 그는 언제나 사업상의 동료들 대부분이, 그리고 친구들이나 이웃들 모두가 그로턴이나 디어필드 아니면 그 비슷한 학교의 잔디밭에서 뛰어놀고 있을 동안 자기는 공공도서관에서 문법과 어휘를 향상하는 방법이 적힌 책을 대출하고 있었다는 사실을 의식하면서도 때로는 은근히 분개하기도 했다. 하지만 자기보다 더 수월한 길을 따라 성장해 온 사람들에 대한 그 은근한 분노를 자기 자신의 인성에 있는 일종의 천박함으로 인식하기도 했다. 단지 자신의 거대한 몸집을 감안한다면, 그가 자신의 이미지를 내내 불이 밝혀진 창문 밖의 빗속에 서 있는 배고픈 젊은이로만 봐왔다는 것은 놀라운 일이었다.

[출전] "Just Tell Me Who It Was" by John Cheever(1912-1982)

## 02

하위내용영역 문학(드라마) A형 서술형 배점 4점 예상정답률 55%

모범답안 Mrs. Reston thinks of David Holmes as a hero, due to the fact that he saved her daughter during the crisis with the ship. Dallas, on the other hand, wants to point attention to the fact that Holmes might have caused a death of one person on a lifeboat. The reason Dallas suspends questioning is Mrs. Reston, the witness, is upset and trying not to give an answer that harms Holmes.

채점기준

+ 2점 : David Holmes에 대한 Mrs. Reston과 Dallas의 서로 다른 관점을 "Mrs. Reston thinks of David Holmes as a hero, due to the fact that he saved her daughter during the crisis with the ship(1점). Dallas, on the other hand, wants to point attention to the fact that Holmes might have caused a death of one person on a lifeboat(1점)"라 서술하였다.
+ 2점 : Dallas가 심문을 더 하지 않고 멈춘 이유를 "Mrs. Reston, the witness, is upset and trying not to give an answer that harms Holmes"이라고 서술하였거나 유사하였다.

[출전] *Survival*

# 36회

본책 p.304

## 01

하위내용영역 문학(시) A형 서술형 배점 2점 예상정답률 50%

모범답안 ⓐ ABCB ⓑ nature

채점기준

- 2점 : 모범답안과 같다. 이것 외에는 답이 될 수 없다.
- 1점 : 둘 중 하나만 맞았다.
- 0점 : 모범답안과 다르다.

[출전] "Nurse's Song" by William Blake(1757-1827)

## 02

하위내용영역 문학(소설) A형 서술형 배점 4점 예상정답률 50%

모범답안 The meaning of the metaphor is that steam-powered machines of the factory look and sound like mad elephants, due to their pipework*(pistons)* and size. In the underlined, the writer is referring to the factory workers, who are servants to the factory and are "quiet" due to their diligence and focus on work.

채점기준

+ 2.5점 : 은유의 의미를 "steam-powered machines of the factory look and sound like mad elephants, due to their pipework *(pistons)* and size"라 서술하였거나 유사하였다.
  ▷ 또는 "the ceaseless working of the steam engine's pistons"을 나타내는 것이라 하였어도 2.5점을 준다.

+ 1.5점 : 밑줄 친 "quiet servants"가 지시하는 것이 "the factory workers, who are servants to the factory and are "quiet" due to their diligence and focus on work"이라 서술하였다.
  ▷ "factory workers"라 하였어도 1.5점을 준다.

**한글 번역**

희미하게 먼동이 트고 괴물 같은 연기의 뱀이 코크타운 위로 길게 꼬리를 뻗은 모습이 드러나기 전부터 요정의 궁궐은 밝게 빛났다. 나막신을 신고 보도를 달려가는 소리와 빠르게 울리는 종소리가 들렸고, 단조로운 일과를 위해 닦고 기름칠이 되어 있는, 우울한 광증에 사로잡힌 모든 코끼리들이 다시 힘겹게 움직였다.
스티븐은 조용하고 조심스럽고 차분하게 직조기 위로 몸을 굽혔다. 그가 일하는 장소인 직조기의 숲속에서 근무하는 모든 노동자들이 그러하듯, 그 모습은 부수고 분쇄하고 찢는 기계장치와 특별한 대조를 이루는 것이었다. 두려워하지 말라, 근심하고 있는 착한 사람들아, 기술이 자연을 망각시킬 것이라고. 신이 만든 것과 인간이 만든 것을 어디에든 나란히 놓고 보라 ; 그러면 전자(신이 만든 것) －비록 신이 만든 것이 아주 보잘것없는 한 무리의 노동자라 하더라도－ 가 그 비교에서 존엄함을 얻게 될 것이라.
이 공장에는 아주 많은 노동자들과 아주 많은 증기력이 있다. 단 일 파운드 무게의 힘까지 그 엔진이 무엇을 해내는지 잘 알려져 있다. 하지만 나랏빚(국채)을 따지는 사람이라 해서 －이들은 침착한 얼굴로 절제된 행동을 하는 이들인데－ 그 기관의 얌전한 하인들의 영혼에 그 힘이 한순간이라도 좋다거나 나쁘다거나, 사랑에 기여한다거나 증오에 기여한다거나, 애국심을 양양한다거나 불만족을 일으킨다거나, 미덕을 악으로 바꾼다거나 그 역이라거나 하는 등의 얘기를 해줄 수 있는 것은 아니다. 노동자들 중 가장 보잘것없는 사람에게도 헤아릴 수 없는 불가사의가 영원히 존재하기 때문에 이 사실이 이상하지 않다. 계산을 물리적 대상에만 한정해야 하고 이러한 끔찍한 미지의 다수는 다른 방법으로 통제해야 한다고 하더라도 말이다!

[출전] <Hard Times> by Charles Dickens(1812-1870)

## 03

하위내용영역 문학(드라마) A형 서술형 배점 4점 예상정답률 45%

**모범답안** The word appropriate for the blank is "stamps". Second, the underlined ⓑ implies that EIGHT is accusing THREE of having an aggressive, murderous temperament because he wants to kill*("pull the switch")* the black boy.

**채점기준**

+ 1.5점 : ⓐ에 들어갈 단어를 "stamps"라 정확히 기술하였다. 이것 외에는 답이 될 수 없다.
+ 2.5점 : 밑줄 친 ⓑ의 의미를 "EIGHT is accusing THREE of having an aggressive, murderous temperament(1.5점) because he wants to kill*("pull the switch")* the black boy(1점)"라 서술하였거나 유사하였다.

[출전] <Twelve Angry Men> by Reginald Rose (1920-2002)

## 37 회

본책 p.309

### 01

하위내용영역 문학(시) A형 서술형 배점 2점 예상정답률 65%

모범답안 ⓐ beloved ⓑ rose

채점기준

- 2점 : 모범답안과 같다.
  - ▷ ⓐ에 "loved"라 하였어도 맞는 것으로 한다. "love"는 답이 될 수 없다.
- 1점 : 둘 중 하나만 맞았다.
- 0점 : 모범답안과 다르다.

### 02

하위내용영역 문학(드라마) A형 서술형 배점 4점 예상정답률 50%

모범답안 From this passage it can be inferred that Tevya is from a large, poor family, wherein three family members share one bed and his daughter wears a shoddy dress. In the underlined sentence, Tevya is saying that the wedding he had arranged for his daughter, or "preordained", will be canceled by him out of consideration for her.

채점기준

+ 2점 : Tevya의 사회적 지위(상태)가 "Tevya is from a large, poor family, wherein three family members share one bed and his daughter wears a shoddy dress."라 서술하였거나 유사하였다.
  - ▷ "가난하다"란 점을 중심적으로 서술하였으면 2점을 준다.
  - ▷ 구체적 근거 없이 "하층 계급"이라고만 답하였으면 1점을 준다.
+ 2점 : 밑줄 친 부분의 의미를 Tevya가 딸의 미래에 대한 의도와 연결시켜 "the wedding he had arranged *("preordained")* for his daughter will be canceled by him out of consideration for her."라 올바르게 서술하였다.
  - ▷ "Tevya intends to cancel the marriage he had arranged for his daughter, out of respect for her wishes"라 하였어도 2점을 준다.

### 03

하위내용영역 문학(소설) A형 서술형 배점 4점 예상정답률 45%

모범답안 The main event of this passage is the formal reception of a famous sculptor's body by the people of his hometown. Second, through the passage there are clues about the deceased's reputation. In his hometown, his reputation is not well-established in that he did not have many close connections there any longer, as most of the men on the platform were "uncertain" and even his family is described as "scattered". For his profile abroad, the covering of his coffin with a palm-leaf is a sign of acclaim, and the mention of his "world-renown" status shows he was acclaimed and honored.

채점기준

+ 2점 : 중심 사건을 "the formal reception of a famous sculptor's (dead) body in his hometown"라 서술하였거나 유사하였다.
  - ▷ "a (famous) sculptor's (dead) body"의 내용이 들어가 있지 않으면 아무리 많이 서술하였어도 0점 처리한다.

+ 2점 : (죽은) 조각가에 대한 고향에서의 평판과 그가 작업하던 바깥 세계에서의 차이를 "In his hometown, his reputation is not well-established while, where he worked, he was acclaimed and honored"라 서술하였거나 유사하였다.

**한글 번역**

한 무리의 마을 사람들이 조그마한 캔자스 마을의 역 안전선에서 벌써 20분이나 연착된 야간 기차를 기다리며 서 있었다. 눈이 세상 모든 것을 두텁게 덮으며 내리고 있었다. 안전선에 있는 사람들은 매서운 추위로 인해 왼발과 오른발을 번갈아가며 서 있었다. 그들은 낮은 어조로 대화를 나누며 안절부절못한 채 이리저리 왔다 갔다 했는데, 자신들에게 기대되는 것이 무엇인지 잘 모르는 듯했다. 이 무리들 중 유일하게 자신이 여기에 왜 왔는지 정확하게 아는 듯 보이는 자가 있었는데, 그는 일행들과는 눈에 띄게 떨어져 있었고, 기차 플랫폼의 끝으로 걸어가고 있었다. 이윽고, 일종의 존경의 눈빛을 띠며, 퇴색된 북군의 군복을 입은 큰 키에 마른 회색머리의 남자가 일행에서 그 남자 쪽으로 발을 끌며 걸어와서는 잭나이프의 사분의 삼이 열린 듯한 각도로 목을 앞으로 구부리면서 말했다.

"오늘밤도 기차가 꽤 연착을 하나보군요, 짐. 아마도 눈 때문인 거 같지요?" 그는 가성이 섞인 새된 소리로 말했다.

"모르겠소." 사방으로 두껍고 거칠게 자란 붉은 수염의 물결을 그리며 약간은 귀찮은 듯 또는 무슨 고민이 있는 듯, 그가 대답했다.

그 마른 군복 입은 남자는 갈대 같이 생긴 이쑤시개를 한쪽 입으로 자근자근 씹으며 말했다. "내 생각인데요. 동부에서 그 시체와 함께 올 만한 사람이 아무래도 없을 거 같네요."

"모르겠소" 전보다도 더 퉁명스럽게 그 사람이 대답했다.

"그가 그 어느 곳에도 속해 있지 않았다는 것은 실로 정말이지 안타깝네요." 그 여윈 남자가 새된 소리로 알랑거리며 계속했다.

바로 그때 멀리서 호각소리가 들렸고 플랫폼 위에서 발을 질질 끄는 소리가 들렸다. 다양한 연령대의 많은 소년들이 천둥소리에 깬 뱀장어마냥 갑작스럽게 그리고 얄상하게 나타났다.

면도하지 않은 붉은 수염의 단단한 체격의 그 남자가 걸으며 모자를 벗었고, 다가오는 기차 쪽 플랫폼으로 재빨리 다가갔다. 그의 뒤에 있던 사람들은 머뭇거리다가 서로를 의심스럽게 바라보았고, 겁쟁이처럼 그의 행동을 따라했다. 기차가 멈췄다.

단단한 박스에서 꺼내어진 관이 눈 덮인 플랫폼에 내려졌다. 마을 사람들은 관이 지나가도록 물러서서 검은 덮게 위에 가로질러 놓여 있는 종려잎을 호기심에 차 바라보면서, 관 주위에 거의 반원을 그리며 모여들었다. 아무도 말을 하지 않았다.

시체를 가지고 온 죽은 유명한 조각가의 제자들 중 한 명인 보스턴 젊은이가 무기력하게 그 주위를 둘러보았다. "메릭 씨의 형제분 안 계십니까?" 그는 확신하지 못한 듯 물었다.

빨간 수염의 남자가 처음으로 걸어나와 다른 무리들 틈에 끼어들었다. "없소, 아직 오지 않았소. 가족이 뿔뿔이 흩어졌답니다. 시체를 곧장 집으로 가져가겠소."

[출전] "The Sculptor's Funeral" by Willa Cather (1873-1947)

# 38회

본책 p.314

## 01

하위내용영역 문학(시) A형 서술형 배점 2점 예상정답률 50%

모범답안 ⓐ practicing ⓑ loved

채점기준

- 2점 : 모범답안과 같다. 이것 외에는 답이 될 수 없다.
- 1점 : 둘 중 하나만 맞았다.
- 0점 : 모범답안과 다르다.

## 02

하위내용영역 문학(드라마) A형 서술형 배점 2점 예상정답률 45%

모범답안 ⓐ morals ⓑ five

채점기준

- 2점 : 모범답안과 같다. 이것 외에는 답이 될 수 없다.
- 1점 : 둘 중 하나만 맞았다.
- 0점 : 모범답안과 다르다.

## 03

하위내용영역 문학(소설) A형 서술형 배점 4점 예상정답률 40%

모범답안 Dramatic irony occurs when there is discrepancy between what characters know and what the reader knows. In this story, the irony comes from the fact that the police officers, when asked to do a "Small favor" by Mrs. Maloney, are, as known to the reader, are unknowingly helping to dispose of*(remove)* the murder weapon, the leg of lamb. She has succeeded in deceiving them by putting the weapon, which is large and should be "easy to find", as one officer remarks, right in front of them.

채점기준

- 4점 : 모범답안과 같거나 유사하다.
- 2점 : 아이러니가 독자가 알고 있는 (객관적) 사실과 등장인물인 경찰들 사이에서 발생한다는 것은 서술하였으나 구체적인 예를 제시하지는 못하였다.
- 0점 : 서술하지 못하였거나 전혀 다르게 서술하였다.

## 39회

본책 p.320

### 01

하위내용영역 문학(드라마) A형 서술형 배점 2점 예상정답률 60%

모범답안 ⓐ tailor's shop ⓑ position

채점기준
- 2점: 모범답안과 같다. Spelling 오류가 있으면 틀린 것으로 한다.
- 1점: 둘 중 하나만 맞았다.
- 0점: 모범답안과 다르다.

[출전] <The Million Pound Bank Note>(1893) by Mark Twain

### 02

하위내용영역 문학(시) A형 서술형 배점 2점 예상정답률 55%

모범답안 ⓐ sunflowers ⓑ seeds

채점기준
- 2점: 모범답안과 같다.
- 1점: 둘 중 하나만 맞았다. ⓑ에 sunflowers라 하였으면 0.5점을 준다.
- 0점: 모범답안과 다르다.

[출전] "By the Wild-Haired Corn"(2004) by Mary Oliver

### 03

하위내용영역 문학(소설) A형 서술형 배점 4점 예상정답률 45%

모범답안 In the underlined part, simile is used. Through the simile, the writer illustrates the destroyed land by the whites and, at the same time, shows the loss*(or "empty-handedness")* of the chief. Then, in the underlined ⓑ, the narrator implies that the interaction between the head of the rubber company and the chief is not fluent due to the chief's weak language ability.

채점기준
+ 0.5점: 비유적 언어를 simile라 하였다.
+ 1.5점: 밑줄 친 ⓐ가 의도하는 바를 "the destroyed land by the whites(0.5점) and, at the same time, shows the loss(or "empty-handedness") of the chief(1점)"라 답하였다.
+ 2점: 밑줄 친 ⓑ의 함축 의미를 "the interaction between the head of the rubber company and the chief is not fluent due to the chief's weak language ability"이라 서술하였거나 유사하게 서술하였다.
  ▷ 둘 사이의 (즉, 두 사람이 누구인지에 대한 언급 없이) 언어 능력 차이에 대한 것이라고만 서술하였으면 1점만 준다.

[출전] <The Color Purple>(1982) by Alice Walker

## 40회

본책 p.326

### 01

하위내용영역 문학(드라마) A형 기입형 배점 2점 예상정답률 55%

**모범답안** ⓐ idea ⓑ robbery

채점기준
- 2점 : 모범답안과 같다. 이것 외에는 답이 될 수 없다.
- 1점 : 둘 중 하나만 맞았다.
- 0점 : 모범답안과 다르다.

[출전] <Glengarry Glen Ross>(1984) by David mamet(1947-)

### 02

하위내용영역 문학(시) A형 서술형 배점 2점 예상정답률 60%

**모범답안** life

채점기준
- 2점 : 모범답안과 같다. 이것 외에는 답이 될 수 없다.
- 0점 : 모범답안과 다르다.

[출전] "The Secret" by Denise Levertov(1923-1997)

### 03

하위내용영역 문학(소설) A형 서술형 배점 4점 예상정답률 45%

**모범답안** The setting of this story is on a small boat lost in the open ocean at night in winter. Second, the correspondent's realization about the poem is that, as a child he blithely ignored the emotional situation of it, but as he faces a similar situation, he then realizes the immense sadness of the poem's contents.

채점기준
+ 1.5점 : 이 작품의 setting을 "on a small boat lost in the open ocean(1점) at night in winter(0.5점)"라 서술하였다.
+ 2.5점 : 기자(correspondent)가 시에 대해 깨달은 바가 "as a child he blithely ignored the emotional situation of it, but as he faces a similar situation, he then realizes the immense sadness of the poem's contents"라 서술하였거나 유사하였다.

[출전] "The Open Boat"(1897) by Stephen Crane (1871-1900)

# 41 회

본책 p.332

## 01

하위내용영역 문학(소설) A형 서술형 배점 4점 예상정답률 50%

**모범답안** gnarled apples

**채점기준**

- 2점 : 모범답안과 같다. 이것 외에는 답이 될 수 없다.
- 0점 : 모범답안과 다르다.

**한글 번역**

의사 리피의 이야기와 그의 아내가 되어 돈을 물려준 키 크고 가무스름한 여성과의 구애 이야기는 아주 희한한 이야기이다. 이 이야기는 마치 와인즈버그의 과수원에서 자라는 뒤틀린 작은 사과들처럼 맛있다. 가을이면 사람들이 과수원에서 걷는데 땅은 발밑에서 서리가 내려 단단하다. 사과는 따는 사람들에 의해 이미 나무에서 다 따졌다. 사과는 통에 넣어져서 도시로 실려가 책, 잡지, 가구와 사람들로 가득 판 아파트에서 사람들이 먹게 될 것이다. 나무에는 이제 사과 따는 사람들이 안 따고 버려둔 마디 많은 사과 몇 개만 매달려있다. 그건 마치 리피의 주먹마디처럼 보인다. 이 사과들을 한 입 베어 물면 그 맛이 좋다. 소수의 사람들만이 그 맛을 안다.
키 크고 까무잡잡한 처녀와 의사 리피는 어느 여름 오후에 구애를 시작했다. 그때 그는 마흔 다섯이었고 주머니를 종잇조각으로 채워 그게 딱딱한 알맹이가 되면 던져 버리는 일을 벌써 시작했었다. 그 처녀는 임신을 했고 겁이 나서 의사 리피에게 진찰받으러 왔다. 그녀는 역시 묘한 일련의 상황들로 인해 그런 상태가 되어 있었다. 아버지와 어머니의 죽음 그리고 물려받은 비옥한 토지는 수많은 구혼자들로 하여금 그녀를 따라다니게 만들었다. 2년간 그녀는 거의 매일 밤 구혼자들을 만났다.
몇 주 동안 키 크고 까무잡잡한 처녀와 의사는 거의 매일 함께 있었다. 그 여자를 그에게 오게 한 상태는 단순한 병으로 지나갔으나 그녀는 옹이진(비틀어진) 사과의 단맛을 발견한 사람 같았고, 도시의 아파트에서 사람들이 먹는 둥글고 흠 없는 사과에 다시는 마음을 집중할 수 없었다. 그와의 교분이 시작된 뒤 가을에 그녀는 의사 리피와 결혼했고 다음 해 봄에 죽었다.

[출전] "Paper Pills" by Sherwood Anderson(1876-1941)

## 02

하위내용영역 문학(시) A형 서술형 배점 4점 예상정답률 40%

**모범답안** The rhyme scheme is AABB CCDD EEFF GG. Second, the poet mainly describes the ongoing conflict between the waves and the shore as they crash non-stop.

**채점기준**

+ 2점 : 각운의 패턴을 "AABB CCDD EEFF GG"라 정확하게 서술하였다. 이것 외에는 답이 될 수 없다.
+ 2점 : 시인이 시에서 중심적으로 묘사한 것을 "the ongoing conflict between the waves and the shore (as they crash non-stop)"이라 서술하였거나 유사하였다.
  ▷ 다음과 같이 서술하였어도 2점을 준다.
  The poet mainly describes a night on an ocean beach when the ocean waves seem to be preparing to destroy the land.

[출전] "Once by the Pacific" by Robert Frost (1874-1963)

## 03

하위내용영역 문학(드라마) A형 서술형 배점 4점 예상정답률 45%

모범답안 Warren compares protons and electrons to personality components in order to support his point of view. Second, Jessica believes that people undergo major changes as they get older, without remaining the same.

채점기준

+ 2점: Warren이 자신의 관점의 근거를 대기 위해 사용한 simile를 "protons and electrons"이라 답하였다.
+ 2점: Warren과 대조되는 Jessica의 관점을 "people undergo major changes as they get older, without remaining the same"라 서술하였거나 유사하였다.

[출전] <This Is Our Youth> by Kenneth Lonergan (1962-)

## 04

하위내용영역 문학(소설) B형 서술형 배점 4점 예상정답률 45%

모범답안 The setting of the story is on a ship in the Mediterranean Sea. Next, it can be inferred that Mrs. Ebbing was unwell (or injured) the day before.

채점기준

+ 2점: 위 작품의 배경을 "on a ship in the Mediterranean Sea"이라 서술하였거나 유사하였다.
+ 2점: 전날 일어났을 것이라 추론할 수 있는 것을 "Mrs. Ebbing was unwell"이라 서술하였거나 유사하였다.

[출전] "On the Gull's Road" by Willa Cather (1873-1947)

# 42회

본책 p.339

## 01

하위내용영역 문학(소설) A형 서술형 배점 2점 예상정답률 50%

모범답안 ⓐ friend ⓑ paralysis

채점기준

- 2점: 모범답안과 같다. 이것 외에는 답이 될 수 없다.
- 1점: 둘 중 하나만 맞았다.
- 0점: 모범답안과 다르다.

한글 번역

이번에는 그에게 희망이 없었다. 세 번째 발작이었다. 밤마다 나는 그 집 앞을 지나다니며(그때가 방학이었다) 불 밝혀진 유리창을 유심히 살펴보았다. 밤마다 창문은 똑같이 희미하면서도 고르게 밝혀져 있었다. 만약 그가 죽는다면, 촛불의 그림자가 침침하게 가려놓은 차양 위에 어른거릴 것이라고 생각했다. 시신의 머리맡에 초 두개를 놓아야 한다는 것을 나는 알고 있었기 때문이다. 그는 가끔 내게 이렇게 말했다. "나는 오래 살지 못해." 나는 그이 말이 공연한 소리라고 생각했다. 이제 보니 그것은 사실이었다. 밤마다 나는 그 창문을 쳐다보며 '마비'라는 말을 가만히 되뇌어 봤다. 그 말은 내 귀에 항상 이상스럽게 들렸다. 기하학의 경절형(磬折形)이라든지 교리문답의 성직매매와 같은 말처럼, 그러나 지금 그 말도 어떤 악하고 죄받을 존재의 이름처럼 들렸다. 그 말은 내게 공포를 자아내게 했다. 그런데도 나는 더 가까이 가서 그것의 무시무시한 장난을 보고 싶어 하는 것이다.
내가 저녁 먹으러 아래층에 내려가 보니 코터 영감은 불가에서 담배를 피우고 있었다. 숙모가 오토밀 죽을 국자로 내게 떠 주는 동안 마치 전에 하다만 말을 계속하는 투로 말했다.
"꼭이 그렇다는 것은 아니지만… 좀 이상스러운 점이 있다 이 말씀이야. 그 사람에게는 좀 괴상한 점이 있어. 내 소견을 말하자면…"

그는 파이프 담배를 빨아댔다. 틀림없이 속으로 소견을 정리해 보는 모양이었다.
"나는 그것에 대해서 일가견이 있는데 말씀이야," 그가 말했다. "그것은 하나의 특수한 병이었다고 할까. 하여간 무어라 말하기가 어렵지…"
그는 그의 일가견에 대해서 밝히지 않고 다시 파이프를 빨기 시작했다. 삼촌은 내가 물끄러미 쳐다보는 것을 보고 내게 말했다.
"그래. 네 오랜 친구가 가 버렸구나. 너도 그 말 들으면 섭섭하겠지."
"누가요?" 내가 물었다.
"플린 신부."
"죽었나요?"
"코터 씨가 지금 막 그 말을 전해 주셨다. 그 집 앞을 마침 지나가셨더란다."

[출전] "Sisters" by James Joyce(1882-1941)

## 02

하위내용영역 문학(시) A형 서술형 배점 4점 예상정답률 50%

**모범답안** The epiphany is revealed in [E]. Second, the epiphany revealed is that the speaker of the poem feels completely at one with nature.

**채점기준**

+ 2점: 에피파니가 드러난 부분이 "[E]"라 정확하게 기술하였다.
+ 2점: 그 에피파니의 내용을 "the speaker of the poem feels completely connected with nature"라 서술하였다.

[출전] "A Blessing" by James Wright(1927-1980)

## 03

하위내용영역 문학(드라마) B형 서술형 배점 4점 예상정답률 45%

**모범답안** The meaning of the underlined selection ⓐ is that people will act like they dislike something that they really don't sense or understand, in order to appear more sophisticated. Second, the best word to match the underlined expression in ⓑ is "hypocrite".

**채점기준**

+ 2점: 밑줄 친 ⓐ의 의미를 "people will act like they dislike something that they really don't sense or understand"라 서술하였거나 유사하였다.
+ 2점: 밑줄 친 ⓑ와 가장 잘 어울리는 한 단어를 "hypocrite"라 정확하게 서술하였다.
  ▷ "hypocracy"라 하였으면 1점을 준다.

[출전] <She Stoops to Conquer> by Oliver Goldsmith (1728-1774)

## 04

하위내용영역 문학(소설) B형 서술형 배점 4점 예상정답률 45%

**모범답안** The reason the king is called "the most progressive monarch" is because he suggested legislative bill of mandatory voting on all issues for women in a time when they had no the right to vote. Second, the two words are "votes-for-women creatures".

채점기준

+ 2점 : 왕이 가장 진보적인 군주라 불리는 이유를 "because he proposed a policy of mandatory voting on all issues for women in a time when they had no voting right."라 서술하였거나 유사하였다.

+ 2점 : 밑줄 친 ⓑ와 가장 잘 상응하는 두 단어를 "votes-for-women creatures"라 서술하였다. 이것 외에는 답이 될 수 없다.

한글 번역

[A] 헤르만 14세(가 왕이 된 것)는 정치에서 일어난 예기치 못한 것 중 하나였다. 여러 가지 면에서 그는 영국의 왕위에 오른 가장 진보적인 군주였다. 백성들은 자기가 어디에 있는지 알기도 전에 이미 다른 곳에 와 있었다. 장관들은 전통적으로 진보적이었지만, 그들조차도 왕이 제안하는 (진보적인) 법률과 보조를 맞추기 어려웠다.
"사실 여성참정권을 주장하는 자들 때문에 정부가 애를 먹고 있습니다." 총리가 인정했다. "놈들은 전국에서 우리 회의를 방해하고 다우닝가(총리관저가 있는 곳) 일대를 정치적 야유 회장으로 바꿔 놓으려 하고 있습니다."
"놈들을 처리해야겠군" 헤르만 왕이 말했다.
"처리한다구요? 맞습니다. 바로 그거예요. 헌데 어떻게 하지요?"
"내가 법안 하나를 만들어 주겠소." 왕이 타자기 앞에 앉으면서 말했다. "여성들은 앞으로 치러질 모든 선거에 반드시 투표해야 한다고 규정하는 법안이오. 반드시 투표해야 한다는 말에 유념하시오. 좀 더 명확하게 표현하면, 투표하지 않으면 안 된다는 뜻이오. 남성들한테는 투표가 전처럼 선택할 수 있는 권리로 남을 것이오. 하지만 21세부터 70세까지의 모든 여성은 국회와 도의회 지역위원회, 교구평의회, 지방자치단체만이 아니라 수영장의 수영강사, 토목공사 도급업자, 성가대 지휘자 그리고 그 밖에 내가 머리에서 떠오르는 대로 추가할 지방 관리에 이르기까지 모든 선거에 반드시 투표해야 하오. 이 모든 직은 모두 선거로 뽑히는 선출직이 될 것이고, 자신의 거주지역 안에서 실시되는 선거에 참여하지 않는 여성 유권자는 벌금 100파운드를 물게 될 거요. 법적으로 충분한 근거가 있는 진단서를 첨부하지 않고 거주지역을 이탈하는 것은 정당한 사유로 받아들여지지 않을 거요. 이 법안을 상하 양원에서 통과시킨 다음 모레 나한테 가져오면 서명하겠소."

[B] '의무적 여성 선거법'은 가장 큰 목소리로 투표권을 요구한 집단에서도 거의 또는 전혀 환영받지 못했다. 영국 여성의 대다수는 참정권 운동에 무관심하거나 적대적이었고, 가장 광적인 여성참정권론자들도 투표용지를 투표함에 넣는 것이 왜 그렇게 매력적으로 보였을까 하고 고개를 갸웃거리기 시작했다. 농촌 지역에서는 새 법의 규정을 시행하는 것이 아주 넌더리 나는 일이었고, 도시에서는 악몽이 되었다. 선거는 끝이 없는 것 같았다. 세탁부와 재봉사들은 일하다 말고 황급히 투표하러 달려가야 했고, 이름도 들어본 적이 없는 후보자를 되는 대로 골라서 투표하는 경우가 많았다.

[출전] "Hermann the Irascible" by Saki(본명 Hector Hugh Munro, 1870-1916)

## 43회

본책 p.346

### 01

하위내용영역 문학(소설) A형 기입형 배점 2점 예상정답률 55%

모범답안 ⓐ eldest ⓑ metaphor

채점기준

- 2점 : 모범답안과 같다. 이것 외에는 답이 될 수 없다.
- 1점 : 둘 중 하나만 맞았다.
- 0점 : 모범답안과 다르다.

한글 번역

다음 날 아침 버넬네 아이들은 충분히 빨리 학교로 걸어갈 수 없었다. 그들은 학교 종이 치기 전에 그들의 인형의 집에 대해서 모두에게 들려주고, 설명해 주고, 아니 자랑하고 싶어서 견딜 수가 없었다. "내가 말할게" 이자벨이 말했다. "내가 맏이니까. 너희 둘은 나중에 끼어들어도 돼. 하지만 내가 맨 먼저 말할 거야."
대답할 말이 아무것도 없었다. 이자벨은 왕초 행세를 했지만 그녀는 언제나 옳았고, 로키와 키자이어 역시 장녀에게 따르는 특권을 너무나 잘 알고 있었다. 그들은 길가의 무성한 미나리아재비를 헤쳐 지나가면서 아무 말도 하지 않았다. "그리고 누가 제일 먼저 와서 그걸 구경하느냐도 내가 선택할 거야. 엄마가 그래도 좋다고 하셨거든." 인형의 집을 안마당에 놓아둔 동안 그들은 학교 친구들을 한 번에 둘씩 데려와서 보여 주어도 좋다고 이미 약속이 되어 있었던 것이다. 물론 남아서 차를 마시거나 집안을 걸어 다니는 것은 허락되지 않았다. 그저 이자벨이 예쁜 점들을 가리키고 로티와 키자이어가 즐거운 표정을 하고있는 동안 정원에 말없이 서있기만 하는 것이다.
하지만 할 수 있는 한 서 둘렀지만 그들이 남학생 운동장의 타르 칠을 한 울타리까지 왔을 때 종이 울리기 시작했다. 그들은 겨우 모자를 벗어젖히고 출석을 부르기 전에 열에 들어설 시간밖에 없었다. 걱정할 것 없었다. 이자벨은 아주 중요하고 신비스러운 일이 있는 듯한 표정으로 손으로 입을 가리고서 가까이 있는 소녀들에게 속삭임으로서 그에 대한 보상이라도 하려 했다. "쉬는 시간에 너희들에게 할 말이 있어."
쉬는 시간이 되자 이자벨은 에워싸였다. 그녀의 반 여학생들은 다투어 그녀를 얼싸안거나 그녀를 따라 딴 데로 가거나 아첨하듯 웃어 보이거나 하며 그녀에게 특별한 친구가 되려 했다. 그녀는 운동장 옆에 있는 거대한 소나무 아래서 그럴싸한 알현식을 거행했다.

[출전] "A Doll's House" by Katherine Mansfield (1888-1923)

### 02

하위내용영역 문학(시) A형 서술형 배점 4점 예상정답률 40%

모범답안 In the fifth stanza, the name written on the outside of a letter is compared to a cloud in the center of the sky. Second, the thematic idea of the poem is that with hands we make contact with the world in all matters from ordinary tasks to the divine.

채점기준

+ 2점 : 5번째 연에서 "the name written on the outside of a letter is compared to a cloud"라 서술하였다.
+ 2점 : 시의 중심 주제를 "with hands we make contact with the world in all matters from ordinary tasks to the divine"이라 서술하였다.
  ▷ 다음과 같이 서술하였어도 2점을 준다.
  - "The little things in life done by hands are sacredly*(divinely)* valuable"
  - "The rather mundane activities by hands have a sacred quality"
  - "The daily handiwork that is done repeatedly is what makes a life so, it should be done well and with meaning"
  - "Mundane and physical labor in a honest and straightforward way is extremely valuable"

[출전] "Daily" by Naomi Nye(1952-)

## 03

하위내용영역 문학(드라마) B형 서술형 배점 4점 예상정답률 45%

**모범답안** Michael moves the things away from Christy because he suspects he could be a thief. Next, the protagonist has not stolen anything nor assaulted a woman.

**채점기준**

+ 2점 : Michael이 주위 물건들을 치우는 이유를 "because he suspects he could be a thief"라 정확하게 서술하였거나 유사하였다.
+ 2점 : 주인공이 하지 않은 두 가지를 "the protagonist has not stolen anything nor assaulted a woman"이라 정확하게 서술하였거나 유사하였다.

[출전] <Playboy of the Western World> by J. M. Synge(1871-1909)

## 04

하위내용영역 문학(소설) B형 서술형 배점 4점 예상정답률 45%

**모범답안** The underlined words in ⓐ mean that Tar Baby was arrested for police for causing a car accident, not only being drunk. Second, it can be implied that "those hills" are an area where a non-white community lives.

**채점기준**

+ 2점 : 밑줄 친 ⓐ의 "그것보다 약간 더한 일 때문이지(Little bit more than that)"가 의미하는 바가 "Tar Baby was arrested for police for causing a car accident"라 정확하게 서술하였거나 유사하였다.
+ 2점 : 밑줄 친 ⓑ의 "those hills"에 대해 유추할 수 있는 것을 "'those hills' are an area where a non-white community lives"라 정확하게 서술하였거나 유사하였다.

**한글 번역**

"타르 베이비를 보지 못해도 섭섭하지 않겠지, 섭섭할까?"하고 그는 물었다.
"섭섭하다니요? 절대 그런 일 없어요. 그런데 그가 어디 있나요?"
에이작스는 그녀의 감미로운 무관심에 미소를 지었다.
"감옥에"
"언제부터죠?"
"지난 토요일부터"
"취해서 잡혀갔나요?"
"그것보다 약간 더한 일 때문이지" 그는 대답하곤 곧바로 타르 베이비의 여러 불운 가운데 자신이 관련된 어떤 사실에 대하여 그녀에게 이야기하기 시작하였다.
토요일 오후에 타르 베이비는 뉴 리버로에서 술에 취해 비틀거리다가 혼잡한 길거리에 넘어졌다. 차를 몰고 가던 한 여인이 그를 피하려고 방향을 바꾸다가 다른 차를 받아 버렸다. 경찰이 왔을 때 그 여인이 시장의 질녀인 것을 알고는 타르 베이비를 구속했다. 나중에 그 말이 퍼지자 에이작스와 다른 두 명이 그를 면회하러 경찰서에 갔다. 경찰은 처음에 그들을 들여보내려 하지 않았다. 하지만 에이작스와 다른 두 사람이 한 시간 반을 주위에 서서 일정한 시간 간격으로 그들의 청원을 반복한 후에야 그들의 태도가 누그러졌다. 감방에 있는 그를 들어가서 봐도 좋다는 허락을 마침내 받아 냈을 때, 그는 몹시 심하게 두들겨 맞아 구석에서 몸이 비틀린 채로 웅크리고 있었고, 옷이라곤 매우 더럽혀진 내의 한 벌밖에 입고 있지 않았다. 에이작스와 다른 이들이 어째서 타르 베이비가 자기 옷을 되돌려 받을 수 없는 가를 담당자에게 물어보았다. "다 큰 사람이 자기가 눈 오줌똥 속에 그대로 누워 있게 하는 게 옳은 일은 아니잖아." 하고 경찰은 답변하였다.
타르 베이비는 백인이라고 언제나 주장했던 에바의 의견과 분명히 같은 의견을 갖고 있었던 그 경찰은 만일 죄수가 오줌똥 속에 살고 싶지 않다면 꼭대기 언덕에서 빠져나와 근엄한 백인처럼 살아야 한다 말하였다.
거칠고 흉악한 말다툼이 더 오갔고, 모든 것은 흑인 세 명의 공소장 작성과 다음 목요일에 있을 민사법정 출두 약속으로 끝이 났다.

[출전] <Sula> by Toni Morrison(1931-2019)

# 44회

본책 p.354

## 01

하위내용영역 문학(소설) A형 기입형 배점 2점 예상정답률 45%

모범답안 dream

채점기준

- 2점 : 모범답안과 같다. 이것 외에는 답이 될 수 없다.
- 0점 : 모범답안과 다르다.

한글 번역

학식이 있어 다채로운 삶을 누리던 사람들일지라도 갑자기 낯선 곳으로 이주해서 자신에 대해 조금도 알지 못하고 전혀 생각이 통하지 않는 사람들 틈에 끼이게 된다든지, 이제까지 그들의 영혼을 살찌우던 곳과는 풍토도 다르고 생활습관도 다른 고장에서 살게 되면 누구나 지금까지 지녔던 세계관이나 보이지 않는 신에 대한 믿음을 고수하기 어려울 것이다. 아니, 과거에 그들이 느낀 기쁨이나 슬픔까지도 실제로 존재했던 경험인지 의심스럽게 느껴지는 법이다. 오래된 신앙과 애정에서 격리된 사람은 아마도 이렇게 레테의 효과를 지닌 망명의 길을 택할 것이다. 그렇게 되면 모든 표상이 사라지기 때문에 과거는 꿈처럼 느껴지고, 과거의 어떤 기억과도 연결되어 있지 않기 때문에 현재 역시 꿈과 같은 것이 되어 버린다. 그러나 그런 경험을 해 본 사람일지라도 사일러스 매너처럼 단순한 직조공이 자기 고장과 이웃을 떠나 래블로에 정착한다는 것이 어떤 결과를 초래하는지 상상하기는 어려울 것이다. 넓게 펼쳐진 산기슭이 내다보이는 그의 고향 마을과 나지막이 자리잡은 이 산림지대는 더 이상 그럴 수 없을 만큼 전혀 딴판이었다. 래블로에서 그는 울창한 나무들과 생울타리 때문에 천국과도 격리된 듯한 느낌이 들었다. 아침의 깊은 적막 속에서 깨어나 이슬 맺힌 가시밭이나 무성하게 자란 잡초를 바라봐도 랜턴 야드를 중심으로 이뤄지던 삶과 관련 있어 보이는 것은 아무것도 없었다. 한때 그에게는 랜턴 야드야말로 하느님의 높으신 섭리가 이루어지는 제단이었던 것이다.

[출전] <Silas Marner> by George Eliot(1819-1880)

## 02

하위내용영역 문학(시) A형 서술형 배점 4점 예상정답률 40%

모범답안 The meaning of the title is that the speaker would want to shoot the neighbor's dog if he had a gun in his house. Second, he transforms the noisy barking into a musical solo.

채점기준

+ 2점 : 시의 제목의 의미를 "the speaker would want to shoot the neighbor's dog if he had a gun in his house"라 서술하였거나 유사하였다.
  ▷ 다음과 같이 서술하였어도 2점을 준다.
  "With a gun in the house perhaps there would have been an easy solution. Shoot the dog"
+ 2점 : 개가 짖는 소음을 "a musical solo"로 변환시켰다고 정확하게 서술하였거나 유사하였다.
  ▷ 다음과 같이 서술하였어도 2점을 준다.
  "the speaker imagines the dog as a performer in an orchestra"

[출전] "Another Reason Why I Don't Keep A Gun In The House" by Billy Collins(1941-)

## 03

하위내용영역 문학(드라마) B형 서술형 배점 4점 예상정답률 45%

모범답안 Two metaphors used by Blair are "scar" used to describe the state of Africa and "kaleidoscope" to describe the moment of change occurring. Next, the major difference between Rumsfeld and Straw's statements is that Straw describes a focus by coalition only on Afghanistan, while Rumsfeld says that the "mission" can go beyond.

채점기준

+ 2점: 두 개의 은유를 "'scar' used to describe the state of Africa(1점) and 'kaleidoscope' to describe the moment(or situations) of change occurring(1점)"이라 명확하게 서술하였거나 유사하였다.

+ 2점: Rumsfeld and Straw의 진술의 핵심적 차이를 "Straw describes a focus by coalition only on Afghanistan, while Rumsfeld says that the "mission" can go beyond"라 명확하게 서술하였거나 유사하였다.

[출전] <Stuff Happens> by David Hare(1947-)

## 04

하위내용영역 문학(소설) B형 서술형 배점 4점 예상정답률 45%

**모범답안** The reasons the narrator thought the savages didn't attack were: the thick fog and the nature of the cries, which is the noise of sorrow caused by the sight of the steamboat. Second, the narrator compares the fog to a mouse and to a heap of cotton-wool.

채점기준

+ 2점: 화자가 야만인들이 공격하지 않을 거라고 생각한 두 가지 이유를 "the thick fog(1점) and the nature of the cries, which is the noise of sorrow caused by the sight of the steamboat(1점)"라고 서술하였다.
  ▷ 둘 중 하나만 맞았으면 1점; "the nature of the noise"라고만 했으면 0.5점을 준다.

+ 2점: 화자는 안개를 "a mouse(1점) and to a heap of cotton-wool(1점)"에 비유했다고 정확하게 서술하였다.
  ▷ 둘 중 하나만 맞았으면 1점을 준다.

**한글 번역**

지배인이 물었을 때 나는 "저 야만족들이 공격할 것 같지 않다"고 대답했지. 그렇게 생각한 데는 몇 가지 이유가 있었지. 짙은 안개가 그 이유 중의 하나였어. 만일 그들이 카누를 타고 강둑을 나선다면 우리 기선이 출발할 경우나 마찬가지로 안개 속에서 길을 잃고 말았을 테니까. 하지만 나는 양쪽 강둑의 밀림은 침투하기 어려우며 그 밀림 속에서 사람들의 눈이 이미 우리를 보았을 것이라고 판단하고 있었어. 강변의 숲이 아주 빽빽한 것은 확실했지만, 그 뒤의 덤불은 분명히 사람들의 출입이 가능했었거든. 안개가 잠시 걷혔을 때 강 유역의 어디에서도 카누는 보이지 않더군. 적어도 기선과 평행을 이루는 거리에서는 카누를 보지 못했어. 하지만 내가 그들이 공격해 올 것이라는 생각이 들지 않도록 한 것은 그 소동의 성격이었어. 우리가 들었던 그 비명의 성격이 그런 생각을 하게 했던 거야. 그 비명 속에는 즉각적으로 적대 행위를 벌일 의도를 예상케 하는 그런 흉포함이 들어 있지 않았던 것이지. 그 난데없이 들려온 소리가 야성적이고 격렬하기는 했지만 그것은 내게 슬픔의 표현이라는 거역할 수 없는 인상을 주고 있었지. 기선이 나타난 것을 보고 그 야만인들은 무슨 이유에서인지 억제할 수 없는 슬픔에 사로잡히게 되었던 거야. 만약 그곳에 위험이 있다면 그것은 거대한 인간 감정이 분출하고 있는 곳 가까이에 가게 된 데서 겪는 위험이라고 나는 해명하고 있었어. 극단적인 슬픔은 궁극적으로는 격렬하게 발산될 수 있겠지만 일반적으로는 냉담한 형태로 나타나는 경우가 더 많아…
백인 순례자들이 안개 속을 응시하고 있는 꼴을 자네들이 좀 보았더라면 좋았을 텐데! 그들에게는 싱긋 웃어 보일 용기가 없었고 심지어는 나를 비난할 용기조차 없었어. 허나 그들은 내가 아마도 공포 때문에 미치게 되었을 거라는 생각을 하고 있었을 것이네. (그래서) 나는 그들에게 정식으로 강의를 했지. 이보게들, 소동을 떨어야 소용이 없다네 하고 계속 지켜보았느냐고? 물론 나는 고양이가 생쥐를 노리듯이 안개가 걷힐 징조만 지켜보고 있었던 걸세. 그러나 우리가 마치 여러 마일 두께의 솜뭉치 더미 속에 묻혀 있듯이 눈에는 다른 아무것도 보이질 않았어. 안개가 솜뭉치 더미처럼 느껴진다고 한 것은 그게 우리를 답답하게 하고 덥게 하고 또 질식하게 했기 때문이지.

[출전] <Heart of Darkness> by Joseph Conrad (1857-1924)

## 45회

본책 p.361

### 01

하위내용영역 문학(소설) A형 기입형 배점 2점 예상정답률 50%

모범답안 silent depository

채점기준

- 2점 : 모범답안과 같다. 이것 외에는 답이 될 수 없다.
- 0점 : 모범답안과 다르다.

한글 번역

[A] 변호사인 그 노신사는 겉으로 보기엔 늙고 낡았지만, 귀족들의 혼인 부동산 계약이나 유언장으로 부를 이룬 것으로 유명했다. 그는 명문가의 비밀에서 비롯되는 신비로운 후광에 둘러싸인 채, 그런 비밀을 묵묵히 지키는 인물로 알려져 있다. 저택 깊숙한 공터에 키 큰 나무와 풀고사리에 둘러싸여 수백 년 동안 자리잡고 있는 고귀한 사당조차도 이 털킹혼 씨의 가슴속에 묻힌 채 사람들 사이를 활보하고 다닐 만큼 많은 비밀은 품고 있지 않다. 그는 이른바 구식 인간으로 —이 단어는 보통 일찍이 한 번도 젊음을 맛본 적이 없을 것 같은 사람을 가리킨다— 반바지를 입고 그 끝단을 얇은 끈으로 묶고 긴 양말 위에 보호대를 덧신었다. 그 검은 양복과 비단인지 털실인지 모를 검은 양말의 특징 가운데 하나는 절대 광택이 나지 않는다는 점이다. 빛에 반응하지 않는 이 복장은 그것을 입은 사람과 닮았다.

[B] 그는 직업상 고객과 상담할 때가 아니면 결코 입을 열지 않는다. 이따금 명문가의 시골 저택에서 열리는 연회장 식탁 구석이나 사교계 수다쟁이들이 좋아하는 살롱 입구 근처에 모습을 드러낼 때는 입을 꾹 다문 채 한가롭게 있다. 하지만 거기 모인 사람들은 모두 그를 알고 있으며, 귀족의 절반쯤은 그 앞에 멈춰 서서 "안녕하십니까, 털킹혼 씨" 하고 인사를 건넨다. 그러면 그는 그 인사를 정중하게 받아들여 다른 여러 지식(비밀)과 함께 마음 깊은 곳에 간직해 버린다.

[출전] <Bleak House> by Charles Dickens(1812-1870)

### 02

하위내용영역 문학(드라마) B형 서술형 배점 4점 예상정답률 50%

모범답안 It can be inferred that Momo has some mental disability. Next, Brigid is originally from Scranton and now lives in Manhattan.

채점기준

+ 2점 : Momo의 상태에 대해 추론할 수 있는 것을 "Momo has <u>some mental disability</u>"라 서술하였거나 유사하였다.
  ▷ <u>senility</u>나 <u>dementia</u>라 하였어도 맞는 것으로 한다.
+ 2점 : Brigid가 살았던 곳을 "<u>Scranton</u>"(1점); 현재 사는 곳을 "<u>Manhattan</u>"(1점)이라 서술하였다.

[출전] <The Humans> by Stephen Karam(1980-)

## 03

하위내용영역 문학(시) B형 서술형 배점 4점 예상정답률 45%

모범답안 The thematic idea is that greatness is not about fame or educational background but about working hard and having integrity. The ONE word is "death".

채점기준

+ 2점 : 시의 핵심 주제를 "greatness is not about fame(or educational background) but about working hard and having integrity(or simplicity or kindness and patience)"이라 명확하게 서술하였거나 유사하였다.
+ 2점 : 밑줄 친 부분이 가리키는 것을 "death (of the speaker's father)"라 명확하게 기술하였다.

[출전] "My father is a simple man" by Luis Omar Salinas(1937-2008)

## 04

하위내용영역 문학(소설) B형 서술형 배점 4점 예상정답률 45%

모범답안 The sentence is "The wind pressed his grey shirt against his chest". Second, the primary concern of the main character is (the burden of) facing the meeting ahead of him as chief.

채점기준

+ 2점 : [A]의 밑줄 친 부분과 상응하는 [B]에 있는 한 문장을 "The wind pressed his grey shirt against his chest"라 정확하게 썼다.
+ 2점 : 주인공의 주된 걱정거리를 "facing the meeting(1점) ahead of him as chief(1점)"라 서술하였거나 유사하였다.

한글 번역

[A] 밀물이 밀려오고 있어서 야자수가 자라고 있는 땅 주변의 하얀 색깔의 걸리적거리는 것과 바닷물 사이엔 겨우 한 가닥의 좁은 단단한 모래사장만 있을 뿐이었다. 랠프는 곰곰이 생각할 필요가 있었기에 그 단단한 모래사장을 택해 (그 위로) 걸어갔다. 발을 쳐다보지 않고서도 걸어갈 수 있는 곳은 거기밖에 없었던 것이다. 물가를 걸어가다가 문득 깨달아지는 바가 있어 그는 놀랐다. 이 세상살이의 권태로움을 깨우친 것 같았다. 이 세상에서의 모든 길은 그때그때의 즉흥적으로 정해지는 것이며, 깨어 살아가는 삶의 대다수는 자기 자신의 발걸음을 조심하는 데 쓰는 것이 아니냐는 생각이 들었던 것이다.
모임을 열 시간이 다 되어 가고 있었기에, 무엇인가를 감추려는 듯한 눈부신 햇살 속으로 걸어가며 그는 모임의 요점을 세심하게 점검하였다. 꿈같은 것을 뒤쫓아도 안 되겠지… 이번 모임은 장난이 되어서는 안 된다. 사무적이어야 한다. 그렇게 생각하자 그의 걸음이 빨라졌다. 긴급하다는 것, 기우는 석양, 빨라진 걸음에 의해 생긴 얼굴에 부딪는 가벼운 바람기가 한꺼번에 갑자기 인식되었다.

[B] 마음의 경련이 일어, 랠프는 온통 더럽고 누더기가 된 것을 발견하였다. 눈을 가리는 더벅머리를 연방 쓸어 넘기는 것, 또 해가 지고 난 뒤 부스럭거리는 소리를 내며 잎사귀에 몸을 뉘는 것 등을 그가 얼마나 싫어했는지도 깨달았다. 순간 그는 종종걸음을 치며 걷기 시작했다. 바람이 그의 셔츠를 그의 가슴에 밀어붙였다.
웅덩이 수영장 근처의 모래사장에는 모임을 기다리는 한 무리의 소년들이 여기저기 흩어져 있었다. 그들은 랠프의 침울한 기분과 불을 꺼트린 잘못을 의식하고 말없이 그에게 길을 내주었다. 그가 서 있는 집회의 장소는 대충 삼각형을 이루고 있었다. 하지만 그들이 만든 모든 것이 그렇듯이 고르지 못하고 불완전하였다. 야자수 그루터기는 모래사장과 평행으로 놓여 있어서 랠프가 걸터앉으면 섬 쪽을 향하게 되고 따라서 소년들 쪽에서 보면 그의 모습은 석호의 번쩍이는 수면을 배경으로 한 거무스레한 형상으로 보였다. 랠프는 초조하게 움직였다. 곤란한 것은 대장이 됐을 경우, 생각할 필요가 있고 현명해질 필요가 있다는 점이다. 그러다가 적절한 상황이 슬쩍 지나가면, 결정을 내려야만 한다. 그러니 생각을 해야만 한다. 생각한다는 것은 소중한 것이고 결과를 낳는 것이기 때문이다.

[출전] <Lord of the Flies> by William Golding (1911-1993)

## 46회

본책 p.369

### 01

하위내용영역 문학(소설) A형 기입형 배점 2점 예상정답률 45%

모범답안 young

채점기준

- 2점 : 모범답안과 같다. 이것 외에는 답이 될 수 없다.
- 0점 : 모범답안과 다르다.

한글 번역

나는 이번 월드컵 경기를 파리 14지구의 변두리의 술집과 카페에서 시청했다. 일부는 젠트리피케이션이 이루어졌지만, 여전히 이민자 인구가 많은 공영 주택단지가 있는 곳이고, 마약, 갱단, 경찰과의 충돌과 같은 낮은 사회 계층의 긴장들이 일상으로 드러나는 혼합 지역이다. 하지만, 지금까지는 월드컵을 시청하는 분위기가 나빠진 않아서 상대적으로 문제가 일어나지 않았다. 프랑스 대표팀의 승전보가 전해질 때마다 울려 퍼지는 경적소리, 맥주 세례가 이어졌다. 뉴스에서 이 모든 것을 보면서 프랑스 축구팬들에 대해 가장 눈에 띄었던 것은, 수많은 민족들이 보였음에도, 그들의 인종 혼합이 아니라 그들이 얼마나 젊었는가 하는 점이었다. 이 세대는 1998년 프랑스 월드컵 우승은 말 그대로 역사적 사건일 뿐인 새로운 밀레니얼 세대이다. 〈르 파리지앵〉에 실린 한 만평은 다음과 같이 말했다: "지난 세기의 이야기를 더 이상 우리에게 하지 말라"고 젊은 세대의 팬들이 나 같은 뚱뚱하고 중년의 백인 남성에게 말한다. 그 메시지는 분명하다: 이것은 우리의 월드컵이고, 축하해야 할 우리 자신의 승리라는 것이다. 어떤 의미에선 이들은 옳다. 프랑스 축구 대표팀은 아주 젊고, 그들은 대체로 과거와 역사의 무게에 무관심하다. 이번 대회에서 스타로 떠오른 킬리앙 음바페처럼 프랑스가 마지막으로 우승컵을 차지했던 1998년에는 태어나지도 않았던 선수들도 있다.

### 02

하위내용영역 문학(시) A형 서술형 배점 4점 예상정답률 40%

모범답안 The meaning of the underlined part is that the speaker is unable to make dumpling dough so has to buy it. Next, in the poem, won tons are compared to: "the fat sun", "misshapen flowers", and "newborns".

채점기준

- + 2점 : 밑줄 친 부분의 의미를 "the speaker is unable to make doughy skin so has to buy it"라 서술하였거나 유사하였다.
- + 2점 : 완탕(중국식 만두)이 비유된 것이 "the fat sun, misshapen flowers, and newborns"라 정확하게 서술하였다.
  - ▷ 이 셋 중 2개만 맞았으면 1점; 1개만 맞았으면 0.5점을 준다.

[출전] "Folding Won Tons In" by Abraham Chang

### 03

하위내용영역 문학(드라마) B형 서술형 배점 4점 예상정답률 50%

모범답안 The source of Ark's grand plan is from God's messages given in her imagination. Next, Ark believes that soldiering is not difficult if God is supporting the person.

채점기준

- + 2점 : Ark의 웅대한 전략(계획)의 원천을 "God's messages given in her imagination"이라 서술하였거나 유사하였다.

+ 2점: Robert의 질문 ("군인 생활이 아무나 할 수 있는 일인 것 같나?")에 대한 Ark의 답을 "soldiering is not difficult if God is supporting the person"이라 서술하였거나 유사하였다.
  - ▷ 다음과 같이 서술하였어도 2점을 준다. "soldiering is not special so anybody can do soldiering if God is on a person's side"

[출전] <Saint Joan> by George Bernard Shaw (1856-1950)

## 04

하위내용영역 문학(소설) B형 서술형 배점 4점 예상정답률 45%

모범답안 The underlined "Fall of Icarus" is a painted scene tattooed onto Henri Deplis' back. Second, the widow presents the masterpiece to Bergamo because she isn't happy with the short offer of Henri Deplis for it.

채점기준

+ 2점: 밑줄 친 "이카로스의 추락"이 "a tattoo(1점) on Henri Deplis' back(1점)"임을 정확하게 서술하였다.
+ 2점: Pincini의 미망인이 남편의 걸작을 베르가모시에 기증한 이유를 "because she isn't happy with the short offer of Henri Deplis for it"이라 서술하였거나 유사하였다.

한글 번역

앙리 드플리는 룩셈부르크 공국에서 태어났다. 심사숙고 끝에 순회 외판원이 됐다. 물건을 팔려고 자주 국경을 넘었는데, 북이탈리아의 작은 마을에 머물고 있을 때 먼 친척이 죽으면서 그의 몫으로 유산을 남겼다는 소식을 듣게 되었다.

그 유산은 드플리의 검소한 관점에서 보더라도 그렇게 큰돈은 아니었지만, 겉보기에 해롭지 않은 정도의 사치로 그를 내몰았다. 특히 그는 현지의 대표적 예술가인 안드레아스 핀치니 씨의 문신을 후원하게 되었다, 핀치니 씨는 이탈리아에서 가장 뛰어난 문신 기술의 대가였지만, 형편이 아주 가난해서 600프랑을 받는 대가로 드플리의 등을 어깨부터 허리까지 '이카로스의 추락'을 묘사한 그림으로 뒤덮는 일을 기꺼이 떠맡았다. 마침내 드러난 밑그림에 드플리는 조금 실망했지만, 막상 작품이 완성되었을 때는 더없이 만족했고, 그것을 감상하는 특권을 누린 사람들도 모두 그것을 핀치니의 대표작으로 인정했다.

그것은 핀치니의 가장 훌륭한 작품이자 마지막 작품이었다. 그 뛰어난 장인은, 사례금을 받을 때까지 기다리지 못하고, 세상을 떴고 화려한 묘석 밑에 묻혔다. 하지만 600프랑을 받아야 할 핀치니의 미망인이 남아 있었다. 그런데 그 직후에 순회 외판원으로서 드플리의 인생에 큰 위기가 닥쳤다. 모처럼 받은 유산도 지출이 ―아무리 사소한 지출이지만― 수없이 누적되자 하찮은 액수로 줄어들었고, 독촉이 심해서 더 이상 지불을 미룰 수 없는 술값과 여러 가지 잡다한 지출 때문에 미망인에게 줄 돈이 430프랑밖에 남지 않았다.

그 미망인은 170프랑을 깎아달라는 요구 때문만이 아니라 죽은 남편의 걸작으로 인정받은 작품의 가치를 떨어뜨리려는 시도에 대해서도 지당하게 분개했다. 일주일 뒤에는 드플리가 가진 돈이 더욱 줄어들어서 문신 값을 405프랑으로 깎아달라고 요구할 수밖에 없었고, 그것은 미망인의 분노를 더욱 부채질했다. 미망인은 예술작품 판매를 취소했고, 며칠 뒤에 드플리는 미망인이 자기 등에 새겨진 문신을 베르가모시에 기증했고, 시 당국은 그것을 고맙게 받아들였다는 것을 알고는 경악했다.

[출전] "The Background" by Hector Hugh Munro (1870-1916)

## 47회

본책 p.376

### 01

하위내용영역 문학(소설) A형 기입형 배점 2점 예상정답률 50%

모범답안 on the road

채점기준

- 2점: 모범답안과 같다. 이것 외에는 답이 될 수 없다.
- 0점: 모범답안과 다르다.

한글 번역

딘을 처음 만난 것은 아내와 헤어지고 얼마 되지 않아서였다. 당시 나는 심한 병을 앓다가 겨우 나은 참이었는데, 이 병에 관해서는 끔찍할 정도로 지긋지긋했던 결별 과정과 세상만사에 무감각해진 나 자신과 관계가 있다는 사실 외에는 더 이야기하지 않도록 하겠다. 딘 모리아티의 등장으로 이른바 길 위에서의 삶이라 할 수 있는 내 삶의 한 시기가 시작되었다. 그 전에도 서쪽으로 가서 시골을 구경하는 것을 자주 꿈꾸기는 했지만, 항상 막연하게 계획만 세웠지 실제로 떠난 적은 한 번도 없었다. 딘은 길 위에서 태어났기 때문에 길동무로는 완벽한 녀석이었다. 1926년 로스앤젤레스로 가고 있던 그의 부모는 솔트레이크시티를 통과하던 중에 고물차 속에서 그를 낳았다. 내가 딘을 알게 된 건 그가 뉴멕시코의 소년원에서 보낸 편지 몇 통을 채드 킹이 보여줬기 때문이었다. 니체같이 지적이고 멋진 것들을 알고 있는 대로 가르쳐 달라는 순진하고 다정한 부탁이 담긴 그 편지에 나는 굉장한 관심을 갖게 됐다. 한번은 그 편지에 관해 카를로와 얘기하다가 딘 모리아티라는 이상한 녀석을 한번 만나보면 어떨까 하는 생각을 했다. 아주 오래전 얘기인데, 그때 딘은 지금과 다르게 신비에 싸인 어린 소년원생이었다. 그 후 딘이 출소를 해서 난생처음 뉴욕에 온다는 소식이 들려왔다. 또 얼마 전에 메릴루라는 여자와 결혼했다는 얘기도 있었다.

[출전] <On the Road> by Jack Kerouac(1922-1969)

### 02

하위내용영역 문학(시) A형 서술형 배점 4점 예상정답률 45%

모범답안 The extended metaphor running through the poem is the speaker's mother is a sunrise. Second, the meaning of the underlined is that the mother makes the father happy and also removes bad moods, or darkness.

채점기준

+ 2점: 확장된 은유(A metaphor that is continued over multiple sentences)를 "the speaker's mother is a sunrise"라 서술하였거나 유사하였다.
+ 2점: 밑줄 친 부분의 의미를 "the mother makes the father happy and also removes bad moods, or darkness"라 서술하였거나 유사하였다.

[출전] "Mama Is a Sunrise" by Evelyn Tooley Hunt(1904-1997)

### 03

하위내용영역 문학(소설) B형 서술형 배점 4점 예상정답률 40%

모범답안 Gabriel realizes that his wife had experienced real love that he had not felt and he loses one sense of himself and decides to find himself. Next, the sentence is: "The time had come for him to set out on his journey westward."

채점기준

+ 2점: Epiphany(a moment where a character experiences a life-changing self-understanding or illumination)를 "Gabriel realizes that his wife had experienced real love that he had not felt and he loses one sense of himself and decides to find himself"라 명확하게 서술하였거나 유사하였다.
  ▷ 다음과 같이 서술하였어도 2점을 준다.
  - "Gabriel realizes that his marriage with his wife never had true love and also that his life in general has been passionless and numb"
  - "he realizes that he cannot separate the past from the present any more than the dead to the living. (He comes to this realization by acknowledging that) Michael Furey, despite both being dead and a part of Gretta's past, is still very much alive.

+ 2점: Gabriel의 미래의 책임에 대한 인식을 나타내는 문장을 "The time had come for him to set out on his journey westward"라 명확하게 기술하였다. 이것 외에는 답이 될 수 없다.

한글 번역

그녀는 깊이 잠이 들었다. 가브리엘은 깊은 숨소리를 들었다. 그러니까 그녀는 생전에 로맨스를 겪었던 것이다. 한 남자가 그녀를 위해 죽었다. 남편인 자신이 그녀의 삶 속에서 얼마나 보잘것없는 역할을 했는가 생각을 해도 그에게 고통이 되지 않았다. 그는 그녀가 잠자는 것을 지켜보았다. 마치 그와 그녀가 부부로서 살아 본 일이 없던 것처럼 말이다. 그의 호기심이 동한 눈이 오랫동안 그녀의 얼굴과 머리털에 머물렀다. 처음 소녀다운 아름다움 속에 있던 시절의 그녀는 어떤 모습이었을까 생각을 하자 이상스럽고도 다정한 동정심이 그의 영혼 속으로 들어왔다.

아마 그녀가 얘기를 모두 다 털어 놓지 않았을 수도 있다. 그의 눈은 의자로 옮겨가서 그 위에다가 던져 놓은 그녀의 옷가지를 보았다. 그는 한 시간 전의 자신이 드러내었던 감정의 폭발에 대해 놀랐다. 어디서 그 감정이 솟아났을까? 이모의 저녁 식사, 자신의 바보 같은 연설, 포도주와 춤, 홀에서 작별 인사할 때의 즐거운 소란, 눈 속에서 강을 따라 걸었던 즐거움에서였다.

밤공기에 그의 어깨가 시렸다. 그는 조심스럽게 이불 밑으로 몸을 뻗어 아내 옆에 누웠다. 하나씩 하나씩 그들은 모두 그림자가 되리라. 나이 들어 끔찍하게 시들고 말라비틀어지느니 차라리 어떤 정열의 충만한 영광 속에 저 세상 속으로 용감하게 들어갈지니라. 그는 옆에 누워 있는 그녀가 가슴속에 아주 오랜 세월 동안, 그녀의 연인이 자기는 살고 싶지 않다고 말할 때의 그 눈의 모습을 간직해 왔다는 사실을 생각해 보았다.

너그러운 눈물이 가브리엘의 눈에 가득 고였다. 그는 어떤 여자에 대해서도 이런 것을 느껴 보지 못했었다. 하지만 이런 느낌이 분명 사랑임을 알고 있었다. 눈물이 눈에 더욱 벅차게 고였고, 어렴풋한 어둠 속에서 그는 한 젊은이가 물이 떨어지는 나무 아래 서 있는 모습을 상상하였다. 다른 형체들도 가까이 있었다. 그의 혼은 거대한 무리의 죽은 사람들이 사는 영역에 접근하였다. 그들의 제멋대로이고 깜빡거리는 존재들을 의식하고 있지만 포착할 수는 없었다. 자기 자체가 회색의 인지할 수 없는 세계 속으로 사라져 가고 있었다. 확고한 세계 그 자체가, 이 죽은 자들이 세우고 살았던 그 세계가 녹으면서 줄어들고 있었다.

유리창에 가벼이 닿는 소리 때문에 그는 창문 쪽을 돌아보았다. 다시 눈이 오기 시작하였다. 그는 졸리는 눈으로 은빛의 어두운 눈송이들이 가로등 불빛에 비스듬히 내리는 것을 보았다. 서쪽을 향한 여행을 출발할 때가 된 것이다.

[출전] "The Dead" by James Joyce(1882-1941)

## 04

하위내용영역 문학(드라마) B형 서술형 배점 4점 예상정답률 40%

**모범답안** Evadne wants to be a "worm" because she is fascinated by the "lower" class and the slums. Second, the gift is most likely to be "sapphires".

**채점기준**

+ 2점 : Evadne이 자신에게 "벌레"라는 은유를 사용한 의미를 "Evadne wants to be a "worm" because she is fascinated by the "lower" class and the slums"라 서술하였거나 유사하였다.
  ▷ 다음과 같이 서술하였어도 2점을 준다.
  "The "worm" metaphor means that Evadne enjoys visiting places like slums more than being a clean, social butterfly"
+ 2점 : 약혼 선물을 "sapphires"라 정확하게 기술하였다. 이것 외에는 답이 될 수 없다.

[출전] <Our Ostriches> by Mari Stopes(1880-1958)

# 48회

본책 p.383

## 01

하위내용영역 문학(소설) A형 기입형 배점 2점 예상정답률 45%

**모범답안** meaninglessness

**채점기준**

- 2점 : 모범답안과 같다. 이것 외에는 답이 될 수 없다.
- 0점 : 모범답안과 다르다.

**한글 번역**

엘리자베스와 그녀의 외아들 조지 사이에는 말로 표현하지는 않았았지만 오래전에 죽어 버린 그녀의 소녀시절의 꿈을 기반으로 하는 깊은 공감대가 있었다. 아들 앞에서 그녀는 소심하고 말이 없었으나 가끔 그가 기자의 의무에 열중하여 마을 여기저기를 분주히 다니는 동안 그녀는 아들의 방에 들어가 문을 잠그고는 창가에 놓인, 부엌 식탁으로 만든 작은 책상 옆에 무릎 꿇었다. 방 안 책상 옆에서 그녀는 하늘에 대고 말하는 의식을 행했는데 반은 기도이고 반은 요구였다. 여자는 한때 자신의 일부였으나 반쯤 잊힌 어떤 것이 소년의 모습에서 재창조되는 것을 간절히 보고 싶었다. 기도는 그것에 관한 내용이었다. "내가 죽더라도 어떻게 해서든 나는 네가 패배하지 않도록 해줄 거야." 그녀는 외쳤다. 그녀의 결심이 너무나 강했기 때문에 몸 전체가 떨렸다. 그녀의 두 눈이 이글거렸고 그녀는 주먹을 꽉 쥐었다. "만약 내가 죽고 내 아들이 나처럼 아무 의미도 없고 재미도 없는 사람이 되는 걸 본다면 난 다시 돌아올 거야"라고 그녀가 선언했다. "그런 특권을 달라고 난 이제 신께 요청할 거야. 난 그걸 요구하는 거야. 신은 주먹으로 날 칠 수 있겠지. 난 내 아들이 우리 둘 모두를 위해 뭔가를 표현하도록 허락되기만 한다면 난 내게 내려쳐질지 모를 어떤 주먹질이라도 견뎌낼 수 있어."
언젠가 혼자 있을 때 엘리자베스는 빵집 주인의 질질 끌면서도 무의미한 분노의 폭발을 지켜보고 난 뒤에 자신의 길고도 하얀 손 위에 머리를 얹고 울었다. 그 후로 그녀는 골목을 지켜보는 일을 더 이상 하지 않았고 그 턱수염 난 남자와 고양이 사이의 경합을 잊으려고 애썼다. 그건 마치 그녀 자신의 인생의 예행연습 같아서 너무나 생생하고 끔찍했기 때문이었다.

[출전] "Mother" by Sherwood Anderson(1876-1941)

## 02

하위내용영역 문학(시) A형 서술형 배점 4점 예상정답률 60%

모범답안 In the third stanza, the poet uses personification (to make the ocean and clouds into a couple). Next, the thematic idea is that companionship makes the world more meaningful.

채점기준

+ 2점: 세 번째 연에서 사용된 비유적 언어를 "personification"이라 정확하게 지적하였다. 이것 외에는 답이 될 수 없다.
+ 2점: 시의 중심 주제를 "companionship makes the world more meaningful(or pleasant)"이라 서술하였거나 유사하였다.
  ▷ 다음과 같이 서술하였어도 2점을 준다.
  • "The world is not a good place to be without someone"
  • "Companion is needed to survive through the difficult times of life"

[출전] "The World Is Not a Pleasant Place to Be" by Nikki Giovanni(1943-)

## 03

하위내용영역 문학(드라마) B형 서술형 배점 4점 예상정답률 40%

모범답안 The strange details supporting Maud's situation are her talking to God, calling her daughter-in-law "mother", and not noticing Helen is present. Next, the cat symbolizes the old woman, Maud.

채점기준

+ 2점: Maud의 상황을 알려주는 이상한 세부사항을 "her talking to God, calling her daughter-in-law "mother", and not noticing Helen is present"라 서술하였거나 유사하였다.
  ▷ 이 가운데 2개만 서술하였어도 2점을 준다.
+ 2점: 고양이가 상징하는 것을 "Maud"라 정확하게 서술하였다. 이것 외에는 답이 될 수 없다.

[출전] <The Nightingale Not the Lark> by Jennifer Johnston(1930-)

## 04

하위내용영역 문학(소설) B형 서술형 배점 4점 예상정답률 55%

모범답안 Mrs. Thompson is upset because Joe has taken a child home to care for. Second, the meaning of the underlined is that she was extremely furious and red-faced.

채점기준

+ 2점: Thompson 부인의 마음이 상한 이유를 "because Joe has taken a child home to care for"라 서술하였거나 유사하였다.
+ 2점: 밑줄 친 은유적 표현의 의미를 "she (Mrs. Thomson) was extremely furious"라 서술하였거나 유사하였다.

[출전] "An Angel in Disguise" by Timothy S. Arthur(1809-1885)

# 49회

본책 p.390

## 01

하위내용영역 문학(소설) A형 기입형 배점 2점 예상정답률 55%

**모범답안** He was a stranger to me.

**채점기준**

- 2점 : 모범답안과 같다. 이것 외에는 답이 될 수 없다.
- 0점 : 모범답안과 다르다.

**한글 번역**

내가 아버지를 마지막으로 본 것은 그랜드 센트럴 역에서였다. 그때 나는 애디론댁스에 있는 할머니 집에서 어머니가 빌린 케이프의 농가로 가는 길이었다. 그래서 아버지에게 내가 기차를 갈아타는 사이 한 시간 반가량 뉴욕에 있을 텐데 함께 점심 식사를 할 수 있겠냐 묻는 편지를 써 보냈었다. 아버지는 나에게 낯선 사람이었다. 아버지의 비서는 내게 정오에 안내 창구 앞에서 그를 만날 것이라는 회신을 보냈고, 나는 열두 시 정각에 그가 사람들을 헤치고 다가오는 것을 보았다. 어머니는 아버지와 삼 년 전 이혼했고, 그 이후로 난 그와 함께 있어본 적이 없었다. 하지만, 그를 보자마자 그가 내 아버지라고, 나의 살과 피이고 나의 미래, 나의 운명이라고 느꼈다. 나는 내가 어른이 되면 그와 비슷해지리라는 것을 알고 있었다. 내 활동 범위가 아버지의 영역 내에서 짜이게 되리라는 것을. 그는 몸집이 큰 잘생긴 남자였고 난 그를 다시 보게 된 것이 엄청나게 기뻤다. 그가 내 등을 철썩 치고 손을 잡아 흔들었다. "안녕, 찰리" 그가 말했다. "반갑구나. 너를 데리고 내 클럽으로 갔으면 좋겠다만 거기는 60번가에 있는데, 네가 이른 기차를 타야 한다면 이 근처 어디에서 뭘 좀 먹는 편이 나을 것 같다." 그가 내 어깨에 팔을 둘렀고 나는 어머니가 장미냄새를 맡듯이 내 아버지의 냄새를 맡았다. 그것은 위스키, 애프터셰이브 로션, 구두 광약, 모직물, 그리고 성인 남자의 사회적 지위가 혼합된 풍요로운 냄새였다. 나는 우리가 함께 있는 것을 누군가가 보았으면 싶었다. 사진을 찍을 수 있었으면 싶었다. 난 우리가 함께 있었다는 어떤 기록을 남기고 싶었다.

[출전] "Reunion" by John Cheever(1912-1982)

## 02

하위내용영역 문학(시) A형 서술형 배점 4점 예상정답률 40%

**모범답안** The literal meaning of the underlined figure of speech is that the couple has bent backs and so is becoming closer to the ground. Next, the contrast drawn is that the tourists reveal a lot of skin in shorts and halter tops but the old couple are entirely covered except their hands and faces.

**채점기준**

+ 2점 : 밑줄 친 비유적 언어의 문자적 의미를 "the old couple has bent backs(또는 the old couple slumped over) and thus are becoming closer to the ground"라 서술하였거나 유사하였다.
+ 2점 : 첫 두 연에서 화자가 드러내는 노부부와 관광객들의 의복의 대조를 "the tourists reveal a lot of skin in shorts and halter tops but the old couple are entirely covered except their hands and faces"라 서술하였거나 유사하였다.
  - ▷ 다음과 같이 서술하였어도 2점을 준다. "tourists wear more modern clothing in contrast to the old couple's faded, more traditional clothing."

[출전] "Los ancianos *(Old People)*" by Pat Mora (1942-)

## 03

하위내용영역 문학(드라마) B형 서술형 배점 4점 예상정답률 35%

모범답안 The whole dialogue is about a child, Vinny, who told Immigration about his uncle and was kicked out of his house. Second, the lesson is that it is impossible to take back your words when you have let out a secret.

채점기준

+ 2점 : 대화가 주로 "about a child, Vinny, who told Immigration about his uncle (and was kicked out of his house)"라 서술하였거나 유사하였다.
  ▷ 다음과 같이 서술하였어도 2점을 준다.
  "the consequences of informing to the police"
+ 2점 : 밑줄 친 부분의 의미를 "it is impossible to take back your words when you've let out a secret"라 서술하였거나 유사하였다.
  ▷ 다음과 같이 서술하였어도 2점을 준다.
  "it is easier to become rich than to take back your words when you've let out a secret"

[출전] <A View from a Bridge> by Arthur Miller (1915-2005)

## 04

하위내용영역 문학(소설) B형 서술형 배점 4점 예상정답률 45%

모범답안 The narrator changes his opinion of his home because he sees it as coarse and common, through the influence of Miss Havisham and Estella. Second, the underlined words refer to the narrator's unpleasant view of home.

채점기준

+ 2점 : 화자의 삶을 바꾸게 한 것이 "because he sees it as coarse and common, through the influence of his Miss Havisham and Estella"라 서술하였거나 유사하였다.
+ 2점 : 밑줄 친 부분이 가리키는 것을 "the narrator's unpleasant view of home"이라 서술하였거나 유사하였다.

한글 번역

자기 집을 부끄럽게 여긴다는 것은 몹시 비참한 일이다. 물론 그것은 사악한 배은망덕에서 비롯된 것이기 쉽고, 따라서 인과응보의 벌을 받아 마땅한 짓이라고 말할 수 있다. 하지만 그보다 더 확실히 말할 수 있는 것은 그것은 비참한 일이라는 것이다. 누나의 성미 때문에 집은 나에게 결코 즐거운 곳이 못 되었다. 하지만 조가 그런 집을 성스러운 곳으로 만들어 주었고, 그래서 나는 집의 소중함을 믿었다. 나는 우리 집의 손님맞이용 거실을 아주 우아한 응접실이라고 믿었고, 우리 집의 정면 출입문을 경건하게 문을 열고 들어가 구운 새고기의 제물을 바치는 장엄한 신전의 신비스러운 입구처럼 생각했다. 나는 또한 우리 집 부엌이 훌륭하지는 못해도 정결한 구역이라 믿었으며, 대장간에 대해서는 사내다움과 독립으로 이끄는 빛나는 길이라고 믿어 왔다. 하지만 채 1년도 안 되는 동안에 이 모든 것이 달라져 버렸다. 이제 이 모든 것은 투박하고 천박했으며, 어떤 일이 있어도 내 사랑하는 에스텔러와 그녀의 양모 해비셤한테는 집을 보여 주고 싶지 않았다. 배은망덕한 이런 내 심리 상태의 얼마만큼이 나의 잘못이고, 얼마만큼이 미스 해비셤의 탓이며, 또 얼마만큼이 누나의 탓이었는가 하는 것은 이 순간 나를 비롯한 어느 누구에게도 전혀 중요하지 않다. 문제는 나에게 변화가 일어났고, 그래서 일이 그렇게 되었다는 사실이다. 잘되었든 잘못되었든, 변명의 여지가 있든 없든, 일은 그렇게 되어버린 것이다. 예전엔 내가 마침내 조의 도제가 되어 셔츠 소매를 걷어 올리고 대장간으로 들어갈 수 있게 되면 자랑스럽고 행복할 것처럼 보였다. 그런데 이제 그것이 현실로 다가오자, 잘게 부서진 석탄재로 먼지투성이가 되었다는 느낌과, 대장간의 모루는 깃털에 불과하게 여겨질 만큼 무거운 돌이 내 매일매일의 삶을 짓누르고 있다는 느낌밖에 없었다.

[출전] <Great Expectations> by Charles Dickens (1812-1870)

## 50회

본책 p.395

### 01

하위내용영역 문학(소설) A형 기입형 배점 2점 예상정답률 50%

모범답안 his wish to retain Eppie

채점기준

- 2점 : 모범답안과 같다. 이것 외에는 답이 될 수 없다.
- 0점 : 모범답안과 다르다.

한글 번역

"매너, 자넨 자네의 삶이 어떻게 될지 불확실하고, 에피의 운명도 자기 아버지의 집에 있을 때와는 전혀 다른 방향으로 결정될 나이에 이르렀다는 것을 기억해야 하네. 내가 못 해준 일을 자네가 다 해준 후에 자네 맘을 상하게 해서 유감이네만, 내 딸을 돌보겠다고 주장하는 게 내 의무라고 느끼고 있다네. 난 내 의무를 다하고 싶은 걸세." 갓프리는 말했다. 매너는 다시 양심의 가책을 느꼈다. 그리고 갓프리의 비난이 사실이 아닐까, 즉 자기가 고집을 세워 에피의 행복에 장애물이 되지는 않을까 하여 놀랐다. 오랫동안 그는 어려운 말을 꺼내기에 필요한 자제심을 회복하려 애쓰며 침묵을 지켰다. 그리고 그 말은 떨리는 목소리가 되어 나왔다.
"전 더 이상 할 말이 없습니다. 좋을 대로 하십시오. 아이한테 얘기하세요. 저는 아무것도 막지 않겠습니다."
대단히 예민한 애정을 지닌 갓프리의 부인 낸시 조차도 남편의 견해에 동조하여, 친아버지가 나섰는데도 에피를 데리고 있겠다는 매너의 바람이 정당치 못하다고 생각했다. 에피가 아주 어릴 때부터 그녀를 큰 사랑으로 길러 온 가엾은 직조공에게는 가혹한 시련일 거라고 느꼈지만, 그녀의 규범은 친아버지의 권리가 양아버지의 권리를 능가하는 것이 당연하다는 데 의문을 허용하지 않았다. 게다가 낸시는 평생 풍족한 환경과 상류계급의 특권에 익숙해 있었으므로, 가난하게 태어난 사람들의 모든 자그마한 목표나 노력과 어렸을 때부터의 양육과 습관에 의해 연결되어 있는 그들 나름의 기쁨을 이해할 수 없었다. 그녀 생각에, 타고난 권리를 되찾은 에피는 오랫동안 지연되기는 했으나 의심할 바 없는 이익을 누리게 된 것이었다. 그래서 매너의 마지막 말을 듣고 갓프리와 마찬가지로 자기네 바람이 이뤄졌다고 안도했다.

[출전] <Silas Marner> by George Eliot(1819-1880)

### 02

하위내용영역 문학(시) A형 서술형 배점 4점 예상정답률 50%

모범답안 The underlined "stars" refer to "starfish". Second, the "approaching darkness" changes the tone from playful to slightly darker with a sense of mortality or doom.

채점기준

+ 2점 : 밑줄 친 "stars"가 가리키는 것을 "starfish"라 서술하였다. 이것 외에는 답이 될 수 없다.
+ 2점 : "다가오는 어둠"에 대한 묘사가 시의 어조를 어떻게 바꾸는가에 대한 질문에 "the 'approaching darkness' changes the tone from playful to slightly darker with a sense of mortality or doom"라 서술하였거나 유사하였다.
  ▷ 다음과 같이 서술하였어도 2점을 준다.
  "the tone from discussion of decoration to the tragedy of deaths as experienced by humans"

[출전] "Starfish" by Lorna Cervantes(1954-)

## 03

**하위내용영역** 문학(드라마) B형 서술형 **배점** 4점 **예상정답률** 50%

**모범답안** It is joked that Martha paints blue circles around her things. Next, George and Martha are married and have a child.

**채점기준**

+ 2점: 그들이 놀리는 Martha의 이교도적 특징을 "Martha paints blue circles around her things"라 서술하였거나 유사하였다.
+ 2점: 그 둘의 관계를 "George and Martha are married and have a child*(son)*"라 서술하였거나 유사하였다.

**한글 번역**

조지: 마사는 거짓말을 하고 있지. 모두들 그걸 알아야 해. 마사는 거짓말을 하고 있어. (마사는 웃는다.) 이 세상에서 내가 확신할 수 있는 건 얼마 없지만… 국경선, 해수면 높이, 정치적 연대, 실생활 속 도덕… 이런 것들엔 더 이상 목숨 걸지 않겠지만… 허나 이 망할 놈의 세상에서 내가 확신하는 한 가지는… 금빛 눈에 푸른 머리카락의… 우리 아들을 만드는 데 내가 염색체상으로 협조한 다는 것이지.
허니: 아 다행이네!
마사: 훌륭한 연설이었어, 조지.
조지: 고마워, 마사.
마사: 아주 잘 대처했어, 조지.
허니: 음… 정말… 잘…
닉: 허니…
조지: 마사는 알지…, 마사가 더 잘 알아.
마사: (자랑스럽게) 나는 더 잘 알아. 나도 남들처럼 대학을 나왔거든.
조지: 마사도 대학 나왔어. 어릴 때는 수녀원에서 자라기도 했지.
마사: 그리고 난 무신론자였어. (자신 없어 하며) 여전히 무신론자이지.
조지: 무신론자는 아니지, 마사… 이교도지. (허니와 닉에게) 마사는 동부 해안의 유일한 이교도이지. (마사가 웃는다.)
허니: 아 멋져요. 여보, 정말 멋지지 않아?
닉: (그녀의 비위를 맞추며) 응… 멋지네.
조지: 그리고 마사는 자기 거시기에다 푸른 원을 그리기도 하지.
닉: 정말?
마사: (농담조로, 변명하듯) 때로는. (손짓하며) 보고 싶어?
조지: (나무라듯) 쯧쯧쯧.
마사: 많이 쯧쯧하셔… 갈보 같으니!
허니: 그는 갈보가 아니지… 갈보가 될 수 없어…, 댁이 갈보지. (낄낄거린다.)
마사: (허니에게 손가락을 흔들어 대며) 너 입조심해!
허니: (명랑하게) 알았어요. 브랜디나 한 잔 더 줘요.
닉: 허니, 너무 마신 것 같아…
조지: 말도 안 되는 소리! 다들 이제야 준비가 됐는데. (술잔들을 거둬 간다.)
허니: (조지를 흉내내며) 말도 안 되는 소리.
닉: (어깨를 으쓱하며) 알았어.

[출전] <Who's Afraid of Virginia Woolf?> by Edward Albee(1928-2016)

## 04

**하위내용영역** 문학(소설) B형 서술형 **배점** 4점 **예상정답률** 45%

**모범답안** The best word for the blank ⓐ is "Brotherhood". Second, the underlined words in ⓑ show that the man doesn't believe he is represented, as a black man, by that flag.

**채점기준**

+ 2점: ⓐ에 들어갈 단어를 "Brotherhood"라 서술하였다. 이것 외에는 답이 될 수 없다.
+ 2점: 밑줄 친 ⓑ에서 알 수 있는 것을 "the man doesn't believe he is represented, as a black man, by that flag"라 서술하였거나 유사하였다.

**한글 번역**

"마음은 순수해야 하고 몸과 정신도 단련시켜야 하오. 내 말을 이해하겠소, 동지?"
"네, 이해할 것 같습니다." 내가 대답했다. "어떤 사람들은 종교에 대해서도 그런 식으로 생각하죠."
"종교?" 그는 눈을 깜박였다. "동지나 나 같은 사람들은 불신으로 가득하지." 그가 말했다. "우리 중 일부는 너무 타락해서 동지회를 믿지 못하는 사람도 있소. 어떤 놈들은 심지어 복수를 원한다니까! 내 말이 바로 그 말이오. 그런 걸 제거해야 한다는 거요. 우리는 다른 동지들을 믿는 법을 배워야 하오. 어쨌든 그들이 우리 동지회를 시작했던 것 아니오? 그들이 다가와서 우리 흑인들에게 손을 내밀고 이렇게 말하지 않았소? '우리는 여러분과 동지가 되길 원합니다.' 안 그렇소? 지금도 그렇지 않소? 그들이 우리를 조직화하고 우리의 투쟁을 도와주며 접근하지 않았소? 확실히 그랬소. 우린 그걸 스물네 시간 내내 기억하고 있어야만 하오. 동지회, 이 말이 우리가 한시도 잊지 않고 마음에 품고 다녀야 할 것이오. 내가 동지를 찾아온 것도 바로 그 때문이오, 동지."
그는 뒤로 물러나 앉으며 커다란 손으로 무릎을 쥐었다. "동지와 의논해 보고 싶은 계획이 있단 말이오." 내가 말했다.
"그게 뭔데요, 동지?"
"음, 말하자면 이렇소. 내 생각에는 우리가 누구인지 보여 줄 방법을 찾아야 할 것 같소. 그러니까 현수막이나, 뭐 그런 걸 준비해야 한단 말이오. 특히 우리 흑인 동지들은 위해서 말이오."
"알겠습니다." 나는 흥미를 느끼며 대답했다. "그런데 왜 그것이 중요하다고 생각하시나요?"
"동지회에 도움이 되니까 그렇소. 그게 이유요. 기억할지 모르지만 우리 민족은 시가 행진이나 장례식을 할 때, 아니면 춤 같은 것을 할 때면 현수막이나 깃발을 내걸지 않소? 그것들이 별 의미는 없다 하더라도 말이오. 그런 게 있으면 그 행사가 더 중요한 것처럼 보이니까. 그러면 사람들이 가던 길을 멈추고 보고 듣게 되오. '저기 뭔 일이 있지?' 하고 궁금해 하죠. 그렇지만 동지나 내가 알고 있듯이 그들에게 진정한 깃발은 하나도 없소."
"네, 알 것 같습니다." 나는 국기가 지나갈 때마다 언제나 소외감을 느꼈던 사실을 떠올리며 대답했다. 내가 동지회를 알기 전까지는 국기는, 그 안에 내 별은 아직 존재하지 않는다는 걸 상기시켜주는 물건일 뿐이었다.

[출전] <Invisible Man> by Ralph Ellison(1914-1994)

## 51 회

본책 p.402

### 01

**하위내용영역** 문학(소설) A형 기입형 **배점** 2점 **예상정답률** 65%

**모범답안** trouble

**채점기준**

- 2점 : 모범답안과 같다. 이것 외에는 답이 될 수 없다.
- 0점 : 모범답안과 다르다.

[출전] "The Trapper Trapped" by Roger Abrahams (1933-2017)

### 02

**하위내용영역** 문학(드라마) B형 서술형 **배점** 4점 **예상정답률** 55%

**모범답안** Knowlt is unreliable because he is shown to be lying for his reason of going to war, saying he was escaping arrest when really he caught Lydia seeing another man. Second, he is now in a grave.

**채점기준**

+ 2점 : Knowlt가 믿을 수 없는 화자인 이유를 "because he is (shown to be) lying for his reason of going to war, saying he was escaping arrest when in reality he caught Lydia dating another man"이라 서술하였거나 유사하였다.
+ 2점 : Knowlt가 현재 있는 곳을 "he is now in a grave"라 정확하게 서술하였거나 유사하였다.

[출전] "Spoon River Anthology" by Edgar Lee Masters(1868-1950)

## 03

하위내용영역 문학(시) B형 서술형 배점 4점 예상정답률 50%

모범답안 The word for the blank is "own". Next, nature rebels against the idea that human beings own a piece of the planet, even though the planet looks after its people.

채점기준

+ 2점: 빈칸에 들어갈 단어를 "own"이라 정확하게 기입하였다. 이것 외에는 답이 될 수 없다.
+ 2점: 자연이 반대하는 것을 "human beings own a piece of the planet"이라 서술하였거나 유사하였다.

한글 번역

오랜 세월 동안 당신이
고된 일과 긴 항해 끝에
당신의 나라, 섬, 80만 평 터, 600평짜리 집의
방 한 가운데 서서 당신이
마침내 어떻게 거기까지 왔나를 생각하며
이것은 내 것이다,라고 말하는 순간

그것은 나무들이 당신을 감싼
그네의 부드러운 두 팔을 풀어 버리고
새들이 그네의 언어를 거두어 버리고
절벽들이 갈라져 무너지고
공기가 파도처럼 당신에게서 빠져나가
당신이 숨을 쉴 수 없는 순간이 된다.

천만에, 하고 그들은 속삭인다. 당신은 아무것도 소유하지 못해.
당신은 방문객일 뿐이었어. 번번이
언덕에 올라가 깃발을 꽂고 제 것이라 선포했지만
우리는 한 번도 당신의 소유물이 아니었어.
당신은 한 번도 우리를 발견하지 못했지.
우리가 언제나 당신을 발견하고 소유했던 거야.

[출전] "The Moment" by Margaret Atwood(1939-)

## 04

하위내용영역 문학(소설) B형 서술형 배점 4점 예상정답률 45%

모범답안 The "magic land" refers to Mexico. Next, the insight of the narrator's post-colonialism shows with the sentence: "The Mexican war, cutting across here with cannon."

채점기준

+ 2점: 마법의 땅이 가리키는 것이 "Mexico"라 정확하게 서술하였다.
+ 2점: 화자의 탈식민주적 통찰이 보이는 한 문장을 "The Mexican war, cutting across here with cannon"이라 정확히 서술하였다.

한글 번역

"됐습니다!" 멕시코 공무원이 싱글거렸다. "다 끝났습니다. 가도 됩니다. 멕시코에 오신 걸 환영합니다. 즐거운 시간 보내세요. 멕시코를 즐기는 것은 어렵지 않습니다."
"예!" 딘이 몸을 부르르 떨었고, 우리는 가벼운 발걸음으로 길을 건너 멕시코로 들어갔다. 차는 그대로 세워놓고 셋이서 나란히 스페인풍 거리를 걸어 희미한 갈색 등불 불빛 속으로 향했다. 밤중에 의자에 앉아 있는 노인들이 동양의 고물상이나 예언자처럼 보였다. 아무도 우리를 보지 않았지만 모두 우리의 움직임을 감지하고 있었다. 왼쪽으로 꺾어 연기가 피어오르는 식당으로 들어가자 1930년대 미국산 주크박스에서 남아메리카 초원 지대의 기타소리가 흘러나왔다. 우리는 세르베사란 이름의 맥주 세 병을 주문했다. 우리는 멋진 멕시코 돈을 물끄러미 바라보고, 갖고 놀고, 주위를 둘러보며 모두에게 미소를 지었다.
미국은 우리 뒤에 있고, 딘과 내가 지금까지 인생에 대해 배운 것들은 전부 그곳에 있었다. 지금 우리는 드디어 길의 끝에서 마법의 땅을 발견한 것이다. 그 마법이 이렇게 굉장한 것일 줄은 꿈에도 몰랐다. "이거 참, 여기 녀석들은 밤새도록 깨어 있군." 딘이 속삭였다. 우리 앞의 커다란 대륙을 생각해 봐. 그곳에는 영화에서 봤던 시에라 마드레 산맥이 있고,

정글이 쭉 펼쳐져 있고, 미국에 있는 것만큼 큰 사막 고원이 있고, 그대로 이어져서 과테말라로, 신만이 아는 땅으로 이어지는 거야. 후! 어떻게 할래? 뭘 할래? 자, 가자!" 우리는 가게를 나와 차가 있는 곳으로 갔다. "정말 야생적인 나라야!" 나는 소리를 질렀다. 딘과 나는 완전히 깨어 있었다. "자, 우리는 모든 걸 버리고 새로운 미지의 국면을 향해 앞으로 가는 거야. 그 모든 세월들, 괴로운 일, 즐거운 일들이 있었지. 하지만 앞으론 이렇게 하자! 다른 것들은 생각하지 말고 곧바로, 이렇게 얼굴을 내밀고, 진정한 의미에서, 다른 미국인이 해온 것과는 다른 식으로 세계를 이해하는 거야. 전에도 미국인들은 여기 왔었지, 그렇지 않아? 멕시코 전쟁(1846-1848) 때 말이야. 대포를 가지고 지나갔었지."

[출전] <On the Road> by Jack Kerouac(1922-1969)

## 52 회

본책 p.408

### 01

**하위내용영역** 문학(소설) A형 기입형 **배점** 2점 **예상정답률** 50%

**모범답안** They are different from you and me.

**채점기준**

- 2점: 모범답안과 같다. 이것 외에는 답이 될 수 없다.
- 0점: 모범답안과 다르다.

**한글 번역**

[A] 이 세상에 유형 같은 것은 없으며, 똑같은 것이 두 개 이상 존재하지 않는다. 지금 여기에 부잣집 젊은이가 한 사람 있는데, 지금부터 내가 이야기하려는 것은 그 청년의 이야기일 뿐 그의 형제들에 관한 것은 아니다. 내 평생을 그의 형제들 사이에서 살아왔지만 이 아이는 나의 친구였다. 아주 돈이 많은 부자들에 대해서 한마디 해야겠다. 그들은 당신과 나와 같은 사람들과는 다르다. 그들은 어렸을 때부터 많은 것을 소유하고 즐긴다. 이런 것이 그들에게 뭔가 영향을 끼친다. 우리가 까다롭게 구는 일을 그들은 부드럽게 대하며, 우리가 신뢰를 보일 때 그들은 냉소적인 태도를 취한다. 부자로 태어나지 않고는 그것을 이해하기 아주 어렵다. 마음 속 깊이 그들은 자신들이 우리보다 우월한 존재라고 생각하고 있는데, 그 이유는 그들과 달리 우리 보통 사람들은 삶의 보상과 피난처를 우리 스스로 찾아야 하기 때문이다. 심지어 우리들과 똑같은 형편으로 전락하거나 또는 우리보다 더 밑바닥으로 떨어지더라도 여전히 자신들이 우리보다 더 낫다고 생각한다. 앤슨 헌터라는 젊은이를 묘사할 수 있는 유일한 방법은 그가 마치 낯선 외국인인 것처럼 접근하고 이런 나의 관점을 끝까지 고수하는 것이다. 만약 잠시라도 그의 관점을 받아들이게 되면 나는 끝장이다. 결국, 황당무계한 영화 같은 것 말고는 아무것도 보여주지 못하게 될 것이다.

[B] 앤슨은 언젠가는 1500만 달러의 재산을 분할 상속받게 될 여섯 남매 중 장남이었다. 그가 철이 들 나이가 된 것은 – 그게 일곱 살이던가? – 대담한 젊은 여성들이 벌써 전기 '가동장치'를 타고 뉴욕의 5번가를 따라 미끄러져 가던 20세기 초엽이었다. 이 무렵 그와 그의 남동생에게는 아주 정확하고 또렷하며 우아한 영어를 구사하는 영국인 가정교사가 있었고, 그래서 그들도 이 가정교사와 같은 말씨를 사용하며 자랐다. 우리가 쓰는 말처럼 이것저것 뒤섞인 말씨와는 달리 낫말과 문장이 산뜻하고 명확했다. 영국 아이들과 똑같이 말했다는 것이 아니라, 뉴욕시의 상류사회 사람들이 구사하는 독특한 말씨를 익혔다는 뜻이다.

[출전] "The Rich Boy" by F. Scott Fitzgerald (1896-1940)

## 02

하위내용영역 문학(시) A형 서술형 배점 4점 예상정답률 60%

모범답안 The cues are a story told in chronological order, linguistically convolution, the use of impersonal phrases or pronouns, and smiling. Next, the underlined words in ⓑ mean that a big smile most likely indicates someone who is trying to deceive.

채점기준

+ 2점: 거짓말인지 구별할 수 있는 모든 신호가 "<u>a story told in chronological order (rehearsed story)</u>, <u>linguistically convolution</u>, <u>the use of impersonal phrases or pronouns</u>, and <u>smiling</u>"이라 정확하게 서술하였다.
  ▷ 4개 중 <u>3개만 서술하였으면 1점</u>; <u>2개만 서술하였으면 0.5점</u>; <u>1개 또는 0개 서술하였으면 0점</u>을 준다.

+ 2점: 밑줄 친 ⓑ의 의미를 "a big smile most likely indicates someone who is trying to deceive"라 서술하였거나 유사하였다.

## 03

하위내용영역 문학(드라마) A형 서술형 배점 4점 예상정답률 55%

모범답안 The outcome of the Orleans battle was defeated. Next, the nobleman prefers to look at books without reading them.

채점기준

+ 2점: 오를레앙 전투의 결과를 "The outcome of the Orleans battle was defeated"라 서술하였다.

+ 2점: Nobleman이 선호하는 것을 "the nobleman prefers to look at books without reading them"이라 서술하였거나 유사하였다.

## 04

하위내용영역 문학(시) B형 서술형 배점 4점 예상정답률 50%

모범답안 The "you" in the poem is the African American's oppressor or white majority. The speaker repeats "I rise" <u>to show that she is able to rise even after they have knocked her down</u>.

채점기준

+ 2점: "you"를 "the African American's oppressor"나 "white majority", 또는 "white racists"라 서술하였거나 유사하였다.

+ 2점: "I rise"를 반복한 이유를 "to show that she was able to rise even after they have knocked her down"이라 서술하였거나 유사하였다.
  ▷ 또는 "to emphasis the continuity of her struggles as well as her resilience"라 하였다.

한글 번역

당신들은 악의적이고 비틀린 거짓말로
나를 역사에 기록할지 모르나
나를 쓰레기에 처박고 짓밟아도
난 먼지처럼 일어설 거야

내가 멋쟁이라서 기분 나빠?
왜 그렇게 죽을상이지?
내 거실에 유전이라도 가진
부자처럼 당당하게 걸어서 그러는 거야?

달처럼 해처럼
어김없는 조수처럼
저 높이 솟는 희망처럼
난 일어설 거야

내가 꺾이는 걸 보고 싶었어?
머리 수그리고 두 눈 내리깔고
두 어깨를 눈물처럼 떨구면서,
슬픔에 울부짖다 지친 모습을?

당신들은 말로 나를 쏘아 버릴 수 있어
눈길로 나를 베어 버릴 수 있어
증오로 나를 죽여 버릴 수 있어
하지만 나는 공기처럼 일어설 거야

내가 섹시해서 언짢은 거야?
내가 허벅지 사이에
다이아몬드를 품은 것처럼 춤을 추니
그렇게 놀라워?

역사의 부끄러운 헛간에서 나와
난 일어서
아픔에 뿌리를 둔 과거를 벗어나
난 일어서
나는 물결 뛰노는 드넓은 검은 대양
솟구치며 출렁이며 물결을 타고
공포와 두려움의 밤을 뒤로하고
난 일어서
기적처럼 해맑은 새벽을 향해
난 일어서
선조들이 물려준 선물을 가져가는
나는 노예들의 꿈과 희망
난 일어서
난 일어서
난 일어서

[출전] "Still I Rise" by Maya Angelou(1928-2014)

## 05

하위내용영역 문학(소설) B형 서술형 배점 4점 예상정답률 45%

모범답안 The word for the blank is "honest." Next, the disease of affirmation is giving positive feedback for the benefit of the listener, even when it isn't truthful.

채점기준

+ 2점: 빈칸에 들어갈 단어를 "honest"라 정확하게 기입하였다. 이것 외에는 답이 될 수 없다.
+ 2점: 긍정의 질병이 "giving positive feedback for the benefit of the listener, even when it isn't truthful"라 서술하였거나 유사하였다.
  ▷ 다음과 같이 서술하였어도 2점을 준다.
  "giving positive feedback for the benefit of the listener, when it is the opposite of one's belief and understanding"

**한글 번역**

자, 이제 여러분은 중요한 부분은 다 들었다. 아니면 적어도 거의 대부분은 들은 셈이다. 나는 보이지 않는 인간이고, 그것 때문에 나는 구덩이 속으로 들어와야 했다. 아니면 그것 때문에 내가 들어온 구덩이를 알게 되었다고도 할 수 있다. 그리고 나는 그 사실을 마지못해 받아들였다. 달리 내가 무엇을 할 수 있었겠는가? 일단 익숙해지면 현실이란 몽둥이만큼이나 저항하기 힘든 것이 된다. 나는 그런 낌새를 알기도 전에 여기 지하실 속으로 쫓겨 들어왔다. 어쩌면 그래야만 했을지도 모른다. 아무튼 나도 모르겠다. 또한 그런 교훈을 받아들인 연유로 인하여 내가 남들보다 뒤처지게 되었는지, 아니면 앞서게 되었는지는 알 수 없었다. 그것이 어쩌면 역사의 교훈일지도 모르겠다.

여러분에게 솔직히 말해 보겠다. 사실, 솔직하게 말하는 것이야말로 내가 아는 것 가운데 가장 어려운 성취(재주)이다. 사람이 보이지 않게 되면, 선과 악이라든가 정직과 부정 같은 문제들이 변화무쌍하여 서로 혼동된다는 걸 안다. 그것은 단지 그 순간 누가 그를 정확히 보는가에 따라 다른 문제이다. 아무튼 나는 나 자신을 정확히 보려고 노력해 왔지만 거기에는 위험이 도사리고 있었다. 솔직하려 할 때 오히려 가장 미움을 받았다. 아무도 만족하지 못했으니 말이다. 심지어 나조차도. 다른 한편, 내가 누군가의 잘못된 믿음을 정당화시키고 긍정해주려고 하면 그 어느 때보다 사람과 감사를 받았다. 또한, 친구들에게 그들이 듣고 싶어 하는, 불합리하고 그릇된 대답을 해주려고 할 때도 마찬가지였다. 내 앞에서 그들은 서로 대화하고 공감할 수 있었다. 그리고 세상을 고정시켜 놓은 채 그것을 즐겼다. 그들은 그렇게 해서 안정감을 얻었다.

하지만 여기에 문제점이 있었다. 그들을 정당화시켜 주려다보니 너무나 자주 나 자신의 멱살을 잡고 숨 막히게 조여서, 두 눈이 튀어나오고 혀가 늘어져 세찬 바람에 덜컹거리며 흔들리는 빈집 문짝 꼴이 돼 버렸다. 그래 맞다. 그것은 그들을 행복하게 했고 나 자신은 병들게 됐다. 그래서 나는 긍정의 병을 앓았으며, 머릿속은 말할 것도 없고 뱃속에서 싫다고 하는 걸 무시하고 "네"라고 말하는 병을 앓았던 것이다.

[출전] <The Invisible Man> by Ralph Ellison (1914-1994)

## 53회

본책 p.416

### 01

**하위내용영역** 문학(소설) A형 단답형 **배점** 2점 **예상정답률** 55%

**모범답안** ⓐ third-person
ⓑ The(또는 Her) pink ribbons

**채점기준**
- 2점 : 모범답안과 같다.
- 1점 : 둘 중 하나만 맞았다.
- 0점 : 모범답안과 다르다.

### 02

**하위내용영역** 문학(에세이) A형 단답형 **배점** 2점 **예상정답률** 65%

**모범답안** past

**채점기준**
- 2점 : 모범답안과 같거나 fathers라 답하였다.
- 0점 : 모범답안과 다르다.

### 03

**하위내용영역** 문학(시) B형 서술형 **배점** 4점 **예상정답률** 30%

**모범답안** In the poem, the speaker uses the extended metaphor, comparing a woman to a silken tent (in a field). By using the figure of speech, the speaker tells the reader some essential aspects of the woman's character vividly and concretely. For instance, the tent's upright pole is likened to the firmness or strong will of the woman's character. Second, the structure of the poem consists of fourteen lines of iambic pentameter rhyming ABAB CDCD EFEF GG, which is called the Shakespearean sonnet.

채점기준

+ 1점 : the extended metaphor가 a woman을 a tent에 비유한 것이란 점을 언급하였다.
+ 1점 : 수직으로 반듯이 서 있는(upright) cedar pole을 여인의 품성의 안정감이나 확고함 등과 연결시켰다.
+ 1점 : 시의 구조가 iambic pentameter의 리듬으로 되어 있다는 점을 서술하였다.
+ 1점 : rhyme은 ABAB CDCD EFEF GG 라는 점을 서술하였다.

## 54회

본책 p.420

### 01

하위내용영역 문학(소설) A형 단답형 배점 2점 예상정답률 60%

모범답안 Ironing

채점기준

• 2점 : 모범답안과 같다.
• 0점 : 모범답안과 다르다.

### 02

하위내용영역 문학(소설) A형 서술형 배점 4점 예상정답률 50%

모범답안 First, the narrator's company's motto — "Here to Help in Time of Need" — proves untrue. Second, the narrator's wife, Brenda is unfaithful to him. Third, the American flag no longer means the same thing to everyone.

채점기준

• 4점 : 모범답안과 같거나 유사하다.
• 3점 : 다음과 같이 서술하였으면 3점을 준다. "There are three examples of the "unreliability of signs": the company's motto, wife-signs, and the American flag."
• 2점 : 3개 중 2개만 올바르게 서술하였다.
• 1점 : 3개 중 1개만 올바르게 서술하였다.
• 0점 : 모범답안과 다르다.

### 03

하위내용영역 문학(시) B형 서술형 배점 4점 예상정답률 30%

**모범답안** First, the speaker uses a metaphor comparing the meatpackers and the rest of those who are involved in the display of packaged meat products in the supermarket to "God of ours, the Great Geometer." Second, in the underlined part ⓑ, a verbal irony occurs when there is incongruity what the speaker says and what he means. Though the speaker says "praise" the meat handler, what he actually means is the opposite: The speaker criticizes him for being mechanical and brutal. By employing this irony, the poet tells the reader the thematic idea: Eating meat is bad and making it look less like meat so that we don't feel guilty about it is worse.

**채점기준**

+1점: 시에서 쓰인 figure of speech가 "metaphor"라 답하였다.

+1점: 밑줄 친 ⓐ에 식육통조림업자(meat-packer)가 비유됐다고 서술하였다.
▷ the meatpacker(s) 이외에 the meat handler(s) 또는 the butcher(s)라 서술하였어도 맞는 것으로 한다.

+1점: 아이러니에 대한 설명을 정확하게 서술하였다.

+1점: 시의 주제를 정확히 서술하였다.
▷ 다음과 같이 서술하였어도 맞는 것으로 한다.
- "God makes the animal nothing like that and eating of meat should be avoided."
- "People do not want to be reminded of the unpleasant parts of anything–specifically not of the food they eat."
- "People prefer to pass over the thought of anything unpleasant."

## 55 회

본책 p.426

### 01

하위내용영역 문학(시) A형 단답형 배점 2점 예상정답률 60%

**모범답안** beggars

**채점기준**
- 2점 : 모범답안과 같다.
- 0점 : 모범답안과 다르다.

### 02

하위내용영역 문학(소설) A형 단답형 배점 2점 예상정답률 60%

**모범답안** ⓐ first person(또는 first-person)
ⓑ knowledge

**채점기준**
- 2점 : 모범답안과 같다.
- 1점 : 둘 중 하나만 맞았다.
- 0점 : 모범답안과 다르다.

### 03

하위내용영역 문학(드라마) A형 단답형 배점 2점 예상정답률 50%

**모범답안** ⓐ struggling
ⓑ stage direction

**채점기준**
- 2점 : 모범답안과 같다. (ⓐ에 struggle이라 답했으면 0.2점 감점한다.)
- 1점 : 둘 중 하나만 맞았다.
- 0점 : 모범답안과 다르다.

한글 번역

시골길 나무 한 그루 서 있다.
저녁
에스트라공이 흙더미 위에 앉아 구두를 벗으려 한다. 기를 쓰며 두 손으로 한쪽 구두를 잡아당긴다. 끙끙거린다. 힘이 빠져 그만둔다. 숨을 헐떡이며 잠시 쉬었다 다시 시작한다. 같은 동작이 되풀이된다.
블라디미르가 들어온다.

에스트라공 : (다시 단념하며) 안 되네!

블라디미르 : (두 다리를 벌리고 종종걸음으로 다가서며) 나는 그 의견에 동의하기 시작했어. 그런 생각을 떨쳐버리려고 오랫동안 속으로 타일러 왔지. '블라디미르, 정신 차려, 아직 다 해본 건 아니잖아' 하면서 말이야. 그리고 다시 투쟁을 계속해 왔단 말이야. (머릿속으로 투쟁을 회상해 보며 생각에 잠긴다. 에스트라공에게.) 아니 또 너로구나.

에스트라공 : 그래서?

블라디미르 : 다시 만나니 반갑다. 아주 떠나 버린 줄 알았는데.

에스트라공 : 나도 그래.

블라디미르 : 드디어 다시 함께로군! 다시 만난 걸 축하해야겠어. 하지만 어떻게 한담? (잠시 생각하더니) 일어나, 껴안아 줄게.

에스트라공 : (짜증스럽게) 조금 있다가. 조금 있다가.

블라디미르 : (기분이 상해서 냉정하게) 나으리께서는 어디서 밤을 지내셨나이까?

에스트라공 : 개천.

블라디미르 : (감탄하며) 개천이라니! 어느 개천?

에스트라공 : (아무 동작 없이) 저기 저쪽.

블라디미르 : 얻어맞지나 않았고?

에스트라공 : 얻어맞았냐고? 확실히 그랬지.

블라디미르 : 같은 녀석들한테?

에스트라공 : 같은 녀석들이냐고? 모르겠다.

블라디미르 : 하긴…. 오래전부터 늘 생각해 온 건데… 넌 내가 없었으면 어떻게 됐을까 하고 말이지… (단호하게) 지금은 죽어서 한 움큼의 뼈다귀만 남았을걸, 틀림없이.

에트스라공 : 그래서 어떻다는 거야?

블라디미르 : (풀이 죽어서) 혼자 감당하기엔 너무 어렵구나. (잠시 사이를 두었다 곧 활기를 띠고) 또 한편으로 생각해 보면, 이제 와서 실망해 봤자 별 수 없다는 생각이 든다. 벌써 오래전부터, 그러니까 90년대쯤부터 그 생각을 해왔어야 하는 건데 말야.

에스트라공 : 그만 지껄이고 이 놈의 신이나 좀 벗겨줘.

블라디미르 : 손을 마주 잡고 에펠탑 꼭대기에서 뛰어내렸겠지. 맨 처음에 뛰어내리는 자들 틈에 끼어 말이야. 우리 그땐 제법 풍채도 좋았는데. 하지만 이젠 너무 늦었어. 이제 우리 같은 건 올라가지도 못하게 할걸. (에스트라공이 구두를 잡아 찢는다.) 뭘 하고 있는 거야?

에스트라공 : 구두를 벗고 있는 거다. 너한텐 이런 일이 한 번도 없었냐?

블라디미르 : 구두는 매일 벗어야 한다고 지겹게 말했잖아? 왜 내 말을 안 듣냐?

에스트라공 : (약한 소리로) 좀 거들어 줘!

블라디미르 : 아프냐?

에스트라공 : (화를 내며) 아프냐고? 그걸 말이라고 하냐?

블라디미르 : 이 세상에 고통을 당하는 게 너 하나밖에 없는 줄 알아? 나 같은 건 안중에도 없는 거지. 네가 내 입장이라면 무슨 소릴 할는지 보고 싶구나. 당해 봐야 알 거다.

에스트라공 : 너도 아팠냐?

블라디미르 : 아팠냐고? 그걸 말이라고 하는 거야?

## 04

하위내용영역 문학(소설) A형 서술형 배점 4점 예상정답률 45%

모범답안 They are in the courthouse because the boy's father has been accused of burning Mr. Harris' barn. Second, the narrator employs two kinds of olfactory images: the smell of food such as cheese and meat and that of "blood." The former represents the boy's hunger; the latter the emotionally-charged smell that denotes fear, grief and despair caused by the blood bond between the boy and his father.

채점기준

+ 1점: 법정에 있는 이유를 "the boy's father has been accused of burning Mr. Harris' barn"이라 서술하였거나 유사하게 서술하였다.
+ 1점: 첫 번째 종류의 냄새를 "cheese"나 "meat"라 기술하였거나; 음식이라 기술하였다.
+ 0.5점: 두 번째 종류의 냄새를 "blood"의 냄새라 기술하였다.
+ 1점: 첫 번째 종류의 냄새의 의미를 "the boy's hunger"를 나타낸다고 서술하였다.
  ▷ "the boy's feelings of fear, despair and grief"라고만 서술하였어도 1점을 준다.
+ 0.5점: 두 번째 종류의 냄새의 의미를 "가족 간(아버지와 아들 간)의 핏줄에서 나오는" 피의 냄새라 서술하였다.

한글 번역

치안판사가 주재하는 재판이 열리고 있는 상점에서는 치즈 냄새가 났다. 사람들이 꽉 들어찬 가게 뒤쪽의 못통을 깔고 앉아 있던 소년은 치즈 냄새와 그 밖의 냄새들이 콧속으로 스며들고 있음을 깨달았다. 그가 앉아 있는 곳에서는 네모나기도 하고 납작하기도 하고 큼직큼직한 갖가지 통조림 깡통들이 꽉 차 있는 여러 층의 선반이 보였다. 통조림들의 상표를 읽어 낸 것은 그의 위장이었다. 그의 머리에 그것은 그저 아무 의미 없는 글자들에 불과했지만 그의 위장에 그것은 매운 양념에 재운 불고기였고, 은빛 곡선을 가진 물고기였다. 치즈 냄새와 그의 내장이 감지한 캔에 들어 밀봉된 고기 냄새들 사이로 끊임없이 나는 다른 냄새가 있었다. 주로 절망과 슬픔으로부터 나오는, 그 오래 된 강렬한 피의 끌림으로부터 기인하는 두려움의 냄새였다. 그가 서있는 곳에서는 치안판사가 앉아 있는 탁자는 보이지 않았다. 판사 앞에 서 있을 아버지와 아버지의 원수도 보이지 않았다(그는 그 절망에 휩싸여 생각했다. '저 원수는 나와 저 사람, 우리 모두의 원수야! 저 사람은 나의 아버지니까!'). 하지만 그들 중 둘의 목소리는 들을 수 있었다. 아버지는 아직 아무 말도 하지 않고 있었기 때문이다.
"하지만, 무슨 증거가 있소, 해리스 씨?"
"말씀 드렸잖아요. 돼지가 우리 옥수수밭에 들어왔습니다. 나는 그놈을 붙잡아서 이 사람에게 돌려보내 주었습니다. 이 사람네 집엔 그놈을 가둘 우리가 없었습니다. 제가 그 점을 지적하고 경고도 했지요. 그런데 또 같은 일이 벌어져 우리 집 우리에 돼지를 넣어뒀다가, 이 사람이 오자 우리를 만들라고 철망까지 넉넉하게 줘서 돌려보냈어요. 그런데 또 같은 일이 벌어졌고, 저는 그놈을 잡아 가둬놓고는 말을 타고 이 사람네로 가 보았더니, 내가 준 철사가 여전히 철사꾸리에 감겨 있는 채로 마당에 나뒹굴고 있더군요. 나는 보관료로 일 달러를 가져오면 돼지를 주겠다고 말했습니다. 그날 밤에 검둥이 하나가 돈을 가지고 와서 돼지를 찾아 갔습니다. 그런데 그 검둥이는 처음 보는 검둥이었습니다. 와서 하는 소리가, '나무와 건초는 불에 탄다고 전하랍니다' 해요. '무어라구?'하고 내가 말했습니다. 검둥이가 하는 말이, '그렇게 전하라고만 했어요. 나무와 건초는 불에 탄다고요'. 그날 밤에 우리 집 헛간이 탔습니다. 가축들은 간신히 꺼냈지만 헛간은 타서 몽땅 없어지고 말았습니다."
"검둥이는 어디 있지요? 잡아 두었소?"
"처음 보는 검둥이라니까요. 어디로 갔는지는 모릅니다."
"하지만 그건 증거가 안 되오. 그게 증거가 안 된다는 것을 모르겠소?"
"저기 저 애를 여기 불러다 주세요. 저 애가 알아요."
소년은 신발도 신지 않은 발바닥 아래 마룻바닥의 감촉이 느껴지지 않았다. 험상궂은 표정으로 자신을 돌아보는 사람들의 힘에 의해 앞으로 끌려가는 듯했다. 그는 그가 지나감에 따라서 돌려지는 냉혹한 얼굴들에서 눌려 오는 무게를 느끼며 걸어 나갔다. 재판을 받기 위해서가 아니라 이사를 가기 위해서, 검은 나들이옷을 차려입은 채 딱딱하게 굳어 있는 그의 아버지는, 그를 쳐다보지도 않았다. 그는 다시금 핏속에서 광분하는 비애와 절망을 느끼며 생각했다. 저 사람은 내가 거짓말하기를 바라는 거야. 그리고 난 그렇게 할 수밖에 없어.

## 56회

본책 p.435

### 01

하위내용영역 문학(시) A형 단답형 배점 2점 예상정답률 60%

**모범답안** live

채점기준

- 2점 : 모범답안과 같다.
- 0점 : 모범답안과 다르다.

### 02

하위내용영역 문학(소설) A형 단답형 배점 2점 예상정답률 60%

**모범답안** fat

채점기준

- 2점 : 모범답안과 같다.
- 0점 : 모범답안과 다르다.

### 03

하위내용영역 문학(드라마) A형 단답형 배점 2점 예상정답률 50%

**모범답안** ⓐ Edmund ⓑ hair

채점기준

- 2점 : 모범답안과 같다.
- 1점 : 둘 중 하나만 맞았다.
- 0점 : 모범답안과 다르다.

**한글 번역**

메리 : (미소 띤 얼굴로 아들들을 돌아보며 조금은 억지로 꾸민 명랑한 목소리로) 지금 너희 아버지 코 고는 걸 갖고 놀리고 있던 참이란다. (티론에게) 제임스, 판단은 당신 아들들에게 맡기겠어요. 걔들도 들었을 테니까. 아니, 제이미 넌 안 되지. 네 코 고는 소리도 너희 아버지만큼 복도 아래까지 들리더구나. 어쩌면 부자지간에 그렇게 똑같은지. 넌 베개에 머리가 닿기가 무섭게 곯아떨어져서 뱃고동(무적)이 아무리 요란하게 울려대도 모르고 자니까. (그녀는 제이미가 탐색하는 듯한 불안한 눈길로 자신을 응시하는 것을 느끼고 얼른 입을 다문다. 얼굴에서 미소가 사라지고 부자연스런 태도가 된다.) 왜 그렇게 보는 거니, 제이미? (그녀의 손이 초조하게 머리로 올라간다.) 내 머리칼이 내려왔니? 이제 머리를 제대로 만지기가 힘들어. 눈이 갈수록 침침해지는데 도대체 안경을 찾을 수가 없네.

제이미 : (죄책감을 느끼듯 시선을 돌리며) 머리는 괜찮아요. 어머니 얼굴이 좋아 보여서요.

티론 : (진심으로) 나도 그 말을 하고 싶던 참이었다, 제이미. 네 어머니 말이다. 이제 살도 찌고 팔팔해서 조금 있으면 안지도 못하겠구나.

에드먼드 : 맞아요, 아주 좋아 보여요, 어머니. (메리는 안심하며 그에게 다정한 미소를 보낸다. 에드먼드는 장난스럽게 씩 웃으며 윙크한다.) 아버지 코 고는 문제는 어머니 말씀이 맞아요. 얼마나 요란한지!

제이미 : 나도 들었어요. (그는 삼류 배우 흉내를 내며 연극 대사를 인용한다.) "무어인입니다, 나팔 소리만 들어도 알지요." (어머니와 동생이 큰 소리로 웃는다.)

티론 : (냉혹하게) 내 코 고는 소리를 듣고 경마 정보지가 아닌 셰익스피어를 생각했다니 앞으로도 계속 코를 골아야겠구나.

메리 : 그만해요, 제임스! 그렇게 발끈할 일도 아닌데. (제이미는 어깨를 으쓱하고는 어머니 오른쪽의 의자에 앉는다.)

에드먼드: (짜증을 내며) 맞아요, 제발요 아버지! 아침 먹기가 무섭게 또 시작이에요! 좀 그만하실 수 없어요? 예? (그는 탁자 왼쪽에 있는 형 옆의 의자에 털썩 앉는다. 티론은 못 들은 체한다.)
메리 : (아들을 나무라며) 아버지가 너한테 뭐라고 하신 게 아니잖아. 넌 항상 제이미 편만 드는구나. 네가 형보다 열 살 위인 것 같구나.
제이미 : (지겨워하며) 왜들 난리에요? 다 그만둬요.
티론 : (경멸하는 태도로) 그래, 그만두자! 다 그만두고 다 피해버려! 야망이라곤 없는 인간에겐 편리한 인생 철학이지. 고작 하는 짓이라곤…
메리 : 제임스 그만해요. (달래듯이 한 팔로 남편의 어깨를 감싸며) 당신 오늘 아침엔 기분이 안 좋은가 봐요. (화제를 바꿔 아들들에게) 너희들 아까 들어올 때 왜 그렇게 히죽거리고 웃었니? 무슨 재미난 얘기를 했는데?

[출전] *Long Day's Journey into Night* by Eugene O'Neill(1888-1953)

## 04

하위내용영역 문학(소설) A형 서술형 배점 4점 예상정답률 40%

**모범답안** The women "stood looking out" with their "children" and kept "silent" indoors, which implies the gender dynamics: the women are passive and have no right to give their opinions on the issue at hand. In other words, this scene indicates the subservience of women to men in the society. Additionally, in the underlined part, the speaker employs simile by describing banks or companies as monsters to illustrate that those institutions trample all over the poor hardworking tenant farmers with an inhuman lack of sympathy for the destruction.

**채점기준**

+ 2점 : 성적 역학관계를 "여성이 남성에게 종속되어 있다"고 서술하고, 위의 내용을 뒷받침하는 구체적인 예(The women "stood looking out" with their "children" and kept "silent" indoors)를 언급하였다.
  ▷ 위의 예 가운데 하나만 쓴 경우 1점을 준다.
+ 2점 : 밑줄 친 부분의 비유적 의미를 "은행이나 회사를 괴물로 비유한 것이 그것들이 가난한 농부들을 냉정하게 짓밟는 존재임을 드러내기 위한 것"이라 서술하였다.

**한글 번역**

지주들이 그 토지로 찾아오기도 했지만 지주의 대리인들이 오는 때가 더 많았다. 그들은 유개(지붕이 있는) 차를 타고 와서는 마른 흙을 손가락으로 만져보고 땅속에 송곳을 박고 지질 시험을 한다. 소작인들은 볕이 내리쬐는 앞마당에서 불안스럽게 그 다가오는 차를 지켜본다. 그러고 나면 드디어 지주 대리인들이 앞마당으로 와서 차 안에 앉은 채 창문 너머로 말을 건넨다. 소작인들은 한참 자동차 옆에서 서 있다가 쭈그리고 앉아 막대기를 찾아 쥐고 먼지 속에 다 그림을 그린다.
열어젖힌 문간에서 여인들이 내다본다. 그 뒤엔 어린 애들이 매달려 있다. 옥수수 대가리 같은 머리와 큰 눈을 가진 아이들이 맨발을 겹쳐놓고 발가락을 놀리고 있다. 여인들과 아이들은 남자들이 지주 대리인들과 이야기하는 모습을 말없이 지켜본다.
지주 대리인들 가운데는 자기가 하는 일이 싫어서 친절하게 대하는 사람도 있다. 잔인하게 굴기가 싫어서 억지로 화만 내는 사람도 있다. 냉정한 사람도 있다. 냉정해야만 지주 행세를 할 수 있다는 걸 오래전 깨달았기 때문이다. 모두가 하나같이 자기보다는 큰 세력에 얽매여 있는 사람들이다. 계산만 해야 하는 자기 신세를 싫어하는 사람도 있고, 꺼려하는 사람도 있다. 또 골치 아픈 생각이나 신경을 쓰지 않아도 되기 때문에 계산하는 것을 오히려 좋아하는 사람도 있다. 토지 주인이 은행이나 금융회사일 경우에 대리인들은, 은행이나 회사의 형편이 꼭 이렇게 해야만 할 형편이라고 말한다. 마치 은행이나 회사가 사람처럼 생각이나 감정을 가진 괴물인 양, 그리고 자기가 괴물에 얽매여 있는 사람인 양 그들은 은행과 회사만 내세운다. 은행은 기계인 동시에 주인이요, 자기네는 한갓 노예 신세여서 책임이 없다는 것이다. 대리인들은 계속해서 요점을 설명한다. 땅이 점점 더 나빠지고 있다고. 목화 농사 때문에 땅에서 기름이 다 빠지고 만다는 것이다.
소작인들은 고개를 끄덕인다. 맞는 말이다. 다른 곡식을 번갈아 심을 수 있다면 땅에 다시 기름이 붙을지도 모른다. 이제는 그 시기를 놓쳤다. 대리인들은 말한다. 은행이나 금융회사는 공기를 못 마시고, 베이컨을 먹지도 않는다. 그들을 이윤을 마신다. 당신들 모두 지금 이 땅에서 떠나야만 한다.

[출전] *The Grape of Wrath* by John Steinbeck (1902-1968)

## 57 회

본책 p.443

### 01

**하위내용영역** 문학(소설) A형 단답형 **배점** 2점 **예상정답률** 60%

**모범답안** ⓐ Setting ⓑ third-person

**채점기준**

- 2점 : 모범답안과 같다.
- 1점 : 둘 중 하나만 맞았다.
- 0점 : 모범답안과 다르다.

### 02

**하위내용영역** 문학(시) A형 서술형 **배점** 4점 **예상정답률** 45%

**모범답안** The thematic idea is that people gravitate toward(s) other people who are joyful and happy but people isolate them from the world when they are in pain. To convey the idea, the speaker vividly portrays(illustrates) two situations in the underlined part. When you hold a "feast," the halls "are crowded" with people, whereas when you go hungry("fast"), people do not share in your pain("the world goes by").

**채점기준**

+ 2점 : 시의 요지를 "사람들은 좋은 때는 함께 하려하지만 고통이나 슬픔 등 괴로운 일이 있을 때는 멀리하려고 한다"로 서술하였거나 이와 유사하게 서술하였다.
  - ▷ 다음과 같이 서술하였어도 2점을 준다.
  - "People tend to enjoy pleasant times together, but avoid those who are in pain or grief."

• "People share joyful and happy moment, whereas they avoid each other when things are going bad."
• "We humans are eager to stay with those in pleasure but flee from those in pain."

+ 2점 : 밑줄 친 부분에 있는 내용을 구체적으로 인용하면서 요지와 연결시켜서 서술하였다. (둘 중 하나만 언급하였으면 1점만 준다.)
When "you" hold a "feast," the halls "are crowded" with people(1점), whereas when "you" go hungry("fast"), people do not share in your pain("the world goes by")(1점).

▷ 다음과 같이 서술하였어도 2점을 준다.
"People gather together in the places of pleasure ("Feast") whereas in the places of distress("Fast") they do not share in other's pain."

## 03

**하위내용영역** 문학(소설) B형 서술형 **배점** 4점 **예상정답률** 45%

**모범답안** The speaker is Death and Death was surprised at seeing the servant in Bagdad in the morning because she was supposed to meet the servant in Samara, not in Bagdad, that evening. The message is that no matter what you do, you will not be able to escape death.

**채점기준**

+ 1점 : 화자가 Death라 서술하였다.
+ 1점 : Death가 놀란 이유가 "그 하인을 바그다드에서 보게 되었기" 때문이라고 서술하였다.
+ 2점 : 소설의 요지가 "아무리 인간이 노력하더라도 죽음은 피할 수 없는" 것이라 서술하였다.

▷ 다음과 같이 서술하였어도 2점을 준다.
• "No matter what you try to escape from death, it will eventually come back to you."
• "It is impossible for person to defeat fate. A person's fate is uncontrollable."
• "Destiny(Death) cannot be escaped."
• "Destiny will always play out no matter what you do."

## 58회

본책 p.448

### 01

하위내용영역 문학(소설) A형 단답형 배점 2점 예상정답률 60%

모범답안 ⓐ lonely ⓑ laughter

채점기준

- 2점 : 모범답안과 같다.
- 1점 : 둘 중 하나만 맞았다.
- 0점 : 모범답안과 다르다.

### 02

하위내용영역 문학(비평) A형 서술형 배점 4점 예상정답률 55%

모범답안 First, it is because only Islamic Orient posed a threat to European powers on the political, intellectual, and economic levels. Second, the commonality is that those nations were all dominated by Western powers.

채점기준

+2점 : 유럽 기독교 세계에 이슬람이 문제적 집단으로 간주되는 이유가 다른 동양의 나라들과는 다르게 "오직 이슬람만이 정치적, 지적, 그리고 경제적 수준에서 유럽의 강력한 경쟁 상대 또는 위협이었기 때문"이라 서술하였다.

▷ 다음과 같이 서술하였어도 2점을 준다.

"only Islam presented Europe with a strong threat(or challenge) on the political, intellectual, and economic levels"

▷ 다음과 같이 서술하였으면 1점을 준다.

- "only Islamic Orient posed a threat to European powers"
- "only Arab and Islamic Orient dominated or effectively threatened European Christianity"

+2점 : 인도, 동인도, 중국, 일본의 공통점으로 "유럽 강국들에 의해 지배당한 적이 있다"고 서술하였다.

### 03

하위내용영역 문학(시) B형 서술형 배점 4점 예상정답률 50%

모범답안 The main theme is the happiness(or blessing) of living in solitude in a (beautiful) small farm(country side) with nature. To convey this theme, in the second stanza, the speaker vividly portrays the healthy products of the farm: "milk," "bread," "attire"(clothing or garments), and "shade" in summer and warm(fire) in winter.

채점기준

+2점 : 시의 핵심 주제가 "자연과 더불어 조그만 농장(시골)에서 고독을 즐기며 사는 것이 행복"이라 서술하였다.

▷ 다음과 같이 서술하였으면 1점을 준다.

- "자연과 더불어 조그만 농장(시골)에서 사는 것이 행복"이다. 즉 고독의 개념을 서술하지 않았다.
- "조그만 농장(시골)에서 고독을 즐기며 사는 것이 행복"이다.

▷ 다음과 같이 서술하였으면 0.5점을 준다.

"혼자 사는 것은 행복한 것이다."

+2점 : 두 번째 연을 핵심 주제와 연결시켜 설명하였다. 핵심 주제를 생생하고 구체적으로 전하기 위해 농장에서 생산되는 모든 것[5가지; "milk," "bread," "attire"(clothing or garments), and "shade" and warm(fire)]을 정확하게 서술하였다.

▷ 4개만을 서술한 경우 1점; 3개만을 서술한 경우 0.75점; 2개만을 서술한 경우 0.5점; 1개 또는 0개 서술한 경우 0점을 준다.

# 59 회

본책 p.452

## 01

하위내용영역 문학(에세이) A형 단답형 배점 2점 예상정답률 60%

모범답안 ⓐ winter ⓑ moral

채점기준
- 2점 : 모범답안과 같다.
- 1점 : 둘 중 하나만 맞았다.
- 0점 : 모범답안과 다르다.

## 02

하위내용영역 문학(소설) A형 단답형 배점 2점 예상정답률 60%

모범답안 ⓐ miners ⓑ shadows
ⓒ industrialization

채점기준

+ 0.5점 : ⓐ에 miners라 정확히 기술하였다. workers라 기술하였어도 맞는 답으로 한다.
  ▷ mining workers 또는 mine workers라 했으면 0.3점을 준다.
+ 0.5점 : ⓑ에 shadows라 정확히 기술하였다.
  ▷ shadow라 했으면 0.3점을 준다.
  ▷ ⓐ에 shadows를, ⓑ에 miners를 기술하였으면 0.5점을 준다.
+ 1점 : ⓒ에 industrialization이라 정확히 기술하였다.
  ▷ the industrial revolution이라 했으면 0.5점을 준다.

## 03

하위내용영역 문학(시) B형 서술형 배점 4점 예상정답률 30%

모범답안 The thematic idea is that a person standing up for something he truly believes in is greater than people who remain away from the reality. To convey the idea, the speaker employs two crucial symbols. The "vulture" symbolizes people who are considered ugly and insane but are endowed with the rarest qualities ever gifted to any human being. On the other hand, the "sparrow" represents ordinary people, who is outwardly nice and tidy but does not perform practical function in society. Second, the underlined ⓐ refers to the sparrow; the underlined ⓑ (refers to) the vulture; the underlined ⓒ (refers to) Noah.

채점기준

+ 1점 : 시의 중심 주제가 "A person standing up for something he truly believes in is greater than people who remain away from the reality"라 서술하였다.
  ▷ 다음과 같이 서술하였으면 1점을 준다.
  - "A person who has the courage can stand for not just themselves but for the people."
  - "One man with courage makes a majority."
  ▷ 다음과 같이 서술하였으면 0.5점을 준다.
  - "We have to think of the motives and objectives of people before we judge them on their appearances and actions that may or may not have turned out well."
  - "Action speaks louder than words."

+ 1점 : "vulture"가 "people who are considered ugly and insane but are endowed with the rarest qualities ever gifted to any human being"을 상징한다고 서술하였다.
  ▷ "다수로부터는 무시당하지만 자기 신념을 가지고 묵묵히 세상에 도움이 되는 행동으로 살아가는 사람"이라 서술하였으면 1점을 준다.
  ▷ "말보다는 실천을 하는 사람"이라 서술하였으면 0.5점을 준다.
+ 1점 : "sparrow"가 "an ordinary people, who is outwardly nice and tidy but does not perform practical function in society"를 상징한다고 서술하였다.
  ▷ "실천보다는 말만 하는 사람"이라 서술하였으면 0.5점을 준다.
+ 1점 : the underlined ⓐ refers to the sparrow; the underlined ⓑ (refers to) the vulture; the underlined ⓒ (refers to) Noah라 서술하였다.
  ▷ 세 가지 모두 올바르게 서술하였으면 1점, 2개만 올바르게 서술하였으면 0.5점, 1개만 서술했거나 전혀 서술하지 못했다면 0점을 준다.

# 60회

본책 p.458

## 01

하위내용영역 문학(소설) A형 단답형 배점 2점 예상정답률 60%

모범답안 unfamiliar

채점기준

- 2점 : 모범답안과 같다.
- 1점 : particular라 답하였다.
- 0점 : 모범답안과 다르다.

## 02

하위내용영역 문학(드라마) A형 단답형 배점 2점 예상정답률 65%

모범답안 ⓐ basement (room)

ⓑ tie his shoelaces(또는 이와 같은 내용이면 맞는 것으로 한다)

ⓒ exposition

채점기준

+ 1점 : ⓐ basement와 ⓑ tie his shoelaces는 각각 0.5점을 준다.
+ 1점 : ⓒ exposition은 1점을 준다.

## 03

하위내용영역 문학(시) A형 서술형 배점 4점 예상정답률 40%

**모범답안** In the first stanza, poet's description of the present is terrifying. The opening two lines describe a world out of control. Also, in the third line, the poet declares "things fall apart." The lines 4-6 vividly illustrate states of "anarchy." The closing lines (of this first section) depict a crisis situation where good people are uncertain what should be done, while "worst" people are full of "passionate intensity"—all too certain in their ignorant minds that they know exactly what is needed. Second, the underlined part refers to Sphinx, or rough beast.

**채점기준**

+2점: 시인이 현재 상태의 세상을 "a world out of control"; "things fall apart"; "anarchy"; "a crisis situation where good people are uncertain what should be done, while worst people are full of passionate intensity"이라 묘사하였다고 서술하였다.

▷ 3개 또는 3개 이상을 서술한 경우 2점; 2개를 서술한 경우 1점; 1개를 서술한 경우 0.5점; 하나도 서술하지 못한 경우 0점을 준다.

+2점: 밑줄 친 부분이 가리키는 것이 Sphinx 또는 rough beast라 서술하였다.

▷ the Second coming이라 답한 경우에도 맞는 것으로 한다.

## 04

하위내용영역 문학(에세이) A형 서술형 배점 4점 예상정답률 45%

**모범답안** The narrator feels she is in limbo because she is in a situation where she seems to be caught in an unclear position, which is between the life just passed and the one to come after her parents' divorce. Second, the boxes marked "Salvation Army" strike the character as ironic, due to the family's break up being finalized, and beyond saving. The whole situation is not salvageable.

**채점기준**

+2점: 타이틀이 Limbo인 이유가 "(제목은 글의 핵심적 생각을 압축적으로 보여주는 것인데) 부모의 이혼 이후의 상황을 화자가 림보와 같이 불확실한 상황에 놓여있는 것이라" 느끼기 때문이라 서술하였다.

▷ 부모의 이혼 이후의 상황과 림보를 연결시켰으면 2점을 준다.

+2점: "Salvation Army"라 쓰인 상자가 아이러니컬한 이유가 "(부모의 이혼 때문에) 가족이 깨진 상황(구원이 불가능한 상황)과 구세군(구원을 해주는)이라는 말이 전혀 어울리지 않기 때문"이라 서술하였다.

# 61 회

본책 p.466

## 01

하위내용영역 문학(소설) A형 서술형 배점 4점 예상정답률 45%

모범답안 The most powerful person is Lengel, the A&P store manager, in that he has the power to publicly put people who he believes dress inappropriately to shame and to make life hard for his staff if he quits his job. Second, the narrator calls the customers "sheep" because they, like compliant sheep, blindly comply with the social norm (or the policy of the store and society) unlike Sammy who goes against the grain (or challenge the rules).

채점기준

+ 1점 : 가장 센 권력을 지닌 자가 Lengel이라 서술하였다.
+ 1점 : 그 이유를 "he has the power to publicly put people who he believes dress inappropriately to shame(0.5점) and to make life hard for his staff(the narrator) if he quits his job(0.5점)"이라고 서술하였다.
+ 2점 : 화자가 고객들을 "양"이라 부른 이유를 "화자와 그들의 차이 즉, 화자는 Lengel로 대표되는 사회적 관습과 규율(또는 정책)에 저항하는 반면(1점), 고객들은 그대로 아무 저항 없이 따르기 때문(1점)"이라 서술하였다.

감점 어색한 표현이나 문법에 어긋난 것이 있으면 각각 0.25점 감점한다.

## 02

하위내용영역 문학(시) B형 서술형 배점 4점 예상정답률 40%

모범답안 The main theme is a conflict between technology (created by human beings) and nature. To emphasize the theme, the poet employs two symbols. First "cars" symbolize technology, which kills nature. Second "gray fox" stands for nature, which is killed by technology. (The gray fox and the cars are the two contrasting elements in the poem.)

채점기준

+ 2점 : 시의 중심 주제가 "a conflict between technology and nature"라 서술하였다.
  ▷ "인간이 만든 과학 기술에 의한 자연의 파괴"라 답하였어도 1점을 준다.
+ 2점 : "gray fox"가 nature를 상징하고(1점); "cars"가 technology를 상징한다고(1점) 서술하였다.

감점 어색한 표현이나 문법에 어긋난 것이 있으면 각각 0.25점 감점한다.

## 62회

본책 p.470

### 01

하위내용영역 문학(비평) A형 단답형 배점 2점 예상정답률 45%

모범답안 ⓐ disorders ⓑ stability

채점기준

- 2점 : 모범답안과 같다. ⓐ를 order나 harmony라고 했으면 0.5점을 준다.
- 1점 : 둘 중 하나만 맞았다.
- 0점 : 모범답안과 다르다.

### 02

하위내용영역 문학(소설) A형 서술형 배점 4점 예상정답률 45%

모범답안 His understanding of the religion shows a remarkable openness of spirit beyond a dogmatic christian fundamentalism. Worship, for him, is to do the will of God, which wants a man to be generous to his fellow-men. Therefore, it is not against the will of God to participate in Queequeg's worship of his idol.

채점기준

+ 1점 : 화자의 기독교 이해가 "도그마에 사로잡혀 있는 것이 아닌 개방성을 지니고 있다"고 서술하였다.
+ 3점 : "진정한 기독교인의 믿음(예배)은 하나님의 뜻을 실천하는 것인데 그 하나님의 뜻은 이웃에게 대접을 받고자 하는 대로 이웃을 대접하는 일(즉, 이웃에게 너그러운 행위를 하는 것)이다. 따라서 화자의 이웃인 Queequeg의 뜻에 따라주는 것이 중요한데 그가 화자와 자기 식의 예배를 보길 원하므로 그와 함께 예배를 보아야 한다"고 서술하였거나 유사하게 서술하였다.
  ▷ 밑줄 친 3개를 모두 서술한 경우 3점; 2개만 서술한 경우 2점; 1개만 서술한 경우 1점을 준다.

### 03

하위내용영역 문학(시) B형 서술형 배점 4점 예상정답률 35%

모범답안 The thematic idea is that focusing only on money, as referred as "it," in life will leave a (greedy) person ruined. To convey the idea vividly, in the third stanza, the speaker employs a simile, comparing money("it") to a pet(dog), which exhilarates people regardless of sex.

채점기준

+ 2점 : 시의 중심 주제가 "focusing only on money, as referred as "it," in life will leave a (greedy) person ruined"라 서술하였다.
  ▷ 다음과 같이 서술하였어도 1점을 준다.
  "money seems to be tamed but actually people are tamed by money"
+ 1점 : "it"이 가리키는 것이 money라 기술하였다.
+ 1점 : 세 번째 문단에 사용된 비유적 언어가 simile이며, 그것의 의미가 "돈이 사람을 즐겁게 해주는 것"이라 명확하게 서술하였다.

## 63회

본책 p.475

### 01

하위내용영역 문학(에세이) A형 단답형 배점 2점 예상정답률 55%

모범답안 human heart

채점기준

- 2점 : 모범답안과 같다. human soul이나 human spirit도 맞는 것으로 한다.
- 0점 : 모범답안과 다르다.

### 02

하위내용영역 문학(시) A형 서술형 배점 4점 예상정답률 55%

모범답안 In the first stanza, the speaker laments the loss of the wonder he once felt in Nature. Second, the rhyme scheme is AABCBCDED. Third, (the summary is as follows.) even though the speaker can still see beautiful nature(the rainbow, the rose, the moon, and the sun), a glory has passed away from the earth.

채점기준

+ 1점 : 시적 화자가 "the loss of the wonder he once felt in Nature"를 탄식한다고 서술하였다.
  - ▷ 다음과 같이 서술하였어도 1점을 준다.
  - "loss of innocence"
  - "loss of the insights and connections with Nature"
  - "his current inability to perceive the world as he once did"
+ 1점 : 각운 형식이 AABCBCD(ED)이라 서술하였다. 7자리까지 맞으면 맞는 것으로 한다.
+ 2점 : 2연을 다음과 같이 요약하였다.
  "Even though the speaker can still see beautiful nature, a glory has passed away from the earth."
  - ▷ 다음과 같이 서술하였어도 2점을 준다.
  - "Even though the speaker can still see beautiful nature, he is no longer able to feel the glory."
  - "Even though the speaker can still see beautiful nature, he feels he is separated from the glory of nature."

감점 요약할 때 10단어 이하나 20단어 이상으로 한 것은 0.3점 감점한다.

### 03

하위내용영역 문학(소설) B형 서술형 배점 4점 예상정답률 50%

모범답안 First, the narrator of <A> likes the museum because it presents him with a vision of life he can understand: it is frozen, silent, and always the same. Second, though the boy can never kiss his lover because he is frozen in time, he should not grieve, because her beauty will never fade.

채점기준

+ 2점 : <A>의 화자가 박물관을 좋아하는 이유를 "거기선 모든 것이 정지되어 있어 변화가 없기 때문"이라 서술하였다. (In the museum, life is frozen, silent, and always the same.)
+ 2점 : 화자가 소년이 슬퍼할 필요가 없다고 말한 이유를 "(항아리 위의 그림에 존재하는) 그의 연인의 아름다움은 영원불멸할 것이기 때문"이라 서술하였다.

감점 어색한 표현이나 문법에 어긋난 것이 있으면 각각 0.3점 감점한다.

## 64회

본책 p.480

### 01

하위내용영역 문학(비평) A형 단답형 배점 2점 예상정답률 55%

모범답안 ⓐ literary theory
ⓑ marketplace

채점기준

- 2점 : 모범답안과 같다.
- 1점 : 둘 중 하나만 맞았다.
- 0점 : 모범답안과 다르다.

### 02

하위내용영역 문학(시) A형 서술형 배점 4점 예상정답률 45%

모범답안 The meaning of the underlined ⓐ is that the speaker's father, who is compared to a gambler, takes the heart pills to cope with his serious heart disease temporarily because he has to pay his bills(rent). This metaphoric expression vividly illustrates the struggle that his father is facing. Second, (the speaker's attitude toward his father is that) he recognizes the sacrificial acts of love and responsibility that his father performed in spite of his own serious disease for his family. To convey his feeling, the speaker employs a metaphor comparing his father to a guitar just like a guitar has a hole in the center, he visualizes his father with a hole in his chest. The speaker wishes he could control his father's pain, to control the strings in his life that are broken so he can feel good.

채점기준

+ 1점: 밑줄 친 ⓐ가 "집세(생활비)를 충당하기 위해서 임시방편으로 약으로 심장병을 다스리며 일할 수밖에 없는 아버지의 힘든 상황"을 의미한다고 서술하였다.
+ 2점: 밑줄 친 ⓑ에서 아버지에 대한 화자의 태도가 "아버지의 가족을 위한 희생과 책임감에 대한 감사와 애정"이라고 서술하였다.
  ▷ 아버지에 대한 화자의 태도를 다음과 같이 서술하였어도 2점을 준다.
  - "the speaker feels sorry for his father's pain and suffering"
  - "the speaker grieves at his father's pain and suffering"
+ 1점: 밑줄 친 ⓑ에서 아버지를 기타에 비유하였다고 서술하고 이 비유를 위의 내용과 연결시켜 서술하였다.

감점 어색한 표현이나 문법에 어긋난 것이 있으면 각각 0.3점 감점한다.

### 03

하위내용영역 문학(소설) B형 서술형 배점 4점 예상정답률 40%

모범답안 The speech Dr. Bledsoe gives above reveals his true position as being somewhat sinister and dissimulative(or deceptive). He is feigning subservience when dealing with the white-dominated power structure to take power for himself, with no regard for anyone else. White folk "support," he says of the university, "but I control it." He admits disinterest for other black people, in the interest of keeping what he has, even if it means "every Negro in the country hanging."

채점기준

+ 4점: Dr. Bledsoe가 "백인 상류층이 지배하고 있는 권력구조에서 그들에게 복종하는 듯하지만 실제로는 자기 자신의 권력을 유지하기 위해서 그렇게 할 따름(3점)"이고 흑인들에 대해서는 "다른 흑인들의 삶에 대해 전혀 관심이 없으며 심지어 자신의 현재의 권력을 유지하기 위해서는 그들 모두가 (린치를 당해) 죽어도 상관없어 한다(1점)"고 서술하였다.

▷ 다음과 같이 서술한 것도 맞는 것으로 해서 4점을 준다.

- Bledsoe reveals how playing the role of the subservient, fawning black to powerful white men has enabled him to maintain his own position of power and authority over the university.
- The speech Dr. Bledsoe gives reveals that he is feigning subservience when dealing with the white-dominated power structure to build himself up with no regard for anyone else. While "rich white folks" control the country, Bledsoe manipulates them by his subservience.
- In regard to his relations with whites, while "rich white folks" control the institute, Bledsoe boasts that he holds power through his subterfuge, and implies that people like him keep the country together. This power, of the white dominance that Bledsoe manipulates, is so strong that it controls whites, blacks, and even the truth. Of the whites' power, he says "they can tell (a lie) so well it becomes the truth."
- Bledsoe mockingly lapses into the dialect of uneducated Southern blacks, saying "I's" instead of "I am." By playing the role of the "ignorant" black man, he has made himself nonthreatening to whites. By telling white men what they want to hear, he can control what they think and thereby control them entirely. In regard to his relations with blacks, he would rather see every black man lynched than give up his current position of authority.

# 65 회

본책 p.486

## 01

하위내용영역 문학 A형 기입형 배점 2점 예상정답률 55%

모범답안 ⓐ death ⓑ soldier

채점기준
- 2점: 모범답안과 같다.
- 1점: 둘 중 하나만 맞았다.
- 0점: 모범답안과 다르다.

한글 번역

"진격하라, 경기병 여단!"
어느 누구라도 두려워했던가?
아니 그 누구도, 비록 병사들은 알았지만,
누군가가 실수했다는 것을.
그들의 명령에 되묻지 않으며,
이유를 따지지 않았네.
명령을 따르고 죽을 뿐이니.
죽음의 계곡으로
육백 명의 기병은 달렸네.

포탄이 그들 오른쪽으로,
포탄이 그들 왼쪽으로,
포탄이 그들 앞에,
날아오고 터졌네.
총알과 포탄의 폭풍 속으로
용감하게 그들은 말을 타고 돌진하였네,
죽음의 턱 밑으로,
지옥의 아가리 속으로
육백 명의 기병은 달렸네.

[출전] "The Charge of the Light Brigade" by Alfred Lord Tennison

## 02

하위내용영역 문학 A형 기입형 배점 2점 예상정답률 60%

모범답안 ⓐ stage direction ⓑ dialogue

채점기준
- 2점: 모범답안과 같다.
- 1점: 둘 중 하나만 맞았다.
- 0점: 모범답안과 다르다.

한글 번역

파리의 고급 레스토랑에 있는 별도 식사 공간(방). 현재. 무대 오른쪽에는 6인용 식탁이 있다. 무대 왼쪽 벽에는 긴 서빙 테이블이 놓여 있는데, 그 테이블엔 샴페인 몇 병과 음식이 담긴 은빛의 큰 그릇이 있고, 샴페인 몇 병은 이미 열려있다. 방 중앙에는 2인용 작은 소파와 소파 양쪽에 의자가 하나씩 있다. 가구부터 벽장식까지 방 안의 모든 것이 프랑스풍이고 은은하게 매력적이다.
커튼이 올라간다.
검은 넥타이를 맨 40대 초반의 클로드 피숑이 방에 홀로 서서 시계를 보며 샴페인을 홀짝거리고 있다. 그는 약간 어리둥절해 보인다. 그는 식탁을 본 뒤, 뷔페 테이블로 건너가 큰 그릇 덮개를 들어올리고 음식 냄새를 맡고 나서 전채가 있는 곳으로 가서 전채 몇 개의 맛을 본다. 돌아서더니 다시 어리둥절해 보인다. 중앙 무대 뒤쪽에 양쪽으로 여는 문이 있다. 옆쪽에 있는 벽에는 좀더 작고 양쪽으로 여는 문이 하나 더 있다. 그 큰 문이 열리고 비슷한 나이의 또 다른 남자가 검은 넥타이를 매고 들어온다. 이 사람은 앨버트 도네이다.

앨버트: 안녕하세요. 제가 제대로 찾아왔지요? 제라드 파티에요?
클로드: 네. 음, 그렇게 생각합니다. 제가 여기 첫 번째로 왔네요. (앨버트가 들어오며 문을 닫는다.)
앨버트: 앨버트 도네라고 합니다.
클로드: 클로드 피숑입니다. (그들은 악수를 한다. 앨버트가 고통 속으로 움찔하며 손을 떼고 고통을 떨쳐내려 한다.)

앨버트 : 아핫… 오오오오.
클로드 : 미안합니다. 제가 그걸 했나요?
앨버트 : 아니, 제가요. 넥타이를 매다가 손가락을 다쳤습니다.
클로드 : 네, 나비넥타이는 참 피곤하게 하죠. 직접 만드셨습니까?
앨버트 : 아니요, 제 아버지 거예요. 아버지는 내 손가락이 올라간 상태에서 그것을 콱 닫으려고 했죠. (손가락을 목구멍에 대고) 이거 너무 좋죠?
클로드 : 음, 여긴 라 카세트입니다… 사람들 말로는 조세핀이 이곳에 살았던 적이 있다고 합니다. 나폴레옹은 저 문을 통해 그녀를 몰래 방문하곤 했답니다. (그가 작은 문을 가리킨다.)
앨버트 : 정말요? 자신의 집에 식당이 있다면 얼마나 편리할까요.
클로드 : 에.. 그 당시엔 여기가 식당은 아니었을 겁니다.

[출전] <The Dinner Party> by Neil Simon

## 03

하위내용영역 문학 A형 서술형 배점 4점 예상정답률 40%

**모범답안** She will be less happy with her life because movies instill in her a scale to judge everyone by their physical beauty, which end in negativity and disillusion. She still goes to the movie because she enjoys the escapism of returning to her earlier dreams.

**채점기준**

- 4점 : 모범답안과 같거나 유사하다.
- 2점 : Pauline이 영화관에 가는 이유를 "이상화된 삶을 보여주는 영화를 통해서 그녀의 (외로운) 삶에서 도피할 수 있기" 때문이라 답하였지만; 그것이 Pauline을 더욱 불행하게 만드는 이유인 "영화에서 본 이상화된 (백인들의) 모습이 그녀의 현실과는 다른데서 오는 좌절감(불일치)"은 서술하지 못하였다.
- 2점 : Pauline이 영화관에 가는 이유를 "이상화된 삶을 보여주는 영화를 통해서 그녀의 외로움에서 도피할 수 있기" 때문이라 답을 못하였지만; 그것이 Pauline을 더욱 불행하게 만드는 이유인 "영화에서 본 이상화된 (백인들의) 모습이 그녀의 현실과는 다른 데서 오는 불일치"를 올바르게 서술하였다.
- 0점 : 모범답안과 다르다.

**한글 번역**

어느 겨울, 아프리카계 미국인 여성인 폴린은 그녀가 임신했다는 것을 알았다. 그녀가 촐리에게 말했을 때, 그가 기뻐하는 것을 보고 그녀는 놀랐다. 그는 술을 덜 마시고 집에 더 자주 오기 시작했다. 그들은 결혼 초기의 편안했던 관계로 돌아갔는데, 그 초기 시절에, 그는 그녀가 피곤한지, 가게에서 그녀에게 무언가를 가져다 주기를 원하는지를 묻곤 했었다. 이 편안한 상태에서, 폴린은 낮일은 중단하고 다시 자신의 살림살이를 하기 시작했다. 그럼에도, 그 두 방에서의 외로움은 사라지지 않았다. 겨울 햇살이 벗겨지는 녹색 페인트의 부엌 의자에 내리쬘 때, 냄비에서 훈제 돼지족발이 끓고 있을 때, 아래층에서 가구를 배달하는 트럭 소리밖에 들리지 않았을 때, 그녀는 집으로 돌아가는 것에 대해 생각했다. 그 때도 대부분 혼자 지냈던 것에 대해 생각했지만, 이 외로움은 달랐다. 그러고 난 뒤, 그녀는 녹색 의자, 배달 트럭을 응시하는 것을 멈추고, 대신 영화를 보러 갔다. 거기 어둠 속에서 그녀의 기억은 되살아났고, 그녀는 예전의 꿈에 굴복했다. 낭만적 사랑에 대한 생각과 함께, 그녀는 또 다른 아이디어, 즉 육체적 아름다움을 소개 받았다. 아마도 인류 사상사에서 가장 파괴적인 아이디어일 것이다. 둘 다 시기심에서 시작되었고, 불안감에서 번성했고, 환멸로 끝났다.
육체적 아름다움을 미덕과 동일시하면서, 그녀는 자신의 정신을 벗겨낸 뒤, 묶고, 자기 경멸을 수집해 쌓아올렸다. 그녀는 육욕과 단순한 보살핌을 잊었다. 그녀는 사랑을 소유적 짝짓기로, 로맨스를 정신의 목표로 간주했다. 그것은 그녀에게는 마르지 않는 샘과 같았으며, 여기에서 그녀는 가장 파괴적인 감정을 끌어내곤 했는데, 이것은 연인을 속이고, 모든 방식으로 자유를 축소함으로써 사랑하는 사람을 감금하려 하는 것이었다.
영화에서 교육을 받은 후, 그녀는 절대적인 아름다움의 척도로 얼굴을 보고 그것을 분류하지 않을 수 없었다. 그리고 그 척도는 그녀가 은막에서 완전히 흡수한 것이었다.

[출전] <The Bluest Eye> by Toni Morrison

# 66회

본책 p.492

## 01

하위내용영역 문학 A형 기입형 배점 2점 예상정답률 60%

모범답안 scent

채점기준
- 2점 : 모범답안과 같다.
- 0점 : 모범답안과 다르다.

한글 번역

담장 너머로 뭔가 익은 냄새가 풍겨 와서
늘 다니던 익숙한 길 버리고
내 발길 멈추게 하는 것을 찾아갔더니
과연 사과나무 한 그루 거기 서 있었네
잎새 몇 개만 걸친 채 사과나무는
여름의 무거운 짐 다 벗어 버리고
여인의 부채처럼 가볍게 숨쉬고 있었지.
더할 수 없는 사과 풍년이 들어
땅은 온통 떨어진 사과들로
빨간 원을 이루고 있었다.

항상 수확하지 않은 채 뭔가가 남아 있기를!
많은 것이 정해진 계획에서 벗어나 있기를,
사과든 뭐든 잊혀져 남겨진 게 있기를,
그래서 그 향기 마시는 게 도둑질이 되지 않기를.

[출전] "Unharvested"(수확하지 않은 것) by Robert Frost

## 02

하위내용영역 문학 A형 기입형 배점 2점 예상정답률 65%

모범답안 destructive

채점기준
- 2점 : 모범답안과 같다.
- 0점 : 모범답안과 다르다.

한글 번역

돈 후안 : 삶은 두뇌를 필요로 하지요, 이 거부할 수 없는 힘 말이오, 무지 속에서 스스로에게 저항할 수 없도록 해야죠. 인간이란 얼마나 대단한 작품인가요!

마왕 : 내가 파우스트에게 그의 영혼 대신 20년의 환락을 주겠다고 약속했을 때 말하지 않았겠소? 인간의 이성이 인간에게 행한 모든 것이 인간을 다른 어떤 야수보다 더 야수적으로 만들어버릴 거라고 말이오. 훌륭한 육체 하나는 소화 불량에다가 허풍이나 떨어대는 철학자의 두뇌 백 개만큼의 가치가 있다오.

돈 후안 : 당신은 두뇌 없는 엄청나게 큰 몸통이 어떠한 것인지 잊고 있군요. 두뇌 빼고 모든 면에서 인간보다 잴 수 없을 정도로 더 큰 것들이 모두 존재했다가 다들 소멸되었소. 메가테리움과 익타이오사우루스는 7리그(21마일)의 걸음으로 지상을 걸어 다니고 구름 같이 방대한 날개로 대낮을 가렸지. 지금 그것들이 어디 있소? 박물관에서 화석이 되어 있지요. 이런 것들도 살았고, 살기를 원했소. 그렇지만 두뇌가 없었기에 자신들의 목적을 수행할 방법을 몰라서, 그래서 자멸한 거지.

마왕 : 그렇다면 인간은 그렇게 자신의 두뇌를 자랑하면서 스스로를 조금이라도 덜 멸망시키고 있는 거요? 당신 최근에 지상 여기저기를 다녀본 적 있소? 난 다녀 봤고 인간의 놀라운 발명도 살펴봤소. 그래서 당신에게 해줄 얘기는, 생명의 기술에서 인간은 아무것도 발명하지 못하고 있지만 죽음의 기술에서는 대자연을 능가하여

화학과 기계를 통해 역병, 전염병, 기아와 같은 온갖 살육을 자행하고 있다는 거요. 오늘 내가 유혹한 농부는 1만 년 전의 농부들이 먹고 마시던 걸 똑같이 먹고 마시고 있더군. 그렇지만 그가 무얼 죽이려고 밖에 나갈 때면 손가락으로 약간 건드리기만 해도 숨어있던 분자의 에너지 모두를 터뜨려 놓는 기적 같은 기계 장치를 들고 가지요. 평화의 기술에 있어 인간의 서투르지. 인간의 마음은 무기에만 가 있소. 당신이 자랑하는 이 경이로운 생명의 힘이란 게 결국 죽음의 힘이오. 인간의 파괴를 통해서 자기의 힘을 측정하고 있소. 인간의 종교가 무엇이지? 나를 증오하는 하나의 핑계요. 인간의 법률은 무엇이지? 당신을 교수형에 처하기 위한 하나의 핑계고, 인간의 도덕은 무엇이지? 상류 계급이 되는 것! 생산하지 않고 소비하기 위한 하나의 핑계요. 인간의 정치는 무엇이지? 독재자를 숭배하거나 – 이유는? 독재자는 죽일 수 있는 존재니까 –, 아니면 의회에서 벌이는 닭싸움 같은 거겠지.

[출전] <Man and Superman> by George Bernard Shaw

OR In the above passage, the irony is situational, in that the headmaster wanted to prove how progressive his school by blocking the long-used path, but the strife this causes earns him a criticism from his uppers. Second, the "path" represents the history and spiritual value of the villagers.

채점기준

+0.5점: situational irony라는 것을 서술하였다.

+2.5점: 아이러니에 대한 내용(The headmaster wanted to prove how progressive his school by blocking the long-used path, but the strife this causes earns him a criticism from his uppers)을 문법 · 표현상 오류 없이 명확하게 서술하였다.

+1점: "path"가 "그 마을의 전통 · 역사 그리고 정신적 가치"를 상징한다고 서술하였다.

**감점**

- 문법적으로 2–3개의 오류 0.5점 감점
- 표현상으로 2–3개의 오류 0.5점 감점
- 문법적으로 4개 이상의 오류 1점 감점
- 표현상으로 4개 이상의 오류 1점 감점

## 03

하위내용영역 문학 A형 서술형 배점 4점 예상정답률 45%

**모범답안** In the ending of the passage, a situational irony occurs when there is an incongruity*(discrepancy)* between what one expects*(what is expected to happen)* and what actually happens. In other words *(or To be specific)*, the headmaster wanted to prove how progressive his school by blocking the long-used path, but the strife this causes earns him a criticism from his uppers. Second, the "path" represents the history and spiritual value of the villagers.

## 04

하위내용영역 문학 A형 서술형 배점 4점 예상정답률 45%

**모범답안** The poem describes a moment when the speaker accidentally killed a hedgehog with his lawn mower while mowing his lawn. The thematic idea is that death can come suddenly in life, just as in nature, so we must appreciate the living and take care of each other.

채점기준

+2점: 시가 "a moment when the speaker accidentally killed a hedgehog with his lawn mower while mowing his lawn"을 묘사한다고 서술하였다.

▷ 다음의 내용과 유사해도 2점을 준다.
"The poem describes the accidental killing of a hedgehog by the speaker during some routine gardening"

+ 2점: 시적 주제를 "death can come suddenly in life, just as in nature, so we must appreciate the living and take care of each other"라 서술하였다.

▷ "사람이 자연과 친하게 잘 지내야 한다"라고 했으면 1점을 준다.

감점

- 문법적으로 2-3개의 오류 0.5점 감점
- 표현상으로 2-3개의 오류 0.5점 감점
- 문법적으로 4개 이상의 오류 1점 감점
- 표현상으로 4개 이상의 오류 1점 감점

한글 번역

잔디 깎는 기계가 멈췄다, 두 번. 무릎을 구부렸을 때, 난
고슴도치 한 마리가 칼날에 꼼짝달싹 못한 채
죽어 있는 것을 발견했다. 고슴도치는 길게 자란 풀 속에 있었다.

난 전에 그것을 본 적이 있고, 심지어 한 번은 먹이도 줬었다.
지금 고슴도치의 고요한 세계를 난 훼손했다
회복이 불가능하게. 매장해 주는 것은 아무 도움도 되지 않았다:

다음 날 아침에 난 일어났지만 고슴도치는 일어나지 않았다.
죽은 후 첫 날, 새로운 부재는
항상 똑같다; 우리는 조심해야 한다

서로서로, 우리는 서로 친절해야 한다
아직 시간이 있을 때.

[출전] "The Mower"(잔디 깎는 기계) by Philip Larkin

유희태 영미문학 ④

# 영미문학 문제은행

모범답안

1판 1쇄 2014년 5월 10일
2쇄 2015년 4월 10일
2판 1쇄 2017년 1월 3일
2쇄 2017년 12월 20일
3쇄 2018년 5월 10일
4쇄 2019년 4월 30일
3판 1쇄 2020년 10월 23일
2쇄 2022년 4월 15일
3쇄 2023년 2월 1일
4판 1쇄 2024년 1월 10일

저자와의 협의하에 인지생략

**저자** 유희태 **발행인** 박 용
**발행처** (주)박문각출판
**표지디자인** 박문각 디자인팀
**등록** 2015. 4. 29. 제2015-000104호
**주소** 06654 서울시 서초구 효령로 283 서경 B/D
**팩스** (02) 584-2927
**전화** 교재 주문 (02) 6466-7202 동영상 문의 (02) 6466-7201



ISBN 979-11-6987-622-3

## Dr. 유희태 전공영어 시리즈

### 유희태 영미문학

① 영미문학개론
② 영미소설의 이해
③ 영미문학 기출
④ 영미문학 문제은행

### 유희태 일반영어

① 2S2R 기본
② 2S2R 유형
③ 2S2R 기출
④ 2S2R 문제은행
⑤ 기출 VOCA 30days

literature

2023 고객선호브랜드지수 1위
교육서비스 부문

2022 한국 브랜드 만족지수 1위
교육(교육서비스)부문 1위

2021 대한민국 소비자 선호도 1위
교육부문 1위 선정

2020 한국 산업의 1등
브랜드 대상 수상

2019 한국 우수브랜드평가대상
교육브랜드 부문 수상

2018 대한민국 교육산업 대상
교육서비스 부문 수상

2017 대한민국 고객만족
브랜드 대상 수상

2017 한국소비자선호도 1위
브랜드 대상 수상

브랜드스탁 BSTI
브랜드 가치평가 1위

유희태 영미문학 ④

# 영미문학 문제은행

교재관련 문의 02-6466-7202
학원관련 문의 02-816-2030
온라인강의 문의 02-6466-7201

박문각 www.pmg.co.kr

ISBN 979-11-6987-622-3